Johann Wolfgang von Goethe

THE SUFFERINGS
OF YOUNG WERTHER
and
ELECTIVE AFFINITIES

The German Library: Volume 19

Volkmar Sander, General Editor

Johann Wolfgang von Goethe

THE SUFFERINGS
OF YOUNG WERTHER
and
ELECTIVE AFFINITIES

Edited by Victor Lange
Forewords by Thomas Mann

CONTINUUM · NEW YORK

1991

The Continuum Publishing Company
370 Lexington Avenue, New York, NY 10017

The German Library
is published in cooperation with Deutsches Haus,
New York University.
This volume has been supported by a grant
from Lufthansa German Airlines.

Printed in the United States of America

Library of Congress Cataloging-in-Publication Data

Goethe, Johann Wolfgang von, 1749–1832.
  [Werther. English]
  The sufferings of young Werther ; and, Elective affinities /
Johann Wolfgang von Goethe ; edited by Victor Lange ; forewords by
Thomas Mann.
      p.   cm. — (The German library ; v. 19)
  Translation of: Werther and Die Wahlverwandtschaften.
  ISBN 0-8264-0329-8. — ISBN 0-8264-0330-1 (pbk.)
  I. Lange, Victor, 1908–   . II. Goethe, Johann Wolfgang von,
1749–1832. Wahlverwandtschaften. English. 1990. III. Title.
IV. Title: Sufferings of young Werther. V. Title: Elective
affinities. VI. Series.
PT2027.W3H813   1990
833'.6—dc20   89-17246
                                                                CIP

Acknowledgments will be found on page 343
which constitutes an extension of the copyright page.

Contents

Introduction

I t was Thomas Mann's fascination as a novelist with the formal
and intellectual characteristics of the masters of European fiction
that produced throughout his life a remarkable canon of critical
reflections, leisurely and occasional rather than systematic or academic in perception and style. His early interest in the Scandinavian
writers of the nineties, such as Jacobsen, is unmistakable in stories
such as "Tonio Kroeger" or *Buddenbrooks*. It was the psychological
subtlety, the historical insight, and the incomparable craftsmanship
of Flaubert, Tolstoy, Turgenev, Dostoevsky, Chekhov, Gide, and Con-
rad that articulated and delineated the substance of his mature work.
On each of these he wrote with a sense of spiritual and, indeed,
personal affinity, with the conviction that they represented in their
human configurations the glories and the agonies, the pride and the
ambiguities of the nineteenth century.

German literature seemed to play a relatively minor part in that
distinguished company: Theodor Fontane offered the urbane elegance, the subtle irony that few other Germans had produced or
were able to achieve. Yet, it would be a mistake to underrate Mann's
profound attachment to the German cultural tradition, its philosophical, political, and aesthetic resources. His lecture on Lessing is
a wide-angled view of the German Enlightenment; Goethe and
Schiller were for him the self-evident monuments of what was to
develop into the Romantic sensibility, in language, imagery, and
musical genius the premise of the modern European experience.
Within that orbit he seems to recognize a recurring tension between
what may be presumed to be the normal, *natural* forms of living, the
average and simple-minded personality, and the puzzling and often

shocking distortions and deviations of the human condition under the pressure of philosophical and existential insights and experiences that create a radical doubt in the efficacy of life. Mann's novels reflect this tension on a variety of levels as the interplay between the pragmatic and the spiritual, the unreflected assertion of health and power, the ever-recurring conflict between convention and individual genius. These are elaborated and explored in memorable figures, striking incidents, and linguistic artistry and ironic detachment.

It is clear and has often been shown that Mann was profoundly aware of his indebtedness to the European narrative tradition, its powerful representatives, and the continuity of certain issues and predilections. He returned again and again to the great Russians and, among European masterpieces, especially, to two of Goethe's most celebrated novels, *Werther* and *Elective Affinities*. These two offer within Goethe's work fiction of a specifically "poetic" sort, free of the "didactic" impulse that gives the coherence of a "message" to the *Wilhelm Meister* novels. Their radiance of mood and sensibility makes each, one early (1774), the other thirty-five years later (1809), a testimonial to an extraordinary and intensely complex state of mind, unique and inexhaustible in its emotional propositions. They are conditioned but not limited by their historical context, and each is propelled by the deeply felt conflict between the claims of private and public passion.

Mann's interpretation of *Werther,* first given in March 1940 to Princeton students, is not so much an original appraisal of the novel as a whole or its technical innovations as a portrait of the authentic human being as the social eccentric, of the inevitable isolation of what in Mann's later work becomes the alienated artist. *Werther* anticipates features of "Tonio Kroeger," the historical constellation produces the personal crisis: Goethe "had personally experienced what agonized and unnerved his generation." Much of Mann's essay is therefore concerned with emphasizing the actual biographical ingredients of the novel, within which Werther plays—as Mann formulates it—the role of the "ingenuous and honest, but also faithless and irresponsible vagabond of feeling." The incidental figures and events—this Mann sees clearly—reinforce as skillful narrative elaborations the main thesis of the book.

Werther's fundamental impulse is his "longing for death," a motif central to Mann's own work and here recognized and critically defined with the perception of the modern novelist. *Werther,* Mann says, "is a masterpiece of necessity, a seamless, intelligently, delicately, and thoughtfully organized mosaic of emotional details, of psychological moments and features which, taken together, produce a picture both of charm and of death."

To the issue of the ambiguity of death, its destructive or redemptive power, Mann himself frequently returns in his own work; and it is the precariousness of life even within the framework of a presumably stable social order that is the theme of one of Goethe's late and most carefully constructed novels, *Elective Affinities,* to which Mann turns in the second critical essay here printed. It is a novel praised and beloved by most German readers for its serenity, its philosophical resonance, and the subtle tension throughout the story between natural and social compulsions. The central characters of Ottilie and Eduard, felt at the time to be more "concrete" than we might admit today, the one the epitome of discretion and "inwardness," the other of an impulsive and indomitable "will to love," reiterate one of Mann's and Goethe's most telling configurations. Recent scholarship has shown alternatives of interpretation that enlarge the horizon within which Mann read the novel; but he recognizes the careful construction as well as the subtle interplay of thematic and philosophical intentions. "It is a miracle of appropriateness and purity of composition, rich in its relationships, linked and concise": "not the biggest," Mann would suggest, "but the most elevated of Goethe's novels."

A modern "novelist of ideas" such as Mann would readily recognize the appropriateness of Goethe's own statement that here, and here alone, he had subordinated the design of a major work to an idea. That idea is not easy to formulate: it ranges from the frailty of the secular order to sustain the institution of marriage, from the power of natural and elemental forces to create and destroy, to the resolution of these discrepancies in the metaphorical resources of Christian faith. Ottilie's clear and inflexible recognition of her own fatal disregard of an order beyond her love for Eduard raises her, in Goethe's language, to the status of a saint. All this Mann recognized with great perception and states in his essay in terms that correspond to his modern vocabulary: "Goethe bows to the moral culture of Christianity, that is to say, to its 'humanity,' its moral and anti-barbarian power." Neither Goethe nor Mann himself was Christian in any orthodox sense; yet each was convinced of the necessary function of Christianity as a system of order against the imponderable temptations and unfathomable energies of a natural world as yet more astonishing than reassuring. When Goethe here and elsewhere speaks of *Entsagung,* of a deliberate confining of natural inclinations, he seems to Mann to elaborate a peculiarly "German" disposition, the German "renunciation" of the "advantages of barbarism." "It is," Mann concludes, "a radiant sign of the possibility of German perfection." That this formula is itself a peculiarly German characteristic of Mann's rhetoric has often been pointed out.

The discretion and discipline implied in the term *Entsagung* has for Goethe compelling formal consequences: it gives to the narrator an extraordinary measure of control and responsibility. We know that in Mann's later novels, in *Krull, Joseph,* or *Doktor Faustus,* the role of the carefully constructed and theatrically effective narrator is the reflection of a distinctly modern formal intention. In *Elective Affinities* the *presence* of the teller of the tale cannot be missed. Yet it is perceptible only in the telling itself. By turns in the conversation, by reflections that challenge the reader, or by discreet touches in the description of the figures, the narrator barely reveals his own judgment of the actions or opinions of the participants in the fatal game. Mann finds a happy formula for the coincidence of sensuality and morality in *Elective Affinities,* of plasticity and analytical abstraction, of immediacy and reflection. The novel, he concludes, once more in the terms of German Romanticism, attempts to create an encounter between *nature* and *mind* in their longing for one another. That is the essence of human striving. "And we may consider a work in which the two wholly absorb one another a superb and humane achievement."

The two examples of Mann's criticism that appear in this volume, of his approach to the intellectual and formal substance of the works of fiction that moved and stimulated him, are never well-considered academic exercises, never intended to convey the full complexity of a literary work. They illustrate the high degree of literacy of a practicing writer, the intensity of his perceptive reading of admired models, and the extraordinary skill not merely of offering critical observations but of arguing and speaking with the appealing voice of a storyteller in the company of receptive and congenial readers and listeners.

V. L.

Foreword to
The Sufferings of Young Werther

On Goethe's *Werther*

The modest little book *Werther*—the complete title of this epistolary novel is *The Sufferings of Young Werther*—was the grandest, most extensive, most sensational success the writer Goethe had ever experienced. The Frankfurt lawyer was no more than twenty-four-years old when he wrote this not very voluminous work, limited also in its conception of the world and in its biographical portrait by the author's youth, yet unbelievably charged with explosive feeling. It was just his second more substantial work. Only *Goetz von Berlichingen,* a drama set during the age of German chivalry and written in the style of Shakespeare, had preceded *Werther,* and due to the power and warmth achieved by the manner with which it infused history with intimacy and life, it had already focused the eyes of the literary world upon the young author. *Werther,* however, presented an entirely diverse side of the author, and was completely different from the earlier work in its character and effect. Its success had in part even a scandalous quality. The unnerving and disrupting sentimentality of this slim book called the guardians of public morals into action and was a terror and source of loathing to the moralists, who saw in its pages a glorification of suicide and its seduction; but precisely these same attributes also triggered the wave of success that exceeded all bounds and made literally the world mad with a death wish: the novel aroused a state of frenzy, of fever, of ecstasy that ran rampant over the inhabited world and had the same effect as the spark that falls into the powderkeg, thereby releasing a dangerous amount of energy through a sudden explosion.

It would not be a simple task to analyze the psychic state that determined the underpinnings of European civilization at that time. Historically, it was the period before the catastrophe and immense atmospheric changes of the French Revolution; intellectually, the epoch Rousseau had impressed with the mark of his sensitive, rebellious spirit. A discontent with civilization, an emancipation of emotions, a gnawing yearning for a return to the natural and elemental, a shaking at the shackles of ossified culture, a revolt against convention and bourgeois confinement: everything converged to create a spirit that came up against the limitations of individuation itself, that allowed an effusive, boundless affirmation of life to take on the form of a death wish. Melancholy and discontent with the rhythmical monotony of life was the norm. In Germany, the movement called *Weltschmerz* intensified because of a fixation with a certain type of graveyard poetry coming out of England at that time. Even Shakespeare contributed to it. Hamlet and his monologues haunted all young people. Ossian and the gruesome, primitive, gloomy heroic moods he imparted shaped the passions of the young.

It was as if readers of all countries, secretly and without knowing it, had waited precisely for the work of an as yet virtually unknown *German* that could do justice to the restrained yearning of the world in a revolutionarily liberating manner—providing the word that would burst the tension. There is the story of a young Englishman who came to Weimar in later years and fainted upon seeing Goethe pass by on the street: he had overtaxed himself, the sight of the author of *Werther* had been too much for him. Goethe later recalls the worldwide success of *Werther* in a Venetian epigram:

> Germany imitated me and France wanted to read me.
> England! amiably you received the broken guest.
> But what does it benefit me that even the Chinese
> paints, with timid hand, Werther and Lotte on glass?

From the start, this couple joined the ranks of the classical love duets of literature and legend: Laura and Petrarch, Romeo and Juliet, Abelard and Heloise, Paul and Francesca. Every young man longed to be able to love so, every young woman to be so loved. An entire generation of young people recognized the disposition of their own hearts in that of Werther's. Impassioned, they ostentatiously wore the garb ascribed to the young doomed hero of the novel: the blue dress coat with yellow vest and pants. The imitation, the melancholic allegiance reached extremes: suicides, obviously and professedly in adherence to Werther's example, took place which, the moralists maintained, the author of the deranged novel had on his conscience. These deluded youths simply forgot that, although the author of *Werther* had portrayed the progression toward suicide in a youthful heart with great skill, he himself by no means committed suicide, but instead overcame this deadly drive in a creative manner, had freed himself from it through literature. In his memoirs, Goethe speaks of the almost grotesque difference between the healing function that *Werther* held in store for his own life and the external effect it exercised. He had experienced personally all that tormented and unnerved his generation. The thought of suicide was no stranger to him: intermittently, it nearly had been his resolve as well. In *Poetry and Truth,* he recalls the time preceding *Werther:* every night before extinguishing the lights he would attempt to thrust the sharp tip of a dagger he possessed a few inches deep into his chest. Unsuccessful at this, he derided himself and opted for life. He sensed, however, that he would be unable to do this unless he executed a literary composition in which all he had thought and felt about this matter would be broached. This confession, this "public cleansing" as Goethe called it, was *Werther.* With the work completed, he felt free and entitled to a new life. While he was relieved and enlightened by transforming reality into poetry, other young people, however, were becoming confused and believed one had to transform poetry into reality, to reenact the novel, and, if necessary, to shoot oneself. Thus, what had proven so beneficial for him was denounced as highly detrimental.

Until his death, Goethe was proud of this work of his youth, on which, beside *Faust,* he prided himself most. "Whoever writes a *Werther* at twenty-four," he states in his old age, "is not exactly a greenhorn." One of the most significant moments in his life—his meeting with Napoleon in Erfurt—is associated with this work. The emperor had read this short novel no fewer than seven times, had even taken it along on his Egyptian campaign. At this famous meeting, the emperor questioned the author about his work. The great life affirmer never renounced the problematic figure of his youth, whose shadow always had accompanied him in brotherly fashion. The seventy-five-year-old, who had to endure the sweet and terrible consternations of love once more for the sake of the young Ulrike, eerily expresses the return of the spirit of his young hero in a poem entitled *To Werther.**

The experience that formed the basis for *Werther,* the idyllic yet painful story of Goethe's love for Lotte Buff, the lovely daughter of the senior civil service clerk in Wetzlar on the Lahn River, became just as famous as the novel itself and justifiably so, since large portions of the book correspond exactly to reality, are faithful and unchanged reproductions of it. Goethe arrived in this charmingly situated country town in the Rhine region in 1772 at the age of twenty-three upon the instructions of his father, who expected the young J. D. to set up practice in the branch of the Reich supreme court located there. His own intention was much more to pursue the arts, to write poetry, and simply to live, and this he did; the court hardly got to see him. The streets of Wetzlar were narrow and dirty, but the surrounding environs were charming; it was May and everything was in bloom, and the poetic idler soon discovered his favorite haunts at fountains, brooks, and romantic lookouts over the Lahn Valley where he could read Homer or Pindar, debate with friends, draw, and reflect. At a country ball for young people, he meets the nineteen-year-old Lotte, who, together with her widowed father and her numerous siblings, lives in the so-called Lodgehouse of the Germanic Order. She is delicate, blonde, blue-eyed, of a cheerful, competent disposition, without advanced education but, in a wholesome way, simultaneously sensitive, childlike, and serious; since the death of her mother she serves as her surrogate for the entire brood of her younger siblings and runs the household for her father. Goethe first lays eyes upon her when he calls for her at the farmstead, where, surrounded by the little ones, she stands distributing

---

*Theodore Ulrike Sophie von Levetzow: During the summer of 1821, the seventy-two-year-old Goethe met Ulrike, then seventeen, in Marienbad. His affection for her grew into a full-blown passion over the next two summers. He asked for her hand in marriage and was flatly refused.—*Tr.*

snacks, already dressed for the ball in a white dress trimmed with pink bows: a scene immortalized precisely so in *Werther* and often reproduced in the fine arts. He spends the evening with her, visits her the next day, and is head over heels in love with her before he discovers she is engaged. He finds out soon enough. The prospective groom is an ambassadorial secretary from Hannover named Kestner, a man of splendid mediocrity who genuinely loves Lotte and whom she, in trusting fashion, loves in return. But mark, this is no passionate affair; it is a cool, if not untender, mutual attraction, focused on a common future, economical goals, and the founding of a family. One waits only that the circumstances of the prospective groom are put in order so as to allow him to enter into marriage.

Goethe enters this relationship as the third party, as an admired and sincerely well-liked friend and companion to both halves of the bridal couple: the poet, the genius, the vagabond of the heart—guileless and honest, but then again unfaithful and unreliable in mundane affairs—who had betrayed and abandoned Friederike Brion because he shrank back from the ties of marriage.* He is the young demon who says of himself in *Faust:* "Am I not the fugitive? The homeless one? The monster without purpose and peace?" A lovable monster: handsome, highly talented, filled with spirit and life, firey, sensitive, exuberant and melancholic—in short, eccentric in an endearing way. The bridal couple, Kestner as well as Lotte, like him very much, the children particularly feel very affectionately toward him, and the threesome spends a peculiar, blissful, and dangerous summer together—although it is quite often a twosome, since Kestner, dutiful and busy as he is, cannot always be, indeed seldom is, present; and while he toils for his envoy, Goethe is at the side of Lotte, the bride-to-be.

He helps her with the housekeeping, in the vegetable and flower garden, picks fruit with her, cuts beans with her. In contrast to the preoccupied groom-to-be, he has all the advantages of a free and lighthearted presence, the advantages of his brilliant youthful personality against which that of the honest Kestner does not stand any kind of chance. Undoubtedly, Lotte loved him, but as the clever,

*Friederike Brion: Daughter of the pastor of Sesenheim. Goethe met her in 1770 during a visit to this town. He and Friederike spent a great deal of time together during his stay and maintained an intense correspondence when he returned to Strassburg for his studies. He broke off the relationship in August 1771.—*Tr.*

sensible girl who knew what she wanted, she knew how to control her feelings for him just as she kept his flitting passions, which he did not always hide, in check. But at least he concealed them most of the time. Once, in the raspberry bushes, he let himself be carried away and kissed her; she was quite indignant about it and did not hesitate to—shall we say tell or confess this to—her fiancé? At any rate they decided to keep a tighter rein on him, to deal with him in a cooler fashion, also spurred by the fact that certain rumors already were circulating regarding the odd relationship. Kestner was a bit irritated; he could not have been very angry. Lotte gave the sinner a good talking to, explained to him once and for all that he could never hope for anything more from her than good companionship. Had he not already known this, standing there so sadly? Had he ever thought he could steal the girl from her good Hans Christian and make her his own, something some people already believed about to happen?* Certainly not, indeed, because of loyalty and decency—and not only due to loyalty and decency, but because his love, vague feelings, aimless passions, in essence evolving poetry—was bankrupt of what Kestner's love possessed: solidity and practicality.

The bridal couple felt compassion for the confusion, the irrational sufferings of this dear person. They gave him rather curious gifts of consolation: a silhouette of Lotte, one of the pink bows she had worn on her dress the day he first saw her. Note well that these offerings came not only from Lotte, but also from Kestner, the prospective groom, and they evoke in us a similar feeling as when we see a prince receiving alms from very simple, good folk.

As autumn arrived, Goethe secretly departed. Suddenly he was gone. The idyllic threesome had lasted four months. The impressions the experience had left upon the poet—in which the richest, painfully devoted sincerity of feeling certainly always was commingled with the intention of literary creation—were complemented in Frankfurt, to which he had fled, by an experience with another woman for whom his life, strangely enough, had room immediately after he had torn himself away from Lotte. This was Maximiliane La Roche from Ehrenbreitstein, an unusually pretty, dark-eyed girl who had just married a rich widower in Frankfurt—the merchant Peter

---

*Hans Christian: Goethe is referring to the real-life Johann Georg Christian Kestner.—*Tr.*

Brentano—and was quite unhappy at his side in their gloomy house, smelly from oil and cheese. Goethe often sat with her, made mischief with her five stepchildren as he had done with Lotte's siblings (since he doted on children, who were immediately drawn to him), accompanied Maxe's piano-playing on the cello, and—there was certainly more. For one day, the merchant Brentano angrily intervened; a furor erupted, there were, as Goethe himself states, "horrible moments," and the friendship disintegrated. The dark eyes, however, that are Lotte's in *Werther*—in reality her eyes were blue—are due to Frau Brentano.

His relationship with her contributed much to complete the plot of the novel. What did this particularly, however, was a death that had just occurred in the poet's circle of acquaintances. The ambassadorial secretary Jerusalem from Braunschweig, a talented, melancholy, suffering soul, had put a bullet through his head, entangled as he was in a hopeless love for the wife of another as well as deeply embittered due to societal discrimination. The incident caused a widespread sensation, and, although it personally affected Goethe very deeply, this did not prevent him from believing that the incident had arrived upon the scene just at the right moment: it lent the Wetzlar composition, still suspended in nebulousness, the actual climax. A process of self-identification with Jerusalem, who had committed an act long familiar to the thoughts of the poet, took place; this character was capable of reflecting all the *Weltschmerz* and ingenious sorrow, all the noblemindedness and misery, all the weaknesses, the yearning, the passion of the time in general and of the individual in particular. Now actually only the form of this attractive plot remained undefined.

Originally, it was to have been a drama, but this did not work. Another genre took its place which united elements of the dramatic, the lyric, and the narrative: the epistolary novel, a tradition created by Richardson and Rousseau. The young author isolated himself completely and dashed off *Werther's Sorrows* in a scant four weeks. The accomplishment would have been even more astonishing had not a number of letters and diary entries, which he himself had written during the Wetzlar period and which he used for the novel almost word for word (even keeping the dates), been immediately at hand.

It is a masterpiece, a nearly unique synthesis of overpowering emotion and precocious artistic sense. Youth and genius are its themes, and from youth and genius it itself is born. I am speaking to people who have read this extraordinary little book and whom I know to be acquainted with the most reliable scholarly commentary on it. What at the most remains for me to do is to draw attention to or recall a few of the beauties and finer points that I myself noticed upon rereading the piece.

A few words about the hero and letter writer himself, the character of young Werther. It is young Goethe himself, without the creative talents nature conferred upon him. In order to portray a deathprone human being, too good or too weak for this life, a writer needs only to reflect himself—with the omission of the creative talents that serve as his own pillar of support, continually luring him back onto the path of the living and (to repeat the term we applied to Goethe)—making him a life affirmer. Goethe did not kill himself because he had *Werther*—and quite a few other things—to write. Werther has no other calling on this earth except his existential suffering, the tragic perspicacity for his imperfections, the Hamletlike loathing of knowledge that suffocates him: thus he must perish. His "novel"—this impossible and illicit love for a girl that belongs to another—is only the disguise that his death wish assumes, the more or less accidental form of his downfall. Lotte, inasmuch as she is flattered by the passion of this extraordinary and, for all his weaknesses, most charming person, inasmuch as this in reality represents a great temptation to her reason and her virtue, has a very sensitive and correct feeling about this state of affairs. "Don't you feel," she asks him, "that you are betraying yourself, that you are willfully destroying yourself? Why me, Werther! Precisely me, the property of another? Precisely that? I fear, I fear it is only the impossibility of possessing me that makes this wish so attractive to you." The bitter mockery with which he reacts to this observation betrays how much in fact it has hit its mark. And this sensitivity is very true to life: the pessimistic psychologist, wallowing in gloomy, despairing insights into the foolish human heart, does not endure it well once psychology turns against him.

This is not to say that Werther spared himself. He is the deeply afflicted expert in relentless introspection, self-observation, self-analysis, the overrefined final product of the Christian-Pietistic cult of the soul and of the emotions. An intellect such as Lessing was displeased by this character; he was inclined to see him as a refutation of the entirety of modern Christian culture because it brought forth such individuals. For, he asked, had a Roman or Greek youth ever killed himself in this manner and for such a reason, namely because of unrequited love? This is a point well taken. But one cannot very well concede that Christian culture is dead ad absurdum when represented by the indulgences and subtle degeneration it produces when exaggerated. The enormous progress that Christianity signifies for the development of human consciousness is not to be questioned because of one such incident of suffering and death depicted, from intimate experience and with precise consistency, by Goethe in the work of his youth.

This short novel is a masterpiece of necessity, a complete mosaic—cleverly, delicately, and deftly assembled—of emotional details, psychological factors, and characteristics, which together impart an image of kindness and death. And in doing this, the author has succeeded in presenting the hero's fatal weakness simultaneously as his exuberant strength. Werther actually is reminiscent of that type of thoroughbred horse mentioned once in the book that, upon becoming terribly heated and aroused, instinctively bites open one of its own arteries in order to help itself breathe. "I'm often in such a state," he says, "I want to slash open one of my arteries and gain everlasting freedom."

"Everlasting freedom." The desire to exchange that which is confining and conditional for that which is infinite and limitless is the fundamental characteristic of Werther's nature, as it is of Faust's. Just read what he writes about spatial distance and time, about the insatiable yearning into space and time, and you will have grasped him completely. The third form of expansion is the emotional: here too, in despair and self-contempt, he collides with human conditionality and inadequacy. "What is man, that exalted demigod! Do not his powers fail him precisely when he needs them most? And when he soars with joy or abandons himself to sorrow, is he not checked in both instances precisely there, restored precisely at these times to his dull icy consciousness, when he longed to lose himself in the wealth of the eternal?" Life, identity, individuality are his shackles: he himself uses this word with regard to his wish to merge with the wildly excited state of nature. "How gladly," he exclaims, "I would have sacrificed my humanness to travel with the stormwinds and tear the clouds, to reign over the floods! Ha! And will this bliss ever be granted to the one in *shackles?*" This emotional pantheism is found once again in Schopenhauer's philosophy of the will.

The greatest and most powerful form of emotional expansion is love; Werther searches for it, is prepared for it from the very start, and it is his death wish that allows him to go to his ruin in a hopeless and disastrous love. Since there is something in his nature that predisposes all people, but especially the common folk and children, to take him into their confidence, he becomes the confessor of a young farmhand nursing a fervent passion for his mistress, a widow who has had a bad marriage and decides to remain alone. Werther is deeply shaken by the rapture of emotion that he catches sight of here. His idle heart is envious from the very first moment. He writes to his friend: "In my entire life I have not seen—I can well say, not thought or dreamed of—urgent desire and hot, ardent longing in such a pure state. Do not scold me when I tell you that upon recalling this innocence and truth my innermost soul burns, and that this image of faithfulness and tenderness pursues me everywhere, and that I, as if enflamed by it, thirst and languish." He is in love even before his love has an object. His next letter tells of his first encounter with Lotte.

What now commences is a romance whose psychological richness ranges from the idyllic, the humorous, the charming to the darkest abyss of emotional temptation; from the beginning, even in its most happy moments, the shadow of death stretches over it. Do you remember the passage in which Werther speaks of his relationship to Albert, the bridegroom, and believes the goodwill the latter shows him certainly to be more Lotte's doing than Albert's own feeling? For in this matter the ladies are clever: if they can keep two suitors on friendly terms with each other, then the advantage is always on their side, as infrequent as this may be the case. I have this same passage in mind when I speak of the novel's lighter features. Werther's state at this time is still open enough, despite being enveloped in passion, to be generally capable of such amusing insights into the diplomacy of "the ladies." But one day he will entertain a death wish for this very same Albert, whom he does not deem worthy of Lotte, a death wish that in the beginning consists only of a hypothetical thought—*what if he died*—ultimately leading Werther to consider an action from which he recoils and which he himself does not reveal, but which we know to be murder.

Not only hate but love also leads him to the brink of an abyss. The fate of the unfortunate, loving farmhand, eerily paralleling his own, thrusts upon his so pure, so properly consciencious heart the idea of rape. The servant is chased off the farm because, in a moment of desperate passion, he had tried to take possession of his mistress by means of violence—a madness for which she may well bear partial responsibility, since, whether consciously or unconsciously, she nurtured his passion through partial approval and small liberties. And Lotte? Is hers not a similar situation? There is a scene in the book whose dangerous sweetness has an outrageous quality: it portrays an innocence enveloped in the coquetry with which this sweet girl fires Werther's passions. It is the scene with the canary: she lets its little beak kiss her before his eyes, she sends it from her lips to his, she offers it crumbs placed upon her smiling mouth. Werther turns his head away. She should not do this he feels; and we, admittedly, feel this way also, since she is astute enough to be aware of Werther's weak state and kind enough to be concerned about it. If she loves him, this should be an additional reason for her to spare him. But again, precisely the love she nurtures for Werther, in spite of her loyalty to Albert, tempts her to engage in those "small liberties" through which that farmer's widow drives her servant to an extreme action.

The novel suggests—in the pointedly psychological and uncovering manner that defines its technique and that has something almost humorously revealing in its insights into the unconscious—that Lotte loves Werther. Lotte feels that it would be dreadfully difficult for her to lose Werther. She wishes he were her brother, or that she could marry him off to one of her friends, which then also would completely restore his relationship to Albert. But as she goes through her friends one by one, she finds something at fault with each of them: she would begrudge her friend any of them. The young poet adds: under such circumstances, Lotte had felt "deeply, without making it clear to herself," that it was her secret desire to keep Werther for herself. He would no longer have expressed this in *Elective Affinities,* whose psychological technique is very much reminiscent of such passages in *Werther.*

I must not be tempted to point out all of the finer points worthy of special mention within these well-stocked pages. To the most daring belongs the episode of the madman searching for flowers in winter; he speaks of a beautiful, happy, and gentle time, referring to the time he spent in the insane asylum, during which he felt as a fish in water. An envy of the advantages of insanity breaks through here, passages that belong to the most extreme emotional expressions in the book.

The discussion of the concept of suicide, which preoccupied the poet himself during the time he was writing *Werther* almost as if it were an *idée fixe,* is given much attention. Werther theoretically defends the idea from the start, long before the decision to carry it out is reached. He rejects the notion that it be presented as an act of weakness: he wants to believe that precisely in this act pride and free will triumph over the enervation that suffering inflicts. "Does not the evil that consumes our strength," he asks, "at the same time rob us of the courage that could free us?" The drive not to be defeated by this dilemma, to prove to himself that his sufferings were not capable of robbing him of the courage to free himself, is revealed as one of the strongest motivations for self-destruction; here one sees clearly how the appropriately artistic externalization of thoughts, which themselves could have become fatal to the young poet, and their unrestrained use as a psychological aid and means of communication, must have been of service in helping him overcome this suicidal state.

One should not overlook the social theme that Goethe included in order to make the setting of Werther's ennui complete: the class conflict he allows his sensitive hero to experience after he has fled from Lotte's side and has become a diplomatic attaché. His clash with snobbish aristocratic society—among which by the way he has a friend, a Rousseauistically tinged Fräulein von B., whose class is a burden to her because it "fulfills none of the desires of her heart"— the humiliating and provocative clash with this detested class is so characteristic for the historical setting of the book and its revolutionary general tendency for even the most superficial of analyses to overlook. Napoleon had criticized this feature. "Why did you do this?" he asked Goethe during their conversation in Erfurt, and Goethe seems to have defended this element of social revolt rather weakly in a purely human romantic tragedy. This was not unfamiliar to his tumultuous youth. Just think of the agitating scene in *Faust* in which Gretchen's wretched seducer rages against society's cruelty, whose victim is the ruined girl. Minister Goethe cut this scene from the production in Weimar, and, as conservative Olympian, he may have been embarrassed by that episode in *Werther* in which the latent, spiritual-emotional revolutionism of the love story manifests itself socially. There is certainly no question, however, that, even without this critical moment, *Werther's Sufferings* is among those books that announced and prepared the way for the French Revolution.

Goethe undoubtedly also was aware of this and always took a certain pride in it. In his old age, he speaks of the book with an affectionate horror. "I have read it only once since its publication," he states in 1824, "and have taken precautions not to do it again. *It is full of firebombs!* I get an uncanny feeling upon reading it, and I fear that I may reexperience the pathological state out of which it emerged."

This rereading already had taken place eight years earlier, in the year 1816. That same year brought the sixty-seven-year-old a singular coincidence and with it a memorable—at least memorable for us—reunion of a personal kind. An elderly lady, only four years younger than he, came to Weimar to visit one of her younger married sisters and called upon him. It was Charlotte Kestner, born Buff: Lotte of Wetzlar, Werther's Lotte. They had not seen each other in forty-four years. She and her husband had suffered quite a bit back then as a result of the inconsiderate exposure of their relationship in *Werther*. Now, however, because of the way things had evolved, the good woman was rather proud of her status as model for the heroine of the early work of such a great man. Her appearance in Weimar caused a stir, which by no means pleased the old gentleman. His excellency invited the Frau Hofrat to lunch and treated her with a stiff civility reflected in the letter she wrote to one of her sons regarding the reunion. It is a tragicomic, human, and literary-historical document. "I have made the acquaintance," she wrote, "of an old man who, had I not known he was Goethe, *and even then,* did not make a pleasant impression on me."

I think this anecdote could be the basis for a reflective story, indeed for a novel, that would deal with emotion and poetry, with pride and the decline of age; it could be the occasion for a penetrating character study of Goethe, of the nature of genius altogether. Perhaps one day the writer who will undertake this will come forth.

Thomas Mann

Translated by Elizabeth Corra

THE SUFFERINGS OF YOUNG WERTHER

I have carefully collected all I could possibly find out about the history of poor Werther, and I lay it before you here, knowing that you will thank me for doing so. You cannot deny his mind and character your admiration and love, or his fate your tears.

And you, good soul, who are feeling the same anguish as he, draw consolation from his sufferings, and let this little book be your friend, if fate or your own fault prevent you from finding a closer one.

First Book

May 4, 1771.

How happy I am to be gone! Best of friends, what is the heart of man! To forsake you, whom I love so much, from whom I was inseparable, and be happy! I know you will forgive me for it. Were not my other associations so chosen by fate as to make a heart like mine uneasy? Poor Leonore! And yet it was not my fault. Could I help it that while the compelling charms of her sister gave me agreeable entertainment, that poor heart developed its own passion? And yet—am I quite without fault? Did I not nourish her feelings? did I not myself delight in those wholly authentic manifestations of nature which so often made us laugh, little laughable as they were? did I not—O what is man, that he has a right to lament what he is? I will, dear friend, I promise you, I will reform, will no longer harp on the misfortunes with which fate presents us, as I have always done; I will enjoy the present, and the past shall be past. You are certainly right, best of men: there would be fewer sufferings among men if they did not—God knows why they are so made—so industriously employ their imagination in recalling the memories of past evils, rather than endure a colorless present.

Please be so good as to tell my mother that I shall attend to her affair as best I can and send her a report of it as soon as possible. I have seen my aunt and find her far from being the vixen that people at home make of her. She is a lively, impetuous woman with the best of hearts. I explained to her my mother's complaints regarding that portion of the inheritance which has been withheld; she gave me her reasons and the facts, and named the conditions under which she would be ready to hand over everything, and even more than we demanded—In short, I don't care to write about it now, but tell my mother that everything will be all right. And in connection with this little matter I have again found, my dear fellow, that misunderstandings and lethargy perhaps produce more wrong in the world than deceit and malice do. At least the two latter are certainly rarer.

For the rest, I like it here very much: solitude in this paradise is a precious balm to my heart, and this youthful time of year warms with all its fullness my oft-shivering heart. Every tree, every hedge is a bouquet of flowers, and one would like to turn into a cockchafer, to be able to float about in this sea of scents and find all one's nourishment in it.

The town itself is unpleasant, but on the other hand all around it lies inexpressibly beautiful nature. It was this which induced the late Count M. to lay out a garden on one of the hills which intersect with the most charming diversity, forming the loveliest valleys. The garden is unpetentious, and you no sooner enter it than you feel that it was designed not by a scientific gardener but by a man with a sensitive heart, who wanted to use it for the enjoyment of himself. I have already shed many a tear for the deceased in the decayed little bower which was his favorite spot and is now mine. Soon I shall be the master of the garden; the gardener has a liking for me, even after so few days, and he will not suffer by it.

May 10.

A wonderful cheerfulness has taken possession of my whole soul, similar to the sweet spring mornings which I enjoy with all my heart. I am alone and glad to be alive in this locality, which was created for such souls as mine. I am so happy, dear friend, so completely immersed in the realization of a tranquil existence, that my art is suffering neglect. I could not draw at all now, not a line, and yet I have never been a greater painter than I am now. When the beloved valley steams around me, and the lofty sun rests on the surface of the impenetrable darkness of my forest with only single rays stealing into the inner sanctuary, then I lie in the tall grass beside the murmuring brook, while on the earth near me a thousand varied grasses strike me as significant; when I feel the swarming life of the little world between the grass-blades, the innumerable, unfathomable shapes of the tiny worms and flies, closer to my heart, and feel the presence of the Almighty, who created us in his image, feel the breath of the all-loving one, who, afloat in eternal rapture, bears and sustains us; O my friend! then when twilight invests my eyes, and the world about me and the heaven above me rests wholly in my soul like the image of a woman one loves—then I am often all longing and I think: ah, could you express all that again, could you breathe onto paper that which lives in you so fully, so warmly, so that it would become the reflection of your soul, as your soul is a mirror of the infinite God! My friend—But this experience is beyond my strength, I succumb to the overpowering glory of what I behold.

May 12.

I don't know whether deluding spirits hover about this region, or whether it is the warm, heavenly fancy in my heart which turns my whole environment into a paradise. Thus, directly outside the town there is a well, one to which I am magically bound like Melusina and her sisters.—You go down a little slope and find yourself in front of a vault in which about twenty steps descend to a spot where the clearest water gushes out of marble rocks. The little wall which serves as coping at the top, the tall trees which give shade all around, the coolness of the spot—all this has a suggestive, mysterious character. Not a day passes without my sitting there for an hour. Then the maids come from the town and fetch water, the most innocent and necessary of employments, which in former days the daughters of kings engaged in themselves. When I sit there, the patriarchal idea is vividly realized about me, as all the men of old make friends or go courting at the well, while beneficent spirits hover about the wellsprings and fountains. O, a man who cannot share that experience must never have been refreshed, after an arduous journey in the summer, by the coolness of a wellspring.

May 13.

You ask whether to send me my books.—Friend, I beg you for the love of God, don't load me up with them. I do not wish to be guided, encouraged, enkindled any more; my heart effervesces enough all by itself. What I need is lullabies, and I have found an abundance of them in my Homer. How often do I lull my agitated blood into quiet, for you have never seen anything as uneven, as unstable, as this heart. Good friend, do I need to tell that to you, who have so often borne the burden of seeing me pass from grief to extravagant joy and from sweet melancholy to disastrous passion? Moreover, I treat my heart like a sick child, granting its every wish. Do not pass this on; there are those who would make it a reproach to me.

May 15.

The lower classes here know me already and love me, especially the children. When I sought their acquaintance to begin with, and put friendly questions to them about this and that, some of them thought I was making fun of them and snubbed me quite rudely. I did not let this bother me; I only felt most keenly what I have often observed before: people of some rank will always keep the common people coolly at a distance, as if they thought they would lose something by approaching them; and then too there are social apostates and practical jokers, who seem to condescend, making their arrogance all the more painful to the poor.

I am quite aware that we are not equal and cannot be equal; but I hold that he who thinks it necessary to withdraw from the so-called rabble in order to keep their respect is just as reprehensible as a coward who hides from his enemy because he is afraid of defeat.

Recently, as I came to the spring, I found a young servant girl who had put her pitcher on the lowest step and was looking around to see if no fellow servant were coming along to help her get it on her head. I descended and looked at her. "Shall I help you, girl?" said I. She blushed up to her ears. "Oh no, sir!" she said. "Don't stand on ceremony." She adjusted her head cushion, and I helped her. She thanked me and mounted the steps.

May 17.

I have made all kinds of acquaintances, but so far I have not found any associates. I don't know, something about me must attract people; so many of them like me and cling to me, and it pains me when our common journey takes us only a short distance. If you ask what the people here are like, I must tell you, "Like people everywhere." Uniformity marks the human race. Most of them spend the greater part of their time in working for a living, and the scanty freedom that is left to them burdens them so that they seek every means of getting rid of it. O fate of man!

But these people are a very good sort. If I forget myself once in a while, tasting with them the joys that are still granted to me, such as exchanging pleasantries in all candor and ingenuousness around a prettily set table, planning a pleasure drive, or arranging for a well-timed dance, and the like, the effect on me is very good; only I must not let myself think that in me lie ever so many other powers, all of which molder for lack of use, and which I must carefully conceal. Ah, and that fetters my whole heart—And yet! to be misunderstood is the fate of such as I.

Alas that the friend of my youth is gone! Alas that I ever knew her?—I could say, "You are a fool! for you are seeking what is not to be found here below." But I did have her friendship, I sensed that heart, that great soul, in whose presence I felt myself to be more than I was, because I was all that I could be. Good God! was there a single force in my soul which remained unutilized? Could I not, when with her, unfold that entire power of feeling with which my heart embraces all nature? Was not our association an endless play of the subtlest feeling, of the keenest wit, a wit whose variations, not excluding some flippancy, bore the stamp of genius? And now!—Ah me, the years of hers which exceeded mine brought her before me to the grave. Never shall I forget her, never her steadfast mind and her divine indulgence.

A few days ago I met a young man named V., an ingenuous youth with a very happy physiognomy. He has just come from the university, and though he does not exactly think himself wise, he does believe he knows more than others. He was diligent, too, as I can tell in all sorts of ways; in short, he is pretty well informed. Having heard that I draw a great deal and know Greek (two rare phenomena in these skies), he sought me out and unloaded much learning, from Batteux to Robert Wood, from Roger de Piles to Winckelmann, assuring me that he had read Sulzer's *General Theory of the Fine Arts,* that is, the first part of it, from beginning to end, and that he owned a MS of Heyne on the study of classical antiquity. I let it go at that.

Furthermore, I have made the acquaintance of a very fine person: a steward of the prince, a frank and ingenuous man. They say it rejoices the soul to see him in the midst of his children, of whom he has nine; in particular they make a great fuss over his eldest daughter. He has invited me to his house, and I will call on him one of these days. He is living in one of the prince's hunting lodges, an hour and a half from here on foot, having received permission to move there after the death of his wife, since he found residence here in the town and in the official dwelling too painful.

In addition, a number of eccentric freaks have crossed my path whom I find insufferable in very respect, most unendurable being their manifestations of friendship.

Farewell! This letter will suit you, for it is nothing but a report.

May 22.

That the life of man is only a dream has seemed to be so to many before now, and I too always carry this feeling about with me. When I behold the narrow bounds which confine man's powers of action and investigation; when I see how all his efficiency aims at the satisfaction of needs which in their turn have no purpose save to prolong our unhappy existence, and then see that all our reassurance regarding certain matters of inquiry is merely a resigned kind of dreaming, whereby we paint the walls within which we are confined with gay figures and bright prospects—All this, Wilhelm, forces me into silence. I return into myself, and find a world! But again a world of groping and vague desires rather than one of clear delineation and active force. And then everything grows hazy to my senses, and in a sort of dream I keep on smiling at the world.

All learned schoolmasters and educators agree that children do not know why they want what they want; but that adults too, as well as children, stagger around on this earth, like them not knowing whence they come and whither they go, pursue true goals just as little as they, and are just as completely governed by biscuits and cakes and birch rods: nobody will believe that, and yet it seems to me palpable.

I am ready to grant—for I know what you would say to this—that the happiest are those who like children live for the day, drag their dolls around, dressing and undressing them, slink with bated breath about the drawer where Mama keeps the candy locked up, and, when they finally get hold of what they want, gobble it down by the mouthful and cry, "More!"—Those are happy creatures. Happy are those, too, who give sumptuous titles to their shabby occupations, perhaps even to their passions, recommending them to the human race as gigantic operations redounding to man's salvation and welfare.—Happy the man who can be like that! But one who recognizes in all humility what all this comes to, who see how amiably every happy citizen manages to shape his little garden into a paradise, and how indefatigably even the unhappy man plods along panting under his burden, while all of them take the same interest in having one more minute to see the light of this sun—ah, he holds his peace, and he too creates his world in himself, and is moreover happy because he is a human being. And then, confined and fettered as he is, still he continues to keep in his heart the sweet feeling of freedom, knowing that he can quit this position whenever he will.

May 26.

You have long known my way of settling down, pitching my tent in some spot I like, and lodging there in a modest fashion. Here too I have again come upon a nook that I found attractive.

About an hour's walk from town lies a place called Wahlheim.* Its situation on a hill is very interesting, and when you leave the village on the upper footpath, all at once you are overlooking the entire valley. A goodhearted hostess, who is obliging and lively for her age, dispenses wine, beer, and coffee; and surpassing everything else are two lindens whose spreading branches cover the small space before the church, which is completely ringed about with farmhouses, barns, and courtyards. So sequestered, so homelike a spot I have not readily found, and I have my little table carried out there

*Note by Goethe. The reader will save himself the trouble of looking for the places mentioned here; it has been found necessary to change the true names given in the original text.—"Wahlheim" means roughly "home of one's choice".—*Tr.*

from the inn, and my chair, and there I drink my coffee and read my Homer. The first time, when I chanced to walk in under the lindens on a fine afternoon, I found the little spot so lonely. Everyone was in the fields, and only a boy of about four was sitting on the ground and holding close to his breast with both arms another one, perhaps half a year old, sitting between his feet, so that he made a kind of armchair for the baby, and, for all the liveliness with which his black eyes looked about him, sat quite still. I found the sight charming: I sat down on a plough across the way and sketched this brotherly posture with great enjoyment. I added the nearest fence, a barn-door, and some broken wheels, all of it just as it stood there, and after the lapse of an hour I found that I had completed a well-disposed, very interesting drawing, without putting in the least imaginary detail. This strengthened me in my resolve to keep hence-forth exclusively to nature. Nature alone is infinitely rich, and she alone forms the great artist. One can say much in favour of rules, about the same things as can be said in praise of civil society. A person who trains himself by the rules will never produce anything absurd or bad, just as one who lets himself be modeled after laws and decorum can never become an intolerable neighbor, never an outright villain; on the other hand any "rule," say what you like, will destroy the true feeling for nature and the true expression of her! I hear you say that that is too severe, that the rule merely restrains, prunes rank shoots, etc.—Good friend, shall I give you a comparison? It may be likened to loving. A young heart is whole-heartedly bound up in a maiden, spends every daytime hour with her, squanders all its talents, all its fortune, in order to employ every moment in expressing its complete devotion to her. And now suppose some pedant comes along, a man who holds a public office, and says to him, "Fine young gentleman, to love is human, only you must be human in your loving! Apportion your hours, keeping some for work, and devote the hours of recreation to your maiden. Figure up your fortune, and whatever is in excess of your needs I will not forbid you to spend on a present for her, only not too often, say on her birthday or name-day, etc."—If the youth obeys, then a useful young person will be the result, and I would even advise any prince to make him a counsellor; however, it will be the end of his love, and, if he is an artist, of his art. O my friends! you ask why the stream of genius so seldom bursts forth, so seldom sends its sublime floods rushing in, to make your souls quake with astonishment?— Dear friends, why, there along both banks of the river dwell the placid conservatives whose summer houses, tulip beds, and cabbage fields would be ruined, and who consequently manage to avert betimes, with dams and drainage ditches, any future threat.

May 27.

I see that I have lapsed into raptures, parables, and oratory, and have thus forgotten to complete the story of my further doings with the children. Wholly engrossed in the feelings of an artist, which my letter of yesterday presents to you in very fragmentary form. I sat on my plough for a good two hours. Then towards evening a young woman with a small basket on her arm came toward the children, who had not moved all this while, calling from a distance, "Philip, you're a good boy." She spoke to me, I thanked her, got up, approached her, and asked if she was the children's mother. She said yes, and giving the older one half a roll, she picked up the baby and kissed it with all a mother's love. "I told my Philip to hold the baby," said she, "and went into town with my oldest boy to get white bread, and sugar, and an earthenware saucepan." I saw all this in the basket, the cover of which had fallen off. "I want to cook my Hans (that was the name of the youngest) a bit of soup for supper; the big boy, the scamp, broke my saucepan yesterday while quarrelling with Philip over the scrapings of the porridge." I asked about the oldest, and she had hardly told me that he was racing around the meadow with some geese when he came running and brought the second boy a hazel switch. I went on talking with the woman and learned that she was the daughter of the schoolmaster, and that her husband had gone on a trip to Switzerland to get the legacy of a cousin. "They wanted to cheat him out of it," said she, "and didn't answer his letters; so he went there himself. I only hope nothing has happened to him; I don't get any word from him." I found it hard to part from the woman, but I gave each of the children a penny, and I gave her one for the youngest, so that she could bring him a roll to go with the soup as soon as she went into town, and so we separated.

I tell you, dear fellow, when my senses are strained to the limit, all the tumult within me is soothed by the sight of such a creature, who moves within the narrow round of her existence in happy tranquillity, gets along somehow from one day to the next, and, seeing the leaves fall, is not moved to think anything but that winter is coming.

Since that day I have often been out there. The children are quite accustomed to me, they get sugar when I drink coffee, and in the evening they share bread and butter and clabber with me. On Sundays they never fail to get a penny, and if I am not there after prayer-time, the hostess has orders to give it to them.

They feel confidential and tell me all sorts of things, and I delight especially in their passions and the simple expressions of their desires when a number of village children are assembled.

It has cost me much effort to rid the mother of her concern lest they should "incommode the gentleman."

May 30.

What I recently told you about painting is certainly true of poetry as well; the only requirement is that one should recognize what is excellent and have the courage to express it, and that to be sure is saying much in few words. Today I experienced a scene which, written down as it was, would produce the finest idyll in the world; but of what use is poetry, scene, and idyll? Must we always start tinkering when we are supposed to share in a phenomenon of nature?

If this introduction leads you to expect much that is lofty and distinguished, then you are once more badly deceived; it is only a peasant lad who so carried me away that I took this lively interest. I shall tell it badly, as usual, and you will as usual, I imagine, think I am overdoing it; it is once more Wahlheim, and always Wahlheim, that produces these rarities.

There was a company outside under the lindens, drinking coffee. Because I did not altogether care for it, I lagged behind under some pretext.

A peasant lad came out of a neighboring house and busied himself with the repair of some part of the plough which I had recently sketched. As I found him pleasing, I spoke to him, asked about his circumstances; we were soon acquainted, and, as usually happens to me with this kind of people, soon on familiar terms. He told me that he was in the service of a widow, and very well treated by her. He told me so much about her, and praised her in such a way, that I could soon tell he was devoted to her, body and soul. She was no longer young, he said, she had been badly treated by her first husband and did not want to remarry, and from his narrative it was so shiningly evident how beautiful, how charming she seemed to him, and how greatly he wished that she might choose him, in order to wipe out the recollection of her first husband's faults, that I should have to repeat word for word to make you visualize the sheer affection, the love and loyalty of this man. Indeed, I should have to possess the gifts of the greatest poet, in order to be able to give you at the same time a vivid depiction of the expressiveness of his gestures, the harmonious sound of his voice, the hidden fire of his glances. No, there are no words to express the gentleness which lay in his whole conduct and expression; anything I could reproduce would be merely clumsy. It touched me especially that he was so afraid I might have a wrong idea of his relation to her and have doubts of her good behavior. How charming it was when he spoke of her figure, or her body, which without the charm of youth attracted him powerfully and held him captive—I can only repeat that to myself in my inmost soul. In all my life I have not seen such urgent desire and ardent, intense yearning in such unmixed purity; indeed I can say that in such purity I have not imagined or dreamed it. Do not chide me when I say that the recollection of this genuine naturalness sets my inmost soul aglow, that the picture of this loyalty and tenderness follows me everywhere, and that I, as if set on fire by it, am languishing and pining.

I will now try to see her too in the near future, or rather, on further reflection, I will avoid that. It is better that I should see her through the eyes of her lover; perhaps she will not appear to my own eyes as she now stands before me, and why should I spoil that lovely picture?

June 16.

Why I don't write to you?—You ask that, and yet you too are one of those who are so learned. You should guess that I am doing fine, in fact—to sum it up, I have made an acquaintance which touches my heart closely. I have—I don't know.

To tell you step by step how it came about that I have learned to know one of the most lovable of creatures will not be easy. I am happy and in high spirits, and that makes me a poor writer of history.

An angel!—pshaw! that's what every man says of his sweetheart, isn't it? And yet I am not in a position to tell you in what respect she is perfect, why she is perfect; enough! she has taken possession of my whole being.

So much simplicity along with so much intelligence, so much kindness with so much firmness, tranquillity of soul and yet fully alive and active.

All this is loathsome twaddle—what I am saying about her—pitiful abstractions, which do not express a single feature of her being. Another time—No, not another time, I'll tell you about it *now*. If I don't do it now, it would never happen. For, between us, since I began to write this I was thrice on the point of laying down my pen, having my horse saddled, and riding off. And yet I swore to myself this morning that I wouldn't ride out, and yet again I go to the window every other minute to see how high the sun still stands. — — —

I wasn't able to resist, I had to go out to see her. Here I am again, Wilhelm, I will sup on my bread and butter and write to you. What a rapture it is for my soul to see her in the midst of the lively, darling children, her eight brothers and sisters!—

If I continue like this, you'll be just as wise at the end as you were to start with. Listen then, I will force myself to go into detail

I wrote you recently about having made the acquaintance of Bailiff S., and about his having invited me to visit him soon in his hermitage, or rather in his little kingdom. I neglected it, and perhaps I should never have gone out there if chance had not revealed to me the treasure which lies hidden in that quiet spot.

Our young people had arranged a dance out in the country, which I willingly agreed to attend. I offered to escort a nice, pretty, but otherwise commonplace local girl, and it was settled that I should hire a carriage, drive my partner and her cousin out to the place of festivities, and on the way stop to take Charlotte S. along. "You will get to know a beautiful woman," said my partner, as we rode through the clearing of the extensive forest toward the hunting lodge. "Be on your guard," added the cousin, "that you don't fall in love?" "Why?" said I. "She is already promised," was the reply, "to a very worthy man, who has gone out of town to arrange his affairs, because his father has died, and to apply for an important position." This information did not interest me much.

The sun was still a quarter of an hour above the mountains when we drove up before the courtyard gate. It was very sultry, and the ladies expressed their concern regarding a thunderstorm, which seemed to be gathering in grey-white, fleecy little clouds all around the horizon. I quieted their fears with a deceptive display of weather-wisdom, although I myself began to suspect that our merrymaking would get a jolt.

I alighted, and a maidservant who came to the gate begged us to wait a moment, saying that Miss Lotte would come soon. I walked through the courtyard toward the well-built house, and when I had mounted the outside steps, and stepped into the doorway, my eyes encountered the most charming spectacle I have ever seen. In the vestibule six children, ranging from eleven to two years old, were crowding around a beautifully formed girl of medium height, who was wearing a plain white dress with pale pink bows on arm and breast. She was holding a loaf of black bread and cutting for the little ones around her slices appropriate to their age and appetite, and she handed over each one with such amiability, and each one called out its "Thank you!" so unaffectedly, stretching its little hands high into the air even before the slice was cut, and now either ran off delighted with its supper, or in accordance with its quieter temperament, walked tranquilly toward the gate, in order to see the strangers, and the carriage in which their Lotte was to ride away. "I beg pardon," she said, "for making you come in and letting the ladies wait. What with dressing, and giving all kinds of directions regarding the house during my absence, I forgot to give the children their supper, and they won't have anyone cut bread for them but me." I paid her some indifferent compliment, for my whole soul was fixed upon her figure, her tone of voice, her whole behavior, and I barely had time to recover from my surprise while she ran into the living room to get her gloves and her fan. The little ones were looking askance at me from some distance, and I walked up to the youngest one, a child with the most attractive face. He was drawing back just as Lotte came out of the door and said, "Louis, shake hands with our cousin." The boy did that very readily, and I could not refrain from kissing him heartily, regardless of his runny nose. "Cousin?" said I, extending my hand to her, "do you think I am worthy of the happiness of being related to you?" "O," said she with an easy smile, "our relationship is very extensive, and I should be sorry if you were the worst among them." As she went she gave Sophie, her next oldest sister, a girl of about eleven, instructions to keep good watch over the children, and to say hello to papa when he came home from his pleasure ride. She told the little ones to obey their sister Sophie as if Sophie were she, and some of them promised this expressly. But a pert little girl of about six said, "All the same, Lotte, she isn't you, and we like you better." The two oldest boys had climbed up onto the back of the carriage, and at my request she gave them permission to ride along to the edge of the forest, if they would promise not to annoy each other, and to hold on tight.

We had scarcely got properly seated, the ladies having greeted each other, with alternate comments on each other's dresses and especially their hats, and having given the company they expected to find a thorough going over, when Lotte bade the driver stop and let her brothers get down; they insisted on kissing her hand again, which the oldest did with all the tenderness appropriate to his fifteen years, the other with much impetuosity and frivolity. She sent her love to the little ones again, and we drove on.

The cousin asked if she had done with the book she had recently sent her. "No," said Lotte, "I don't like it, you can have it back. And the one before that was no better." I was astonished when, on my asking what the books were, she answered,*—I found so much personality in all that she said, and every word showed me new charms, new rays of intellect bursting forth from her face, which seemed little by little to blossom out with pleasure, because she could feel by my bearing that I understood her.

"When I was younger," she said. "I liked nothing so much as novels. God knows how content I was when on a Sunday I could just settle into a corner, to participate with all my heart in the fortune and misfortune of some Miss Jenny. Nor do I deny that such reading

---

*Note by Goethe. It has been found necessary to suppress this passage in the letter, in order to give no one any occasion for complaint. Although, ultimately, no author can care much about the judgment of an individual girl and an unstable young man.

still has some charm for me; but since I so rarely have time to read a book, it must be something that just suits my taste. And that author is my favorite in whom I find my own world again, in whose work life goes on like my own, and yet whose story becomes as interesting and as heartfelt as my own domestic life, which to be sure is no paradise, but still on the whole a source of unspeakable happiness."

I strove to conceal the agitation which these words produced in me. This did not do much good, to be sure; for when I heard her in passing speak with such truth about "The Vicar of Wakefield," about*—I was soon beside myself, told her everything I could not help saying, and only observed after some time, when Lotte shifted the conversation to take in the others, that they had sat there wide-eyed the whole time, as if they were not present. The cousin looked at me more than once with a mocking upturn of her nose, which however mattered nothing to me.

The conversation took up the pleasure of dancing. "If this passion is a fault," said Lotte, "I readily admit nevertheless that I know nothing to surpass dancing. And if anything troubles me and I hammer out a quadrille on my old piano, out of tune as it is, that makes everything all right again."

How I feasted on her black eyes during this conversation! How the vivacious lips and the fresh, hearty cheeks drew to them my whole soul! How I, wholly absorbed in the glorious ideas she was expressing, often failed completely to hear the words with which she conveyed her meaning!—You have some picture of that, because you know me. In short, I got out of the carriage as if dreaming, when we came to a halt before the pavilion, and was so lost in dreams, in the twilit world around me, that I scarcely gave a thought to the music which flooded down toward us from the illuminated ballroom.

The two gentlemen who were the partners of the cousin and Lotte, Mr. Audran and a certain N. N.—who can remember all the names?—met us at the carriage, took charge of their ladies, and I escorted my partner upstairs.

We wound around each other in minuets; I claimed one lady after another, and it was just the most unattractive ones who could not manage to clasp one's hand and make an end. Lotte and her partner

---

*Note by Goethe. Here too the names of some native authors have been omitted. Whichever of them enjoys Lotte's approval will surely feel it in his heart if he should read this passage, and of course no one else needs to know.

began an English square dance, and you can appreciate how happy I felt when in due course she began to dance the figure with us. One must *see* her dance! You see, she is so wrapped up in it with her whole heart and her whole soul, her whole body one single harmony, so carefree, so unaffected, as if the dance were really everything, as if she were thinking nothing else, feeling nothing else; and in that moment, surely, everything else fades away.

I asked for the second quadrille; she promised me the third, and with the most amiable ingenuousness in the world she assured me that she loved the German style of dancing. "It is the fashion here," she went on, "for every couple that belong together to stay together during the German dance, and my partner is a poor waltzer and will thank me if I spare him the trouble. Your lady can't waltz either, and doesn't like to, and during the quadrille I saw that you waltz well; now if you will be mine for the German dance, then go and request it of my gentleman, and I will talk to your lady." I shook hands on it, and we agreed that during that time her partner should converse with mine.

Now the dance began! And for a while we took pleasure in interlacing our arms in various ways. With what charm, with what fleetness she moved! and now when it actually came to waltzing, and we revolved about each other like the spheres, at first there was a little confusion, to be sure, because very few are skilled at it. We were astute and let them romp their fill, and when the clumsiest couples had quit the field, we swung in and held out valiantly with one other couple, Audran and his partner. Never have I been so light on my feet. I was no longer human. To hold in my arms the most lovable creature, and flying about with her like lightning, so that everything about me faded away, and—to be honest, Wilhelm, I did swear to myself all the same that a girl I loved and had a claim upon should never waltz with anyone but me, and even if I lost my life over it. You know what I mean!

We walked around the hall a few times to catch our breath. Then she sat down, and the oranges which I had previously put aside, and which by now were the only ones left, had an excellent effect, except that with every slice she handed to a demanding lady beside her for politeness' sake I felt a stab through my heart.

During the third quadrille we were the second couple. As we were going down the line, and I, clinging to her arm, was gazing with

God knows how much rapture into her eyes, which were filled with the sincerest expression of the frankest, purest pleasure, we encountered a woman whom I had already observed because of the amiable effect of a face no longer young. She looks at Lotte with a smile, lifts a menacing finger, and as she speeds past us she says "Albert" twice in a very significant manner.

"Who is Albert?" said I to Lotte, "if it is not presumptuous to ask." She was on the point of answering when we had to separate in order to dance the big eight, and when our paths crossed it seemed to me that I detected a pensive cast on her brow.—"Why should I disavow it?" she said, as she gave me her hand for the promenade. "Albert is a fine person to whom I am as good as engaged." Now this was no news to me (for the girls had told me about it in the carriage), and yet it *was* utterly new to me, because I had not yet related it in my thoughts to her, who had become so dear to me in such a short time. Anyway, I got confused, forgot what I was doing, and danced in between the wrong couple, so that everything was sixes and sevens, and it required all Lotte's presence of mind, with tugging and twisting, to restore order without loss of time.

The dance was not yet ended when the flashes which we had been seeing for some time along the horizon, and which I had steadily declared to be heat lightning, began to increase greatly, and the thunder drowned out the music. Three ladies ran out of the square, followed by their gentlemen; the disorder grew general, and the music stopped. It is natural that when a misfortune or something terrible surprises us in the midst of merriment, it makes a stronger impression on us than usual, partly on account of the contrast, which is so vividly experienced, partly, and more, because our senses have become more perceptive and therefore receive an impression all the more rapidly. To such causes I must ascribe the extraordinary contortions into which I saw several ladies fall. The smartest one sat down in a corner with her back to the window and held her ears shut. Another knelt down before her and hid her head in the first one's lap. A third pushed in between the two and embraced her dear sisters, with endless tears. Some wanted to go home; others, who were still less aware of what they were doing, did not have enough presence of mind to stave off the importunities of some of our young gourmets, who seemed to find an occupation in anticipating all the anxious prayers which were meant for Heaven, and in gathering them from the lips of the distressed beauties. Some of our gentlemen had gone below to smoke a pipe in peace; and the rest of the company raised no objection when the hostess hit upon the shrewd idea of putting at our disposal a room which had shutters and curtains. Scarcely had we got into it when Lotte busied herself with placing chairs in a circle, and, when the company had sat down at her request, she proposed that they play a game.

I saw more than one purse up his lips and stretch his limbs in the hope of a juicy forfeit. "We'll play counting," said she. "Now pay attention! I will circle from right to left, and so you are to count in the same way, each saying his proper number, and that must go like wildfire, and whoever hesitates or makes a mistake gets a box on the ear, and so on up to a thousand." Now that was a merry sight. She walked around the circle with her arm outstretched. "One," said the first, his neighbor said Two, the next one Three, and so on. Then she began to walk faster, and faster and faster; soon there was a mistake and slap! went her hand, and the laughter confused the next one and slap! And still faster. I myself got two slaps, and with keen pleasure I thought I observed that they were harder than the ones she usually dealt the others. Universal laughter and commotion ended the game before it had even got up to a thousand. The most intimate friends drew each other away, the storm was over, and I followed Lotte into the ballroom. As we went along she said. "The ear-boxing made them forget the storm and everything!" I couldn't say a word. "I was one of the most timid," she continued, "and by pretending to be courageous in order to give the others courage I took heart myself." We stepped to the window. Off to one side there was thunder, and the splendid rain was trickling down upon the land; the most refreshing fragrance rose up to us from the rich abundance of the warm atmosphere. She stood leaning on her elbows, with her gaze searching the countryside; she looked up to heaven and at me; I saw her eyes fill with tears, and she laid her hand on mine, saying, "Klopstock!" I recalled at once the glorious ode* she had in mind, and became immersed in the stream of emotions which she had poured over me by uttering this symbolic name. I could not bear it, I bent down over her hand and kissed it and amid

---

*Klopstock's poem in free rhythms, "Die Frühlingsfeier" (the festival of spring), had a sensational appeal in eighteenth century Germany.—*Tr.*

tears of the utmost rapture. And looked into her eyes again—Noble poet! would that you had seen your apotheosis in that gaze, and would that your name, so often profaned, would never reach my ears from any other lips.

June 19.

I no longer know where I stopped in my story the other day; but I know that it was two o'clock in the morning when I got to bed, and that if I could have chatted with you instead of writing, I might have kept you up until morning.

What happened on our return drive from the ball I haven't told you yet, and this is no day for it, either.

It was the most glorious sunrise. The dripping woods, and the refreshed earth round about! Our other ladies fell into a doze. She asked me, didn't I want to join them? I shouldn't be uneasy on her account. "As long as I see those eyes open," I said, looking steadily at her, "there's no danger." And we both held out, all the way to her gate, which the maidservant quietly opened for her, assuring her in response to her questions that her father and the little ones were well, and all of them still asleep. Then I parted from her with the request that I might see her again that same day; she consented, and I went there; and since that time sun, moon, and stars can calmly go about their business, but I am conscious neither of day nor night, and the whole world around me is fading away.

June 21.

I am living through such happy days as God sets aside for his saints; and let become of me what will. I may never say that I have not tasted the joys, the unalloyed joys of life.—You know my Wahlheim; there I am completely settled, from there it is only a half hour's walk to Lotte, and there I feel all that I am and the full bliss that is given to man.

If I had thought, when I chose Wahlheim as the goal of my pleasure walks, that it was situated so close to Heaven! How often, in the course of my lengthy wanderings, I have seen the hunting lodge, that embraces all my desires, now from the height, now from the plain across the river!

Dear Wilhelm, I have had all sorts of reflections concerning man's desire to expand, to make new discoveries, to rove about; and then again concerning his deep urge to accept willingly his confining limits, to drift along in the rut of habit, giving no heed to what lies either to right or left.

It is a wonder how, when I came here and looked down into the lovely valley from the hilltop, I was attracted by everything around me.—That grove yonder!—Oh, if I could mingle with its shade!—That mountain top!—Oh, if I could survey the broad expanse from there!—Those hills linked together and the intimate valleys!—Oh, if I could lose myself in them!—I hastened thither, and I returned, and had not found what I hoped. Ah, distance affects us like the future! Before our soul lies a vast, dimly outlined whole in which both feeling and sight lose themselves, and we yearn, ah! to surrender our whole being, to let ourselves be filled with all the rapture of one great, glorious emotion—But alas! when we hasten thither, when the There becomes the Here, everything is just as it was, and we stand there in our poverty, in our limitation, and our soul thirsts for quickening water that has eluded us.

So it is that even the most restless rover finally longs for his native land, to find in his cottage, on the breast of his wife, in the circle of his children, in the affairs that furnish their support, the joy that he vainly sought in all the wide world.

When I walk out to my Wahlheim in the morning, at sunrise, and, having picked my own sugar peas in the garden of the inn, sit down and string them, reading now and then in my Homer; then when I select a pot in the little kitchen, dig out a piece of butter, put the pods on the flame, cover the pot, and sit down there so that I can shake them up occasionally: then I feel so vividly how Penelope's impudent suitors* slaughter oxen and swine, cut them up, and roast them. There is nothing that could fill me so completely with a quiet, genuine feeling as those traits of patriarchal life which I, thank God, can weave into my kind of life without affectation.

How fortunate it is for me that my heart can feel the plain, naïve delight of the man who puts on the table a cabbage that he has grown himself, and for whom it is not merely the vegetable, but all the good days, the fine morning when he planted it, the pleasant evenings when he watered it, taking his pleasure in its thriving growth—that he enjoys again in one comprehensive moment.

*Odyssey XX, 251.—Tr.

The day before yesterday the town doctor came out to see the steward and found me on the floor among Lotte's children, some of them scrambling over me, others teasing me, while I tickled them and provoked a great outcry on their part. The doctor, who is a very dogmatic puppet, smooths the folds of his cuffs while talking, and pulls out a shirt-frill that has no end, considered this to be beneath the dignity of an intelligent person; I could tell by the tilt of his nose. But I paid not the least attention, let him discourse on very sensible matters, and rebuilt for the children the card houses they had knocked down. This also led to his going about town and complaining that the steward's children were spoilt enough as it was, but Werther was now ruining them completely.

Yes, dear Wilhelm, of all living things on earth, children are closest to my heart. When I watch them, and see in the little creatures the seeds of all the virtues, all the powers, of which they will one day be so much in need; when I perceive in their obstinancy future steadfastness and firmness of character, in their mischievousness good humour and the ease with which they will slide over the perils of the world, and all of it so unspoiled, so complete!—then I repeat over and over again the golden words of the Teacher of men: "Except ye become as little children!" And now, best of friends, these children, who are like ourselves, whom we should look upon as our models, we treat as subjects. They are not supposed to have a will of their own!—Well, don't we have one? on what do we base our prerogative!—The fact that we are older and wiser!—Good God, from your Heaven you see old children, and young children, and that is all, and your son proclaimed long ago in which of them you take the greater pleasure. But they believe in him without hearing him—that too is an old story—and form their children after themselves, and—Adieu, Wilhelm! I have no desire to prattle on further.

I feel in my own poor heart, which is worse off than many a one languishing on a sickbed, what Lotte must mean to a patient. She will spend some days in town at the house of an excellent woman who, the physicians say, is nearing her end, and who wishes to have Lotte near her in these last moments. Last week I went with her to call on the pastor of St.***, a hamlet that lies off to one side in the hills, an hour's walk from here. We got there about four. Lotte had taken her second sister along. When we stepped into the parsonage yard, which is shaded by two tall walnut trees, the good old man was sitting on a bench before the front door, and when he saw Lotte, he was as if rejuvenated, forgot about his stick, and boldly rose to go toward her. She ran up to him and forced him to sit down, seating herself beside him, brought him many greetings from her father, and hugged his odious, filthy, youngest boy, the pet of his old age. You should have seen her as she held his full attention, raising her voice to make herself audible to his half-deaf ears, telling him about young, robust persons who had died unexpectedly, about the excellence of Karlsbad, and praised his resolve to go there in the following summer, telling him that he was looking much better, much livelier than the last time she had seen him. Meanwhile I had paid my respects to the pastor's wife. The old man grew quite lively, and since I could not refrain from praising the handsome walnut trees which were shading us so pleasantly, he began, though with some difficulty, to tell us their history.

"As for the old tree," he said, "we don't know who planted it: some say this pastor, some the other. But the younger one back there is as old as my wife, fifty years come October. Her father planted it in the morning of the day towards the evening of which she was born. He was my predecessor in office, and there are no words to tell how dear the tree was to him; it is certainly no less dear to me. My wife was sitting under it on a wooden beam, knitting, when I came into this yard as a poor student twenty-seven years ago."

Lotte asked after his daughter and was told that she had gone out with Mr. Schmidt to the meadow to talk to the workmen. The old man went on with his story, telling how his precedessor, and the latter's daughter also, had come to like him, and how he had first become his vicar and then his successor. The story had hardly been finished when the pastor's daughter and the aforementioned Mr. Schmidt came up through the garden; she welcomed Lotte with heartfelt warmth, and I must say I found her not unpleasing: a sprightly, well-formed brunette, who could have made our short stay in the country quite entertaining. Her lover (for Mr. Schmidt promptly presented himself as such), a nice but quiet person, who would not take part in our conversation, although Lotte kept drawing him into it. What distressed me most was that I thought I could read in his features that it was obstinacy and ill humour, rather than a limited intelligence, which prevented him from speaking his mind. Subsequently this became only too plain; for when Friederike during a stroll walked with Lotte, and occasionally with me too, the gentleman's face, which was of a brownish hue to start with, darkened so visibly that it was opportune for Lotte to pluck me by the sleeve and give me to understand that I had been too attentive to Friederike. Now nothing annoys me more than when people torment each other, but most of all when young people in the bloom of life, when they could be supremely open to all joys, spoil the few good days they have together with silly notions, and only too late realize that what they have thrown away is irretrievable. This vexed me, and when we returned to the parsonage toward evening, eating clabber around a table, and the conversation turned upon the joy and sorrow in the world. I could not resist picking up that thread and talking very earnestly against ill humor.

"We often complain," said I, "that there are so few good days, and so many bad ones, and mostly we are wrong, it seems to me. If we always had our hearts open to the enjoyment of the good which God prepares for us day by day, then we would also have strength enough to bear the bad when it comes."

"But we have no control over our feelings," replied the pastor's wife; "how much depends on our body! If we don't feel well, nothing pleases us."

I conceded that. "Let us then," I went on, "regard it as a disease and inquire if there is no remedy for it."

"A good suggestion," said Lotte, "I at least believe that much depends on us. I know that by experience. If something annoys me and tries to make me vexed, I jump up and sing a couple of quadrilles, prancing up and down the garden, and right away it's gone."

"That is what I was going to say," I rejoined: "bad humor is to be treated just like indolence, for it is a kind of indolence. Our nature inclines to it very much, and yet if we once have the force to brace ourselves, the work will go briskly through our hands, and we shall find a true pleasure in being active."

Friederike was very attentive, and the young man raised the objection that one is not master of himself and is least of all able to control his emotions.

"The question here," I replied, "is that of an unpleasant emotion, which surely everyone is glad to be rid of; and no one knows how far his powers will extend until he has tried them out. Certainly, one who is sick will consult all the physicians around, and he will not reject the greatest deprivations or the bitterest drugs in order to regain his cherished good health."

I observed that the honest pastor was straining to hear, so as to take part in our discussion, and I raised my voice as I turned to address him. "They preach against so many vices," I said; "I have never yet heard that anyone has combatted ill humor from the pulpit."*

"That would be something for city preachers to do," he said, "peasants have no ill humor; yet once in a while it would do no harm, it would at least be a lesson to the peasant's wife, and to the Bailiff."

Everyone laughed, and laughed heartily too, until he fell to coughing, which interrupted our discussion for a while; thereupon the young fellow resumed: "You called ill humor a vice; that seems to me an exaggeration."

"Not at all," I answered, "if that deserves such a name wherewith we injure ourself and our neighbor. Is it not enough that we cannot make each other happy; must we also rob each other of the pleasure that every heart can occasionally give itself? And give me the name of the person who is in an ill humor and at the same time is so noble as to conceal it, to bear it all alone, without spoiling the joy of those around him! Or isn't it rather an inner vexation at our own unworthiness, a displeasure with ourself, always bound up with a hostility egged on by foolish vanity? We see people happy whom *we* are not making so, and that is unendurable."

Lotte smiled at me, seeing the agitation with which I was speaking, and a tear in Friederike's eyes spurred me on to continue. "Woe to those," I said, "who make use of the power they have over another's heart to rob it of the simple joys which are an outgrowth of its own nature. All the gifts, all the little kindnesses in the world will not make up for one moment of enjoyment of oneself which a malice-filled discomfort of our tyrant has embittered."

My whole heart was full at that moment; the recollection of so

---

*Note by Goethe. We now have an excellent sermon on this by Lavater, among those dealing with the Book of Jonah.—Johann Kaspar Lavater (1741–1801) also wrote a work on physiognomy, to which Goethe contributed.—Tr.

much that is past pressed in upon my soul, and tears came to my eyes.

"If each one would only say to himself every day," I cried out, "you can have no influence over your friends save by leaving them their joys and increasing their happiness, insofar as you enjoy it with them. If their soul is tortured by a disturbing passion, or distracted by grief, have you the power to give them one drop of balm?

"And then when the last dread disease falls upon the creature that you have undermined in the days of her prime, and now she lies there in a pitiful lassitude, her eyes looking passively heavenward, the sweat of death shifting on the pale brow, and you stand at her bed like one condemned, feeling to your depths that you can do nothing with all that you own, and fear convulses you inwardly, so that you would like to surrender everything in order to be able to infuse in this perishing creature one drop of invigoration, one spark of courage."

The recollection of such a scene at which I had been present fell upon me at these words with all its force. I put my handkerchief to my eyes and left the room, and only the voice of Lotte, calling to me that we were going to leave, brought me to my senses. And how she scolded me as we went, saying that I took everything too much to heart, and that it would bring me to my death! and that I should spare myself!—Oh, angel! For your sake I must go on living!

July 6.

She is constantly with her dying friend, and she is always the same, always the attentive, lovely creature who, wherever she turns, quiets pain and makes people happy. Yesterday evening she took a walk with Marianne and little Amalia; I knew about it and met them, and we went on together. After a walk of an hour and a half we came back toward the town and reached the spring which has meant so much to me and now means a thousand times more. Lotte sat down on the little coping, we standing before her. I looked about, ah! and the time when my heart was so alone again came to life for me. "Dear spring," I said, "of late I have ceased to rest near your coolness, and passing you in haste I have sometimes not even looked at you." Looking down, I saw Amalia very busily climbing the steps with a glass of water. I looked at Lotte and felt all that she is to me. Meanwhile Amalia came up with the glass. Marianne wanted to take it from her—"No!" cried the child with the sweetest look, "no, Lotte, you must drink first!" I was so enchanted by the sincerity, by the affection of her cry that the only way I had of expressing my emotion was to lift up the child from the ground and kiss her heartily, whereupon she began to weep and wail. "You have done wrong," said Lotte. I was taken aback. "Come, dear," she went on, taking the child by the hand and leading her down the steps, "come and wash yourself with the cool water, quick, quick, then it will be all right." As I stood there and saw with what zeal the little one rubbed her cheeks with her little wet hands, with what faith that the miraculous spring would wash away every impurity and avert the disgrace of growing an ugly beard; as Lotte said, "That's enough," and still the little one kept on eagerly rubbing, as if more would be more effective than little—I tell you, Wilhelm, I have never witnessed a baptism with greater reverence, and when Lotte came up, I would have liked to cast myself down before her as before a prophet who has washed away with holy water the sins of a nation.

That evening I could not refrain, in my heartfelt joy, from relating the incident to a man whom I thought to have human feeling, since he has common sense; but how I put my foot in it! He said that Lotte had done very ill; one should not misinform children; such actions gave rise to countless errors and superstitions, against which one must guard children at an early age.—Now it occurred to me that the man had had a child baptised a week before, and so I let it pass, retaining in my heart fidelity to this truth: we should deal with children as God deals with us, for He makes us happiest when He lets us grope our way in a pleasant illusion.

July 8.

What children we are! How greedy we are for a certain look! What children we are!—We had walked to Wahlheim. The ladies drove out, and during our strolls I thought that in Lotte's black eyes—I am a fool, forgive me! you should see them, those eyes.—To make it short (for my eyes are falling shut with sleepiness)—look, the ladies got in, and round the carriage were standing young W., Selstadt and Audran and I. So then there was chat through the carriage door with these lads, who I admit were airy and animated enough.—I sought Lotte's eyes; ah, they were wandering from one to the other! But on me! me! me! who stood there intent upon her alone, they did not fall!—My heart spoke a thousand farewells to her! And she did not see me! The carriage drove past, and there was a teardrop in my eye. I looked after her, and saw Lotte's headdress push out through the door, and she turned to look, ah, for me?— Friend! This is the uncertainty I am suspended in; this is my consolation: perhaps she was looking for me! Perhaps! Good night! O what a child I am!

July 10.

You should see what a silly figure I cut when she is mentioned in society! And then if I am even asked how I like her—Like! I hate that word like death. What sort of person must that be who likes Lotte, in whom all senses, all emotions are not completely filled up by her! Like! Recently someone asked me how I like Ossian!

July 11.

Mrs. M. is in a very bad state; I pray for her life because I suffer with Lotte. I rarely see her at the house of my lady friend, but today she told of a marvellous incident.—Old M. is a stingy, niggardly miser, who has roundly tormented and restricted his wife all her life; yet she always contrived to get along. A few days ago, when the physician told her she could not live, she sent for her husband— Lotte was in the room—and addressed him like this: "I must confess to you a matter which might cause confusion and vexation after my death. I have kept house all this time as properly and economically as possible; but you will forgive me for having deceived you all these thirty years. At the beginning of our marriage you fixed a small sum for the expenses of the kitchen and other domestic needs. When our establishment grew and our business increased, you could not be induced to increase my weekly allowance in proportion; in short, you know that in the times when our requirements were at the peak, you demanded that I should get along on seven florins a week. So I took them without demur, and every week I took the rest out of the till, since nobody suspected that a wife would rob the cash box. I didn't waste anything, and I would have confidently faced eternity without this confession, but for the fact that the one who will have to run the house after me would not know what to do, since you could always insist that your first wife had got along on that much."

I discussed with Lotte this incredible self-deception of the human mind: that a man should not suspect some unrevealed explanation when a person gets along on seven florins, although the visible expenditure is perhaps twice that much. But I myself have known people who would have assumed without surprise that their house contained the prophet's never-failing curse.*

July 13.

No, I do not delude myself! I read in her black eyes true sympathy for me, and for my fate. Yes, I feel, and in this I can trust my heart, that she—O may I, can I utter the heaven that lies in these words?—that she loves me!

Loves me!—And how precious I become to myself, when—I think I may say this to you, for you have understanding for such things—how I adore myself, now that she loves me!

Is this presumptuousness, or a feeling for things as they really are?—I do not know any person whose share in Lotte's heart might cause me apprehension. And yet—when she speaks of her betrothed, speaks of him with such warmth, such love—then I feel like one who is deprived of all his honors and dignities, and whose sword is taken from him.

July 16.

Ah, how it courses through my every vein when my finger unexpectedly touches hers, or when our feet encounter each other under the table! I pull back as if singed, and a mysterious force draws me forward again—all my senses reel so.—O! and her innocence, her unsuspecting soul does not feel how the little intimacies torture me. If in conversation she even lays her hand on mine, and moves closer to me in the interest of the discussion, so that the heavenly breath of her lips can reach mine—I think I am fainting, as if struck by lightning.—And, Wilhelm, if I should ever dare to violate this heaven and this confidence—! You know what I mean. No, my heart is not so ruined! It is weak! weak enough!—And doesn't that mean ruin?

She is sacred to me. All physical desire is mute in her presence. I

*1 Kings 17:14–16—*Tr.*

can never tell how I feel when I am with her; it is as if my soul were awhirl in every nerve.—There is a melody that she plays on the piano with the touch of an angel, so simple and so full of meaning. It is her favourite tune, as soon as she plays the first note of it I find myself cured of all grief, bewilderment, and cares.

To me nothing that is said about the magic power of ancient music is improbable, seeing how simple singing affects me. And how she has the wit to employ it, often at a time when I should like to put a bullet through my head! Then the darkness and delusion of my soul is dispersed, and again I breathe more freely.

July 18.

Wilhelm, of what value to our heart is a world without love? The same as a projector without a light! No sooner have you put in the little lamp than the gayest pictures are shining on your white wall! And even if it were no more than that, mere transient phantoms, still our happiness is in them when we stand before them like unspoiled youngsters, delighting in the wondrous sights. Today I could not go to see Lotte, being detained by an unavoidable engagement. What was to be done! I sent out my servant, merely to have a human being around me who had been near her today. With what impatience I waited for him, with what joy I saw him return! I would have clutched his head and kissed him, if I had not been ashamed to.

They say of Bologna rock that if you lay it in the sun it will draw in the rays and shine for a while at night. So it was with my lad. The feeling that her eyes had rested on his face, his cheeks, his coat buttons, the collar of his overcoat, made all of it so holy to me, so precious! At that moment I would not have given up the lad for a thousand talers. I felt so happy in his presence.—God help you if you laugh at this. Wilhelm, when we feel happy, are we seeing phantoms?

July 19.

"I shall see her!" I cry in the morning as soon as I am awake, looking toward the beautiful sun with unmixed delight; "I shall see her!" And then for the rest of the day I have no further wish. Everything, everything merges in that one prospect.

July 20.

Your idea, yours and Mother's, that I should accompany the ambassador to * * *, is not as yet acceptable to me. I am not overly fond of being a subordinate, and besides, we all know that he is an obnoxious person. You said that my mother would like to see me engaged in some activity; that made me laugh. Am I not active as it is! and isn't it basically the same whether I count peas or lentils? Everything in the world comes down to mere trumpery, and a man who wears himself out because others want him to, without gratifying his own passion or satisfying his own needs, but seeking money, or prestige, or whatever, is bound to be a fool.

July 24.

Since it means so much to you that I should not neglect my sketching, I would rather skip the whole subject than tell you that little is being done all this while.

Never was I happier, never was my feeling for nature more complete and intimate, down to the pebbles, down to the grass-blades, and yet—I don't know how to express it, my power of visualization is so feeble, and everything sways and swims so before my soul, that I cannot hold any outline fast; but I have the fancy that if I had clay or wax I could mould it quite well. And if this goes on too long, I *shall* take clay, and knead it, and even if it should turn into a cake!

Three times I have begun a portrait of Lotte, and three times I have made myself ridiculous; which vexes me all the more since I had a very sure hand some time ago. So then I made a silhouette of her, and thus must suffice me.

July 26.

Yes, dear Lotte, I will take care of and see to everything; just keep on giving me commissions, and do so often. But I have one request of you: strew no more sand on the notes you write me. Today I put it promptly to my lips, and got grit between my teeth.

July 26.

I have sometimes resolved not to see her so often. As if a man could stick to that! Every day I succumb to temptation, and then I promise myself solemnly, 'Tomorrow for once you will stay away', and when the morning comes, once again I find some irresistible pretext, and before I know it I am with her. Either she has said in the evening, "You're coming tomorrow, aren't you?" And who could stay away after that? Or she gives me some commission, and I find it proper to take the answer to her in person; or the day is just too lovely, I'll go out to Wahlheim, and once I am there, it's only an extra half hour's walk to her!—I am too close to her aura—Click! and there I am. My grandmother would tell a tale about the magnet-mountain. Ships that came too close were suddenly robbed of all their iron: the nails flew off to the mountain, and the poor wretches drowned, caught in the collapsing hull.

July 30.

Albert has come, and I shall go; and even if he were the best and noblest of men, to whom I should be ready to yield in every respect, it would be unendurable to watch him have possession of so many perfections.—Possession!—Enough, Wilhelm: the betrothed is here! A good and agreeable man whom one cannot but like. Fortunate that I was not present to witness his reception! That would have rent my heart. Yes, and he is so decent that he has not kissed Lotte a single time in my presence. God reward him! I have to love him because of the reverence he shows for the girl. He wishes me well, and I surmise that that is Lotte's doing rather than his own feeling. For in that respect women have a fine instinct, and a sound one: if they can keep two admirers on good terms with each other, that is bound to be to their advantage, however rarely it succeeds.

At the same time I cannot deny Albert my esteem. His outward calm contrasts very vividly with the restlessness of my character, which cannot be concealed. He has deep feeling, and he knows what he has in Lotte. He seems to be rarely in an ill humor, and you know that that is the vice in people which I hate worse than any other.

He regards me as a man of intelligence; and my devotion to Lotte, the warm pleasure I take in all her actions, increases his own triumph and makes him love her all the more. I will leave the question open whether he doesn't sometimes torment her with little jealousies; I at least, were I in his position, would not remain wholly free from such devilry.

Be that as it may! the joy I had in being with Lotte is gone. Shall I call that stupidity or blindness?—What need of names? The story tells itself!—I knew everything I know now before Albert came; I knew that I had no claims on her and I made none—that is to say, insofar as it is possible not to desire so lovable an object.—And now the simpleton looks on wide-eyed when the other really comes and takes the girl away from him.

I clench my teeth, and mock at my own misery, and would mock twice and thrice over at those who might say that I should resign myself, and that, since it simply can't be otherwise—Take these passionless people off my neck!—I rove around in the woods, and when I get to Lotte's and Albert is sitting outside with her in the summer house, and I can't do anything else, I lapse into foolish extravagance and begin all sorts of silly and nonsensical talk.—"For heaven's sake," said Lotte to me today, "I beg of you, no such scene as you made last evening! You frighten me when you are so gay."— Between you and me, I watch for times when he is busy; then whoosh! out I dash, and I always feel happy if I find her alone.

August 8.

I beg you, dear Wilhelm, not to think I was pointing at you when I called unendurable those people who require us to submit to inevitable destiny. Truly, I was not thinking that you too might be of a similar opinion. And basically you are right. Just one thing, however: it is very rare in this world that we can get along with an Either-Or; feelings and modes of behaviour shade off as diversely as there are gradations between a Roman and a snub nose.

So you will not take it amiss if I concede your whole argument, and still try to squeeze through between your Either-Or.

Either, you say, you have hopes of Lotte, or you have none. All right, in the first case seek to realize your hope, seek to embrace the fulfilment of your wishes; in the other case, pull yourself together and try to get rid of a wretched emotion which is bound to consume all your powers—My dear fellow! that is well said, and—quickly said.

And can you, if there is a wretch whose life is slowly, irresistibly giving way to a creeping disease, can you demand of him that he should seize a dagger and put a sudden end to his torment? And does not the ailment which is consuming his powers rob him at the same time of the courage to free himself from it?

True, you could answer with a related analogy: Who would not rather have his arm cut off than by hesitating and haggling put his life in jeopardy?—I don't know!—and let us not go on bickering with metaphors. Enough—Yes, Wilhelm, sometimes I have a moment of leaping courage and could shake off everything, and then—if I only knew where—I think I would go—

Evening.

My diary, which I have been neglecting for some time, got into my hands again today, and I am astonished to see with what awareness I walked into all this, step by step! How I kept a clear picture of my condition, and yet acted like a child, just as right now I see so clearly, and there is no sign of any improvement.

August 10.

I could lead the happiest of lives if I were not a fool. It is not often that such favourable circumstances come together to delight the soul of a man as are those in which I find myself at present. Ah, just as certain is it that our heart alone creates its own happiness.—To be a member of that lovable family, loved like a son by the father, like a father by the little ones, and by Lotte!—then there is honest Albert, who does not spoil my happiness by any capricious ill temper; who encompasses me with a heartfelt friendship; to whom after Lotte I am the dearest person in the world—Wilhelm, it is a joy to hear us when we go strolling and converse about Lotte: nothing has been discovered in the world more ridiculous than this relationship, and yet it often causes tears to come to my eyes.

When he tells me about her admirable mother: how on her deathbed she entrusted her house and her children to Lotte, and commended Lotte to his care, how since that time a wholly different spirit has animated Lotte, how she, in her concern for the household and in a natural seriousness, has become a true mother, how not a moment of her time has been spent without loving action, without some toil, and yet how her cheerfulness, her sprightly spirit has never forsaken her.—I walk along beside him, pick flowers by the wayside, form them very carefully into a bouquet, and—fling them into the passing stream, looking after them as they gently toss their way down.—I don't know whether I have written you that Albert will stay here and receive a post, with a very pretty income, from the court, where he is a great favorite. I have seen few to equal him in orderly and zealous despatch of duties.

August 12.

There is no doubt that Albert is the best person in the world. Yesterday I had an extraordinary experience with him. I called on him to take leave of him; for I took a fancy to ride off into the mountains, from where I am just now writing to you, and as I was walking up and down the room, his pistols met my eye. "Lend me the pistols for my trip," said I. "I don't mind," said he, "if you want to take the trouble of loading them; I just hang them up for the looks." I took one down, and he continued, "Since my cautiousness once played me such a mean trick, I don't care to have anything more to do with the things." I was curious to hear what had happened. "I lived for a good three months," he said, "in the country house of a friend, had a couple of unloaded pistols, and slept undisturbed. One rainy afternoon, as I was sitting idle, the thought came to me, I don't know how: we might be attacked, we might need the pistols and might—well, you know how it is.—I gave them to my servant to clean and load; and he dallies with the maids, tries to frighten them and, God knows how, the gun goes off with the ramrod still in it and drives the ramroad into the ball of one girl's right thumb, crushing the thumb. So I had an earful, and had to pay the doctor besides, and since that time I leave all guns unloaded. My dear fellow, what is caution? the forms of danger are infinite! To be sure—" Now you may know that I love this man very much, all but his 'to be sure'; for isn't it obvious that every generalization is subject to exceptions? But that's the way this fellow will correct himself! If he thinks he has said something precipitate, too general, half true, then he never stops limiting, qualifying, adding to it and taking from it, until at last there is nothing left of what he said. And on this occasion he got very deeply involved; finally I stopped listening to him altogether, fell into freakish thoughts, and suddenly leaping up I pressed the mouth of the pistol to my forehead above the right eye. "For shame!" said Albert, pulling the pistol down, "what are you doing?" "It's not loaded," said I. "What if it isn't, why do you do it?" he replied impatiently. "I can't imagine how a person can be so silly as to shoot himself; the mere thought of it repels me."

"O that you people," I burst out, "when you mention something, have to say: that is silly, that is wise, that is good, that is bad! And what does it all mean? Has it made you explore the conditions underlying an action? are you able to unfold with precision the reasons why it happened, why it had to happen? If you had, you wouldn't be so ready with your judgments."

"You will admit," said Albert, "that certain actions remain morally wrong, no matter what their motivations may be."

I shrugged my shoulders and admitted it. "And yet, my good fellow," I went on, "here too there are some exceptions. It is true that theft is a wrong; but does the man who sets out to steal in order to save himself and his family from imminent starvation deserve sympathy or punishment? Who will cast the first stone against the husband who, in righteous wrath, sacrifices his faithless wife and her contemptible seducer? or against the girl who in an hour of rapture loses self-control in the irresistible joys of love? Even our very laws, coldblooded pedants that they are, let themselves be moved and withhold their penalties."

"That is an entirely different thing," replied Albert, "because a person who is carried away by his passions loses all power of deliberation and is as good as drunk or mad."

"Oh, you rationalists!" I cried with a smile. "Passion! Drunkeness! Madness! You stand there so calm, so unsympathetic, you moral men! chide the drinker, abhor the irrational, walk past like priests, and like the Pharisee thank God that he has not made you like one of these. I have been drunk more than once, my passions were never far from madness, and I repent of neither: for in my own measure I have learned to understand how it is that all extraordinary beings, who have accomplished something great, something seemingly impossible, have always and necessarily been defamed as drunk and mad.

"But even in ordinary life it is unendurable to hear men exclaim in response to almost any halfway deliberate, noble, unexpected deed: the fellow is drunk, he is crazy! Shame on you sober ones, shame on you sage ones!"

"Here we have some more of your wild ideas," said Albert, "you overdo everything, and in this case you are at least wrong in comparing suicide, which was our last topic, with great actions: since it can certainly not be regarded as anything but a weakness. For it is admittedly easier to die than to endure a life of torment with steadfastness."

I was on the point of breaking off; for no argument robs me so of composure as when a man comes along with an insignificant commonplace when I am expressing the depths of my heart. But I composed myself, because I had often heard that, and had often been vexed by it, and retorted with some vivacity, "You call that weakness? I beg you not to let yourself be misled by appearances. If a nation is sighing under the unendurable yoke of a tyrant, do you dare speak of weakness if the people rise up in rage and rend their fetters? If a man, gripped by the terror of having his house seized by fire, feels all his strength heightened and carries off with ease burdens which he can scarcely move when his mind is calm; if another, furious with outrage, stands up against six others and overpowers them; are they to be called weak? And, my good fellow, if exertion is strength, why should overexertion be the opposite?"

Albert looked at me and said, "Don't take it amiss, but the examples you cite don't seem to be pertinent here." "That may be," said I; "I have often been told that my way of combining things sometimes borders on absurdity. Let us see, then, whether we can imagine in some other way how a man must feel who resolves to cast off the otherwise agreeable load of life. For only insofar as we have fellow feelings are we entitled to discuss such a matter.

"Human nature," I continued, "has its bounds: it can endure joy, sorrow, pain, up to a certain degree, and it perishes as soon as that degree is exceeded. In this case it is then not a question of whether a man is weak or strong, but whether he can outlast the measure of his suffering—be it spiritual or physical; and I find it just as strange to say that the man who takes his life is a coward, as it would be improper to call a man cowardly who dies of a malignant fever."

"Paradoxical! most paradoxical!" cried Albert. "Not as much as you think," I replied. "You will admit that we call it a mortal sickness when a body is so assailed that in part its forces are consumed, in part robbed of effectiveness, that it is no longer capable of restoring itself, or of resuming, by any fortunate turn of things, the customary course of life.

"Now then, my friend, let us apply this to the mind. Behold the human being in his confined state and see how impressions affect him, take a firm hold on him, until at last a growing passion robs him of all calm power of thought and drives him to destruction.

"In vain does a calm, rational person diagnose the unhappy man's condition, in vain does he try to give him courage! Just as a healthy man who stands at the bedside of a sick one cannot infuse into him the least bit of his own strength."

For Albert this exposition was too general. I reminded him of a girl that had recently been found dead in the water, and repeated her story to him.—A young, good creature who had grown up in the narrow round of domestic occupations, definite weekly chores, who had no other prospect of pleasure than perhaps to go strolling about the town with her companions on a Sunday, in finery that she had acquired little by little, perhaps to go dancing when the chief holidays came around, and for the rest to spend an occasional hour, with all the vivacity of sincere interest, in chatting with a neighbor woman about some quarrel, some bit of evil gossip—whose ardent nature at last feels some more tender needs, which are increased by the flatteries of men; her previous pleasures gradually lose their savor for her, until finally she meets a man to whom she is irresistibly drawn by an unfamiliar emotion, on whom she pins all her hopes, forgetting the world around her, and hears nothing, sees nothing, feels nothing but him, the only one, yearns only for him, the only one. Not spoiled by the empty diversions of an inconstant vanity, her desire goes straight to the point: she wants to become his, to find in a lasting union all the happiness that she lacks, to taste in one concentration all the joys for which she has longed. Repeated promises that put the seal on the certainty of all her hopes, bold caresses which heighten her desires, encompass her whole soul; she is afloat in a vague awareness, in a foretaste of all joys, her tension attains the highest peak, at last she stretches out her arms to embrace all she has wished for—and her beloved forsakes her.— Paralyzed, without sensation, she sees herself before an abyss; all is darkness about her, no prospects, no consolation, no hope! for *he* has forsaken her in whom alone she felt her existence to be. She does not see the wide world that lies before her, nor the many souls who might make up for her loss; she feels herself alone, forsaken by everyone—and blindly, driven into a corner by the fearful affliction of her heart, she flings herself down, to stifle all her torments in one all-embracing death.—Look, Albert, that is the story of so many a human being! and tell me, is that not the same as a disease? Nature finds no way out of the labyrinth of tangled and contradictory forces, and the human being has to die.

"Woe to him who could look on and say, 'Foolish girl! Had she waited, had she let time have its effect, despair would surely have abated, and surely someone else would have come forward to comfort her,' Just as if one should say, 'What a fool to die of fever! Had he waited until his powers had recovered, his life-forces improved, the tumult of his blood abated, then all would have gone well, and he would be alive today!' "

Albert, who still could not visualize this comparison, made some objections, including this one: I had spoken only of a simple-minded girl; but he could not comprehend how a man of reason, who was not so limited, who had a broader grasp on things, could be excusable. "My friend," I cried, "human beings are human, and the bit of common sense a man may have counts for little or nothing when passions rage and the bounds of humanness press in on us. Say rather—We'll come back to this," said I, reaching for my hat. O, my heart was so full—And we parted without having understood each other. As indeed it is not easy in this world for one person to understand the next one.

August 15.

It is surely a fact that nothing in the world but love makes a person indispensable. Lotte makes me feel that she would dislike to lose me, and the children have no other idea but that I would keep coming morning after morning. Today I had gone out to tune Lotte's piano, but I couldn't get to it, for the little ones pursued me with a request for a fairy tale, and Lotte herself said that I should give them their way. I cut the bread for their supper—they now take it from me almost as willingly as from Lotte—and told them the capital tale about the princess who is served by hands. I learn much in doing so, I assure you, and I am astonished at the impression it makes on them. Because I sometimes have to invent a detail that I forget the next time, they say right away that last time it was different, so that I am now training myself to recite them unalterably in a singsong and as straight as a string. I have learned from this that an author must necessarily injure his book by issuing a second revised edition of his story, even though it should be poetically ever so much improved. The first impression finds us willing listeners, and man is so made that one can persuade him of the most fantastic happenings; but they also stick fast in his memory, and woe to him who tried to erase and obliterate them again!

August 18.

Was it necessary, I wonder, that that which makes the happiness of a man should also become the source of his misery?

The warm, rich feeling of my heart for living nature, which flooded me with so much rapture, which turned the world around me into a paradise, is now becoming an unendurable tormentor to me, a torturing spirit that pursues me on all my ways. Whereas formerly I would survey the fruitful valley from the cliffs, looking across the river toward yonder heights, and seeing everything around me sprouting and swelling; whereas I saw those mountains, from the foot all the way to the summit, clad with a dense growth of tall trees, and those valleys in their manifold windings shaded by the loveliest groves, while the gentle stream flowed along among the whispering reeds and mirrored the beloved clouds that the light breeze wafted across the evening sky; and then I would hear the birds around me bring the woods to life, and the millions of swarming mites danced bravely in the last red rays of the sun, whose last quivering glance freed the buzzing beetle from its grass, and the humming and stirring about me drew my attention to the earth, and the moss, which wrests its nourishment from my resistant rocks, and the underbrush that creeps down the sandy slope would reveal to me the glowing inner holy life of nature—how I would take all that into my warm heart, feeling myself as it were deified in the overflowing abundance, and all the glorious forms of this infinite world come to life within my soul. Monstrous mountains invested me, abysses lay before me, and mountain torrents plunged downward, the rivers flowed below me, and woods and wilds resounded; and I saw all the unfathomable forces in the depths of the earth working and creating within each other; and now above the ground and under the sky swarm the living creatures in their untold diversity. Everything, everything peopled with myriads of forms; and then the people seeking joint security in their little houses, and building their nests, and ruling in their minds over the wide world! Poor fool that you are! deeming everything so insignificant because *you* are so small.—From the inaccessible mountains across the desert that no foot has trodden, and on to the end of the unknown ocean, breathes the spirit of the eternally creating One, rejoicing in every speck of dust that hears Him and is alive.—Ah, in those days, how often did my longing take the wings of a crane that flew overhead and carried me to the shore of the uncharted sea, to drink from the foaming cup of the infinite that swelling rapture of life, and to taste but for an instant, despite the limited force of my soul, one drop of the bliss of that being which produces all things in and by means of itself.

My brother, the mere recollection of those hours does me good. Even this present effort to recall those unspeakable feelings, to utter them again, lifts my soul out of itself, and then makes me feel doubly the anxiety of the state which surrounds me now.

It is as if a curtain had pulled aside before my soul, and the stage of infinite life is transforming itself before me into the abyss of an eternally open grave. Can you say, "This is!" when everything is transitory? when everything rolls by with lightning speed and so seldom expands the entire potential of its existence, ah! is swept away in the stream, sucked under, and dashed to bits on the rocks? There is no moment which does not consume you and yours with you, no moment when you are not, and of necessity, a destroyer; the most innocent stroll costs a thousand crawlers their life, as *one* step destroys the laborious structures of the ants, trampling a little world into an ignominious grave. Ha! it is not the great, rare catastrophes in the world, the floods that wash away your villages, the earthquakes that engulf your cities, which touch me; what undermines my heart is the consuming power which lies hidden in the whole of nature; power which has formed nothing that does not destroy its neighbor, destroy its own self. And so I stagger on in terror! Heaven and earth and their interplaying forces all around me! I see nothing but a monster which, eternally swallowing, chews its eternal cud.

August 21.

In vain I stretch out my arms toward her, in the mornings, when I rouse vaguely from bad dreams, in vain I seek her by night in my bed, when some happy, harmless dream has deluded me into thinking that I was sitting beside her on the meadow, holding her hand and covering it with a thousand kisses. Ah, then when I grope for her, still half drugged with sleep, and thus wake myself up—a flood of tears bursts from my straining heart, and I weep disconsolate toward a gloomy future.

August 22.

It is a misfortune, Wilhelm: my active powers are dulled into a restless lassitude, and I cannot be idle and yet I cannot do anything, either. I have no power of imagination, no feeling for nature, and books disgust me. If we lose ourselves, we lose everything else, too. I swear to you, sometimes I would wish to be a day labourer, merely to have on awaking in the morning a prospect for the day to come, an urge, a hope. Often I envy Albert, whom I see buried in documents up to his ears, and I imagine that I would be happy if I were in his place. Several times before this I have suddenly taken the notion of writing to you and to the minister of state, to apply for that position in the embassy which, as you assure me, would not be refused me. I believe that. The minister has liked me for a long time, and has long been urging me to devote myself to some fixed occupation; and for an hour I may feel like doing so. Later, when I think of it again, and I recall the fable of the horse which, dissatisfied with its freedom, has saddle and bridle put on it and is ridden half to death*—I don't know what I should do—And listen! isn't the longing in me for a change of state perhaps an uncomfortable impatience of soul which will pursue me everywhere?

August 28.

It is true that if my sickness could be cured, these people would cure it. Today is my birthday,† and the first thing in the morning I receive a little package from Albert. On opening it I immediately catch sight of one of the pale pink bows which Lotte was wearing when I made her acquaintance, and for which I have asked her several times since then. There were two booklets in duodecimo with it, the little Wetstein edition of Homer, one which I have so often wanted, so as not to have to carry the big Ernesti edition when I went walking. Look! thus they anticipate my wishes, go looking

---

*In a fable of La Fontaine the horse, unable to outrun the deer, asks man's help. —*Tr.*

†Goethe was born on August 28.—*Tr.*

for all the little favors of friendship, which mean a thousand times more than those ostentatious gifts whereby the giver's vanity humiliates us. I kiss this bow a thousand times over, and with every breath I sip the recollection of the raptures with which those few happy, irretrievable days filled me to overflowing. Wilhelm, it is a fact, and I do not grumble at it: life's flowers are merely without permanence! How many of them fade away without leaving a trace, how few of them set as fruit, and how few of those fruits ripen! And yet there are still enough of them on hand; and yet—Oh, my brother!—can we see such ripened fruits and neglect or despise them, let them decay untasted?

Farewell! It is glorious summer weather, and I often sit in the fruit trees in Lotte's orchard with the fruit-picker, that long pole, and pull down the pears from the treetop. She stands below and takes them when I lower them to her.

August 30.

Unhappy man! Are you not a fool? aren't you deceiving yourself? What avails this raging, endless passion? I have no more prayers to say except to her; my imagination perceives no other figure than hers, and I see everything in the world around me merely in relation to her. And that does give me many a happy hour—until I again have to tear myself away from her! Ah, Wilhelm! what my heart often urges upon me!—When I have sat beside her, two hours, or three, and have feasted myself on her figure, on her behavior, on the divine expression of her sayings, and little by little all my senses come under tension, and it grows dark before my eyes, and I scarcely hear anything, and it clutches at my throat like the hand of an assassin, and then my heart tries to relieve my straining senses by its wild throbbing and only increases their distraction—Wilhelm, I often don't know whether I am on the earth! And—if sorrow does not gain the upper hand, occasionally, so that Lotte allows me the wretched consolation of weeping out my anguish upon her hand— then I have to leave, go far off! and then I rove far afield; then it is joy to me to climb a steep mountain, to work my way through a pathless forest, through hedges that wound me, through brambles that tear my flesh! Then I begin to feel somewhat better! Somewhat! And if I sometimes lie still en route because of exhaustion and thirst, or sometimes, in the dead of night when the full moon hangs high above me, in a lonesome wood, seat myself on a gnarled tree, merely to give some relief to my sore feet, and then doze off in a sleep of exhaustion in that dim radiance! O Wilhelm! solitary housing in a hermit's cell, a haircloth garment and a belt of thorns, would be restoratives for which my soul is languishing. Adieu! I see no end to this misery save the grave.

September 3.

I must go! I thank you, Wilhelm, for having confirmed my wavering resolve. For two weeks now I have been thinking of leaving her. I must go. She is in town again at the house of a friend. And Albert—and—I must go!

September 10.

That was a night! Wilhelm! now I can survive anything. I shall not see her again! O that I cannot rush to fall on your neck, cannot express to you, best friend, amid a thousand tears and transports, the emotions that are assailing my heart. Here I sit and gasp for air, try to calm myself, and await the morning, and the horses are ordered for sunrise.

Ah, she is sleeping peacefully and does not know that she will never see me again. I tore myself away, and was strong enough not to betray my intention in a conversation lasting two hours. And good heavens, what a conversation!

Albert had promised me that he would be in the garden with Lotte after supper. I stood on the terrace under the tall chestnut trees and looked after the sun as it set, for the last time for me, over the lovely valley, over the gentle stream. So often I had stood there with her and watched that same glorious spectacle, and now—I walked up and down the avenue that was so dear to me; a secret bond of sympathy had so often held me here, even before I knew Lotte, and how glad we were when we discovered, at the beginning of our acquaintance, our mutual affection for this spot, which is in truth one of the most romantic that I have ever seen portrayed by an artist.

First you have, between the chestnut trees, the extensive view— Oh, I remember, I think I have already written you much about it, how tall walls of beech finally invest one, and how an adjacent grove makes the avenue more and more dark until at last everything ends in a small, enclosed spot around which all the tremors of solitude seem to float. I can still feel how homelike it seemed when I stepped into it for the first time at high noon; I had a faint premonition of what a stage that was to become for bliss and bane.

I had basked for perhaps a half hour in the languishingly sweet thoughts of departure and of return, when I heard them mounting the terrace. I ran toward them, and with a shiver I seized her hand and kissed it. We had just reached the top when the moon rose behind the shrubs on the hill; we talked about various things and approached unawares the dark arbor. Lotte went in and sat down, Albert at her side, and I too; but my unrest would not let me sit long; I got up, stepped in front of her, paced back and forth, sat down again: it was a disquieting situation. She called our attention to the beautiful effect of the moonlight, which was illuminating the entire terrace before us at the end of the walls of beech: a glorious sight, which was all the more striking since we were invested all around by pronounced twilight. We were silent, and after a while she began, "I never go walking in the moonlight, never, without encountering the thought of my departed ones, without having the feeling of death and of the future come over me. We shall live!" she continued in a voice of the most glorious feeling; "but, Werther, shall we find each other again? know each other again? what is your premonition? what do you say?"

"Lotte," said I, as I held out my hand to her and my eyes filled with tears, "we shall see each other again! here again and there again!"—I could not say more—Wilhelm, did she have to ask me that when I had this fearful parting on my mind?

"And I wonder if the dear departed know about us," she went on, "if they feel, when we were well off, that we recall them with warm affection. O! the form of my mother always hovers about me when I sit of a quiet evening among her children, among my children, and they are gathered about me as they used to be gathered about her. Then when I look heavenward with a yearning tear, and wish that she might look in for a moment to see how I am keeping my word, that I gave her in the hour of her death: to be the mother of her children. With what emotion I exclaim, 'Forgive me, dearest mother, if I am not what you were to them. Ah! surely I do all that I can; surely they are dressed, nourished, yes, and what is more than all else, cared for and loved. Could you see our harmony, dear saint!

you would glorify with the most fervent thanks the God whom you besought with your last and bitterest tears for the welfare of your children.' "

So she spoke! O Wilhelm, who can repeat what she said? How can cold, lifeless letters represent this glorious flower of the spirit? Albert interrupted her gently: "This is too hard on you,* dear Lotte! I know that your soul inclines much to these ideas, but I beg you—" "O Albert," said she, "I know that you have not forgotten the evenings when we would sit togther at the little round table when Papa was away and we had put the little ones to bed. You often had a good book, and so rarely found time to read anything—Was not our intercourse with that wonderful soul more than all else? that beautiful, gentle, cheerful, and always active woman! God knows about the tears with which I often cast myself before Him in my bed, praying that He would make me like her."

"Lotte," I cried, as I cast myself down before her, took her hand, and moistened it with a thousand tears, "Lotte, the blessing of God rests upon you, and the spirit of your mother!" "If you had known her," she said, as she pressed my hand,—"she was worthy of your acquaintance!" I thought I would swoon. Never had a greater, prouder thing been uttered about me—and she continued, "And this woman had to go in the prime of her life, when her youngest son was not six months old! Her sickness did not last long; she was calm, resigned, and only the thought of her children caused her grief, especially the baby. When the end neared, and she said to me, 'Bring them up here,' and I led them in, the little ones knowing nothing, and the older ones beside themselves as they stood around the bed, and how she lifted her hands and prayed over them, and kissed one after the other and sent them away, and said to me, 'Be a mother to them!'—I gave her my hand on it!—'You are promising much, my daughter,' said she, 'the heart of a mother and the eyes of a mother. I have often seen by your grateful tears that you feel what that is. Have that for your siblings, and have for your father the loyalty and the obedience of a wife. You will console him.' She asked for him, but he had gone out to spare us the unbearable grief he was feeling, for the man's heart was rent.

---

*Albert addresses her as "Sie," not "du," thus bearing out Werther's observation of Albert's deep respect for her.—*Tr.*

"Albert, you were in the room. She heard someone's footsteps and inquired, and had you come to her, and when she looked at you and me, with the calm and comforted gaze that knew we would be happy, happy together—" Albert flung his arms around her and kissed her and cried, "We are happy! we shall be!"—Our quiet Albert was quite beside himself, and I had forgotten who I was.

"Werther," she recommenced, "to think that this woman should be gone! Heavens! sometimes I think how we let the dearest thing in life be borne away, and how no one but the children feel that so keenly, the children who kept complaining that the black men had carried off their mama."

She got up, and I, restored to reality and shaken, remained sitting and held her hand. "Let us go," said she, "it is time now." She tried to withdraw her hand, and I held it more tightly. "We shall see each other again," I cried, "we shall find each other, we shall recognize each other amid all the figures there are. I am going," I continued, "going willingly, and yet, if I were to say 'for ever,' I should not endure it. Farewell, Lotte! Farewell, Albert! We shall meet again." "Tomorrow, I imagine," she replied in jest. I felt that 'Tomorrow!' Ah, she did not know, as she drew her hand out of mine—They walked out through the avenue, and I stood and looked after them in the moonlight, and flung myself on the ground and cried myself out, and leaped up, and ran out onto the terrace in time to see her white dress shimmering toward the garden gate, down yonder in the shade of the tall lindens: I stretched out my arms and it vanished.

Second Book

October 20, 1771.

We arrived here yesterday. The ambassador is not well, and so he will stay in for some days. If only he were not so ungracious, all would be well. I see, I see, fate has assigned severe tests to me. But courage! A light heart endures everything! A light heart? It makes me laugh that that word gets into my pen. O, a little lighter blood would make me the happiest man under the sun. What! when others are strutting around here in my presence in complacent self-satisfaction with their bit of talent and ability, I should despair of my ability, of my gifts? You, good God, who gave me all this, why did you not withhold the half of it and make me self-confident and contented?

Patience, patience! things will improve. For I tell you, Wilhelm, you are right. Now that I am pushed around among these people every day, and see what they do and how they do it, I am in much greater favour with myself. It is certain that since we are so made as to compare everyone with ourselves and ourselves with everyone, happiness or misery lies in those circumstances with which we associate ourselves, and then nothing is more dangerous than solitude. Our imagination, impelled by nature to assert itself, nourished by the fantastic images of the poet's art, invents a hierarchy of being of which we are the lowest, while everyone else appears more splendid, more perfect. And that is a wholly natural affair. So often we feel that much is lacking in us, and another often seems to possess just that which we lack, to whom we then ascribe all that we do have, and a certain ideal degree of contentment besides. And thus the happy man stands there complete, our own creation.

If on the other hand we just keep working straight ahead, with all our weakness and strain, we very often find that we get farther with our tacking and tardiness than others with their sailing and rowing—and—surely one has a true feeling of one's worth when one keeps pace with others or even outruns them.

November 26.

I am beginning to feel quite at ease here, considering. The best of it is that there is enough to do; and then the various kinds of people, all sorts of new figures, present a motley spectacle to my soul. I have made the acquaintance of Count C., a man for whom I feel a greater veneration every day, a great and capacious mind, and one who is not cold because of his broad knowledge; whose conversation radiates so much feeling for friendship and love. He took an interest in me when I carried out a commission that took me to him and he observed at our first words that we understood each other, and that he could talk with me as he could not with everyone. Also, I cannot praise too highly his frank behaviour toward me. There is no such true, warm pleasure in the world as to see a great soul which opens up to us.

December 24.

The ambassador causes me much vexation, as I foresaw. He is the most punctilious fool that can exist; one step at a time and as fussy as an old woman; a person who is never content with himself, and whom consequently no one else can satisfy. I like to work straight ahead, and let it stand as it stands; but he is capable of handing a report back to me and saying, "It is good, but look it over: one can always find a better word, a neater particle." That makes me wild. No 'and,' no connective may be left out, and he is a mortal foe of all inversions, which I sometimes let slip; if you don't drone out your periods according to the traditional melody, he doesn't understand a word. It is a pain to have to do with such a person.

The confidence of Count C. is as yet the only thing that makes up for it. Lately he told me quite frankly how dissatisfied he is with the slowness and inanity of my ambassador. "Such people make things hard for themselves and others; yet," said he, "one must resign oneself to that, like a traveller who has to cross over a mountain: to be sure, if the mountain were not there, the way would be much easier and shorter; but it *is* there, and it must be crossed!"—

I think that my chief also detects the preference that the Count gives me over him, and that annoys him, and he takes every opportunity to talk ill of the Count to me; I naturally take the opposite side, and that only makes the matter worse. Yesterday he really aroused me, for I was involved too: he said the Count was quite good at general affairs, for he could work quickly and wrote in a good style, but he was lacking in thorough scholarship, like all literary folk. He wore an expression that seemed to say, 'Do you feel the stab?' But it failed to affect me; I despised a man who could think and behave like that. I stood my ground and fought back with considerable vehemence. I said that Count was a man for whom one must feel respect, on account of his character as well as his knowledge. "I have not known anyone," I said, "who has succeeded so well in enlarging his mind so as to cover countless subjects, while continuing to be active in public affairs." This was all Greek to his mind, and I took my leave to avoid swallowing more gall in response to some further twaddle.

And for this all you are to blame who talked me into undergoing this yoke, and prated so much about activity. Activity! If a man who plants potatoes or rides into town to sell his corn doesn't do more than I, then I will spend ten years wearing myself out in the galley to which I am now chained.

And the resplendent misery, the boredom among the repulsive crowd that finds itself thrown together here! the petty rivalry among them, as they just watch and wait to get one single step ahead of each other; the wretchedest, most pitiful passions, quite unmasked. There is a woman, for example, who converses with everyone about her rank and her country, so that every stranger must think, 'This is a fool woman who puts on great airs concerning her bit of noble blood and the prestige of her nation.'—But it is even much worse: this very woman was born right here in the vicinity as the daughter of a secretarial clerk—Look, I can't understand the human race, when it has so little sense as to make such a downright fool of itself.

To be sure, I observe more clearly every day, my friend, how silly we are to judge others by ourselves. And because I am so much concerned with myself, and because this heart is so tempestuous— ah, I am glad to let the others go their way, if only they could let me go mine.

What piques me most is the odious social distinctions. Now I know as well as the next man how necessary differences in rank are, how many advantages they give even to me; but they shouldn't get in my way just when I might enjoy a little pleasure, a gleam of happiness on this earth. While out walking lately I got to know a Miss von B., an agreeable person, who has preserved much naturalness in the midst of this formal existence. We took pleasure in conversing, and as we parted I asked for permission to call on her. She granted it with so much ingenuousness that I could hardly wait for a suitable moment to call. This is not her home, and she is living in an aunt's house. The old lady's physiognomy did not please me. I was very attentive to her, I addressed myself mostly to her, and in less than half an hour I had pretty well guessed what the girl herself confessed later on: that her beloved aunt has a lack of everything in her old age, has no decent income, no intellect, and no support except the long line of her forebears, no protection but the rank which she employs like a barricade, and no pleasure except that of looking down from her top storey upon the heads of the common citizens. In her youth she is said to have been beautiful and to have frittered away her life, first tormenting many a poor youth with her capriciousness, and in maturer years submitting to the tyranny of an old officer, who in return for this price and a tolerable living spent her bronze age* with her, and died. Now she finds herself alone in her iron age, and no one would look at her if her niece were not so lovable.

January 8, 1772.

What sort of people are they whose whole soul is wrapped up in ceremony, whose entire striving and contriving is devoted to the goal of moving their chair one place nearer the head of the table? And it isn't as if they had nothing else to do: no, on the contrary, the work piles up, just because the little vexations keep people from taking care of the important matters. Last week there was a quarrel during the sleighing party, and all the fun was spoiled.

How foolish not to see that the place you occupy really makes no difference, and that the one who occupies the first place so seldom plays the first role! How many kings are ruled by their ministers, how many ministers by their secretaries! And then who is first? it is he, I think, who surveys the rest, and who has so much power or cunning as to harness their abilities and passions to the execution of his plans.

January 20.

I must write you, dear Lotte, here in the good room of a poor peasant inn, in which I have taken refuge from a hard storm. As long as I moved about that sad hole of a town, D., amid alien people, wholly alien to my heart, I never had a moment, not one, in which my heart bade me write to you; and now in this humble hut, in this solitude, in this confinement, while snow and hail are pounding furiously on my little window, here my first thought was of you. As I stepped in, upon me descended your figure, your memory, O Lotte! so sacred, so warm! Kindly God! the first happy moment in all this time.

If you saw me, best of women, in this surge of distractions! and saw how desiccated my senses become; not *one* moment of heartfelt being, not *one* hour of bliss! nothing! nothing! I stand as before a peep show, and watch the mannikins and tiny horses move about,

---

*The allusion is to Ovid's four ages of man. The bronze age is one's forties and fifties; the iron age embraces the last quarter of a normal life.—*Tr.*

and often ask myself whether it is not an optical illusion. I play too, or rather, I am played with, like a marionette, and sometimes I seize my neighbor by his wooden hand and draw back shuddering. Of an evening I will resolve to enjoy the sunrise, and yet I don't quit my bed; by day I hope to be gladdened by the moonlight, and yet I stay in my room. I don't rightly know why I get up, why I go to bed.

The leaven which set my life in motion is lacking; the stimulus which kept me awake in the dark of night is gone, and that which woke me from sleep in the morning is no more.

There is only one female creature whom I have met here, a Miss von B., who resembles you, dear Lotte, if it is possible to resemble you. 'Well,' you will say, 'this fellow is going in for pretty compliments!' Not altogether false. For some time I have been very gallant, because I can't be otherwise. I display much wit, and the ladies say that no one manages to utter praise as finely as I (and lies, you will add, for that is an essential part of it, you understand?). But I was going to speak of Miss B. She has a great soul, which is plainly visible in the gaze of her blue eyes. Her rank is burdensome to her, satisfying none of the desires of her heart. She longs to escape from this turmoil, and we spend many an hour in imagining ourselves in rural scenes of unmixed happiness; ah! and in your company! How often she has to pay homage to you: no, she doesn't have to, she does so voluntarily, likes so much to hear things about you, loves you.—

O, I wish I were sitting at your feet in the dear, familiar little room, with our little treasures playfully tumbling all around me, and if they grew too noisy for you, I would gather them about me and quiet them with some hair-raising tale.

The sun is setting in glory over the land with its glittering snow, the storm has passed by, and I—must lock myself up in my cage again—Adieu! Is Albert with you? And how—? God forgive me that question!

February 8.

For a week we have been having the most abdominable weather, and to me that is a benefit. For during all the time I have been here not a single fine day has shown itself to me in the sky that someone has not spoiled or embittered for me. So when it rains very hard, or drizzles, or freezes, or thaws—ah ha! I think, it can't be any worse in the house than it is outside, or vice versa, and then I'm content. If the sun at rising in the morning gives promise of a fine day, I can never help crying out: there again they have a divine gift of which they can deprive each other. There is nothing of which they don't deprive each other. Health, good repute, joyousness, recreation! And mostly because of silliness, lack of sense, and narrow-mindedness, and, if they are to be believed, with the best intentions. Sometimes I should like to beg them on my knees not to attack their own bowels so furiously.

February 17.

I fear that my ambassador and I will not endure each other's company much longer. The man is utterly unendurable. His manner of working and doing business is so ridiculous that I cannot refrain from opposing him and frequently doing something according to my ideas and my system, which naturally enough, never suits him. In this regard he lately complained of me at court, and the minister gave me a rebuke which was to be sure gentle, but a rebuke for all that, and I was on the point of requesting my dismissal, when I received from him a private letter,* one before which I fell on my knees, paying homage to that lofty, wise, and noble mind. How he reproves my excessive sensitiveness, how he respects, to be sure, as good and youthful spirit, my extreme notions of effective work, of influencing others, of carrying affairs to success, and does not attempt to extirpate them, merely to mitigate and lead them into channels where they will have their proper play and can have the most powerful effect. So I too am strengthened for another week, and again at one with myself. Calmness of soul is a glorious thing, and contentment with oneself. Ah, my friend, if only that jewel were not just as frail as it is precious and beautiful.

February 20.

God bless you, my dear ones, and give you all the good days He subtracts from mine!

I thank you, Albert, for having deceived me: I was waiting to hear

---

*Note by Goethe. Out of respect for this excellent man, the above-mentioned letter has been withdrawn from this collection, as well as another which is referred to later on, because it was not thought that such an indiscretion could be excused even by the warmest gratitude of the reading public.

when your wedding day was to be, and I had resolved to remove Lotte's silhouette solemnly from the wall on that day, and to bury it among other papers. And now you are a pair, and her image is still here! Well, then let it remain so! And why not? I know that I am with you too, that I am, without injury to you, in Lotte's heart, and have, yes, have the second place in it, and I will and must keep that. O, I should go mad if she could forget—Albert, all hell lies in that thought. Albert, farewell! Farewell, angel of Heaven! Farewell, Lotte!

March 15.

I have suffered a vexation which will drive me away from here. I am grinding my teeth! Devils! It is not to be made good, and at bottom you are to blame for it, you who goaded and drove and tormented me to put myself into a position which was not to my liking. And now I have it! and you have it! And to keep you from saying once more that my extravagant notions ruined everything, here you have an account, my dear sir, neat and plain, such as a chronicler would set down.

Count von C. loves me, singles me out; this is well known, and I have told you so a hundred times. Now I was at dinner yesterday at his house, and it was the very day when the aristocratic company of lords and ladies assemble there, a fact which I did not remember, nor did it occur to me that we inferior beings have no right to be in it. Good, I dine with the count, and after dinner we walk up and down in the great hall, I talking with him and with Colonel B., who joins us, and so the hour for the assembly approaches. God knows, I don't give it a thought. In walks my supersnobbish Lady von S. with her noble consort, and her nobly hatched goose of a daughter with the flat breast and the dainty bodice, and in passing they widen their nostrils and stare with traditionally aristocratic eyes, and since that tribe is heartily distasteful to me I was just going to take my leave, and was only waiting until the count should be free of that dreadful twaddle, when my Miss B. comes in. As I always feel a little lifting of the heart when I see her, I remained, placed myself behind her chair, and only observed after some time that she was talking to me with less candor than usual, with some embarrassment. I was struck by this. Is she too like all these others? I thought, and was hurt and wanted to leave, and yet I stayed, because I would have liked to find an excuse for her, and was incredulous, and was hoping for another kind word from her and—what you will. Meantime the company was filling up. Baron F. with his entire wardrobe from the days of the coronation of Francis I, Councillor R., designated here, however, *in qualitate* as von R., with his deaf wife, etc., not forgetting the poorly equipped J., who fills up the gaps in his antiquated garb with newfangled trappings—such folk come in droves, and I speak with a few acquaintances, all of whom are very laconic, I thought—and paid heed to no one but my B. I did not observe that the women at the end of the hall were whispering into each other's ears, that it was percolating to the men, that Lady von S. was talking to the Count (Miss B. told me after all this afterward), until at last the Count walked up to me and drew me over to a window.—"You know," said he, "our quaint ways: the company is displeased, I observe, at seeing you here; I would not for the world—" "Your Excellency," I broke in, "I beg a thousand pardons; I should have thought of this sooner, and I am sure you will forgive me this forgetfulness; I was going to take my leave some time ago, but some evil spirit held me back," I added with a smile, bowing.—The Count pressed my hands with a warmth of feeling that was unmistakable. I stole quietly out of the aristocratic gathering, went out, got into a cabriolet, and drove to M. to watch the sunset from the height there, reading at the same time in my Homer the fine canto in which Ulysses enjoys the hospitality of the excellent swineherd. All that was good.

In the evening I came back to dinner, there being but few in the dining-room; they were playing dice on a corner of the table, with the cloth turned back. Now honest Adelin comes in, lays down his hat on seeing me, comes up to me, and says softly, "You suffered a vexation?" "I?" said I. "The Count expelled you from the company." "To the devil with them!" I said. "I was glad to get out into the fresh air." "It's good," said he, "that you take it so lightly; only it does vex me, for everyone is talking about it." Now for the first time the affair began to annoy me. All who came to dinner and looked at me made me think, 'that is why they are looking at you.' That created a bad feeling.

But worse than that, when I am pitied today wherever I show up, when I hear that my rivals are triumphing and saying that this just shows what happens to the upstarts whose bit of intelligence makes them conceited, so that they think they have a right to override all the social conventions, and all the rest of the vile gossip—you feel like sticking a knife into your heart; for whatever may be said about being independent, I'd like to see the man who can endure to let the rascals talk against him when they have an advantage over him; if their talk is baseless, yes, then it's easy to ignore them.

March 16.

All the hounds are after me. Today I met Miss B. in the avenue, and could not refrain from speaking to her, and, as soon as we were somewhat separated from the rest, revealing my hurt at her recent behaviour. "O Werther," she said with a sincere tone, "could you so interpret my confusion, you who know my heart? What I suffered on your account, from the moment when I entered the hall! I foresaw everything, and a hundred times it was on my tongue to tell you. I knew that Lady von S. and Lady von T. would sooner leave with their husbands than remain in your company! I knew that the Count must not spoil his friendship with you,—and now all this to-do!" "How so, dear lady?" I said, concealing my alarm; for all that Adelin had said to me the day before yesterday ran at that moment through my veins like boiling water. "How much it has cost me up to now!" said the sweet creature, with tears in her eyes. I was no longer master of myself, and was on the point of casting myself at her feet. "Explain yourself," I cried. The tears ran down her cheeks. I was beside myself. She wiped them away without trying to conceal them. "You know my aunt," she began; "she was present, and she saw it, O, with what eyes did she see it! Werther, last night I endured a sermon about my intercourse with you, and this morning, and I have had to hear you disparaged and degraded, and I could and might only half defend you."

Every word she said went through my heart like a knife. She did not feel how compassionate it would have been to conceal all this from me, and now she went on to say what else would be gossiped, and what sorts of people would use it as a triumph. How people would now gloat and rejoice over the punishment of my arrogance and my disdain of others, with which they have long been reproaching me. To hear all this from her, Wilhelm, in a tone of the warmest sympathy—I was annihilated, and I am still raging inside. I wish that someone would dare to throw it up to me, so that I could run my sword through his body; if I saw blood, I should feel relief. Oh, a hundred times I have seized a knife, to ease this burdened heart. It is said of a noble breed of horses that when they are fearfully heated and jaded, they instinctively bite open a vein, in order to help them get their breath. So I often feel, but I should like to open a vein that would procure me eternal freedom.

March 24.

I have petitioned the court for my dismissal and hope to receive it, and you both will forgive me for not having first obtained your permission. Once and for all, I had to get away, and I know all the things you had in mind to say in order to induce me to remain, and so—Feed this to my mother in a sweet syrup, for I cannot help myself, and she must put up with the fact that I cannot help her either. Of course it is bound to be painful to her. To see all at once the fine course halted, which her son had just begun as a road to Privy Councilor and Ambassador, and back to the stall with the little steed! Make of it what you will, and put together all the possible cases in which I could and should have remained; enough to say that I am going, and that you may know where I shall land, I'll tell you that Prince * * * is here, who finds much pleasure in my company; hearing of my intentions, he has invited me to go with him to his estates, to spend the lovely springtime there. I have his promise that I am to be left to myself, and since we understand each other, up to a certain point, I'll take a chance and go with him.

April 19.

For your information.
Thanks, Wilhelm, for your two letters. I did not answer, because I let this sheet lie until my dismissal should have arrived from the court; I was afraid my mother might apply to the minister and make my resolve more difficult. But now it is done, and my dismissal is here. I do not like to tell you how reluctantly it was given to me, and what the minister writes to me—you would burst out into new lamentations. The Crown Prince sent me twenty-five ducats as a parting gift, with a note which moved me to tears; so I do not need to have my mother send me the money for which I lately asked.

May 5.

Tomorrow I shall go from here, and since my birthplace lies only a few miles from the road, I will revisit that too, and will recall the days of old, so happily dreamed away. I will enter by the very gate through which my mother drove out with me, when she left the dear, familiar spot after the death of my father, to imprison me in her unbearable town. Adieu, Wilhelm, you shall have a report of my journey.

May 9.

I completed the visit to my former home with all the veneration of a pilgrim, and some unexpected emotions laid hold upon me. By the great linden, which stands a mile from town on the road to S., I ordered a halt, got out, and bade the postillion drive on, so as to taste on foot every recollection as something quite new, vivid, and as my heart willed it. So there I stood under the linden which in former days of boyhood had been the goal and the limit of my strolls. How different? In those days I yearned in happy ignorance to get out into the unfamiliar world, where I hoped to find so much nourishment, so much enjoyment for my heart, wherewith to fill and to satisfy my aspiring, yearning bosom. Now I am returning from the wide world—O, my friend, with how many disappointed hopes, with how many ruined plans!—I saw lying before me the mountains which had been so many thousands of times the object of my desires. For hours on end I could sit here, reaching over yonder with my longing, losing myself with all my soul in the woods and valleys which presented themselves to my eyes in such a pleasant vagueness; and then when I had to turn at the appointed time, with what repugnance did I abandon that beloved spot!—I approached the town, and all the old familiar summer houses were saluted, but the new ones were distasteful to me, as well as all the other alterations that had been made. I entered the gate, and at once and immediately I found myself again. I don't care to go into detail; charming as I found it, just so monotonous would it be in the recital. I had resolved to dwell on the market-place, right next to our old house. As I walked along I observed that the school house, where an honest old woman had herded us together in childhood, was converted into a general shop. I recalled the uneasiness, the tears, the apathy, the heartfelt terror, which I had endured in that hole.—There was not one step I took which was not noteworthy. A pilgrim in the Holy Land does not encounter as many stations of religious recollection, and his heart is scarcely as full of sacred emotion.—One more item must serve for a thousand. I strolled down the stream as far as a certain farm; that had formerly been my course, too, and the places where we boys would try to skip flat stones over the water the largest number of times. I recalled so vividly, when I stood still and looked after the flowing water, with what wonderful premonitions I used to follow its course, how thrilling I imagined the regions to be where it was bound, and how I had soon reached the limits of my imaginative power; and yet the water must go on, on and on, until I lost myself completely in the contemplation of an invisible distance.—See, my good friend, just so confined and blissful were the glorious patriarchs! so childlike was their feeling, their poetry! When Ulysses speaks of the unmeasured sea and of the unending earth, that is so true, human, heartfelt, intimate, and mysterious. What good does it do me that I can now parrot with every schoolboy the fact that it is round? Man needs but few clods of earth to base his happiness upon, less to cover his final rest.

Now I am here in the Prince's hunting-lodge. It is quite easy to get along with this gentleman, for he is candid and simple. Strange people surround him whom I do not understand at all. They seem not to be rascals, and yet they do not have the look of honest folk. Sometimes they seem honest to me, and yet I cannot trust them. Another thing that I regret is that he often speaks of things which he has only heard and read, always from the point of view which the other wanted to present to him.

Also, he prizes my intelligence and my talents more than he does this heart, which is after all my sole pride, which is the only source of everything I have, of all my force, all my bliss, and all my misery. Oh, anyone can know what I know—only I possess my heart.

May 25.

I had something in mind of which I was going to tell you nothing until it should be carried out; now that nothing is to come of it, it's perhaps just as well. I wanted to volunteer for war service; I have had that at heart for a long time. That was chiefly the reason why I followed the Prince here, he being a general in the service of * * *. During a stroll I revealed my resolve to him; he advised me against it, and it would have had to be more a passion than a notion with me if I had not been willing to lend an ear to his reasoning.

June 11.

Say what you will, I cannot stay here any longer. What am I to do here? Time hangs heavy. The Prince keeps me as well as one can, and yet I am not in my element. At bottom we have nothing in common. He is a man of sense, but of a very common sense; intercourse with him does not entertain me any more than the reading of a well-written book. I'll stay one week more, and then I shall resume my aimless roving. The best thing I have done here is to sketch. The Prince has a feeling for art, and would have a still stronger feeling if he were not hemmed in by his miserable scientism, and by the customary terminology. Sometimes I grit my teeth when guiding him through nature and art with warm imagination, and he suddenly blunders in with some stereotyped dictum and thinks he is doing just the right thing.

June 16.

True, I am but a wanderer, a rover on earth! Are you more than that?

June 18.

Where I am bound for? let me tell you in confidence. For another fortnight I must stay here after all, and then I have persuaded myself that I wanted to visit the mines in ***; but actually there is nothing to that, and I only wish to get closer to Lotte, that is all. And I scoff at my own heart—and do its will.

June 29.

No, it is all right! Everything is all right!—I—her husband! O God who made me, if you had granted me that bliss, my whole life should be one continuous prayer. I offer no challenge, and forgive me these tears, forgive me my vain desires!—She my wife! If I had clasped in my arms the dearest creature under the sun—A shiver goes through my whole body, Wilhelm, when Albert puts his arm around her slender waist.

And, may I say this? Why not, Wilhelm? She would have been happier with me than with him! O, he is not the man to gratify all the desires of that heart. A certain lack of sensitivity, a lack—take it as you will; that his heart does not beat in sympathy at—oh!—at the passage in a loved book where our hearts, Lotte's and mine, came together; or in a hundred other cases, when it chances that we utter our feelings regarding an action or a third person. Dear Wilhelm!— True, he loves her with all his heart, and what does such a love not deserve!—

An unendurable person interrupted me. My tears are dried. I have lost the thread. Adieu.

August 4.

I am not alone in this. All people are deceived in their hopes, duped in their expectations. I called on my good young woman under the linden. The oldest boy ran to meet me, and his cry of joy brought out his mother, who looked very depressed. Her first word was, "Good sir, alas, my Hans has died!" That was her youngest boy. I was silent. "And my husband," said she, "came back from Switzerland and brought nothing with him, and without the help of good people he would have had to beg his way out, for he had caught a fever on the way." I could say nothing to her, but gave something to the youngster; she begged me to accept some apples, which I did, and then forsook the place of sad recollection.

August 21.

In the turn of a hand things change with me. Sometimes a joyous ray of life is about to dawn again, ah! but only for a moment!— When I lose myself like this in dreams, I cannot fight off the thought: what if Albert were to die? You would! yes, she would— and then I run after that fantasm until it leads me to abysses from which I shrink back trembling.

If I go out of the gate along the road on which I drove for the first time to fetch Lotte for the dance, how very different that was! Everything, everything has gone by! No hint of that former world, not one pulse-beat of the feeling I knew then. I feel as a spirit must, if it returned to the fire-gutted, ruined castle which as a thriving prince he had once built and furnished with all the attributes of splendor, and which at death he had hopefully bequeathed to his beloved son.

September 3.

Sometimes I do not understand how any other *can* love her, is permitted to love her, since I love her so exclusively, so deeply, so fully, and neither know nor have anything but her!

September 4.

Yes, it is so. As nature inclines toward the fall, so it is becoming fall in me and about me. My leaves are turning yellow, and the leaves of the neighbouring trees have already fallen. Did I not write you once about a peasant lad, just after I came here? Now I have inquired about him in Wahlheim; they said he had been harshly dismissed, and nobody claimed to know anything more about him. Yesterday I met him by chance on my way to another village; I spoke to him, and he told me his story, which touched me doubly and trebly, as you will readily understand when I retell it to you. Yet why all this, and why don't I keep to myself what frightens and wounds me? why do I sadden you too? why do I keep giving you opportunities to pity me and to scold me? So be it, that too may be a part of my fate!

With a quiet melancholy, in which I seemed to detect some timidity, the young man answered my first questions; but very soon more candidly, as if all at once he knew himself and me again, he confessed his failings, bewailed his unhappiness. Could I, my friend, refer every one of his words to your judgment? He admitted, indeed he recounted with a kind of enjoyment and the happiness of remembrance, that his passion for his mistress had increased in him day by day, so that at last he did not know what he was doing, nor, as he expressed it, where to turn. He had been unable to eat or drink or sleep, and had felt choked; he had done what he should not and had forgotten what he was ordered to do, and it had been as if he were pursued by an evil spirit; until one day, when he knew she was in an upstairs room, he had followed her, or rather had been drawn after her. As she had lent no ear to his pleading, he had tried to take possession of her by force; he did not know what had come over him, and he called God to witness that his intentions toward her had always been honorable, and that he had desired nothing more earnestly than that she would marry him, that she might spend her life with him. When he had spoken thus for awhile, he began to hesitate, like a man who has something more to say and does not dare to utter it; at last he also admitted to me, shyly, all the little liberties she had allowed him, and how close she had let him come to her. He broke off two or three times, repeating the most animated protestations that he was not saying this to blacken her, as he put it, that he loved and valued her as before, that such words had never crossed his lips, and that he was only saying this to me in order to convince me that he was not a wholly perverted and unreasonable person—And here, my friend, I strike up my old song again, the one I shall sing eternally: If I could only place this man before you as he stood before me, as he still stands before me! If I could tell you everything properly, so that you should feel how I sympathize with his fate, and must do so! But enough: since you also know my fate, and me as well, then you know only too well what draws me to all those who are unhappy, and especially to this unhappy one.

Now that I read this page over, I see that I have forgotten to tell the end of the story, which however is easy to imagine. She resisted him; her brother came up, who had long hated him and had long wanted him out of the house, because he feared that a new marriage would make his sister withdraw from his children the inheritance which right now raises his hopes since she is childless. The brother had kicked him out of the house at once and made such a fuss over the affair that the woman, even if she had wished, could not have taken him back. Now, he said, she had hired another servant, and on his account too, it was said, she had heard she had fallen out with her brother, and it was positively asserted that she was going to marry him, but he was firmly resolved not to see that happen.

What I am telling you is not exaggerated, not sentimentalized, and indeed I may well say that I have told it feebly, feebly, while I have coarsened it by reporting it with our conventional moral words.

So then, this love, this loyalty, this passion, is no poetic invention. It is alive, and in its complete genuineness it exists amid that class of people whom we call uncultured, whom we call crude. We refined ones—refined until there is nothing left! Read this story with reverence, I beg you. I am quiet today as I write this down; you see by my handwriting that I am not smearing and splashing as usual. Read, my dear fellow, and think as you do so that it is also the story of your friend. Yes, so it was with me, so it will be with me, and I am not half as good, not half as resolute as that poor, unhappy fellow, with whom I am almost afraid to compare myself.

September 5.

She had written a note to her husband, whom business affairs had kept for some time in the country. It began, "Dearest and best, come as soon as you can. I shall be overjoyed to see you back." A friend who came in brought word that certain circumstances would keep him from returning so soon. The little note was not sent and got into my hands that evening. I read it and smiled: she asked me why. "What a divine gift is the imagination," I cried, "for a moment I was able to conceive that this was written to me." She dropped the subject, seeming displeased, and I said no more.

September 6.

It was hard for me to resolve to put away the plain blue dress-coat in which I had my first dance with Lotte, but it finally became too shabby. But I also had a new one made that was just like its predecessor, with collar and facings, and with it again a yellow waistcoat and trousers.

Yet the effect is not precisely the same. I don't know—I believe that in time I shall get to like this one better.

September 12.

She was out of town for some days, having gone to fetch Albert. Today I entered her room, she came toward me, and I kissed her hand overjoyed.

A canary left the mirror and flew to her shoulder. "A new friend," she said, enticing it to perch on her hand, "it was bought for my little ones. It is just too sweet! Look at it! If I give it bread, it flutters its wings and pecks so daintily. It kisses me, too, look!"

As she held out her mouth to the little creature, it pressed into the sweet lips as charmingly as if it could have felt the bliss it was enjoying.

"It shall kiss you, too," she said, handing the bird to me. The tiny beak made its way from her lips to mine, and the pecking contact was like a breath, a faint suggestion of a lovely pleasure.

"Its kiss," I said, "is not quite without greed: it seeks nourishment and returns unsatisfied after an empty caress."

"It will also eat out of my mouth," she said. She fed it some crumbs with her lips, whose smiles expressed the joys of an innocently shared love.

I turned my face away. She should not do it! should not goad my imagination with these pictures of heavenly innocence and blissfulness, not awaken my heart out of the slumber into which it is rocked at times by the indifference of life!—And why not?—She has such confidence in me! She knows how much I love her!

September 15.

It is infuriating, Wilhelm, that there are human beings without feeling or appreciation for the few things on earth that still have some value. You know the walnut trees under which I sat with Lotte at the house of the honest pastor of St. * * *, those magnificent trees which, God knows, filled my soul with the greatest joy! How familiar they made the parsonage, how cool! and how splendid the branches were! and recollection extending back to the honest pastor-couple that planted them so many years ago. The schoolmaster often told us one of their names, which he had heard from his grandfather; and he is said to have been such a good man, and his memory was always sacred to me under those trees. I tell you, the schoolmaster had tears in his eyes as we spoke yesterday of their having been cut down—Cut down! I could go mad, I could murder the cur that struck the first blow. I, who could grieve myself to death if such a pair of trees stood in my yard and one of the died of old age, I have to see this done. My dear fellow, there is one compensation all the same! What a thing is human feeling! The whole village is murmuring, and I hope the pastor's wife will be made to feel, by a lack of butter and eggs and of other marks of confidence, the wound she has dealt her village. For it is *she*, the wife of the new pastor (our old one has died too), a lean, sickly creature, who has every reason to take no interest in the world, for no one takes an interest in her. A silly fool she is, who makes pretensions to being learned, who meddles with the problem of which books of the Bible are genuine, works a great deal at the new-fashioned moral and critical re-evaluation of Christian ethics, and shrugs her shoulders at Lavater's enthusiasms, and whose health is thoroughly broken down, for which reason she has no joy on God's earth. Nor would it have been possible for any other creature to cut down my walnut trees. See, I can't get over it! Just imagine, the falling leaves make her yard disorderly and dank, the trees rob her of daylight, and when the nuts are ripe the boys throw stones at them: that gets on her nerves, that disturbs her deep mediations when she is weighing Kennikot, Semler, and Michaelis one against the other. When I saw that the people in the village, especially the old ones, were so discontented, I said, "Why did you permit it?" They said, "If the mayor is willing, here in the country, what can be done?" But one thing was rightly done. The major and the pastor, who was hoping to get some advantage from the silly notions of his wife—which don't make his soup any more savory—thought they would divide the profit; but the treasury got wind of it and said, "Hand it over!" For it still had old claims to that part of the parsonage where the trees stood, and it sold them to the highest bidder. They are down! O, if I were the prince! I would see to it that the pastor's wife, the mayor, and the treasury—Prince!—Well, if I were the prince, what would I care about the trees in my land?

October 10.

If I merely see her black eyes, I feel better at once! Look, and what vexes me is that Albert does not seem to be as happy as he—hoped— as I—think I should be—if—I am not fond of writing dashes, but in this case I have no other way of expressing myself—and I think it is plain enough.

October 12.

Ossian has displaced Homer in my heart. What a world it is into which the glorious one leads me! To stroll across the heath, with the gale roaring around me, which leads in steaming mists the spirits of our fathers through the vague light of the moon. To hear from yonder mountains, amid the roar of the forest stream, the half-obliterated groaning of the spirits from the caves, and the lamentations of the girl who is grieving herself to death, hovering about the four moss-covered, grass-grown gravestones of her beloved, fallen noble. Then when I find him, the grayhaired, roving bard, who seeks on the spacious heath the footprints of his forebears, and ah!

finds their gravestones, and then looks wailing toward the good evening star which conceals itself in the rolling waves of the ocean, and the past ages come to life in the soul of the hero, days when a friendly ray illumined the perils of the brave, and the moon shone upon their beribboned ship on its victorious return. When I read on his brow his deep distress, see this last forsaken hero totter in complete exhaustion toward the grave noting how he keeps drinking in ever new, painfully glowing joys in the enfeebled presence of the shades of his departed ones, and how he looks toward the cold earth, the tall, waving grass, and exclaims, "The wanderer will come, who knew me in my beauty, and will ask, 'Where is the singer, Fingal's excellent son? His footstep goes over my grave, and he asks in vain after me on the earth.' "—O, my friend! I would like to draw my sword like an ancient man-at-arms, free my prince at one stroke from the quivering torment of a life of slow death, and send my own soul after the liberated demigod.

October 19.

Oh, this void! this fearful void which I feel here in my breast!—I often think to myself: if you could press her just once to this heart, just once, then this entire void would be filled.

October 26.

Yes, it is becoming certain to me, friend, certain and ever more certain, that little importance attaches to the existence of any being, very little. A woman friend came to see Lotte, and I went into the adjoining room to get a book, but could not read, and then I took a pen to do some writing. I heard them speaking quietly; they were telling each other unimportant matters, town gossip: this girl is getting married, that one is sick, very sick. "She has a hacking cough, her face is only skin and bones, and she has fainting spells; I wouldn't give a penny for her life," said the one. "And Mr. N. N. is in a bad way too," said Lotte. "He is already bloated," said the other. And my vivid imagination took me to the bedside of these poor people; I saw with what reluctance they were turning their backs upon life, how they—Wilhelm! and my little ladies were talking about it as people do talk about the fact that a stranger is dying.—And when I look about me and survey the room, and around me are Lotte's dresses and Albert's writings and these furnishings, with which I am on such friendly terms, including this inkwell, and I think, 'See what you mean to this household! All in all. Your friends honor you! You are often a joy to them, and to your heart it seems as if that joy were indispensable, and yet—if you were to go, if you parted from their circle? Would they, and how long would they feel the void that the loss of you would inflict upon their destiny? how long?'—O, man is so transitory that even where he finds the only evidence for his existence, even where his presence makes its only true impression, namely, in the memory, in the souls of his loved ones, even there he must be extinguished and disappear, and how quickly!

October 27.

Often I would like to rend my breast and knock in my brain, seeing that people can be so little to each other. Ah, the love, joy, warmth, and rapture which I cannot bestow will not be given to me by the other, and even with a whole heart full of bliss I shall not delight one who stands before me cold and sapless.

I have so much, and my feeling for her engulfs it all; I have so much, and without her I find everything turned into nothing.

October 30.

If I have not been a hundred times on the point of flinging my arms about her! The great God knows how it feels to see so much loveliness go crisscross before me and be forbidden to reach for it; and yet reaching for things is the most natural impulse in man. Don't children reach for everything they see?—And I?

November 3.

God knows, I often get into bed with the desire, indeed at times with the hope, of not awaking again; and in the morning I open my eyes, see the sun again, and am wretched. O that I could be capricious, could put the blame on the weather, on a third party, on a frustrated undertaking, then I would only have to bear half the unendurable burden of ill-humor. But woe is me! I feel too plainly that all the guilt is mine alone,—no, not guilt! Bad enough that in me the source of all my misery lies concealed, as formerly the source of all my joys. Am I not still the very one who formerly revelled in all the fullness of his feeling, whose every step was followed by paradise, who had a heart that could lovingly embrace an entire world? And that heart is dead now, no raptures issue from it any more, my eyes are dried up, and my thoughts, no longer regaled with refreshing tears, draw my brow into anxious folds. I suffer much, for I have lost what was the sole rapture of my life, that holy, animating force with which I created worlds all about me; it is gone!—When I gaze out of my window toward the distant height, seeing how the morning sun breaks through the mist above it and lights up the quiet valley meadow, and the gentle stream meanders toward me between its leafless willows.—O, when that glorious natural scene stands before me as lifeless as a chromo, and all this rapture cannot pump one drop of bliss from my heart up into my brain, and this whole fellow stands before the countenance of God like a dried-up well or a leaky bucket. I have often flung myself on the ground and begged God for tears, as a ploughman prays for rain when the sky is brazen above him and around him the earth is parching.

But alas, I feel that God does not give rain and sunshine in response to our impetuous requests, and those former days whose memory torments me, why were they so blissful? why else than because I awaited his spirit with patience, and welcomed the rapture which he poured over me with undivided, deeply grateful heart.

November 8.

She has rebuked my excesses! ah, but so lovably! My excesses, whereby I sometimes let myself be seduced by a glass of wine into drinking a bottle. "Don't do it!" she said, "think of Lotte!" "Think!" said I, "need you bid me do that? I think—I don't think! You are always present to my soul. Today I was sitting at the spot where you lately dismounted from the carriage—" She spoke of something else, so as not to let me enlarge upon the subject. Best of friends, I am done for! she can do with me whatever she will.

November 15.

I thank you, Wilhelm, for your heartfelt sympathy, for your well-meant advice, and beg you to be calm. Let me endure to the end: for all my wearisomeness I still have force enough to hold out. I honor religion, as you know, and I realize that it is a staff to many a weary wanderer, refreshment to the languishing. Only—can it, must it be so for every one? If you behold the great world, you will see thousands who did not find it so, thousands who will never find it so, whether preached to them or not—and must it be so to me? Does not even the Son of God say that those would be around him whom the Father has given to him? What if I am not given to him? what if the Father wants to keep me for Himself, as my heart tells me?—I beg you not to misinterpret this; do not see a mockery in these innocent words; it is my whole soul that I am laying before you: else I should wish I had held my peace: just as I am reluctant to say anything about all those matters of which everyone knows as little as I do. What is human destiny other than to endure his measure of suffering, drink his cup to the dregs?—And if the God from heaven found the cup too bitter for his human lips, why should I exalt myself and act as if it tasted sweet to me? And why should I be ashamed, in the terrible moment when my whole existence is trembling between being and not-being, when the past shines like a flash of lightning over the dark abyss of the future, and everything about me is sinking, and the world going to destruction with me—Isn't it then the voice of the creature which is being driven back into itself, fails to find a self, and irresistibly tumbles to its fall, that groans from the inner depths of its vainly aspiring powers, 'My God! my God! why hast thou forsaken me?' And should I be ashamed of that saying, should I be afraid of that moment, seeing that he who rolls up the heavens like a robe did not escape it?

November 21.

She does not see, she does not feel, that she is preparing a poison which will destroy me and herself; and I sip to the bottom, with fullest enjoyment, the cup she hands me for my ruin. Of what avail is the kind gaze with which she often—often?—no, not often, but sometimes looks at me, the complaisance with which she receives an involuntary expression of my emotion, the sympathy with my suffering that is delineated on her brow?

Yesterday, as I was departing, she held out her hand and said, "Adieu, dear Werther!"—Dear Werther! It was the first time that she had called me "dear," and it sent a shiver all through me. I have repeated it to myself a hundred times, and last evening, as I was about to go to bed and was chatting about all sorts of things with myself, I said all at once, "Good night, dear Werther!" and afterwards I had to laugh at myself.

November 22.

I cannot pray, "Let me have her!" and yet she often seems to me to be mine. I cannot pray, "Give her to me!" for she belongs to another. I indulge in all sorts of quibbles about my griefs; if I let myself go, the result would be a whole litany of contradictions.

November 24.

She feels what I am suffering. Today her gaze penetrated deeply into my soul. I found her alone; I said nothing, and she looked at me. And I no longer saw in her the charming beauty, no longer the shining of her excellent mind; all that had vanished before my eyes. A much more glorious gaze stirred me, full of the expression of the deepest sympathy, of the sweetest compassion. Why could I not fling myself at her feet? why could I not weep my answer on her neck with a thousand kisses? She took refuge in her piano, and with sweet and low voice she breathed out tones in harmony with her playing. Never have I seen her lips so charming; it was as if they opened in a famishing desire to sip in those sweet sounds that welled forth from the piano, and as if only the mysterious echo responded from that pure mouth—O, if I could only tell you how it was!—I resisted no longer, bowed my head, and vowed: 'never will I dare, you lips, to press a kiss upon you, on which the spirits of heaven hover—, And yet—I will—! Ha! do you see, that stands before my soul like a barrier—this bliss—and then, lost forever to expiate that sin—Sin?

November 26.

Sometimes I tell myself: your fate is unique; consider all others fortunate—no other has ever been so tormented. Then I read a poet of past times, and it is as if I were looking into my own heart. I have so much to endure! Ah, have people before me ever been as wretched as I?

November 30.

It is, it *is* my fate not to come to my senses! Wherever I go, I encounter some apparition which robs me of all composure. Today! O fate! O humanity!

I was strolling along the stream in the noon hour, having no desire to eat. All was desolate, a moist, chill west wind blew down from the mountain, and the grey rain clouds were drifting into the valley. From afar I saw a man in a worn green coat, who was crawling about among the rocks and seemed to be seeking herbs. When I came closer, and he turned around at the noise I made, I saw a most interesting face, in which a quiet sorrow was the main feature, but which otherwise expressed nothing but a good, straightforward mind; his black locks were put up in two rolls with hairpins, the rest being into a heavy plait that hung down his back. As his clothing seemed to me to indicate a man of lowly station, I thought he would not take it amiss if I paid attention to his occupation, and so I asked him what he was seeking. "I am seeking flowers," he answered with a deep sigh, "and I find none." "Nor is this the season," I said with a smile. "There are so many flowers," he said, coming down to me. "In my garden there are roses and two kinds of honeysuckle, one of which my father gave me, and they grow like weeds; I have been looking for them for two days, and I can't find them. Out yonder, too, there are always flowers, yellow and blue and red ones, and the centaury has a pretty little flower. I can't find any of them." I saw that something was wrong, and so I asked a roundabout question: "What do you want to do with the flowers?" A strange, twitching smile puckered his face. "If you will not give me away," he said, putting a finger on his lips. "I have promised my sweetheart a bouquet." "That is nice," I said. "O," said he, "she has lots of other things, she is rich." "And yet she loves your bouquet," I responded. "O!" he continued, "she has jewels and a crown." "Why, what is her name?" "If the States-General would pay me," he replied, "I'd be a different person! Yes, there once was a time when I was so happy! Now it's all over with me. I am now—" A moist glance toward the sky expressed everything. "So you were happy?" I asked. "Oh, I wish I were again like that!" said he. "At that time I was as happy, as merry, as unburdened as fish in water!" "Heinrich!" called an old woman who came long the path, "Heinrich, where are you hiding? we have been looking for you everywhere, come to lunch!" "Is that your son?" I asked, approaching her. "Indeed, my poor son," she replied. "God has given me a heavy cross to bear." "How long has he been so?" I asked. "In this calm state," she said, "he has been for half a year now. Thank God that it is no worse than this; before that he was raving for a whole year and lay chained up in the mad house. Now he harms nobody, only he is always having to do with kings and emperors. He was such a good, quiet person, wrote a fine hand, and helped to support me; all at once he grew melancholy, fell into a high fever, which turned into madness, and now he is as you see him. If I were to tell you, sir—" I broke in upon the stream of her words by asking, "What kind of a time was it that he praises so, saying that he was so happy then, so well off?" "The foolish fellow!" she cried with a compassionate smile, "he means the time when he was out of his mind, he is always praising that; that is the time when he was in the mad house, when he knew nothing about himself—" This struck me like a thunderclap, and I put a coin in her hand and left her in haste.

"When you were happy!" I exclaimed, walking rapidly toward the town, "when you felt as cheerful as a fish in water!"—God in heaven! have you made that to be that fate of men, that they are not happy until they have acquired some sense and then lose it again?—Poor wretch! and yet how I envy your clouded mind, the confusion of thought in which you are languishing! You go out in the hope of picking flowers for your queen—in the winter—and mourn because you find none, and fail to understand why you can find none. And I—and I go out without hope, without purpose, and return home the same as when I went.—You dream of what a man you would be if the States-General paid you. Happy creature! able as you are to ascribe your lack of happiness to an earthly obstacle. You do not feel! you do not feel that in your ravaged heart, in your deranged brain, your misery lies, from which you cannot be freed by all the kings of the earth.

That man should die disconsolate who scoffs at a sufferer journeying toward the remotest well-spring, which will augment his illness, make his death more painful! or who looks down upon the hard-pressed heart which, in order to rid itself of pangs of conscience, and to lay aside the sufferings of his soul, makes a pilgrimage to the Holy Sepulchre. Every step which cuts through his shoes on his pathless way is a drop of balm for the terrified soul, and with every completed day's journey his heart is relieved of many distresses as it lays itself down.—Have you a right to call that a delusion, you phrasemongers on your beds of ease?—Delusion!—O God, you see my tears! Having created man with poverty enough, must you also endow him with brothers who would rob him of even the little he had, of his bit of trust in you, in you, you all-loving one? For man's trust in a healing root, in the tears of the grapevine, what is that but trust in you, trust that you have put into all that surrounds us the curative and alleviating force of which we have an hourly need? Father whom I do not know! Father who once filled my whole soul, and who has now turned his countenance away from me! call me to you! keep silence no longer! your silence will not sustain this thirsting soul—And would a man, a father, be able to show anger, if his unexpectedly returning son should fall upon his neck and cry, "I am here again, my father! Be not angry that I am cutting short the journey which it was your will that I should endure still longer. The world is everywhere the same, reward and joy following upon effort and toil; but what does that mean to me? I only feel content where you are, and in your presence I wish to suffer and to enjoy."—And you, dear heavenly Father, should you thrust him from you?

December 1.

Wilhelm! the man about whom I wrote to you, that happily unhappy man, was a clerk employed by Lotte's father, and a passion for her which he cherished, concealed, and revealed, and which caused his dismissal from the steward's service, made him demented. Feel as you see these prosy words with what a turmoil this story gripped me, when Albert told it to me just as calmly as you will perhaps read it.

December 4.

I beg of you—You see, it is all up with me, I can bear it no longer! Today I was sitting with her—sitting, and she was playing on her piano, various melodies, and all that expression! all!—all!—what would you?—Her little sister was on my knee dressing her doll. Tears came into my eyes. I bent down, and her wedding ring struck my gaze—my tears flowed—And all at once she dropped into that old, divinely sweet melody, all of a sudden, and through my soul passed a feeling of consolation, and a recollection of things past, of the times when I had heard that song, of the gloomy intervals of vexation, of frustrated hopes, and then—I walked up and down the room, my heart suffocating under all that flooded into it.—"For God's sake," I said, going up to her in an impetuous outburst, "for God's sake, stop!" She stopped and stared at me. "Werther," she said with a smile that pierced my soul, "Werther, you are very sick, even your favorite dishes disagree with you. Go now! I beg you, calm yourself." I tore myself away from her, and—God! you see my misery, and you will end it.

December 6.

How that figure pursues me! Waking and dreaming it fills my whole soul! Here, when I close my eyes, here in my brow, where the power of inner vision unites, are her black eyes. Here! I cannot put it into words for you. If I close my eyes, there they are; like an ocean, like an abyss they lie still before me, in me, filling all the thoughts within my brow.

What is man, the eulogized demigod? Does he not lack force at the very point where he needs it most? And when he soars upward in joy, or sinks down in suffering, is he not checked in both, is he not returned again to the dull, cold sphere of awareness, just when he was longing to lose himself in the fullness of the infinite?

The Editor to the Reader

How deeply I should wish that of the last remarkable days of our friend so many personal testimonials had remained to us that I should not need to interrupt the sequence of his posthumous letters with my own narrative.

I have been at pains to collect precise information from the lips of those who could be well apprized of his story; it is simple, and all the accounts of it, apart from a few details, agree with each other; only with regard to the states of mind of the actors do opinions differ, and judgments are divided.

What is left for us save to narrate conscientiously what we have been able to learn by dint of repeated, diligent inquiry, to insert the letters left behind by the departing one, and not to disregard even the tiniest scrap of paper; especially since it is so difficult to discover the true and peculiar motives of even a single action, if it takes place among persons not of the common stamp.

Discontent and moroseness had taken deeper and deeper root in Werther's soul, becoming more firmly intertwined, and had gradually filled his entire being. The harmony of his mind was wholly destroyed, and an inner fever and fury, which threw all the forces of his nature into confusion, produced the most contradictory effects and finally left him with nothing but exhaustion, from which he strove to free himself even more anxiously than he had previously struggled with all his other trials. The intimidation of his heart consumed all other forces of his mind, his vivacity and his perceptiveness; he became a sad figure in society, steadily more unhappy, and his injustice to others grew with his unhappiness. At least this is said by Albert's friends; they maintain that Werther was not able to judge the conduct of a quiet man who had finally become possessed of a long-desired happiness, and who sought to preserve this happiness for the future, Werther being a man who consumed his entire fortune, as it were, each day, whereupon each evening saw him suffer pain and want. Albert, they say, had not altered in that short time, he continued to be the same person that Werther had known from the outset, and that he had so greatly esteemed and honored. Albert loved Lotte more than anything else, he was proud of her, and he likewise wished to see her recognized by everyone as the most glorious of creatures. Was he then to be blamed if he desired to avert even the least shadow of a suspicion, if at that stage he had no wish to share this precious possession with anyone, even in the most innocent fashion? They admit that Albert often left his wife's room when Werther was with her, but not out of hatred or aversion toward his friend, only because he felt that the latter was oppressed by his presence.

Lotte's father had been seized by an ailment which kept him indoors; he sent her his carriage, and she drove out to see him. It was a fine winter day; the first snow had fallen heavily, covering the whole landscape.

Werther followed after her on the next day, in order to escort her back, in case Albert did not come to fetch her.

The bright weather was unable to have much influence on his

melancholy mood: a dull weight burdened his soul, the pictures of sadness had established themselves firmly within him, and his spirit knew no activity save to shift from one painful thought to another.

As he lived in eternal conflict with himself, so the state of others seemed to him all the more dubious and confused; he believed that he had disturbed the fine relationship between Albert and his wife, and he reproached himself for this, feeling at the same time a secret anger against her husband.

His thought touched again upon this subject as he walked along. "Yes, yes," he said to himself, privately gritting his teeth, "that is the familiar, amiable, tender association, sharing in all things, the calm, lasting loyalty! Satiety and indifference, that is what it is! Does not any miserable business matter attract him more than his precious, delicious wife? Does he know how to appreciate his good fortune? Does he know how to esteem her as she deserves? He has her; all right, he has her—I know that, as I also know something else, and I believe myself accustomed to the idea, but it will yet make me mad, it will yet deprive me of my life—And has his friendship with me held water? Does he not already see in my attachment to Lotte an invasion of his rights, in my attentiveness to her a silent reproach? I know very well, I feel, that he does not like to see me, that he wishes my removal, that my presence is burdensome to him."

Repeatedly he checked his rapid pace, often he stood still, seeming to be about to turn back; but again and again he redirected his course forward, and in the midst of these thoughts and soliloquies he at last reached the hunting lodge, against his will as it were.

He entered the door and asked about Lotte and her father, finding the house in some commotion. The oldest boy told him that an accident had taken place over in Wahlheim, that a farmer had been slain.—This made no impression upon him.—He entered the living room and found Lotte trying to dissuade her father, who despite his illness wanted to go over and investigate the affair on the spot. The slayer was as yet unknown, but the victim had been found in the morning before the door of the house, and there were surmises: the victim was the servant of a widow who had previously had another man in her service, whom discord had driven from her house.

When Werther heard this, he started up vehemently. "Is it possible!" he exclaimed, "I must go over there, I can't wait one minute." He hurried toward Wahlheim, every recollection came to life in him, and he did not doubt for a moment that the crime had been committed by that man with whom he had had a number of talks, and whom he had come to like so much.

As he had to go through the lindens to get to the tavern where they had deposited the body, he was horrified at the sight of the spot he had loved so much. The threshold on which the neighbor's children had so often played was sullied with blood. Love and loyalty, the fairest human feelings, had turned into violence and murder. The stately trees stood bare and covered with frost, the fine hedges which arched over the low wall of the churchyard were denuded, and the gravestones, covered with snow, were visible through the gaps.

As he approached the tavern, before which the whole village was assembled, suddenly a clamor arose. From afar a troop of armed men was seen, and everyone cried that they were bringing the slayer. Werther looked in that direction and was not long in doubt. Yes! it was the servant who had loved the widow so much, and whom Werther had encountered some time before, going about in his silent wrath, in his hidden despair.

"What have you done, unhappy man!" exclaimed Werther, as he went toward the prisoner. The latter looked at him quietly, and in silence, and finally replied quite calmly, "No one shall have her, and she will have no one." They led the captive into the tavern, and Werther hurried away.

As a result of this frightful, violent contact, everything in his nature had been thrown into turmoil. For a moment he was suddenly torn out of his sadness, his discontent, his apathetic resignation; sympathy took hold of him invincibly, and an unspeakable desire came over him to save that man. He felt him to be so unhappy, he found him so guiltless even as a criminal, he put himself so profoundly in his situation, that he was confident he could persuade others as well. Already he felt a desire to be able to speak for the man, already the most animated plea was on his lips, he hurried toward the hunting lodge, and on the way he could not refrain from uttering under his breath all the arguments he was going to present to the steward.

When he entered the room, he found Albert there, and this vexed him for a moment; but he soon composed himself again and recited his ideas to the steward with ardor. The latter shook his head a couple of times, and although Werther brought forward with the greatest vivacity, passion, and truth all that a man could say in exculpation of another, yet the steward, as can easily be imagined, was not moved by it. On the contrary, he did not let our friend finish, opposed him strongly, and rebuked him for taking the side of an assassin! showing him that in this fashion all law would be annulled, all the security of the state destroyed; and he also added that in such an affair he could no nothing without taking upon himself the greatest responsibility: everything, he said, must be done in order and follow the prescribed course.

Werther did not yet admit defeat, but he merely requested the steward to look the other way if the man should be helped to escape. This too the steward rejected. Albert, who finally entered into the conversation, likewise sided with the older man. Werther was outvoted, and in fearful suffering he set out again, after the steward had said to him repeatedly, "No, he cannot be saved!"

How sharply these words must have struck him we see from a little note which was found among his papers, and which was undoubtedly written on that same day.

"You cannot be saved, unhappy man! I see clearly that we cannot be saved."

What Albert had at last said about the case of the prisoner in the presence of the steward had been most repugnant to Werther: he thought he had observed in it some resentment against himself, and although upon repeated reflection it did not escape his keen mind that both men might be in the right, yet it was as if he must renounce his own inmost existence in order to confess it, in order to admit it.

We find among his papers a page which refers to this, and which perhaps expresses his entire relation to Albert:

"Of what avail that I say to myself, over and over, that he is good and honest: it tears my entrails apart, I cannot be just."

Since it was a mild evening, and the weather was beginning to encourage a thaw, Lotte walked back on foot with Albert. On the way they looked about them now and then, just as if they missed Werther's escort. Albert began to speak of him, censuring him while at the same time doing him justice. He touched upon his unhappy passion, wishing that it might be possible to get him away from there. "I wish that for our sakes, too," he said, "and I beg you," he went on, "take measures to give his behavior toward you a different direction and to reduce the frequency of his visits. People are beginning to notice, and I know that in some places it has been discussed." Lotte was silent, and Albert seemed to have felt her silence; at least from that time on he did not speak of Werther to her again, and if she mentioned him, he would drop the conversation or turn it in some other direction.

The vain attempt which Werther had made to rescue the unfortunate man was the last flare of the flame of a failing candle; he sank all the deeper into pain and inactivity; especially, he grew almost beside himself when he heard that he would perhaps even be summoned to testify against the man, who had now had recourse to denial.

All the disagreeable things that had ever come his way in his active life, his vexation while with the embassy, all else in which he had failed, all that had ever wounded him, kept going back and forth within his soul. He seemed to himself justified in his inactivity by all this, he seemed cut off from all future prospects, incapable of getting anywhere a handhold such as one uses on the affairs of common life, and so in the end, wholly surrendered to his strange feeling, his mode of thinking, and an endless passion, in the eternal monotony of an unhappy association with the lovable and loved creature whose calm he was disturbing, tearing at his own powers, which he wore down without purpose or prospect, he moved ever closer to a melancholy end.

The strongest evidence of his bewilderment and passion, his unquiet striving and driving, his weariness of life, is some letters left by him, which we will insert here.

"*December 12.*

"Dear Wilhelm, I am in such a state as those unfortunates must have been, of whom it was believed that they were driven about by an evil spirit. Sometimes I feel a seizure: it is not fear, not desire—it is an inner and unknown storm which threatens to rend my breast, which squeezes my throat shut! Woe, woe! and then I rove about in the fearful nocturnal scenes of this hostile winter season.

"Yesterday evening I felt I must go out. A sudden thaw had set in, and I had heard that the river had overflowed, that all the brooks were swollen, and that from Wahlheim down, my beloved valley was flooded! I ran out after eleven at night. A terrible spectacle, to see the raging floods, descending from the rocks, swirling in the moonlight, cover fields and meadows and hedges and all, and the broad valley in both directions turned into a surging lake in the roar of the wind! And then when the moon came out again and rested above the dark cloud, and out in front of me the waters rolled and rang in the fearfully magnificent reflection: then a shiver came over me, and once more a longing! Ah, with open arms I stood facing an abyss, and murmured 'down! down!' and was lost in the rapture of having my torments, my suffering go sweeping down there! surging along with the waves! Oh!—and you were unable to lift your feet from the ground and put an end to all torments!—My clock has not yet run down, I feel that! O Wilhelm, how gladly I would have given all my human existence in order to rend the clouds with that gale, or to take hold of the flood waters! Ha! and will the imprisoned one not enjoy that rapture, some time?

"And as I looked mournfully down at a spot where I had rested under a willow with Lotte, during a walk on a hot day—that too was flooded, and I could barely recognize the willow! Wilhelm. 'And her meadows,' I thought, 'the lands around the hunting lodge! how ruined now is our summer arbor by the rushing river,' I thought. And the sunshine of the past looked in at me, as a prisoner dreams a dream of flocks, meadows, and dignities! I stood still!—I do not rebuke myself, for I have courage to die.—I might have—Now I am sitting here like an old crone who gleans firewood from fence posts and begs her bread, in order for one moment to lengthen and to lighten her fading, joyless existence."

"*December 14.*

"What is this, my friend? I shrink from myself! Is not my love for her the holiest, purest, most brotherly love? Have I ever felt a culpable desire in my soul?—I will make no protestations—And now, dreams! O how true was the feeling of men who ascribed such contrary effects to alien powers! Last night! I tremble to say it, but I held her in my arms, firmly pressed to my breast, and covered her mouth, which murmured love, with unending kisses; my eyes were afloat in the intoxication of hers! God! am I culpable, that even now I feel a bliss in recalling those ardent joys in all their intensity? Lotte! Lotte!—And it is all over with me! my thoughts blur, for a week now

I have had no more self-control, my eyes are full of tears. I am nowhere content, and everywhere content, I wish nothing, demand nothing. It would be better for me if I went away."

The resolve to quit the world had, at this time and under such circumstances, gained more and more power over Werther's soul. Since his return to Lotte this had always been his final prospect and hope; but he had told himself that it should not be an overhasty or precipitate deed: he would take this step with the soundest conviction, with a resoluteness of the greatest possible quietude.

His doubts, his struggle with himself, are evident from a note which is probably the beginning of a letter to Wilhelm, and which was found undated among his papers.

"Her presence, her fate, her sympathy with my fate, is squeezing the last remaining tears out of my desiccated brain.

"To lift the curtain and step behind it! that is all! And why this delay and lagging? Because we don't know how things look over yonder? and we don't return? And because that is a trait of our mind, to surmise confusion and darkness in that about which we know nothing definite."

At last he became more and more akin to and befriended with this sad idea, and his resolve grew firm and irrevocable, of which evidence is given by the following ambiguous letter which he wrote to his friend.

"December 20.

"I owe thanks to your love, Wilhelm, for taking my words as you did. Yes, you are right: it would be better for me if I went away. Your proposal that I rejoin you does not entirely suit me; at least I should like to make a detour, especially since we hope to have lasting frost and good roads. And I like it very much that you want to come to fetch me; just wait another fortnight, and look for one more letter from me with further information. It is needful that nothing should be picked before it is ripe. And a fortnight more or less can do much. Tell my mother this: that she should pray for her son, and that I beg her forgiveness for all the distress I have caused her. That had to be my fate, to sadden those to whom I owed it to bring happiness. Farewell, my dearest friend! All the blessings of heaven upon you! Farewell!"

What went on in Lotte's soul during this time, how she felt toward her husband, toward her unhappy friend, we scarcely dare to express in words, although knowing her character we think we can form a private idea of it, and although a fine womanly soul can think its way into hers and feel with her.

So much is certain, that she had made a firm resolve to do everything that would keep Werther away, and if she delayed, then it was a heartfelt, friendly desire to spare him, because she knew how much it would cost him, indeed that it would be almost impossible for him. Yet she came under greater pressure to act in earnest; her husband said nothing about this relationship, as she too had maintained silence, and she was all the more intent upon proving to him through her actions that her principles were worthy of his own.

On the very day on which Werther wrote the letter to his friend which we have just inserted, it being the Sunday before Christmas, he went to see Lotte in the evening and found her alone. She was occupied with putting in shape some small playthings which she had made up as Christmas presents for her small brothers and sisters. He spoke of the pleasure the little ones would have, and of the times when the unexpected opening of a door and the display of a decorated tree, with its wax candles, candy ornaments, and apples, could produce the delights of paradise. "You too," said Lotte, concealing her embarrassment behind a sweet smile, "you too shall have a present, if you are very good; a wax candle and something besides." "And what do you call being good?" he exclaimed; "how am I to be? how can I be? dear Lotte!" "Thursday evening," she said, "is Christmas Eve, and then my children will come here, and father too, and each one will get his present; come then yourself—but not sooner." Werther was taken aback. "I beg you," she went on, "things are that way, I beg you for the sake of my peace of mind: things cannot, they cannot go on this way." He turned his eyes from her, paced up and down the room, and murmured, "Things cannot go on this way," between his teeth. Lotte, who sensed the terrible state into which these words had plunged him, tried to divert his thoughts by all sorts of questions, but in vain. "No, Lotte," he exclaimed, "I shall not see you again!" "Why do you say that?" she replied, "Werther, you can, you must see us again, only be moderate. O, why must you be born with this vehemence, this unconquerably clinging passion for everything on which you once lay hold! I beg you," she continued, taking him by the hand, "be more moderate! Your mind, your knowledge, your talents, what diverse enjoyments they afford you! Be a man! turn this unhappy attachment away from a creature who can do nothing but feel sorry for you." He ground his teeth and looked gloomily at her. She held his hand: "Just for a moment, keep a calm mind, Werther," she said. "Don't you feel that you are deceiving yourself, deliberately destroying yourself? And why me, Werther? just me, the property of another? just that? I fear, I fear that it is only the impossibility of possessing me that makes this desire so appealing to you." He drew his hand away from hers, looking at her with rigid, angry gaze. "Wise!" he cried, "very wise! Was it perhaps Albert that made that observation? Diplomatic! very diplomatic!" "Anyone can make it," she retorted. "And should there be no girl in the whole wide world to fulfill the desires of your heart? Prevail upon yourself to go in search of one, and I swear to you that you will find her; for I have long been afraid, for you and us, of the limitation which you have imposed upon yourself all this time. Prevail upon yourself! a journey will and must divert your mind! Seek and find a worthy object of your love, and then return, and let us enjoy together the happiness of a true friendship."

"One could have that printed," he said with a cold smile, "and recommend it to all teachers of the young. Dear Lotte! give me peace for a little while, and all will be fulfilled." "Only this, Werther, that you do not come here before Christmas Eve!" He was about to reply, when Albert entered the room. They bade each other a frosty Good Evening, and in embarrassment they walked up and down side by side. Werther began some insignificant conversation, which was soon exhausted; Albert did the same, whereupon he asked his wife about certain commissions, and when he heard that they had not yet been taken care of, he spoke to her some words which seemed to Werther cold and indeed quite harsh. He wanted to leave but could not, and delayed till eight, discontent and anger increasing in him all the while, until the table was set and he took his hat and cane. Albert invited him to stay, but he, in the belief that he was merely receiving an insignificant compliment, returned cold thanks and went away.

He got home, took the candle from the hand of his boy, who was going to light the way for him, and went alone into his room; he wept aloud, talked excitedly to himself, paced vehemently up and down the room, and finally threw himself in his clothes on the bed, where the servant found him, venturing to enter towards eleven o'clock in order to ask whether he should pull off his master's boots. Werther permitted this then and forbade the servant to enter the room the next morning until he should call him.

Monday morning, the twenty-first day of December, he wrote to Lotte the following letter, which was found sealed on his desk after his death and was brought to her, and which I will insert here a paragraph at a time, in accordance with the writing of it, as revealed by the circumstances.

"It is resolved, Lotte, I want to die, and I write this to you without any romantic extravagance, calmly, in the morning of the day on which I shall see you for the last time. When you read this, my dear, a cool grave will already be covering the rigid remains of the restless unfortunate who knows no greater sweetness to fill the last moments of his life than to converse with you. I have had a terrible night, and ah! a beneficent night. That night has confirmed and fixed my decision: I want to die! When I tore myself away from you yesterday, in the fearful revolt of my mind and with everything rushing to my heart, and I was gripped in chilling horror by my hopeless, joyless existence beside you—I had scarcely reached my room when I flung myself on my knees, beside myself, and you, O God! granted me the bitterest tears as my last refreshment! A thousand projects, a thousand prospects went storming through my soul, and as last of all the thought stood before me, firm and whole, the last and only one: I want to die! I lay down to sleep, and this morning, in the calm of awaking, that thought still remains firm, still quite strong in my heart: I want to die!—It is not despair, it is the certainty that my sufferings are complete, and that I am sacrificing myself for you. Yes, Lotte! why should I conceal it? one of us three must go, and I will be the one! O my dear! in this torn heart the frenzied thought has slunk about, often—to murder your husband!—or you!—or me!—So be it then!—When you climb up on the mountain, on some fine summer evening, then remember how I often came up the valley, and then look across toward my grave in the churchyard, and see how the wind makes the tall grass wave back and forth in the rays of the setting sun—I was calm when I began, but now, now I am weeping like a child, since all that is growing so vivid around me."

At about ten o'clock Werther called his servant, and while dressing he told him that he would go away on a journey in a few days, and so he should take out all the clothes and get everything ready for packing; he also gave him orders to ask everywhere for the bills, to bring back some books he had lent, and to pay for two months in advance the stipulated amounts to some poor people, to whom he was wont to give something each week.

He had his lunch brought to his room, and after lunch he rode out to see the steward, whom he did not find at home. Deep in thought he walked up and down the garden, seeming to wish to heap upon himself, in this last hour, all the melancholy of recollection.

The little ones did not leave him long in peace, they pursued him, jumped up on him, and gave him the news: that when tomorrow, and again tomorrow, and one more day came, they would go to Lotte to get their Christmas presents, and they told him the wondrous things that their little imaginations promised them. "Tomorrow!" he exclaimed, "and again tomorrow! and one more day!" and he kissed them all heartily and was about to leave them, when the little boy asked to whisper something else in his ear. The child revealed to him that his big brothers had written out fine greetings for New Year, *so* big! and one for papa, one for Albert and Lotte, and one for Mr. Werther, too; they were going to deliver them on New Year's Day in the morning. This overwhelmed him, and he gave each of them something, got on his horse, sent good wishes to the steward, and rode away with tears in his eyes.

Towards five o'clock he got home and ordered the maid to see to the fire and keep it burning on into the night. He bade the servant pack books and linen into the bottom of the trunk and sew up his outer clothing into a bundle. Thereupon, probably, he wrote the following paragraph of his last letter to Lotte.

"You are not expecting me! you thought I would obey and that you would not see me again until Christmas Eve. O Lotte! it is today or never again. On Christmas Eve you will hold this paper in your hand, trembling and wetting it with your precious tears. I will, I must! O how happy I feel that I am resolved."

Lotte had meanwhile got into a strange frame of mind. After the last conversation with Werther she had felt how it would be for her to part from him, and what he would suffer when he should go away from her.

It had been said in Albert's presence, as if casually, that Werther would not come again before Christmas Eve, and Albert had ridden out to see an acquaintance in the vicinity with whom he had business to transact, and with whom he had to stay overnight.

Now she was sitting alone, none of her brothers and sisters being with her, and abandoned herself to her thoughts, which hovered quietly about her circumstances. She saw herself now united forever with the husband whose love and loyalty she knew, to whom she was devoted with all her heart, whose calm and reliability seemed veritably destined by heaven to be such that a good wife might found the happiness of her life upon them; she felt what he would always be to her and her children. On the other hand, Werther had become so dear to her, from the very first moment of their acquaintance the agreement of their souls had shown itself so beautifully, and the long and lasting association with him, together with a number of situations they had gone through together, had made an indelible impression on her heart. She was accustomed to share with him everything of interest which she felt and thought, and his removal threatened to make a breach in her whole being which could never be filled again. O, if she could have transformed him into a brother in that moment! how happy she would have been!—had it been allowed her to marry him off to one of her friends, and could she have hoped to restore his relation to Albert to all that it had once been!

She had thought over her friends, one after the other, and found something to object to in each one, found none to whom she would not have begrudged him.

Amid all these reflections she only now felt deeply, without making it plain to herself, that it was her secret, heartfelt desire to keep him for herself, and she was saying to herself the while that she could not keep him, might not keep him; her pure, fine, generally lighthearted spirit, so ready to help itself, felt the burden of a melancholy which knows that the prospect of happiness is sealed off. Her heart was oppressed, and a cloud of sadness rested on her eyes.

So it had come to be half past six when she heard Werther coming up the steps and soon recognized his step and his voice as he asked for her. How her heart beat, and for the first time, we may almost say, at his approach. She would have been glad to refuse to see him, and when he entered she went toward him with a kind of passionate perplexity: "You did not keep your word." "I promised nothing," was his reply. "Then at least you should have heeded my request," she responded, "I made it to give us both peace."

She did not rightly know what she was saying, and knew just as little what she was doing when she sent for a couple of her friends so as not to be alone with Werther. He laid down some books which he had brought, asked about others, and now she wished that her friends would come, now that they would stay away. The maidservant came back, bringing word that both asked to be excused.

She was going to have the maid sit in the adjoining room with her work; then she changed her mind again. Werther walked up and down the room, and she went to the piano and began to play a minuet, but it refused to go smoothly. She collected herself and sat down quietly beside Werther, who had taken his accustomed seat on the sofa.

"Have you nothing to read?" she said. No, he had nothing. "In there in my drawer," she began, "lies your translation of some of the songs of Ossian; I have not read them yet, for I always hoped I might hear them from you; but there was never any time or any opportunity." He smiled and fetched the songs, and a shiver went through him as he took them in his hand; his eyes filled with tears as he looked closer at the sheets. He sat down and read.

"Star of descending night! fair is thy light in the west! thou liftest thy unshorn head from thy cloud; thy steps are stately on thy hill. What dost thou behold in the plain? The stormy winds are laid. The murmur of the torrent comes from afar. Roaring waves climb the distant rock. The flies of evening are on their feeble wings; the hum of their course is on the field. What dost thou behold, fair light? But thou dost smile and depart. The waves come with joy around thee: they bathe thy lovely hair. Farewell, thou silent beam! Let the light of Ossian's soul arise!

"And it does arise in its strength! I behold my departed friends.

Their gathering is on Lora, as in the days of other years. Fingal comes like a watry column of mist; his heroes are around. And see the bards of song, grey-haired Ullin! stately Ryno! Alpin, with the tuneful voice! the soft complaint of Minona! How are ye changed, my friends, since the days of Selma's feast? when we contended, like gales of spring, as they fly along the hill, and blend by turns the feebly-whistling grass.

"Minona came forth in her beauty; with downcast look and fearful eye. Her hair flew slowly on the blast, that rushed unfrequent from the hill. The souls of the heroes were sad when she raised the tuneful voice. Often had they seen the grave of Salgar, the dark dwelling of white-bosomed Colma. Colma left alone on the hill, with all her voice of song! Salgar promised to come: but the night descended around. Hear the voice of Colma, when she sat alone on the hill!

"COLMA. It is night; I am alone, forlorn on the hill of storms. The wind is heard in the mountain. The torrent pours down the rock, No hut receives me from the rain; forlorn on the hill of winds!

"Rise, moon! from behind thy clouds. Stars of the night arise! Lead me, some light, to the place, where my love rests from the chase alone! his bow near him, unstrung: his dogs panting around him. But here I must sit alone, by the rock of the mossy stream. The stream and the wind roar aloud. I hear not the voice of my love! Why delays my Salgar, why the chief of the hill, his promise? Here is the rock, and here the tree! here is the roaring stream! Thou didst promise with night to be here. Ah! whither is my Salgar gone? With thee I would fly, from my father; with thee, from my brother of pride. Our race have long been foes; we are no foes, O Salgar!

"Cease a little while, O wind! stream be thou silent a while! let my voice be heard around. Let my wanderer hear me! Salgar! it is Colma who calls. Here is the tree, and the rock. Salgar, my love! I am here. Why delayest thou thy coming? Lo! the calm moon comes forth. The flood is bright in the vale. The rocks are grey on the steep. I see him not on the brow. His dogs come not before him, with tidings of his near approach. Here I must sit alone!

"Who lie on the heath beside me? Are they my love and my brother? Speak to me, O my friends! To Colma they give no reply.

Speak to me: I am alone! My soul is tormented with fears! Ah! they are dead! Their swords are red from the fight. O my brother! my brother! why hast thou slain my Salgar? why, O Salgar! hast thou slain my brother? Dear were ye both to me! what shall I say in your praise? Thou wert fair on the hill among thousands! he was terrible in fight. Speak to me; hear my voice; hear me, sons of my love! They are silent; silent for ever! Cold, cold are their breasts of clay! Oh, from the rock on the hill; from the top of the windy steep, speak, ye ghosts of the dead! speak, I will not be afraid! Whither are ye gone to rest? In what cave of the hill shall I find the departed? No feeble voice is on the gale: no answer half-drowned in the storm!

"I sit in my grief! I wait for morning in my tears! Rear the tomb, ye friends of the dead. Close it not till Colma come. My life flies away like a dream: why should I stay behind? Here shall I rest with my friends, by the stream of the sounding rock. When night comes on the hill; when the loud winds arise; my ghost shall stand in the blast, and mourn the death of my friends. The hunter shall hear from his booth. He shall fear but love my voice! For sweet shall my voice be for my friends: pleasant were her friends to Colma!

"Such was thy song, Minona, softly-blushing daughter of Tor-man. Our tears descended for Colma, and our souls were sad! Ullin came with his harp; he gave the song of Alpin. The voice of Alpin was pleasant: the soul of Ryno was a beam of fire! But they had rested in the narrow house: their voice had ceased in Selma. Ullin had returned, one day, from the chase, before the heroes fell. He heard their strife on the hill; their song was soft but sad! They mourned the fall of Morar, first of mortal men! His soul was like the soul of Fingal; his sword like the sword of Oscar. But he fell, and his father mourned: his sister's eyes were full of tears. Minona's eyes were full of tears, the sister of car-borne Morar. She retired from the song of Ullin, like the moon in the west, when she foresees the shower, and hides her fair head in a cloud. I touched the harp, with Ullin; the song of mourning rose!

"RYNO. The wind and the rain are past: calm is the noon of day. The clouds are divided in heaven. Over the green hills flies the inconstant sun. Red through the stony vale comes down the stream of the hill. Sweet are thy murmurs, O stream! but more sweet is the voice I hear. It is the voice of Alpin, the son of song, mourning for the dead! Bent is his head of age; red his tearful eye. Alpin, thou son of song, why alone on the silent hill? why complainest thou, as a blast in the wood; as a wave on the lonely shore?

"ALPIN. My tears, O Ryno! are for the dead; my voice for those that have passed away. Tall thou art on the hill; fair among the sons of the vale. But thou shalt fall like Morar; the mourner shall sit on thy tomb. The hills shall know thee no more; thy bow shall lie in the hall, unstrung!

"Thou wert swift, O Morar! as a roe on the desert; terrible as a meteor of fire. Thy wrath was as the storm. Thy sword in battle, as lightning in the field. Thy voice was a stream after rain; like thunder on distant hills. Many fell by thy arm: they were consumed in the flames of thy wrath. But when thou didst return from war, how peaceful was thy brow! Thy face was like the sun after rain; like the moon in the silence of night; calm as the breast of the lake when the loud wind is laid.

"Narrow is thy dwelling now! dark the place of thine abode! With three steps I compass thy grave, O thou who wast so great before! Four stones, with their heads of moss, are the only memorial of thee. A tree with scarce a leaf, long grass, which whistles in the wind, mark to the hunter's eye the grave of the mighty Morar. Morar! thou art low indeed. Thou hast no mother to mourn thee; no maid with her tears of love. Dead is she that brought thee forth. Fallen is the daughter of Morglan.

"Who on his staff is this? who is this, whose head is white with age? whose eyes are red with tears? who quakes at every step? It is thy father, O Morar! the father of no son but thee. He heard of thy fame in war; he heard of foes dispersed. He heard of Morar's renown; why did he not hear of his wound? Weep, thou father of Morar! weep; but thy son heareth thee not. Deep is the sleep of the dead; low their pillow of dust. No more shall he hear thy voice; no more awake at thy call. When shall it be morn in the grave, to bid the slumberer awake? Farewell, thou bravest of men! thou conqueror in the field! but the field shall see thee no more; nor the dark wood be lightened with the splendor of thy steel. Thou hast left no son. The song shall preserve thy name. Future times shall hear of thee; they shall hear of the fallen Morar!

"The grief of all arose, but most the bursting sigh of Armin. He remembers the death of his son, who fell in the days of his youth. Carmor was near the hero, the chief of the echoing Galmal. Why bursts the sigh of Armin, he said? Is there a cause to mourn? The song comes, with its music, to melt and please the soul. It is like soft mist, that, rising from a lake, pours on the silent vale; the green flowers are filled with dew, but the sun returns in his strength, and the mist is gone. Why art thou sad, O Armin! chief of sea-surrounded Gorma?

"Sad! I am! nor small is my case of woe! Carmor, thou hast lost no son; thou hast lost no daughter of beauty. Colgar the valiant lives; and Annira fairest maid. The boughs of thy house ascend, O Carmor! But Armin is the last of his race. Dark is thy bed, O Daura! deep thy sleep in the tomb! When shalt thou awake with thy songs? with all thy voice of music?

"Arise, winds of autumn, arise; blow along the heath! streams of the mountain roar! roar, tempests, in the groves of my oaks! walk through broken clouds, O moon! show thy pale face, at intervals! bring to my mind the night, when all my children fell; when Arindal the mighty fell; when Daura the lovely failed! Daura, my daughter! thou wert fair; fair as the moon on Fura; white as the driven snow; sweet as the breathing gale. Arindal, thy bow was strong. Thy spear was swift in the field. Thy look was like mist on the wave; thy shield, a red cloud in a storm. Armar, renowned in war, came, and sought Daura's love. He was not long refused: fair was the hope of their friends!

"Erath, son of Odgal, repined: his brother had been slain by Armar. He came disguised like a son of the sea: fair was his skiff on the wave; white his locks of age; calm his serious brow. Fairest of women, he said, lovely daughter of Armin! a rock not distant in the sea, bears a tree on its side; red shines the fruit afar! There Armar waits for Daura. I come to carry his love! She went; she called on Armar. Nought answered, but the son of the rock, Armar, my love! my love! why tormentest thou me with fear? hear, son of Arnart, hear: it is Daura who calleth thee! Erath the traitor fled laughing to the land. She lifted up her voice; she called for her brother and her father. Arindal! Armin! none to relieve your Daura!

"Her voice came over the sea. Arindal my son descended from

the hill; rough in the spoils of the chase. His arrows rattled by his side; his bow was in his hand: five dark grey dogs attend his steps. He saw fierce Erath on the shore: he seized and bound him to an oak. Thick wind the thongs of the hide around his limbs; he loads the wind with his groans. Arindal ascends the deep in his boat, to bring Daura to land. Armar came in his wrath, and let fly the grey-feathered shaft. It stung; it sunk in thy heart. O Ardinal my son! for Erath the traitor thou diedst. The oar is stopped at once; he panted on the rock and expired. What is thy grief, O Daura, when round thy feet is poured thy brother's blood! The boat is broken in twain. Armar plunges into the sea, to rescue his Daura, or die. Sudden a blast from the hill came over the waves. He sunk, and he rose no more.

"Alone, on the sea-beat rock, my daughter was heard to complain. Frequent and loud were her cries. What could her father do? All night I stood on the shore. I saw her by the faint beam of the moon. All night I heard her cries. Loud was the wind; the rain beat hard on the hill. Before morning appeared, her voice was weak. It died away, like the evening-breeze among the grass of the rocks. Spent with grief she expired; and left thee Armin alone. Gone is my strength in war! fallen my pride among women! When the storms aloft arise; when the north lifts the wave on high; I sit by the sounding shore, and look on the fatal rock. Often by the setting moon, I see the ghosts of my children. Half-viewless, they walk in mournful conference together."

A flood of tears, which burst from Lotte's eyes and gave her oppressed heart relief, checked Werther's reading. He threw down the papers, seized her hand, and wept the bitterest tears. Lotte rested her head on the other hand and hid her eyes with her handkerchief. Both were in a fearful agitation. They felt their own wretchedness in the fate of those noble souls, felt it jointly, and their tears united. Werther's lips and eyes were aglow on Lotte's arm; a shudder seized upon her; she tried to withdraw, yet pain and sympathy lay upon her like lead, laming her. She took a deep breath for her recovery, and begged him, sobbing, to continue, begged with all the force of heaven in her voice. Werther trembled, his heart ready to burst, and he lifted the paper and read half brokenly,

"Why dost thou awake me, breath of spring? Thou wooest me, saying, 'I bedew thee with the drops of heaven!' But the time of my wilting is near, near in the blast that will strip me of my leaves! Tomorrow the wanderer will come; he that saw me in my beauty will come; his eyes will seek me everywhere in the field, and will not find me.—"

The whole force of these words descended upon the unhappy man. He flung himself down before Lotte in the fullness of despair, seized her hands, pressed them into his eyes and against his brow, and a premonition of his terrible intention seemed to flit through her soul. Her senses grew confused, she pressed his hands, pressed them against her breast, bent down with a sorrowful movement to him, and their glowing cheeks touched. The world was lost to them. He flung his arms about her, pressed her to his breast, and covered her trembling, stammering lips with frenzied kisses. "Werther!" she cried with stifled voice, turning away from him, "Werther!"—and with feeble hand she pushed his breast from hers;—"Werther!" she cried with the composed accents of the noblest dignity. He did not resist, released her from his arms, and cast himself down senselessly before her. She drew herself up, and in alarmed confusion, quivering half in love, half in anger, she said, "That is the last time! Werther! You will not see me again." And casting a glance of the fullest love upon the wretched man, she hurried into the adjoining room and locked the door behind her. Werther stretched out his arms towards her, but did not venture to restrain her. He lay on the floor, his head on the sofa, and in this position he remained for more than half an hour, until a noise brought him to. It was the maid, who was about to set the table. He paced up and down the room, and when he again found himself alone he went to the door of the cabinet and called in a low voice, "Lotte! Lotte! just one word more! a farewell!" She was silent. He persevered and pleaded and persevered; then he tore himself away and cried, "Farewell, Lotte! forever, farewell!"

He came to the city gate. The guards, who had long grown used to him, let him out without a word. There was a light drizzle half between rain and snow, and it was nearly eleven when he rapped again. His servant observed, when Werther got home, that his master's hat was missing. He did not venture to say anything, but helped him undress and found everything wet. Later, his hat was found on a cliff which overlooks the valley from the slope of the hill, and it is inconceivable how he climbed it on a wet, dark night without falling.

He laid himself down in bed and slept long. The servant found him writing when he brought him coffee the next morning at his call. He was writing the following portion of his letter to Lotte.

"For the last time, then, for the last time I open these eyes. They are, alas, not to see the sun any more, for a dreary, misty day is keeping it concealed. Well, then mourn, nature! your son, your friend, your beloved is approaching his end. Lotte, this is a feeling without compare, and yet it is closest to a half-conscious dream, to say to oneself, 'this is the last morning.' The last one! Lotte, I have no feeling for that word 'last.' Am I not standing here in my full strength? and tomorrow I shall lie outstretched and limp on the ground. Die! what does that say? Look, we are dreaming when we speak of dying. I have seen many a man die; but mankind is so hemmed in that it has no feeling for the beginning and end of its existence. As yet, still mine and yours! yours, O beloved! And in a moment—separated, parted—perhaps for ever?—No, Lotte, no— How can I perish? how can you perish? Why, don't we *exist?*— Perish!—What does that mean? That is again just a word! an empty sound! without anything for my heart to feel.— —Dead, Lotte! interred in the cold ground, so confined! so dark!—I had a friend who was everything to my helpless youth; she died, and I followed her corpse, and stood at the grave as they let the coffin down, and the ropes rolled down beneath it with a humming sound, and came up again with a rush, and then the first shovelful of earth rattled down, and the frightened lid gave out a dull sound, and duller and ever duller, and at last was all covered!—I flung myself down beside the grave—moved, shaken, terrified, my innermost being rent apart, but I did not know how I felt—how I shall feel—Die! Grave! I do not understand the words!

"O forgive me! forgive me! Yesterday! It should have been the last moment of my life. O you angel! for the first time, for the first time without any doubt my inner, inmost being was permeated with the glow of the rapturous feeling: She loves me! she loves me! On my lips the sacred fire is still burning that flowed out from yours, and new, warm rapture is in my heart. Forgive me! forgive me!

"Oh, I knew that you loved me, knew it from your first soulful glances, from the first pressure of your hand, and yet, when I was away from you again, or when I saw Albert at your side, I was again despondent in feverish doubts.

"Do you recall the flowers that you sent me after you were unable to say a word to me in that wretched company, or extend your hand to me? O, I knelt before them half the night, and they gave me the assurance of your love. But alas! those impressions passed by, as the feeling of God's grace gradually retreats once more from the soul of the believer, though it had been bestowed upon him with all the fullness of heaven in a sacred and visible symbol.

"All that is transitory, but no eternity shall extinguish the glowing life which I tasted yesterday on your lips, which I feel in my soul now! She loves me! This arm has embraced her, these lips have quivered on her lips, this mouth has stammered words on hers. She is mine! you are mine! Yes, Lotte, for ever.

"And what of the fact that Albert is your husband? Husband! That would be for this world, then—and for this world a sin that I love you, that I would like to draw you out of his arms into mine? Sin? Very well, and I am punishing myself for it; I have tasted it in all its heavenly ecstasy, that sin, have drawn into my heart the elixir of life and strength. From that moment you are mine! mine, O Lotte! I shall go before you! go to my Father, to your Father. To him I will make my complaint, and he will comfort me, until you come, and I will fly to meet you and clasp you and abide with you in the sight of the Infinite One in eternal embraces.

"I am not dreaming, I am in no delusion! When nearing the grave my inner light increases. We shall be! we shall see each other again! And see your mother! I shall see her, shall find her, ah, and pour out my whole heart to her! Your mother, your image."

Toward eleven, Werther asked his servant if Albert had perhaps returned. The man said, yes, he had seen his horse being led away. Thereupon his master gave him an unfolded note with this written on it:

"Would you kindly lend me your pistols for a journey I have in mind? May all go well with you!"

The sweet woman had slept little during the night; what she feared was now decided, and decided in a manner which she could neither have surmised nor feared. Her blood, which was wont to course so purely and freely, was in a feverish turmoil, and a thousand warring feelings rent her noble heart. Was it the fire of Werther's embraces that she felt in her bosom? was it anger at his presumptuousness? was it a mournful comparison of her present condition with those other days of wholly candid, untrammelled innocence and carefree confidence in herself? How should she meet her husband? how confess to him a scene which she might so easily confess, and yet which she did not dare to confess? They had maintained a mutual silence for so long, and should she be the first to break the silence and make so unexpected a disclosure to her husband at an inopportune time? She was already afraid that the mere report of Werther's call would make an unpleasant impression on him, and now there was even this unexpected catastrophe! Could she rightly hope that her husband would see it in quite the right light, and accept it wholly without prejudice? and could she wish that he might read in her soul? And then again, could she dissemble before the man to whom she had always been like a glass of bright crystal, open and clear, and from whom she had never concealed, never been able to conceal, any of her feelings? Whatever she thought of doing, it caused her concern and made her uneasy; and again and again her thoughts reverted to Werther, who was lost to her, whom she would not give up, whom she, alas! must abandon to himself, and to whom, when he had lost her, nothing more would be left.

How heavily lay upon her now—a thing which at the moment she could not make clear to herself—the burden of the barrier which had developed between them! Sensible and good as they were, they began to observe silence toward each other with respect to certain hidden differences, each one feeling right on his side, wrong on the other, and circumstances became so complex and so critical that it was impossible to disentangle things at the decisive moment on which everything depended. Had a happy confidingness brought them closer together again, sooner, had love and indulgence come to life mutually between them, causing their hearts to open, perhaps our friend might still have been saved.

One more strange circumstance must be added. Werther, as we know from his letters, had never made a secret of his longing to quit this world. Albert had often opposed this, and at times Lotte and her husband had talked about it. The latter, seeing that he felt a decided repugnance to such an act, had very often indicated, with a kind of irritation which was otherwise quite foreign to his character, that he had much cause to doubt the seriousness of such a resolve, and he had even allowed himself an occasional jest on the subject, and had imparted his disbelief to Lotte. This quieted her on the one hand, to be sure, when her thoughts presented such a sad picture to her mind, but on the other hand she felt herself prevented thereby from communicating to her husband the anxieties which were torturing her at that moment.

Albert returned, and Lotte went toward him with an embarrassed haste; he was not cheerful, his transaction had not been completed, for he had found the neighboring bailiff to be a stubborn, petty person. Moreover, the bad roads had made him peevish.

He asked whether anything had happened, and she replied over-hastily that Werther had been there on the previous evening. He asked whether letters had come, and received the answer that letters and some parcels were in his room. He went there, and Lotte remained alone. The presence of the man whom she so loved and honored had made a new impression upon her heart. The thought of his nobility, his love and kindness, had brought more calm to her spirit, she felt a secret impulse to follow him, and she took her work and went to his room, as she was frequently wont to do. She found him occupied in opening the parcels and reading the letters. Some seemed not to have the most agreeable contents. She put some questions to him which he answered curtly, then he went to the desk to write.

So they had been together for an hour, and in Lotte's soul the darkness kept deepening. She felt how hard it would be for her to disclose to her husband, even if he were in the best of moods, what she had on her heart; she lapsed into a melancholy which became the more frightening to her as she sought to conceal it and to check her tears.

The entrance of Werther's servant brought her embarrassment to the highest pitch; he handed the note to Albert, who turned calmly to his wife and said, "Give him the pistols."—"I wish him a happy journey," he said to the lad. This struck her like a thunderbolt, and she staggered to her feet, not knowing what she was doing. Slowly she went over to the wall, with trembling hand she took down the weapons, wiped off the dust and hesitated, and she would have delayed still longer if Albert had not hurried her by an inquiring look. She handed the unhappy instruments to the boy without being able to utter a word, and when he had left the house she folded up her work and went to her room in a state of the most inexpressible uncertainty. Her heart predicted to her all possible terrors. Now she was on the point of flinging herself at her husband's feet and disclosing everything to him, the story of the preceding evening, her guilt and her premonitions. Then again she saw no way out of her difficulty, and least of all could she hope to persuade her husband to go to Werther. The table was set, and a good woman friend who only came to ask a question and was going to leave at once—and remained—made the conversation at table endurable; they controlled themselves, they chatted, they related things, they forgot themselves.

The lad came back to Werther with the pistols, and the latter took them from him with delight upon hearing that Lotte had handed them to him. He had bread and wine brought, bade the lad go and eat, and sat down to write.

"They have passed through your hands, you wiped the dust off them, and I kiss them a thousand times, for you touched them; and you, spirit of heaven, favor my resolve! and you, Lotte, hand me the instrument, you, from whose hands I have wished to receive my death, and, ah! receive it now. O, I asked my lad about everything. You trembled as you handed them to him, you spoke no farewell! Woe! woe! no farewell!—Should you have locked your heart against me, for the sake of the moment which attached you to me forever? Lotte, not in a thousand years can that impression be effaced! And I feel that you cannot hate him who has such a glowing love for you."

After eating, he bade the lad complete the packing, tore up papers, went out, and took care of some small bills. He came home again, went out again, passed through the gate, heedless of the rain, went into the count's park, roved further around the countryside, came back as night was falling, and wrote the following.

"Wilhelm, for the last time I have seen fields and woods and sky. Farewell to you, too! Dear mother, forgive me! Console her,

Wilhelm! God bless you both! My affairs are all in order. Farewell! we shall see each other again, and more happily."

"I have rewarded you ill, Albert, and you will forgive me. I have disturbed the peace of your house, I have brought distrust between you. Farewell! I will end it. O that you two might be made happy by my death! Albert! Albert! make that angel happy! And so may God's blessing abide with you!"

That evening he did much rummaging among his papers, tore up many of them and threw them into the stove, and sealed some packets addressed to Wilhelm. They contained short essays and detached thoughts, a number of which I have seen. At ten o'clock, after he had had more fuel put on the fire, and had a bottle of wine brought, he sent the servant to bed, whose bedroom as well as those of the domestics were far to the rear; the lad lay down in his clothes so as to be on hand early in the morning, for his master had said that the post horses would be at the house before six.

Past eleven.

All is so still about me, and my soul so calm. I thank you, God, for granting me in these last moments this warmth, this strength.

"I step to the window, dear one! and look out, and even through the passing, flying storm clouds I see single stars of the eternal sky. No, you will not fall! the Eternal bears you on his heart, and me. I saw the stars in the handle of the Great Wain, the most loved of all the constellations. When I used to leave you at night and walked out of your gate, it would be facing me. With what intoxication I often gazed at it! often with upraised hands made of it a symbol, a sacred marker of my present blessedness! and even now—O Lotte, what does not remind me of you? do you not surround me? and have I not like an insatiable child snatched and kept all sorts of trifles that had felt your sacred touch?

"Dear silhouette! I bequeath it back to you, Lotte, and beg you to honor it. Thousands, thousands of kisses I have pressed upon it, a thousand times I have waved to it, when I went out or came home.

"I have written your father a note asking him to protect my corpse. There are two linden trees in the churchyard, in a rear corner towards the fields; there I wish to rest. He can and will do that for his friend. You ask him too. I will not demand from pious Christians that they should lay their bodies next to a poor unfortunate. Oh, I wish you would bury me by the roadside, or in the lonely valley, so that priest and Levite should bless themselves as they passed the stone marker, and the Samaritan should drop a tear.

"Here, Lotte! I do not shudder to seize the cold and terrible cup from which I am to drink the intoxication of death! You handed it to me, and I do not quail. All! all! Thus all the desires and hopes of my life are fulfilled! So coldly, so rigidly to knock at the brazen portal of death.

"That I could have gained the happiness of dying for *you!* Lotte, to offer myself up for *you!* I would die courageously, I would die joyously, if I could restore to you the peace and the rapture of your life. But alas! to few noble souls is it given to shed their blood for their dear ones, and by their death to enkindle a new, hundredfold life for their friends.

"In these clothes, Lotte, I wish to be buried, for you have touched them, hallowed them; and I have made this request of your father. My soul is hovering over the coffin. Let no one search my pockets. This pale pink bow which you wore on your bosom, the first time I found you among your children—O kiss them a thousand times and tell them of the fate of their unhappy friend. The dear ones! they are swarming around me. Ah, how I attached myself to you! and from the first moment could never let you go!—This bow is to be buried with me. On my birthday you gave it to me! How I drank in all those things!—Ah, I did not think that the way would lead me to this!——Be calm! I beg you, be calm!—

"They are loaded—The clock strikes twelve! So be it, then!—Lotte! Lotte! farewell! farewell!"

A neighbor saw the flash of the powder and heard the shot; but as all remained still, he gave it no further attention.

At six in the morning the servant steps in with a light. He finds his master on the floor, finds pistols and blood. He calls, he takes hold of him; no answer, only a death rattle. He runs for the doctors, runs to Albert. Lotte hears the bell pulled, and trembling seizes on all her limbs. She wakes her husband, they get up, crying and stammering the servant tells his news, and Lotte drops in a faint at Albert's feet.

When the physician reached the unhappy man, he found him on

the floor, not to be saved; his pulse was still beating, his limbs were all paralyzed. Over his right eye he had shot himself through the head, brains had oozed out. Uselessly, they opened a vein in his arm; blood flowed, and he was still drawing breath.

From the blood on the arm of the chair it could be inferred that he had done the deed while sitting at the desk; then he had slumped down, rolling convulsively around the chair. He lay on his back, powerless, towards the window, fully dressed and booted, in the long blue coat with the yellow waistcoat.

The house, the neighborhood, the town got into a turmoil. Albert entered. They had laid Werther on the bed with bandaged brow; his face was already like that of a dead man, and he did not move a muscle. There was still a fearful rattle in the lungs, now weak, now stronger; his end was expected.

Of the wine he had drunk only one glass. *Emilia Galotti** lay open on the desk.

Let me say nothing about Albert's consternation and Lotte's grief.

The old steward came on a gallop at the news, and kissed the dying man amid burning tears. His older sons soon followed him on foot, dropped down beside the bed, expressing the most uncontrollable grief, and kissed his hands and his mouth, and the oldest, whom he had always loved the most, clung to his lips until he had expired and they tore the boy away by force. At twelve noon he died. The presence of the steward and the measures he took quelled a commotion. At night toward eleven he had him buried at the spot Werther had chosen. The steward followed the body, and his sons, but Albert found it impossible. There were fears for Lotte's life. Workmen carried him. No clergyman escorted him.

Translated by Bayard Quincy Morgan

---

*A tragedy by G. E. Lessing, which was found open beside the body of the young man whose suicide moved Goethe deeply and was one of the motivations for *Werther.*—Tr.

Foreword to
Elective Affinities

About Goethe's *Elective Affinities*

The author of these lines admits to having had some influence on the decision as to which novel by Goethe should be included in the epic pantheon of this collection: *Wilhelm Meister* or *Elective Affinities*. The attraction of the former was great. When a work of great literature is unhurriedly republished and redesigned, what is always implied is that a national possession is being successfully revitalized and brought up to date. The unaffected modern guise, a presentation free of philology, creates the possibility of being seen with youthfully direct and ahistorical eyes. Free of the aroma of the museum, the masterpiece becomes again nature and life, and spurs the reader, who thereby achieves a higher level of existence, to perceive and understand it afresh, and, in perhaps unforeseen ways, to make it once again fertile for his interior household, as well as for the household of time. To bring the German public in its present-day level of maturity and experience into new and free contact with the world of *Wilhelm Meister*, that world of adventure and cultivation in which the educational springs in such a purely organic way from the confessional, and the social idea and the idea of the state spring similarly from the educational—this was the attractive thought we allowed ourselves to be tempted by, so as to experience the necessity of justifying to ourselves our ultimate decision in favor of *Elective Affinities*.

Most importantly, we did not, with this decision, prove unfaithful to the sphere of *Wilhelm Meister's Years of Wandering or the Renouncers.* We know that *Elective Affinities* was originally intended as a novella to be inserted into the body of this epic life's work, no different than, for instance, *The Fifty-year-old Man* and *The Wandering Fool* and other such stories and fairy tales. The author had been mistaken about the spatial requirements of his theme: his original vision of the work had been too small. The work itself wanted, as it sometimes happens, to be longer than its creator had meant it to be. "Such a work," Goethe later said about it, thankful that a perceptive friend had understood the book to be a whole entity, existing in its own right, endowed with its own life: "such a work grows under one's very hands and imposes the necessity of exerting all of one's force to remain master over it, and to finish it." And what thus surfaced at Cotta in Tübingen in 1809, after two years' worth of work and after the sixty-year-old "had devoted to it all that he was capable of," was the principal work of a poet, a well developed novel in two parts and two volumes. It was not the greatest, but it was the most exalted novel that the Germans called their own.

Elective Affinities is indeed our most exalted novel, and that is why we chose it. It is a creation as elegant as it is German, a marvel of achievement, purity of composition, and richness of interrelation, connection, and completion. For Rochlitz was correct when he wrote to Goethe that "if it is true that there are digressions which appear contradictory when taken in isolation, it is also true that they affirm its unity when taken as part of the whole, in the whole." It is a work of such tender and uncompromising knowledge of the human heart, so balanced between kindness and severity, clarity and secrecy, wisdom and emotion, form and feeling, that it is only with amazement that we call it our own. But since it is really ours, we would like to raise it up as a shining proof to ourselves and others of the possibility of Germanic perfection.

In our impatience to do justice to what we love and also to satisfy

the impatience of those who have newly absorbed this work, we
have hastily and prematurely snatched at a few words of praise
without even grounding what we say. For these lines are intended not
as a foreword but really as an afterword. We want not so much to
prepare the reader for excellence, but, in a friendly way, to
give expression to the satiety of the reader who has just come
from reading, and thereby, at the most, bringing the reader's
emotion back upon itself. Is this not indeed the duty of love to which
a writer, among all men, is essentially appointed? And should we
not become especially aware of this noble call under Goethe's influence? How he depicted mankind, what a "Man of Letters"
he was to have ingenuously assigned himself this title instead
of the one of "Poet," even at the risk of offending the German ear!
For within this highly humanist concept of *depiction*, the
difficult and often clumsily handled contrast between "Man of Letters" and "Poet" disappears. Goethe memorably employed this contrast when he characterized himself as a Man of Letters in
comparison to Shakespeare, the Poet, but he forgot the contrast
altogether at the moment when the desire to depict something
created in him the confidence that he was "truly born to be a man of
letters." That is why there should be something else inserted at this
point in praise of our book, inasmuch as it is the work of a man of
letters, and inasmuch as it is prose. It is best accomplished with the
words of Zelter, the musician, who, on October 27, 1809, wrote to
Goethe:

> There are certain symphonies by Haydn whose free and easy
> flow sets my blood agreeably into motion, and makes me want to
> be useful to the world. . . .That is how I always feel when I read
> your novels, and that is how I felt today as I read your *Elective
> Affinities*. You will never falter in your mischievous and secretive
> game with the things of the world, or with the characters whom
> you place in it and direct, regardless of complications that run
> through it or attempt to make space for themselves. Furthermore,
> there is your *style,* clear as that transparent element whose agile
> inhabitants swim to and fro, shimmering or flashing darkly
> without ever getting lost or going astray. It could drive one to
> poetry, reading such prose, and the devil knows I am incapable of
> writing a single line such as yours.

These words do justice to the elegance and precision of Goethe's prose, to the purity of its humanism, and to the magic of its rhythms. This magic is a reasonable one, the clearest fusion of Eros and Logos, and it pleasantly and irresistibly guides us through the work, carrying us along.

We have used words that already indicate the very equilibrated nature of the work, that aspect of the work which lends it its humanity and nobility. It is this that we primarily want to address: the undisturbed balance between sensuality and morality, or, artistically speaking, between art and criticism, or between spontaneity and calculation. This relates as well to that often thoughtlessly handled opposition between Poet and Man of Letters, if only to the extent that these are but a designation and subdesignation for the most important opposition, which is that between nature and freedom—that which articulates the question of mankind itself.

For the present, let us keep to the realm of art, pointing out that *Elective Affinities* is, as Goethe himself testified in a conversation with Eckermann, his most intellectual work. Goethe said that it was not, on the whole, his habit as an author to strive to embody an abstract idea. The only longer work in which he was conscious of having attempted the representation of a thought-out idea, he explained, may have been his *Elective Affinities.* This is clearly reminiscent of Schiller's immortal treatise on naïve and sentimental poetry. Although this classic German essay actually makes all others obsolete since what they say is included within it, it nevertheless creates an antithetical environment in which reality and life are never completely incorporated. The world of art has always contained mixtures of both elements. Schiller's critical separation errs theoretically on one point: he depicts the spirit exclusively as striving, striving in particular toward nature, and toward materialization, whereas nature, the naïve, is depicted as self-contained. It is not only the spirit that strives, but the place toward which the spirit strives. Nature is likewise sentimental; its goal is spiritualization. Man *is* the sublime encounter between nature and spirit as they yearn toward one another, and we may refer to a work in which they truly mesh as a great and most human work.

In fact, *Elective Affinities* is a spiritual construction to a degree not easily found a second time in the work of Goethe, the son of nature. Thus, its self-awareness and artistic intelligence were immediately recognizable to Goethe's contemporaries, in part in the sense that it was admired, and in part in the sense that it was criticized. Noticed was a certain poverty of form and symmetry of proportion, as well as the brevity of the narration in relation to the long and frequent reflective passages. At that time Solger wrote to Goethe himself that, "according to general opinion, the story could almost be called only the *skeleton* of a novel." He admired as "profoundly artistic" the way that the characters were contrasted exclusively in groups, and the way that, although the members of each group were to no small degree connected, they were still separated so widely, so surely, and so rationally: "Indeed, the group members appear even in their difference to be grouped so cleverly together." He conceded that "several times the characters seemed to act somewhat more for the sake of the poet, and especially more for the sake of the situation the poet wanted to create, than out of themselves and out of the characters' inner beings." Solger also emphasized, however, with satisfaction, that they, the characters, were "not immaterial ideas" but "real people" and individuals without, he added, an emphasis put upon what are commonly called their idiosyncracies. "These idiosyncracies seem, similar to small last-minute touches put on a painting, rather to be only applied in order to give a more deceiving impression of reality, as deceiving as Worthy Art can possibly be." Worthy Solger! Not the illusion of a wax figure in a museum, in front of which the rabble stands gaping, but life in the light of thought, the ideal transparency of characters who are not immaterial ideas, but people—that is what Solger perceived *Worthy Art* to be, and thus he defines the poetic. The characters of *Elective Affinities* are full of warm individual life. Riemer recounts how in Karlsbad they literally kept company with these imagined fantasy figures as if they were real, and how these figures even compelled one to compare them to real people. Soon a Charlotte was found among the visitors at the spa. Found as well were a captain, a lord, and also a Mittler. To top it off, the architect—the character who met with perhaps the most approval—was, so it was claimed, an outright portrait, and this fact quickly spread. The original was recognized, and fingers were pointed at Engelhardt, the tall young artist from Kassel whose traits Goethe had borrowed for his character. People were eager, as well, to find likenesses to society figures in other characters of this sensational novel: to the duchess Luise in

Charlotte, to a Baron von Müffling in the Captain, to a Fräulein von Reitzenstein in Luciane and so forth. *At the same time,* however, these characters are symbolic, like symmetrically arranged chess pieces, moved back and forth in a sophisticated game of the mind, representing that mysticism of nature that gave them the names Otto and Ottilie, their corresponding headaches, and which made them bear other people's children. . . .We say "at the same time," and not "besides" or "as well as," for we are dealing with the interlacing of form and idea, of spiritualization and materialization, with the interweaving of naïve and sentimental being. We should consider that in the whole history of art, this has never again so felicitously occurred.

On the level of morality, the correspondences are no different, and the artistic and the critical, the poetic and the intellectual, bear the names sensuality and morality, or the historical names, of paganism and Christianity.

In fact, Goethe's supposed resolute non-Christianity is, all in all, rather questionable. It is all too simple to prove through quotations his humanist antipathy to "the Cross." It is at least in better taste to draw upon those quotes which so expressively concede to a certain respect for Christian thought. The Pedagogical Province's* sanctity of suffering is as significant as it is surprising. Goethe found in the gospels "a reflection of splendor emanating from Christ, that was of such a divine nature, as divinity has never before appeared on this earth." "The grandeur and *moral culture* of Christianity, as it shimmers and sparks in the gospels," he said with sympathy and obvious feelings of partisanship, "will never be surpassed by the human mind." Goethe was a pupil of Spinoza, and, if indeed the dualistic separation between God and Nature is the basic premise of Christianity, then Spinoza was a pagan and Goethe was one along with him. However, the world is not defined by God and nature alone. The human—the humane—belongs within it, and Spinoza's definition of humanity is Christian inasmuch as it characterizes the human phenomenon as the process of becoming aware of man's Godly nature, as the breaking through of previously stifled being and action, thus as the process of detaching from nature, and thereby as spirit. Additionally, the well-known "reconciliation of the

---

*From *Wilhelm Meister's Years of Wandering.*—Trs.

passions through their analysis" is not necessarily pagan, and neither is Spinoza's motif of renunciation *(Entsagung)* which became in
time the principal motif of Goethe's life and work (just as the idea of
freedom was the motif in Schiller and the idea of redemption was
that in Wagner).

Although there is not sufficient space here, there would be much
to say about the emanation of this central motif, the motif which is
already heard in the subtitle of *Years of Wandering,* the work of
which *Elective Affinities* is an offshoot. All we want to express is
this: that whatever has restraint and whatever has form in Goethe—
as well as his character, his stature as the nation today conceives it—
is the achievement of renunciation. We are not speaking generally or
speaking about the sense of sacrifice, which is the sense of all art. We
are not speaking about the struggle with chaos, the giving up of
freedom, or the creative modesty of which the inner being of the
work consists. Goethe's pathos of renunciation, or—since we are
dealing with something permanent and interwoven with existence—
his *ethics* of renunciation, is of a personal sort. It was his destiny, the
instinctive summons of a singular national mission, a mission which
was essentially moral. Or could this destiny and this mission, this
connection, circumstance, and control, this pedagogical duty of
renunciation, be, after all, less particular to Goethe than it seemed
to us before? Could it be a characteristic native to the German
intellect that it is compelled, to a degree unshakable even by the
threat of severe spiritual punishment, by this dictate of destiny,
which in some way and to some degree will grow to become an
educational responsibility?

We spoke previously of feelings of partisanship with Christianity
that at times apparently touched Goethe. Of what did this partisanship consist, and to what did it relate? Goethe bowed before the
"moral culture" of Christianity. In other words, he bowed before its
humanity, its moral, antibarbarian tendencies, which coincided so
closely with his own. His occasional homage to Christianity doubt-
lessly derives from his understanding of the relationship between his
own mission and that of Christianity within the Germanic race. In
other words, the profound, Germanic meaning of this "renunciation," we may say at this point, lies in the fact that Goethe understood his duty, his national mission, as essentially a civilizing one.
Who could doubt that there lay within Goethe possibilities of a

greatness—a wilder, more abundant, more dangerous, and more "natural" greatness—than the one his inbred self-control allowed him to reveal, the one which is revealed in the highly pedagogical image of him we hold today? In his *Iphigenie,* it is the idea of humanity as opposed to barbarity which achieves the stamp of civilization—not in the polemical sense, and certainly not in the political sense in which the word is used nowadays, but in the sense of "moral culture." It was a Frenchman, Maurice Barrès, who called *Iphigenie* a "civilizing work" that "upholds the rights of society against the arrogance of the intellect." This remark pertains almost more to that other work of self-discipline, self-chastisement, and, yes, of self-mortification: *Tasso,* a work often looked down upon because of its atmosphere of sophistication, courtliness, and prudery. These are works of renunciation, works of Germanic pedagogy that dispense with those advantages of barbarism that the hedonist, Richard Wagner, allowed himself with such enormous effect (with the logical negative result that his ethnosensual oeuvre daily gains in brutish popularity).

We place *Elective Affinities* next to *Iphigenie* and *Tasso.* In their language, spirit, attitude, and conviction, they achieve the highest level of German cultivation. It is wonderful how we may find here a unified social and religious "not-nature" (which is not an "anti-nature," but a "moral culture") and how cultivation becomes morality. *Elective Affinities* is Goethe's *most Christian* work, and it is to *Elective Affinities* that he appealed when he was anxious to defend himself against accusations of paganism. "I, a pagan?" he once exclaimed. "But I had Gretchen executed, and Ottilie die of starvation! is that not Christian enough for people? What more could they want?" But his words betray a deep sorrow for those enchanting children of nature, his sisters and creations, Gretchen and Ottilie, and for the sacrifice he had to make by destroying them in the name of morality. Sulpiz Boisserée described a drive he took with Goethe from Karlsruhe to Heidelberg one starry night, six years after the novel had been completed: "He spoke of his relationship to Ottilie, how he loved her and how she made him unhappy. Finally, his talk became full of an almost mysterious foreboding." Kind, magnanimous man who, in utter obedience to the call of the spirit, still did not become unfaithful to nature, his element! He paid tribute to morality in a tragic, masculine manner, but he depended upon the feminine, and murmured foreboding words under the stars about the enigmatic fate of mankind, which he loved and which made him unhappy.

"The very simple text of this complicated little book," Goethe wrote, "paraphrases the words of Christ: 'Whosoever looketh on a woman to lust after her, etc.' I do not know if anybody has recognized them." But that is Tolstoy! But, by God, it is *not* Tolstoy, because it is *not* about the asceticism of the absurd, nor about the heartwrenchingly helpless yearning after spiritualization by the untamed children of nature, nor—and we are repeating this—is it about anti-nature. It is, however, about moral culture, about a deep, heartfelt sympathy with the natural, despite an obedience to a higher order. It is about a tragic, moral victory over love, resulting in a transfiguration that instructs men to sense the sanctity of the insurmountable tragedy of their fate.

For Ottilie is a saint, even if she wasn't recognized as such when her novel appeared. Can it be believed? The book was shocking. "Every aspiring Luther in Germany," as Nietzsche would say, cried murder over its sinfulness, as if Christianity dealt with anything other than sin, and as if saintliness could grow out of anything other than sin. Ottilie is a saint. Wieland felt this, even if he did not appreciate or understand it. For his part, he was "shocked" by the "moral tendencies" of the book. This opposite reaction occurred as well. Wieland called *Elective Affinities* "a truly horrible work," thus expressing the radicalness of its Christianity (which is, in the end, no less absolute than in the *Kreutzer Sonata),* the aroma of the crypt that makes us shiver with horror at the end, and "the horrid tranquility," to which, as Knebel says, "the story climbs toward the end." It was from this tranquility that Wieland escaped, to the humorous, human qualities of the book, to such charming moments as when Eduard says, after his first encounter with Ottilie, "She is such a delightful, entertaining girl," to which Charlotte replies, "Entertaining? But she has not yet opened her mouth." If he were duke, said Wieland, he would present Goethe with an entire estate for those words. We agree with him completely, without assuming, however, that the unprejudiced old gentleman understood very much of this saintly story.

The first seeds of the novel were early implanted in Goethe's soul. He was a student when he went on the hiking trip from Strassburg to Saint Odilie Mountain in Lower Alsace that he described in *Poetry and Truth:*

> There, where the foundation of a Roman citadel is still standing, it is said that the beautiful daughter of a count dwelt for reasons of piety in the cracks and stone crevices of the ruins. Not far from a chapel where hikers edify themselves, her well is pointed out and many a charming story is told. The image I formed of her and her name engraved themselves deep within me. I carried both with me for a long time until at last I endowed one of my later, but no less beloved, daughters with it, the daughter who was so favorably received by the pious and pure of heart.

By the pious and pure of heart. But is he not speaking about the book that, after all, provoked something of a scandal, as if it was a Life of a Saint? The scientific was added later. It consisted in the idea to apply the term "elective affinities," or chemical affinities, to the human, social sphere, as well as the oddest, mystical, deeply felt eroticization of the attractive forces of natural elements, something so little understood that philistines asked one another how Goethe could have written two volumes about this chemical phenomenon, when he was only reiterating what was popularly known and could easily be found in any chemistry textbook. *Reiterating*—it could not be more stupidly put. The sense of how daring this novel was, however, is difficult to capture even today, a daring that lay in contrasting the idea of man's subjection to nature—his passionate necessity, couched in the symbols of that science in which, as in no other science, the exact has always been mixed in with the mystical—with the idea of man's freedom, that unpredictable power of the human soul to surmount the immensity of nature, a power that is out of the reach of the laws of man and belongs, perhaps, to a higher order.

Ottilie is the sweetest child of nature that was ever fashioned by an artist's hand. In her gentleness, her smiling silence, and somnambulistic charm, she has something of one of the elemental beings of Romanticism, of an Undine. Her sympathetic connection to nature comes straight from her creator's heart, atmospherically surrounding her: in her hand the pendulum swings above metal; her left-sided headache appears in the vicinity of a coal deposit, the existence of which no one had previously suspected. All of nature's guilt and innocence is expressed in the sensitive obliviousness of this enchanting figure. She loves according to the law of nature and against the imperative of morality. She becomes, as does Gretchen, her sister, free of sin—all that drove her to it, God, was so dear, ah, was so sweet.* It is quite obvious that Goethe himself was in love when he created Ottilie. The image of the sainted Odilie came to life in the form of a living being just as he had begun to write his story. He was in the midst of one of his late passions: the fifty-eight-year-old had become smitten with the eighteen-year-old Herzlieb, foster child of the bookseller Frommann of Jena. He put into the bosom of his creation the renunciation that he, the "resolute pagan," employed in this as in all of the more meaningful cases of his love life. It is from this renunciation that the very peculiar, sweet, utterly mysterious, and peaceful atmosphere toward the end of the novel comes, when Eduard, Charlotte, and Ottilie apparently live together again as before. It is certainly this renunciation that motivated him to write the awe-inspiring, sublime ending: the wasting away of Ottilie (for which we were wisely prepared early on by the news of her strange moderation in eating and drinking even during her stay at boarding school), the popularly held belief in the power of her corpse to work miracles, and the seraphic finale. The student's boyish dream of the sainted Odilie mingles with the graying gentleman's renunciatory passion for a young life, becoming a tragic poem celebrating both the power of nature and the power of a human super-nature, which salvages its freedom through death.

Elective Affinities is of the highest form of art in its unity of structure and idea. In its artistic incarnation, it genuinely *is* what it portrays: the spiritualization of nature and "moral culture." Great art has always been the herald of the third empire. Art sets an example for mankind and the poet, in alliance with both the forces of nature and spirit, may indeed be called the master of all mankind.

THOMAS MANN

Translated by Jessica Chalmers and Jo Eckardt

---

*A well-known quote from *Faust, Part One,* in which Gretchen recalls her love for Faust.—*Trs*.

ELECTIVE AFFINITIES

Part One

Chapter One

E duard, a wealthy landowner in his early middle years, had
been spending the loveliest hour of an April afternoon in his
tree nursery, grafting fresh shoots on young stocks just sent him. His
task finished, he gathered his tools into their case and was con-
templating his work with satisfaction when the gardener approached, pleased by his master's interest and assistance.

"Have you seen my wife, by any chance?" Eduard inquired, just
as he was on the point of leaving.

"She is over there on the newly laid out grounds," the gardener
replied. "The summer house which she has been building against
the rock wall opposite the castle will be finished today. Everything
has turned out beautifully and will certainly please Your Grace. The
view from there is remarkable: the village is below; a little to the
right is the church, whose steeple you can almost look over; and,
opposite, the castle and the park."

"Quite so," Eduard said. "Not far from here I could see the men
working."

"And, then," the gardener went on, "to the right, the valley opens
out, and you look over the meadows with their many trees, far into a
serene and bright distance. The path up to the rocks has been very

prettily laid out. Her Ladyship is ingenious; it is a pleasure to work for her."

"Please go and ask her to wait for me," said Eduard. "Tell her that I should like to see and enjoy her latest achievement."

The gardener hurried away, and Eduard followed after a little while. He walked down the terraces and, in passing, looked into the greenhouses and at the hotbeds. When he came to the brook, he crossed a foot bridge and arrived at a point where the way branched in two directions. He did not take the path which ran across the churchyard in an almost straight line toward the rock wall, but followed the other, which wound gently upward, leading a little farther to the left through pleasant shrubbery. He sat down for a moment, on a bench where the paths rejoined; and then he started the climb which brought him, by a steep and uneven way, over all sorts of steps and ledges, finally to the summer house.

At the door Charlotte welcomed her husband and led him to a seat where he could take in at a single glance, through door and windows, the different views of the landscape, as though set in frames. He was delighted and expressed his hope that spring would soon bring new life to the surroundings. "I have only one criticism," he added. "The pavilion seems to me rather small."

"Certainly large enough for two," Charlotte answered.

"Yes, and there may be room even for a third person."

"Why not? And for a fourth as well. If we have company, we can always make other arrangements."

"Since we are now here alone and undisturbed, and in a calm and relaxed mood," Eduard began, "I must make a confession concerning something that has been on my mind for some time, something that I should tell you, but for which I haven't yet found an opportunity."

"I had the impression that something was troubling you," said Charlotte.

"Then I shall be quite frank in saying," Eduard continued, "that I should probably have kept silent still longer if the mail were not going out tomorrow, so that we must make a decision today."

"What is it?" asked Charlotte, kindly encouraging him.

"It concerns our friend, the Captain," Eduard replied. "You know the unfortunate position in which, like so many others, he has been placed through no fault of his own. How distressing it must be for a man of his education, talents, and abilities to find himself without anything to do. I'll not hold back my personal wish any longer: to have him here with us for a while."

"This needs serious consideration and must be looked at from more than one angle," Charlotte replied.

"I shall tell you my point of view immediately," Eduard answered. "In his last letter he sounded deeply discouraged; not that he is in want—he knows how to live economically, and I have taken care of his necessities—besides, it does not embarrass him to accept money from me. All our lives we have mutually borrowed and lent to such a degree that we cannot any longer figure out the sum of our credit and debit. That he is without any occupation, constitutes his real problem. His only pleasure—his passion, really—is to use for the benefit of others, day by day and hour by hour, those manifold abilities in which he has trained himself. To sit idle, or to go on studying in order to acquire still more skill, while he is unable to use what he already possesses to such a high degree—but enough, dearest. It is a humiliating situation for him, and it tortures him the more acutely since he is so much alone."

"I had reason to believe that he received offers from various quarters," Charlotte said. "I myself have written to many influential friends, men and women, to recommend him. And so far as I know, this has not been entirely without effect."

"That is true," Eduard answered. "But even these various opportunities and offers bring him new distress and embarrassment. None of them is at all suitable to the sort of person he is. He has never been asked to play an active part; he is asked to sacrifice himself, his time, his opinions, and his way of life; and that is impossible for him. The more I think about it all, the more I understand his situation and the stronger is my wish to see him here with us."

"It is very noble and lovable of you to feel your friend's predicament so deeply," Charlotte said; "but let me remind you to think also of yourself and of us."

"That I have done," Eduard answered. "For us, his presence certainly promises only pleasure and profit. There is no question of additional expense; this will be even less if he lives with us, especially since his visit will not cause the least inconvenience. He can have his own quarters in the right wing of the castle; everything else will be solved in due time. How much he will gain by this arrangement, and how many agreeable things *we* shall gain from his company—even some profit! For a long time I have wanted the estate and the whole countryside surveyed; he will arrange and supervise this. You have suggested that we take over the farms as soon as the leases of the present tenants have expired. How precarious such an enterprise is! How much preliminary and useful information he will be able to give! I feel very strongly that I should always have had here a man of his kind. Country folk may have practical experience; but what they say is usually vague and not always straightforward. Educated people from the city and the universities may be clear-headed and logical, but they lack the practical approach to the problems. From my friend I can expect both knowledge and experience. I can easily imagine that a hundred other circumstances will develop from this arrangement, and some are in your interest as well; and these will, as I foresee, do immense good. Thank you, first of all, for having listened so patiently. Now have your say, quite frankly and in detail. Tell me everything that is in your mind; I shall not interrupt you."

"Very well then," Charlotte replied. "First let me begin with a general observation. Men always think more of the individual case—of the Immediate; and they are right, because they are called upon to plan and to act. Women, on the other hand, must think more of things in their sequence; and rightly, because their personal destiny—and the destiny of their families—depends on continuity and because it is just this continuity which it is their mission to preserve. Let us therefore briefly glance over our present and our past life; and you will have to admit that the invitation to the Captain does not completely fall in with our original intentions, plans, and arrangements.

"How I enjoy thinking of our earliest relationship! We fell deeply in love with each other when we were young. You were separated from me—because your father, in his insatiable passion for wealth, married you to a rich woman considerably older than yourself. I was separated from you because, being without particular prospects, I was forced to marry a wealthy man whom I respected but did not love. We both regained our freedom—you first, when your wife left you a large fortune; I much later, at the time when you returned from your travels. So we met once more. We could speak of the past without sadness; we enjoyed our memories. We could live undisturbed. You insisted on marriage. I did not immediately consent; although we were about the same age I, the woman, had aged earlier than you, the man. At last, I could not refuse you what you thought your greatest happiness. You wished by my side to find peace from your restless years at court, in the army, and on your travels. You wanted to collect yourself, to enjoy life, but with me alone. I sent my only daughter to a boarding school, where she certainly receives a far more complete education than would be possible here in the country; and I also sent my niece Ottilie to the same school, although she would perhaps have received a better training—under my own supervision—as my companion and a help in our household. All this was done with my consent, for the single purpose that we might live our own lives, one for the other, and enjoy our so long-desired and so late-achieved happiness in peace and quiet. In this way we started our life together in the country. *I* took over the domestic duties; *you* the outside tasks and the general management of the estate. I have arranged my life to comply with all your wishes, to live for you alone. Let us try, at least for a while, to see how long we can be sufficient to each other."

"Since continuity, as you say, is woman's special element, one either should not listen continuously to your words or should admit at once that you are right; and I shall admit that you have been right—until now," Eduard replied. "The plan by which we mapped out our life is a good one; but should we add nothing new to it—should nothing new grow out of it? *My* work in the garden, *yours* in the park—is this for a pair of recluses?"

"You are right, perfectly right!" Charlotte answered. "We should only avoid introducing anything that might interfere with our way of life—any alien factor. Do not forget that our projects, even our diversions, were, in a way, exclusively dependent on our being alone together. You wanted to read to me the daily record of your travels, and doing so, collect and arrange any loose notes; then, with my help, compile from these invaluable but scattered notes and memoranda, a complete Journal which would give pleasure to us and to others. I promised you my help in copying; and we thought it would be so convenient and enjoyable, so delightful and intimate, to travel, in memory, through that world which we had not been allowed to see together. The beginning has already been made. In the evenings, moreover, you have started playing your flute again, while I accompany you at the piano. And there has been no lack of visits to or from our neighbors. I, for one, had promised myself, with all this, the first truly happy summer I had ever imagined."

"Still, I cannot help thinking while I hear you repeat all this so kindly and sensibly," Eduard said, rubbing his forehead, "that, after all, nothing would be changed by the presence of the Captain; on the contrary, everything would be quickened and stimulated. He has accompanied me on some of my wanderings; he, too, has made many notes, and from a different point of view. Only if we put all that together would the work become a perfect whole."

"Well, then, I will confess quite honestly that my feeling is against this plan," Charlotte declared, with a touch of impatience. "My instinct warns me that nothing good will come of it."

"When you speak in this way," Eduard sighed, "you women are indeed invincible. First, you are so sensible that we cannot contradict you; then, you are so charming that we readily surrender; so emotional that we hesitate to hurt you; and so full of forebodings that we are alarmed."

"I am not superstitious," Charlotte replied. "I should not take these dark intimations too seriously if they meant nothing further; but they are usually subconscious recollections of the fortunate or unfortunate consequences which, as we have observed, follow on our own or other people's actions. Nothing is more momentous in any situation than the appearance of a third person. I have known friends—brothers and sisters, lovers, husbands and wives—whose circumstances were completely reversed, whose mutual relationship changed completely through the accidental or intentional intrusion of a new person."

"This may perhaps happen in the case of people who always blindly grope their way through life." Eduard admitted, "but not to those who, once enlightened by experience, possess more self-awareness."

"The conscious mind, dearest, is no adequate weapon; it is even at times a dangerous one for the person who handles it," Charlotte insisted. "From all this, one fact at least becomes clear—that we should on no account act too hastily. Give me a few more days in which to think it over; do not make any decision."

"As the matter now stands, we are bound to act too quickly in any case, even after the lapse of a day or two," Eduard pleaded. "We have exchanged arguments for and against the plan; now it is the conclusion that matters, and it seems to me best to leave the matter to chance."

"I know that, when you are at a loss and must make a decision, you like to resort to a wager or to the dice." Charlotte said, "but in such a serious matter I should consider that a sin!"

"But what am I to write to the Captain?" Eduard exclaimed. "I must sit down and write a letter at once."

"Write him a calm, sensible, and encouraging letter," advised Charlotte.

"That would be as good as none at all," Eduard replied.

"And yet in certain cases it is necessary and kind to write a letter, even if it says nothing, rather than not to write at all," was all Charlotte said.

Chapter Two

Eduard was alone in his room. His sensitive nature had been agreeably excited by Charlotte's summingup of the different phases of his life and by her evocation of their mutual situation and projects. He had been so happy to be close to her, to be with her, that he now drew up in his mind a warm, understanding, but sensible and noncommittal letter to the Captain. But when, going to his desk, he took up and reread his friend's letter, the sad plight of this talented man again rose vividly before him; the emotions which had distressed him during the last few days rushed on him again, and he felt that it would be impossible for him to leave his friend in such a desperate situation.

Eduard was not used to denying himself anything. The only child of wealthy parents, he had been spoiled from early youth. They had succeeded in persuading him into an unusual but extremely advantageous marriage to a woman much older than himself, who had pampered him in every possible way, trying to repay his kindness to her by extreme generosity. After her early death he became his own master, free to travel anywhere, able to afford any diversion, any change—not caring for extravagant pleasures but for many and varied interests. He was broad-minded, generous, and gallant—

courageous when necessary. What in the world could obstruct his desires!

Up to now everything had gone as he wished. Charlotte had become his wife; he had finally won her by his long, obstinate, romantic loyalty; but now he found himself for the first time contradicted, for the first time frustrated at precisely the moment when he wished to have his friend near him in order to make, as it were, the circle of his life complete. He was vexed and impatient; he took up his pen several times only to put it down again, because he could not make up his mind what to write. He did not wish to go against the wishes of his wife, neither could he do what she had advised him to do; in his restless state it would have been impossible for him to write a calm note. It was most natural that he should try to put the whole matter off. In a few words he apologized to his friend for not having written earlier and for not writing today at greater length; and he promised to send him more important and reassuring news soon.

The next day, while they walked to the summer house, Charlotte took the opportunity to return to their earlier conversation, convinced, perhaps, that the safest way to weaken a project is to discuss it repeatedly.

This suited Eduard perfectly. He expressed himself in his usual manner, kindly and pleasant. Although his natural sensitiveness easily flared into anger, although his temperamental desires could become too insistent, and although his stubbornness was at times hard to bear, yet everything he said was always tempered by a perfect consideration for the other person so that it was impossible not to find him charming even if, at the same time, rather difficult.

Accordingly, this morning he began to put Charlotte in a good mood; and later completely disarmed her with all sorts of lover's talk, so that at last she exclaimed, "I know; you want me to grant to the lover what I refused to the husband.

"You can at least be sure, dearest, that your wishes and the warmth with which you express them do not leave me unmoved and do not find me unresponsive," she added. "They force me to make a confession. I, too, have kept something from you all this time. I find myself in a position similar to yours, and I have practiced the same self-control I am now asking of you."

"I am glad to hear this," Eduard answered, "and I see that it is sometimes necessary for a husband and wife to quarrel; they come to know each other better."

"I want to tell you now," Charlotte said, "that I feel about Ottilie just as you feel about the Captain. I hate to see the dear child in a boarding school where she has to face a rather embarrassing situation. My daughter Luciane, born as she is to play a part in society, is being trained in this school for this part. She learns languages, history, and any other subjects, just at a glance, as she plays her piano sonatas and musical variations at sight. With her lively temperament and excellent memory one might almost say that she forgets everything and remembers everything in a flash; she distinguishes herself among all the others by the freedom of her behavior, by her graceful movements when dancing, and by her perfect ease in conversation; and she has established herself as queen of a little circle of girls by her innate domineering nature. The headmistress of the school sees in her a little goddess who can be shaped into something precious under her direction, who is going to be a credit to the school and will gain her reputation and an increase of pupils. While the first pages of the headmistress' letters and monthly reports are always pure hymns to the perfection of such a child—hymns which I am quite capable of translating into my own prose—everything she finally says concerning Ottilie consists of recurrent apologies that a young girl, although growing into such great physical beauty, should not show any real development toward either spiritual or manual accomplishments. And the little she says in addition does not puzzle me, because I recognize in this dear child the complete character of her mother, who was my closest friend. She grew up with me, and I am certain that I could educate and train her daughter to become a wonderful human being if I could be her teacher and her guardian.

"But since this does not fall in with our own plan, and because we should never pluck and pull too much at our conditions of life, always introducing something new, I prefer to bear with the situation and even repress an uneasy feeling that my daughter—who knows perfectly well that poor Ottilie is entirely dependent on us—may use her advantage over her with thoughtless arrogance and so to a certain extent blight our kindness.

"But who is so well educated that he does not sometimes show his superiority over others in a cruel way? Who is so superior that he may not suffer at some time or other under such arrogance? Ottilie's character will be strengthened by these trials; but, since I have realized her painful situation more acutely, I have made continued efforts to place her somewhere else. I expect an answer very soon; and then I shall not hesitate. This is *my* care, my dearest. You see that we both have the same kind of worry and the same loyal and feeling hearts. We shall bear our troubles together, for they do not counteract each other."

"Human beings are very strange," Eduard said, smiling. "If we can only dismiss from our thoughts something that troubles us, we believe that it no longer exists. We are capable of making sacrifices in a general way, but we are seldom ready to sacrifice ourselves in particular. My mother was like that: so long as I lived with her, as a boy and a young man, she was not for one moment free of anxiety about me. If I came home later than expected from a ride on horseback, she immediately imagined an accident; if I became soaking wet in a heavy shower, she was sure that I should catch a fever. But when I went abroad, and I was far away from her—then I scarcely seemed to belong to her.

"If we look more deeply into all this," he went on, "it seems evident that we are both acting in a foolish and irresponsible way in leaving two fine human beings—both very close to our hearts—in this predicament and distress, only because we will not take risks. If this is not selfish, what can be called so? I propose that you take Ottilie and let me have the Captain—and let us try it, for Heaven's sake."

"We might take this chance," Charlotte reflected, "if we two alone were to run the risk. But do you think it advisable to bring the Captain and Ottilie together under the same roof—the Captain being a man of about your age, an age—I make this flattering statement to your face—when a man has just become capable of loving as well as of being loved; and a young girl as attractive as Ottilie?"

"I really cannot understand how you come to think so highly of Ottilie," Eduard objected. "I can explain it only by supposing that you have transferred your affection for her mother to her. She *is* pretty, no doubt, and I remember that the Captain called my attention to her when we returned, a year ago, and met you both at your aunt's house. She *is* pretty; her eyes in particular are beautiful; but I do not remember that she made the slightest impression on me."

"That was nice of you," said Charlotte, "for, after all *I* was there; and, although she is much younger than I, the presence of your old friend had so much attraction for you that you overlooked the promises of a budding beauty. That is the way you are, and it is the reason why it is so pleasant to share your life."

Although Charlotte seemed to speak in all sincerity, she did not betray a little secret—that at the time, when Eduard had just returned from abroad, she had intentionally introduced Ottilie to him in order to make a favorable match for her beloved foster-daughter. She had given up thinking of herself in connection with Eduard. The Captain, too, had been drawn by her into the plot; he was to bring the young girl to Eduard's attention. But Eduard, stubbornly loyal in his heart to his early love, had looked neither to right nor left and had been happy only in the feeling that it was at last possible to secure the highly desired treasure which a former series of events had apparently denied him forever.

Husband and wife were about to descend toward the castle through the newly laid out grounds when a servant hurried to meet them, and, laughing, called from some distance below: "Will Your Grace please come quickly? Herr Mittler has just galloped at full speed into the courtyard. He shouted to us to find you and to ask if he were needed. 'Am I needed?' he called after us. 'Do you hear? Hurry, hurry!' "

"The queer fellow!" Eduard exclaimed. "But does he not come just at the right moment, Charlotte? Quickly!" he ordered the servant. "Tell him that he should stay—that I need him, that we need him badly. Take care of his horse. Show him into the dining hall and give him something to eat. We shall come at once."

"Let us take the nearest road," Eduard said to his wife, as he chose the path across the churchyard which he usually avoided. Here also he saw, to his great surprise, traces of Charlotte's loving care. With the greatest possible respect for the old memorials, she had had the place leveled and rearranged, creating in this way a pleasant spot where eye and imagination equally could rest with delight. The oldest tombstones had been given a place of honor, ranged along the wall according to their date; either standing, or let into the wall, or otherwise fastened, they surrounded the high foundation of the church like an ornamental frieze. Eduard was strangely moved when he entered by the little gate; he pressed Charlotte's hand, and tears rose to his eyes. But the tears soon disappeared at the sight of their odd guest, who, not being able to sit still in the castle, had mounted his horse and ridden straight through the village and up to the churchyard gate, where he stopped and called out to his friends: "Are you really serious? If you really need me, I shall stay for dinner. But don't keep me too long; I still have a great deal to do today."

"Since you took the trouble to come so far, do ride in, at least," Eduard welcomed him. "We meet here in a solemn place. Look how beautifully Charlotte has softened its sadness."

"I—enter this place? Never!" protested the rider. "Never! Neither on horseback, nor in a carriage, nor on foot. Those who rest in peace are no concern of mine. I must put up with it when I am carried here some day, feet foremost. Well, is it serious?"

"Yes, very serious!" cried Charlotte. "It is the first time in our married life that we have been in trouble and need help."

"It does not look so," he answered, "but I will believe you. If you are deceiving me, I shall not help you another time. Follow me quickly; my horse deserves some rest."

Soon the three were sitting together in the hall; dinner was served, and Mittler told them what he had done that morning and what he still planned to do. This strange man had once been a clergyman and, apart from his untiring activity in his ministry, had distinguished himself by his skill in pacifying and settling quarrels in his own parish as well as in the neighborhood—at first between individuals and then between communities and between landowners. As long as he had been in his ministry, not one married couple had been divorced; and the district courts had never been bothered with quarrels and lawsuits from his part of the country. Early in life he realized the necessity of a thorough acquaintance with the law; and he devoted himself zealously to that science, soon finding himself a match for the shrewdest lawyer. The sphere of his activity widened remarkably, and some people tried to persuade him to move to the city where he could carry on in more influential circles the ministrations he had begun at a lower level. But, having won a large sum in the lottery, he bought with this money a small estate, which he leased and made the center of his activities. He was firmly determined—or rather followed an old habit and his inclination—never to stay in a house where there was no quarrel to settle or no assistance of any sort needed. People who were superstitious about the significance of names insisted that the name *Mittler* ("mediator") had compelled him to choose this strangest of all vocations.

The dessert had been served when the guest seriously pressed his host and hostess not to keep back their news any longer, since he would have to leave immediately after his coffee. Husband and wife then made their confessions in complete detail; but hardly had he heard what it was all about when he jumped angrily from his chair, rushed to the window, and ordered his horse to be saddled.

"Either you don't know me or don't understand me," he exclaimed, "or you merely make fun of me. Is this a question of a quarrel? Does this call for help? Do you think I am in the world to give advice? Of all the stupid occupations ever undertaken by man, that is the most stupid. Everyone should listen to his own advice and do what he cannot help doing. If it turns out well, he should be glad of his wisdom and his luck; if badly—I shall be at hand. The person who wants to get rid of an evil always knows what he wants; but one who wants something better than he has is stone-blind. Yes, yes, laugh at me—he plays at blindman's buff; perhaps he'll snatch something—but what? Do as you like; it does not make any difference! Invite your friends or leave them alone; it is all the same! I have seen the most reasonable things go wrong, the most foolish succeed. Do not rack your brains; and should the whole matter turn out badly in one way or another, don't worry either; send for me—I'll help you! Until then, good-bye!"

With these words he jumped on his horse and left, without waiting for his coffee.

"Now you see of how little use a third person really is when two close friends are not completely in agreement," Charlotte said. "You must admit that we now are, if possible, more confused and uncertain than before."

Both would probably have still wavered for some time if an answer from the Captain to Eduard's last letter had not arrived. He had made up his mind to accept one of the positions offered him, although it was by no means worthy of his abilities. He was supposed to share the boredom of some rich people of rank who expected him to keep them amused.

Eduard at once saw the situation as a whole and filled in the picture with unsparing comments. "Could you bear to see our friend in such a sad predicament?" he exlaimed. "You cannot be so cruel, Charlotte!"

"That strange fellow, Mittler, may be right after all," Charlotte admitted. "All such undertakings are gambles. No one can foresee how they will turn out. New combinations can have fortunate or unfortunate results; and we cannot even claim that the outcome is due to our own merit or our own guilt. I do not feel strong enough to oppose you any longer. We will try; but I ask you to promise me one thing: let everything be planned only for a short time. Give me your permission to investigate further with his interest in mind and to use my influence and my connections to find him a position which will really satisfy him or give him at least some satisfaction."

Eduard thanked his wife very warmly and with his usual charm. With a relieved and happy heart he left to send his friend their invitation; and he then asked Charlotte to add a few words in her own handwriting, saying that she approved the plan and joined him in his friendly suggestion. She wrote with an easy flow of the pen, expressing herself affably and politely, but in a sort of haste which was not her habit; and—which was very unlike her—she finally smudged the paper with a blot of ink, to her great annoyance; and the blot only became larger when she tried to dry it up.

Eduard joked about this and added—as there was still space—a second postscript, saying that his friend should take this as proof of their impatience to see him and should match his coming to the haste in which the letter had been written.

The messenger left, and Eduard thought he could not give a more convincing expression of his gratitude than by insisting again and again that Charlotte should immediately send for Ottilie. She asked him to give her some time to decide and that same evening succeeded in stimulating Eduard to playing a duet with her. Charlotte played the piano extremely well. Eduard performed not quite so well on the flute; for, although he practiced diligently from time to time, he was by nature not patient or persevering enough to train such a talent successfully. Therefore he played his part unevenly—some passages well but perhaps too quickly; in others he had to slow down because he was not familiar enough with the music; and it would have been difficult for any one but Charlotte to go through an entire duet with him. But Charlotte knew how to cope with it; she slowed down, and then allowed him to run away with her, fulfilling in this way the double duty of a good conductor and an intelligent housewife, both of whom always know how to preserve a general moderate measure, even if single passages may not always be in the right tempo.

Chapter Three

The Captain arrived. Previously, he had written a letter which had put Charlotte completely at ease. So much frankness about himself, such a clear insight into his own circumstances as well as into the situation of his friends, promised a good and cheerful outcome.

Conversation during the first few hours, as generally happens with friends who have not seen each other for some time, was animated and very nearly exhaustive. Toward evening Charlotte suggested a walk to the new grounds. The Captain was delighted with the entire setting and noticed every beautiful spot which, thanks to the new paths, had come into better view and could now be enjoyed to the full. He had a trained eye but, at the same time, was easily satisfied. Although he could see that all was not perfect, he did not—as is often the case—dampen the good spirits of friends who showed him their property by asking for more than the circumstances allowed; nor did he remind them of anything more perfect he had seen elsewhere.

When they came to the summer house, they found it gaily decorated. Although composed only of artificial flowers and evergreens intermixed with lovely sheaves of wheat and other fruits of field and forest, the whole arrangement showed remarkable taste. "Even though my husband does not wish us to celebrate his birthday or name day, he will not scold me because today I dedicate these few garlands to the celebration of a triple occasion."

"A triple occasion?" Eduard exclaimed.

"Certainly!" Charlotte replied. "Should we not celebrate our friend's arrival; and, then, you both have probably forgotten that today is your name day. Are you not both called 'Otto?' "

The two friends' hands clasped across the small table. "You remind me of our youthful pledge of friendship," Eduard said. "When we were children, we were both called by that name, but later, when we were in school together, the name was the cause of so much confusion that—voluntarily—I yielded my nice laconic name to him."

"Don't boast too much of your generosity," mocked the Captain. "I remember fairly clearly that you liked the name 'Eduard' much better; and indeed it sounds very pleasant, especially when pronounced by pretty lips."

All three were seated around the same little table at which Charlotte had so fervently opposed the invitation to their guest. Eduard, being happy, did not wish to remind his wife of that hour; but he could not refrain from saying: "There is even room here for a fourth person."

At this moment they heard the sound of hunting horns from the castle, affirming and confirming, as it were, the innermost thoughts and wishes of the friends here gathered together. They listened in silence, all three lost in their own thoughts, each moved by his or her own happiness and in perfect harmony with the happiness of the others.

Eduard first broke the silence; he got up and walked out into the open. "Let us take our friend to the top of the hill at once," he said to Charlotte. "He must not think that this narrow valley is our only inheritance and domain; high up there he can have a wider view, and we can breathe more freely."

"This time we have still to climb up the old rather difficult footpath," Charlotte said; "but I hope that my little steps and paths will soon lead us more conveniently to the top."

And so they arrived, over rocks and through bushes and shrubbery at the summit, which was not level but consisted of a succession of grassy ridges. Village and castle, at their back, were no longer visible. Below they saw ponds stretching along the valley, backed by wooded hills; where these ended, steep rocks formed a perpendicular wall behind the last expanse of water, which reflected their magnificent forms on its surface. In a ravine, where a rushing brook poured down into one of the ponds, was a grist-mill; almost hidden among surrounding trees it seemed to offer a pleasant and quiet retreat. In the entire semicircle which they overlooked, a great

variety of depths and heights, of thickets and of forests, spread out
before them, promising with their early green a future abundant
prospect. Here and there single clusters of trees caught their eyes,
especially one group of poplars and plane trees directly below them
on the edge of the central pond. The trees were all full grown; strong
and flourishing, they tapered upward and widely spread their
branches.

Eduard asked his friend to take particular notice of them. "I
planted those myself when I was a boy. They were saplings that I
saved when my father, laying out a new part of the great park, had
them removed in the middle of summer. They will, no doubt, show
their gratitude again this year by sending out new shoots."

Pleased and in good spirits, the friends returned to the castle. The
Captain was assigned comfortable and spacious quarters in the
castle's right wing, where he was soon established and where he
arranged his books, papers, instruments in order to continue his
usual occupations. But Eduard, during the first days, did not allow
him one peaceful moment; he took him, either on horseback or on
foot, to see everything about the place; made him acquainted with
the surroundings and the estate itself; and told him, on these excursions, his long-cherished plans to improve his knowledge of everything in order to put all to more profitable use.

"The first matter we should attend to is for me to map out the
entire terrain with a compass," suggested the Captain. "It is an easy
and pleasant task, and, though not entirely exact, it will always be
useful and is a good starting point; we can also carry it through
without much assistance, and we shall know for certain that it can
be finished. If you should ever consider a more precise job of
surveying, that can easily be managed later."

The Captain was very skilful at this kind of mapping. He had
brought the necessary instruments with him and started at once. He
instructed Eduard, as well as some foresters and peasants, to assist
him in his work. The weather was favorable. The Captain spent his
evenings and early morning hours in making shaded drawings; and
in a very short time all was also worked out *au lavis* and in color.
Eduard watched while his possessions emerged like new creations
upon paper; and it seemed to him as if only now they really
belonged to him. Opportunities arose to discuss the environs as a
whole and the laying-out of new grounds, which would be much

more successful when a map of the entire estate existed than formerly, when they had only experimented with nature in details and
according to chance impressions.

"We shall have to explain all this to my wife," Eduard said.

"Don't do it!" warned the Captain, who never liked to impose his
own opinions on other people. Experience had taught him that the
opinions of human beings are much too varied to be united upon a
single point, even by means of the most sensible arguments. "Don't
do it! She might easily become uncertain of herself. Like all persons
who occupy themselves with that kind of thing as a hobby, she feels
that it is more important for her to do something than that something ought to be done. She resembles those who potter about with
nature, who have a preference for this spot or that, who do not dare
to remove this or that obstacle, who do not have the courage to
sacrifice anything, who cannot imagine beforehand what they want
to create. They experiment, and this turns out well and that badly;
they make changes, changes perhaps where things should have been
left as they were, and leave things unchanged which should perhaps
have been changed; and in this way everything remains forever a
patchwork which is delightful and stimulating but unsatisfactory."

"Now tell me quite frankly—you are not satisfied with her new
arrangements?" Eduard asked.

"If the finished effect were equal to the original conception—
which is really quite good—I should have nothing to criticize. She
has tortured herself with the difficulty of getting through the rocks,
and now tortures everyone (if I may say so) whom she takes up to the
crest of the hill. For neither side by side, nor in single file, is it
possible to walk with any ease. One's step may be interrupted at any
moment—and I could make many other objections!"

"But could it have been done in a different way?" Eduard asked.

"Easily," explained the Captain. "She had only to break away one
corner of the projecting cliff, which is really quite insignificant, since
it consists of small pieces, and she would have gained a graceful
sweeping curve for her ascending path and, moreover, plenty of
stones which the masons could use to widen the road and to fill the
bad spots in it where the path has become narrow and tortuous. But
all this is in strict confidence, between friends; any mention of it
would confuse and annoy her. What has been done must be left as it
is. If you will spend more money and labor, there is still plenty to do

from the little summer house up to the crest and beyond; and we can manage this the way we wish."

Even while the two friends were so busy with their present problems, there was opportunity for animated and pleasurable exchange of memories of former times in which Charlotte could share. And they decided to begin the journal of their travels, as soon as the more urgent work was finished, and in this way recall the past.

When Eduard and Charlotte were alone together, they had fewer subjects of conversation than before, especially since the Captain's criticism of the new grounds, which Eduard found to the point, weighed on his mind. He kept silent about it for a long time; but at last, when he saw her toiling up her little steps and paths again from the summer house to the top of the hill, he could no longer refrain and told her, after some evasions, of his new ideas.

Charlotte was completely taken aback. She was intelligent enough to see at once that the friends were right; but her own work, so differently planned, already existed and could not be undone; she had thought it right and liked it; she even liked every one of the details that were criticized. She did not wish to be convinced and defended her little achievements. She blamed the two men for planning everything on too large a scale, for wanting to make an important work out of a playful idea and pleasurable occupation, without considering the expense which a more elaborate plan would inevitably involve. She was upset, hurt, and annoyed. She was unwilling to drop her former plans, although she could not quite deny the advantages of the new ones; but, determined as she was, she stopped the work at once, in order to gain time to think over the whole matter and let it mature in her mind.

Now, while Charlotte was missing her active pastime, the two men were more and more together and looked into everything, especially the nurseries and hothouses. During the intervals of their work they continued their usual country gentlemen's sports—hunting and buying and bartering horses and breaking these into rein and harness; and Charlotte was left more and more to herself. She devoted more of her time to her correspondence and also wrote letters on behalf of the Captain; but she had many lonely hours. She therefore enjoyed the reports she received from the boarding school all the more and read them with great interest.

A long and detailed letter came from the headmistress, who, as usual, after expressing her satisfaction with the progress of Charlotte's daughter, added a short postscript and enclosed a note written by the young man who was her tutor. Both follow:

The Headmistress's Postscript

"In regard to Ottilie, your Ladyship, I can only repeat what I have said in my previous reports. I cannot find fault with her, but I also cannot say that I am happy about her. She is, as she has always been, modest and polite toward others; but I do not quite like her self-effacement and her submissiveness. Your Ladyship the other day sent her a sum of money and material for dresses. She has not touched the money, and the material has not yet been used. Of course, she keeps her things clean and neat and obviously changes her dresses for that reason alone. I also cannot approve of her extreme moderation in eating and drinking. We do not have extravagant meals; but there is nothing I like better than to see the children eat enough good and wholesome food. Everything that is served after careful selection should be eaten, and I never can bring Ottilie to do this. She even manages to find some task to perform, or goes to fetch something that the servants have forgotten or neglected, when she wants to skip some course or the dessert. On the other hand, one must consider that she frequently suffers—as I have only lately been told—from a pain on the left side of her head which is only temporary but probably disturbing and severe. So much for this otherwise dear and lovely child."

Enclosure of the Tutor

"Our excellent headmistress usually passes on to me the letters in which she sends the parents and guardians of her pupils her observations about them. I have always read the letters addressed to Your Ladyship with special attention and pleasure; for, while we congratulate you on having a daughter who combines in herself all those brilliant qualities which will help her to rise in society, I think that you are no less fortunate in possessing in your foster-daughter a child born to be useful and a blessing to others and, without any doubt, destined for happiness, as well. Ottilie is almost our only pupil concerning whom our admirable headmistress and I do not agree. I do not at all blame that untiring lady when she wishes to see the fruits of her efforts appear in a tangible and visible form, but there are some fruits which, although shut into a shell, nevertheless have a sound core, and will sooner or later develop into rich maturity. Your foster-daughter, I am convinced, is such a nature. So long as I have been her teacher, I have seen her ever moving at the same pace, slowly, slowly forward—never back. Just as it is necessary for a small child to start with beginnings, so it is with her. Everything that does not follow from something she has already learned she is unable to grasp. She is incapable, even inaccessible, when confronted with an easily understandable subject—on which, however, she cannot connect with any former experience; but, as soon as one can find the connecting links and explain them to her, nothing is too difficult for her comprehension.

"Because she progresses so slowly, she is far behind her companions, who, with totally different abilities, always hurry on learning everything easily—even unrelated subjects—remember them easily, and can apply them without difficulty. This is not Ottilie's way; she is almost paralyzed when a teacher proceeds too quickly, as happens in a few classes given by excellent but impatient instructors. There have also been complaints about her handwriting and her inability to grasp the rules of grammar. I have looked closely into this. It is true that she writes slowly and tensely, if one may say so; but her letters are neither timid nor badly formed. When I tutored her in French (although that is not my subject), I taught her by going forward step by step; and she easily understood. Of course it is strange, although she knows many things and knows them well, when she is asked questions she does not seem to know anything at all.

"If I may conclude with a general observation, I should like to say that she does not learn like a person who receives an education but like one who herself wishes to educate others; not like a pupil but like a future teacher. Your Ladyship will think it strange that I, a teacher and educator, cannot think of higher praise to give a person than to pronounce her my equal. Your Ladyship's great insight and deeper knowledge of the world and of human nature will read my inadequate but well-meant words with the best understanding. You can be assured that this child, too, is promising. With my best compliments, I ask your Ladyship's permission to write again as soon as I have something important and pleasant to report."

Charlotte was very happy about this note. Its contents closely corresponded to the idea she had herself formed of Ottilie; at the same time, she could not help smiling at the Tutor's warm interest which seemed greater than the perception of good qualities in a pupil usually rouses. In her quiet unprejudiced way of thinking, she looked at this relationship as she had in many similar cases; she appreciated the sympathy felt by this sensible man for Ottilie, having learned from many experiences during her life how precious true affection is in a world where indifference and dislike are so much at home.

Chapter Four

The topographical map of the estate and its environs was finished. In pen-and-ink and colors it showed clearly all the characteristic features on a fairly large scale. Its exactness was well founded on trigonometrical measurements made by the Captain. Hardly anyone but this active man could have gone with so little sleep; his days were always devoted to an immediate purpose, so that every evening showed that something had been accomplished.

"Now let us turn our attention to the rest," he said to his friend; "that is, a descriptive survey of the estate. There must already be enough documents from which evaluation of the leases and other matters will naturally develop. But we should firmly decide on one principle and strictly observe it: to separate business from pleasure. Work requires serious thinking and firmness; life should be lived more flexibly. Work demands a clear sequence; in life one has at times to be inconsequential; this is delightful and even exhilarating. If you are firm in the first, you can be more free in the second; otherwise, if you mix the two, firmness will be swept away and canceled by freedom."

Eduard felt a slight reproach in his friend's remark. Although by nature not without orderly habits, he could never bring himself to arrange his papers in files. His correspondence with others and the papers which concerned his personal affairs were not kept separately. In the same way, he was liable to confuse business with mere occupation and conversation with entertainment. Everything was now easier for him since his friend, acting as a second self, took care of all these matters and brought about a division which the single self often refuses to make.

In the Captain's wing they constructed a depository for their present transactions as well as an archive for past ones. They collected there all the documents, papers, and communications received, from different places—from rooms, garrets, and cupboards—where they had formerly been kept; and in no time the chaos was cleared, and the marked files lay in gratifying order in their labeled pigeonholes. The friends found the necessary documents more complete than they had expected. An old clerk was extremely helpful—he did not leave his desk all day, even spending part of the night there—although Eduard had previously found him unsatisfactory.

"He does not seem the same person!" he exclaimed. "He is so active and useful!"

"The reason is that we do not burden him with new work before he has finished the old at his convenience," the Captain explained. "In this way he accomplishes a great deal, as you see; if you disturb him, he can do nothing."

Although they spent their days together in this manner, the two friends never failed to keep Charlotte company in the evenings. If no visitors from the neighboring towns and estates arrived—which was frequently the case—they read and talked, mostly on topics concerned with the improvement of conditions, the privileges and the comfort of the middle class.

Charlotte, whose habit was to make use of the present moment, felt that it was to her own personal advantage if her husband was happy and contented. Various domestic arrangements which she had always wished to make but had not known how to start were now realized with the help of the Captain. Her private medicine chest, until now poorly stocked, received new supplies of medicines; and Charlotte herself, aided by popular books on the subject and through discussion, was now in a position to exercise her active and charitable nature more frequently and more efficiently than before. After the three had discussed the usual emergencies, which in spite of their frequent occurrence only too often take us by surprise, they began, first of all, to provide everything which might be required for the resuscitation of a drowned person. This sort of accident happened very frequently in this region, since they lived near so many ponds, lakes, rivers, and mill dams. The Captain took extensive care of this special department, and Eduard let fall the remark that a strange case of this kind had marked a memorable point in the life of his friend. But the Captain said nothing, evidently wishing to avoid sad memories; and Eduard immediately became silent. Charlotte, who had a general knowledge of the incident, passed quickly over the allusion.

"All these precautions are very valuable," the Captain began one evening, "but we lack the most essential factor: a good man who knows their practical use. I can warmly recommend a former army surgeon whom I know well, and whose services are at present available at moderate terms. He is an excellent man in his profession, and he treated me frequently, in the case of a violent internal trouble, more skilfully than a famous physician. Immediate medical care is the thing one misses most in the country."

They wrote to the surgeon at once; and Eduard and Charlotte were glad that a sum of surplus money, set aside for extra expenses, could now be used for essential needs. In this way Charlotte used the Captain's knowledge and his practical judgment for her own purposes; she gradually became completely reconciled to his presence and at ease concerning any possible consequences. She usually prepared certain questions she wished to ask him; and, as she loved life, she wished to eliminate anything harmful or of a fatal nature. The lead glaze of pottery and the verdigris on copper vessels had worried her very often. She asked him to explain all this to her; and they naturally had to go back to elementary physics and chemistry.

Eduard's special liking for reading aloud to others gave an occasional and always welcome motive for this sort of conversation. He had a very musical deep-pitched voice and, in former years, had been famous for his lively and moving recitals of poetry and dramatic prose. At present he was interested in other subjects; and the books from which he now read to them were, for the most part, works on physics, chemistry, or technical problems.

One of his most striking peculiarities—which he very likely shared with many others—was that he could not bear to have anyone look over his shoulder at the book he was reading.

Formerly, when he used to read poems, plays, or stories aloud, this antipathy had been the natural consequence of a desire which is equally strong in the reader, the poet, the actor, and the narrator: to surprise, to pause, and to work up suspense. These intended effects are, of course, thwarted when another person's eyes can run ahead over the page. For this reason Eduard usually chose a seat where no one could sit behind him. In the present case—in their little circle of three—such a precautionary measure was unnecessary; and, as the reading matter offered no cause for emotional excitement or for imaginative surprise, he did not trouble to be particularly careful in his choice of a seat.

One evening, however, when he had seated himself to read, without giving much thought to the place, he suddenly noticed that Charlotte was looking into his book. His old impatience returned, and, speaking in a rather unkind tone, he chided her: "That is one of the annoying habits I wish people would drop once and for all! When I read aloud to you, is it not as though I were speaking directly to you? The written and the printed words take the place of my own thoughts, my own heart. Would I make the effort to talk if a little window had been set into my forehead or breast, so that the person to whom I communicate my thoughts and emotions, one by one, would know all the while, in advance, what I was driving at? If someone glances into the book I am reading, I always feel as if I were being pulled apart."

In a large as well as in a small circle, Charlotte had shown a special talent for quietly passing over any unpleasant, violent, or even any too outspoken remark. She knew how to interrupt a long-winded conversation or, on the other hand, how to stimulate one that threatened to exhaust itself; and now this wonderful gift did not fail her. "I am sure you will forgive me my tactlessness if I confess what occurred to me just now," she said. "I heard you reading about 'relationships' and 'affinities,' and I immediately thought of certain relatives—two cousins who just now are giving me a good deal of trouble. My attention turned again to your reading; I heard that it concerned inanimate matter; and I glanced into your book to pick up the lost thread."

"It is the analogy which misled and confused you," Eduard answered. "The book here deals only with earth and minerals; but man is a true narcissus; he likes to reflect himself everywhere; he spreads himself under the whole world like the foil of a mirror."

"Yes," the Captain added. "He treats everything outside himself in this fashion. His own wisdom and his folly, his will and his whim, he attributes to the animals, the plants, the elements, and the gods."

"Would you explain to me quite briefly—as I do not want to lead you too far away from the present subject—what is meant here by— 'affinities'?" Charlotte asked.

"I shall do that with pleasure and as clearly as I can," the Captain, to whom Charlotte had directed her question, answered. "Whatever I have learned and read about these matters dates back about ten years. Whether the scientific world still accepts this theory, or if the theory agrees with modern doctrines, I cannot say."

"It is a pity that nowadays we cannot learn anything to last a lifetime," Eduard exclaimed. "Our forefathers relied on what they were taught in their youth; *we* have to learn something different every five years or so in order not to fall completely behind the times."

"We women are not so particular," said Charlotte. "Quite frankly, I am mainly interested in the exact meaning of the word; nothing makes one more of a laughing stock in society than to use a foreign or a technical term incorrectly. I only wish you would tell me in what sense this term is used in connection with the matters you mentioned. I am quite content to leave its scientific implications to the scholars who will not (by the way) ever agree easily among themselves, as I have had the opportunity to observe."

"How are we to begin, in order to come to the point in the quickest possible way?" Eduard asked the Captain, who, after reflecting for a short time, began:

"If I begin farther back, we shall come to the point all the quicker."

"I shall certainly be very attentive," said Charlotte, putting her needlework away.

The Captain then began:

"The first thing we notice in all natural elements is that they have a relation to themselves. It may sound strange for me to state something so obvious; but only if we completely agree about the known, can we proceed together to the unknown."

"I think," interrupted Eduard, "we can make everything clearer for Charlotte and for ourselves if we give a few examples. Just think of water, or of oil, or of mercury—and you will see a unity, a cohesion, of their parts. This unity is never lost except when broken by force or by some other determining factor. If this factor is eliminated, the parts immediately combine again."

"No doubt that is very true," Charlotte agreed. "Raindrops quickly unite and form a flood. Even as children, we used to play with quicksilver and separate it into small pellets which, to our great surprise, always ran together again."

"Then perhaps I may briefly mention an important point," the Captain added, "namely, that this perfectly clear relation of parts, made possible by the liquid state, always distinguishes itself by a definite globular shape. The falling water drop is round, and you yourself mentioned just now the small mercury pellets; but even a drop of molten lead, if it has time to harden as it falls, lands on the ground in a globular shape."

"Wait a moment and see if I have understood what you are driving at," Charlotte said. "Just as everything relates to itself, so it must have some relation to other things."

"And that relation will be different according to a difference in the elements involved," Eduard eagerly went on. "Some will meet quickly like friends or old acquaintances and combine without any change in either, just as wine mixes with water. But others will remain detached like strangers and refuse to combine in any way— even if they are mechanically mixed with, or rubbed against, each other. Oil and water may be shaken together, but they will imme- diately separate again."

"From this point it is only a step to imagine that one sees in these simple forms the people one has known," said Charlotte. "I am particularly reminded of the societies in which we have lived. But the strongest resemblance to these soulless elements shows in the groups which confront one another in the world: the trades and professions, the aristocracy and the commoners, soldiers and civil- ians."

"But just as all these can be unified by common laws and morals, so also in our chemical realm intermediate links exist which join mutually hostile elements," Eduard said.

"In this way we combine oil and water by means of alkaline salt," the Captain interjected.

"Please don't go too fast with your lecture and let me prove that I can keep up with you," Charlotte said. "Have we not by now arrived at the 'affinities'?"

"You are right!" the Captain replied. "In just a moment we shall become acquainted with them in their full force and determination. The tendency of those elements which, when they come into contact, at once take hold of, and act on one another, we call 'affinity.' The alkalis and the acids reveal these affinities in the most striking way—although by nature opposites, perhaps for that very reason they select one another, take hold of and modify each other eagerly; and then together form an entirely new substance. You have only to think of lime, which shows a decided inclination for all sorts of acids—a distinct desire to combine with them. As soon as our chemistry cabinet arrives, we will show you many kinds of interesting experiments which will give you a much better idea of all this than words, names, and technical terms can do."

"I must confess that when I hear you say that these odd things are 'related,' they seem to me not so much blood relations as relations in spirit and soul," Charlotte said. "In just the same way truly deep friendships can develop between people because opposite dispositions are the best basis for a very close union. I shall now wait for the moment when you will show me some of these mysterious effects. I'll not interrupt your reading again," she said, turning to Eduard. "You have taught me so much that now I shall be a more attentive and understanding listener."

"No, my dear," Eduard replied. "You have challenged our instruction, and you will not get off so easily. It is precisely the complicated cases that are most interesting. Only through them can you learn to know the degrees of affinity—the closer and stronger, as well as the more remote and weaker, relationships. Affinities really become interesting only when they bring about separations."

"How terrible!" Charlotte cried. "Is that depressing word, which, unfortunately, we hear so often nowadays, also in nature's textbook?"

"Of course it is," Eduard answered. "The title of honor formerly given to chemists was 'artist in separating.'"

"But that title is probably no longer given, and it is just as well," Charlotte said. "*Uniting* is a greater and more deserving art. An artist in *uniting* would be welcome in any profession, the world over. But, as you both seem to be in a teaching mood, tell me more of your cases."

"We will, then, take up where we left off in our talk," said the Captain. "For instance, what we call limestone is a more or less pure calcareous earth in close combination with a volatile acid known to us in a gaseous form. If we put a piece of this limestone in a weak solution of sulphuric acid, the latter will take possession of the lime and appear with it in the form of gypsum; but the delicate gaseous acid will escape. Here we see a case of separation, and of a new combination, so that we think we are correct in using here the term 'elective affinity,' as it really looks as though one relation had been deliberately chosen in preference to another."

"Excuse me as I excuse the scientist," said Charlotte. "But in this case I should never think of a choice but of a compelling force—and not even that. After all, it may be merely a matter of opportunity. Opportunity makes connections as it makes thieves. As to your chemical substances, the choice seems to be exclusively in the hands of the chemist who brings these elements together. But once united, and they *are* together, God have mercy on them! In the present case I am only sorry for the poor gaseous acid which must again roam about in infinite space."

"The acid has only to combine with water to refresh the healthy and the sick as a mineral spring," the Captain retorted.

"That is easy for the gypsum to say," said Charlotte. "The gypsum is taken care of; it is a *substance;* but that other displaced element may have much trouble until it finds a home again."

I am very much mistaken if there is not a bit of malice behind your words," said Eduard, smiling. "Out with your mischievous thoughts! Perhaps *I* am (in your eyes) the lime which has been taken into possession by the Captain, who is the sulphuric acid, and am torn away from your amiable company and changed into refractory gypsum."

"If your conscience prompts you to make remarks like that, I have no reason to worry," said Charlotte. "These parables are entertaining, and who does not like to play with analogies? But man is placed many degrees higher than these elements; and if we have here used fine words like 'choice' and 'elective affinity' a little too broadly, we would do well to turn back into our own hearts and, in so doing, think seriously about the value of such terms. Unfortunately, I know enough cases where a close union of two hearts, apparently indissoluble, has been dissolved by the accidental introduction of a third person; and where one or the other of a once happily united couple has been driven out into an uncertain world."

"You see how much more chivalrous the chemists are," said Eduard. "They provide a fourth element, so that no one feels neglected."

"That is true!" added the Captain. "And those cases are indeed the most important and remarkable, wherein this attraction, this affinity, this separating and combining, can be demonstrated, the two pairs, as it were, crossing over; where four elements, until then joined in two's, are brought into contact and give up their former combination to enter a new one. In this dissociating and taking possession, this flight and seeking, we actually imagine we see some higher pre-determination; we believe these elements capable of exercising some sort of willpower and selection, and feel perfectly justified in using the term 'elective affinities'!"

"Why don't you describe such a case!" Charlotte asked.

"Such matters cannot easily be described in words," replied the Captain. "As I said before, as soon as I can demonstrate to you the experiments themselves, everything will become intelligible and simpler for you. As it is I should be forced to put you off with formidable scientific terms which would have no meaning for you. You must see with your own eyes these apparently lifeless but actually very dynamic elements and observe with interest how they attract, seize, destroy, devour, and absorb each other and then emerge out of that violent combination in renewed and unexpected form. Only then will you agree that they might be immortal or even capable of feeling and reasoning, because we feel our own senses to be almost insufficient for observing them properly and our reason too limited to understand their nature."

"I will not deny that the strange scientific terms must seem difficult and even absurd to anyone who has not become familiar with them by direct observation and by general conceptions," Eduard said; "but meanwhile we can easily express in symbols, for this occasion, the relations of the elements we have been discussing here."

"If you will not think me too pedantic, I can very easily sum up the whole matter by using letters," the Captain said. "Imagine an *A* so closely connected with a *B* that the two cannot be separated by any means, not even by force; and imagine a *C* in the same relation to a *D*. Now bring the two pairs into contact. *A* will fling itself on *D,* and *C* on *B,* without our being able to say which left the other first, or which first combined itself with the other."

"Now then!" said Eduard. "Until we have seen all this with our own eyes, we shall take this formula as a useful allegory and draw from it a practical lesson. You, Charlotte, represent the *A,* and I am your *B;* for, to be honest, I completely depend on you and follow you as *B* follows *A. C* obviously stands for the Captain, who just at present draws me away from you to some extent. It is only to keep you from escaping into infinite space that we should try to find a *D* for you; and that is, no doubt, your darling Ottilie, whose coming you should really no longer resist."

"Very well!" Charlotte agreed. "Even if, in my opinion, the example does not quite fit our case, I think it very fortunate that today we all agree for once perfectly and that these natural and elective affinities have encouraged me to tell you, earlier than I had intended, that I made up my mind this afternoon to send for Ottilie, for my faithful housekeeper is about to leave to be married. This decision is in my own interest and for my own sake. Why I decided in Ottilie's interest, you shall read aloud to us. I'll not look into the letter while you are reading. Of course, I already know what it says. Here, read; do read!"

With these words she produced a letter and gave it to Eduard.

Chapter Five

The Headmistress's Letter

"Your Ladyship will excuse me if I am very brief today. I must write reports to all the parents and guardians concerning the results of the public examinations which are just over and which will show what we have accomplished with our pupils during the past year. I may be brief since I can tell you much in a few words. Your daughter has turned out to be in every sense the first in her class. The enclosed certificate and her own letter, with its description of her awards and her delight at her success, will be a great satisfaction and pleasure to you. My own feelings are somewhat sad ones, because I expect that soon there will be no longer any reason for keeping with us a young lady who is so far advanced. I send my compliments to your Ladyship. In my next letter I shall submit my suggestions concerning the best plans for her future. My assistant will write you about Ottilie."

The Tutor's Letter

"Our respected headmistress has left it in my hands to write you concerning Ottilie, partly since she is embarrassed, because of her attitude in these matters, to report what must be reported; partly because she herself feels guilty and prefers that I offer apologies in her name.

"Knowing only too well how inarticulate our dear Ottilie is about herself and the things she really knows, I had been worried about this public examination, for which it is not possible to prepare a student—least of all Ottilie—who could never be prepared for mere show and make-believe, as such preparation is usually made. The result of the examination has only too well justified my uneasiness. She did not receive any award and is, besides, among those who did not receive a certificate. What more can I say? Her handwriting is very good; her letters are better shaped than those of the other pupils, but these others have much more freely flowing pens. They were all quicker with their answers in arithmetic; and no difficult problems—which she can solve better than the rest—came up. In French the others outtalked and outshone her. In history she was not prompt with her names and dates; and in geography she did not show enough knowledge of political division. During the music recital there was neither time nor quiet for her few simple tunes. In drawing she would certainly have received the first prize. Her outlines were clear, the details carefully done and yet full of imagination. Unfortunately, she had set herself too large a task and was not able to complete it.

"After the pupils were dismissed, the examiners went into a conference to which we teachers were also admitted, and where we could say a few words. I soon noticed that Ottilie was either not mentioned at all or mentioned with indifference if not with disapproval. I hoped to improve her chances by frankly describing her personality as a whole, which I could do with great warmth, because I was deeply convinced of what I said and because, when young, I had found myself in a similar predicament. Everyone listened with attention; but, when I had finished my plea, the chairman of the board of examiners said, kindly but laconically, 'Aptitudes are taken for granted; they should become accomplishments. This is the aim of all education; it is the clear and pronounced wish of parents and guardians as well as the unexpressed and perhaps only half-realized wish of the children themselves. It is also the purpose of examinations, where both teachers and pupils alike are tested. From all you have said, there seems to be a possibility of promise in this child; and it is certainly to your credit that you so conscientiously watch the capacities of the pupils. If, during the next year, you can develop her aptitudes into accomplishments, you and this pupil you are so warmly interested in will certainly receive our full approval.'

"I had already resigned myself to the consequences, but I had not anticipated the disturbing scene which occurred soon afterward. Our dear headmistress, who, like a good shepherd, cannot bear to see one of her flock lost or as was here the case unadorned, after the departure of the examiners could no longer conceal her disappointment. She said to Ottilie, who was standing quietly near a window, while the other pupils rejoiced in their awards, 'Now for Heaven's sake tell me, how can any intelligent person appear so stupid?'

"Ottilie calmly answered, 'Excuse me, dear Mother. I feel my headache again today, and it is very painful.'

" 'No one could know that,' the headmistress, who is usually so sympathetic, said dryly; and she unkindly turned away.

"Well, it *is* true that no one could realize it, for Ottilie's face does not change; and I have never seen her once move her hand to her temple.

"But this was not all. Your Ladyship's daughter, by nature lively and outgoing, was in high spirits after her triumph, and almost arrogantly so. She danced through the rooms with her prizes and her certificate and waved them in Ottilie's face. 'You have done very badly today,' she cried.

"Ottilie quietly answered, 'This was not the last test.'

" 'But you will always be the last,' the young lady answered and ran off.

"To any other person, Ottilie might have seemed unmoved; but not to me. An inner agitation, against which she fights, always shows in the uneven color of her face: her left cheek flushes for a moment while the right turns pale. I saw this symptom and felt so sorry for her that I talked for a long time with the headmistress alone. We seriously discussed the whole matter, and the kind lady saw that she had made a grave mistake. Without going into details, I shall submit to your Ladyship our final decision and our mutual request that you take Ottilie into your home for a short period. The reasons will gradually become clear to you. If you agree, I shall tell you more about the best way to treat the good child. Your daughter—we expect—will soon leave our school; and then we shall be glad to have Ottilie with us once more.

"One further point which I might forget later. I have never seen Ottilie ask for anything, much less ask for anything urgently. But there are rare occasions when she tries to decline doing something she is asked to do. She does this with a gesture, irresistible to anyone who has caught its meaning. She raises her hands, palms pressed together, and brings them back to her breast, at the same time slightly bending forward and looking into the person's eyes with an expression of such pleading that the asker is glad to give up all he has asked or wished. If you ever see that gesture—which is not likely while she is in your Ladyship's care—remember my words and spare Ottilie."

Eduard finished reading these letters—not without occasional smiles and shaking of the head. They now, naturally, exchanged remarks about the different people involved and the situation as a whole.

"Very well! The long and short of it is that a decision has been made at last; she is coming!" Eduard cried. "You are taken care of, my dear and now *we* can come out with *our* scheme. It is absolutely necessary that I move into the Captain's wing. The late evening and the early morning are the best time for us to work together. You will then have room enough for yourself and Ottilie in the left wing of the house."

Charlotte did not object to this arrangement; and Eduard thereupon outlined his plans for their future way of living. In the course of so doing, he remarked: "It is really very charming of your niece to suffer from a headache on the left side. I myself feel one sometimes on the right side. If it should happen that we suffer at the same time, and sit opposite each other, I leaning on my right elbow, she on her left, our heads resting on our hands as we look in different directions—what a pretty pair of 'companion pictures' we shall make!"

The Captain thought this highly dangerous; but Eduard cried: "Beware of the *D,* my dear fellow! What would become of *B* if *C* should be captivated by *D!*"

"Well, I should think there would be only one possible solution," replied Charlotte.

"You are right. He would return to his *A*—to his Alpha and Omega," exclaimed Eduard, who jumped up and took Charlotte in his arms.

Chapter Six

The carriage which brought Ottilie drove up, and Charlotte went out to meet it. The girl hurried to her and knelt before her, clasping Charlotte's knees.

Charlotte was a little embarrassed, and, trying to raise her she asked—"Why so humble?" "This is not meant as a sign of humility." Ottilie answerd, and remained on her knees. "I love to think of the time when I did not reach much higher than your knee but I was already certain that you loved me."

She rose to her feet, and Charlotte embraced her with affection. She then introduced her to the two men, and all three immediately began to treat her with particular consideration. Beauty is everywhere a very welcome guest. Ottilie listened to their conversation with great attention but did not join in.

The next morning Eduard remarked to Charlotte, "What a charmng and entertaining girl!"

"Entertaining?" Charlotte asked, smiling. "She has not yet once opened her mouth."

"Really?" said Eduard, puzzled. "How strange!"

Charlotte gave the newcomer only a few hints about the management of the household. Ottilie had quickly indeed taken in the whole arrangement with a sort of intuitive grasp. She easily understood what she was to do in general, and what for each person in particular. Everything was done punctually. She knew how to give directions without appearing to give orders. If something had not been done, she did it herself.

As soon as she realized how much leisure she had, she asked Charlotte to allow her to use this spare time for her school work, which she did conscientiously. She worked at her assignments exactly as the tutor had reported to Charlotte. No one interfered, but occasionally Charlotte did resort to indirect suggestions. For instance, she slipped a few worn quill pens among Ottilie's own, to stimulate a bolder sweep to her handwriting; but afer a short time these were always resharpened.

The two women had decided to converse in French when they were alone; Charlotte in particular held firmly to the plan, since Ottilie was much more talkative when she spoke this foreign language—which, incidentally, she had promised her teacher to practice regularly. In French she often said more than she apparently intended; Charlotte particularly enjoyed one occasion when Ottilie unexpectedly gave her an accurate and sympathetic description of the school. Charlotte found her an agreeable companion and hoped one day to see her become a trusted friend. She now looked through Ottilie's earlier school reports again, because she wished to refresh her memory about everything the headmistress or the tutor had said about the girl and to compare it with her own observations of Ottilie's personality. It was Charlotte's conviction that we cannot too quickly become acquainted with the disposition of those with whom we have to live, so that we may know what to expect of them, what we can hope to improve in them, and what we have to understand and tolerate, once and for all.

These comparisons did not reveal anything unexpected; but much that was already known to her now became more significant and obvious. Ottilie's moderate habits of eating and drinking, for instance, really began to worry her.

The most urgent matter which engaged the two women was Ottilie's wardrobe. Charlotte wanted her to dress better and more elegantly. Ottilie, who was never idle, at once began to cut out the materials which had previously been given to her; and quickly and skilfully, with very little help from others, soon made some dresses that fitted her perfectly. These new and fashionable dresses set off her figure in an admirable way. A woman expresses her natural beauty in her clothes; we imagine we see a new and lovelier person whenever she wears a different dress.

So we can well say that more and more, from the very beginning, Ottilie was, for the two men, a joy to behold. Just as the emerald pleases the eye by its superb color, and may even have some healing power for that precious organ of sight, so human beauty, with a much stronger force, acts on our senses and feelings. He who looks at Beauty is proof against the breath of Evil; he is in harmony with himself and the whole world.

Ottilie's arrival had benefited all of them, in many respects. The two men became punctual, even to the minute, when they were to join the ladies; they were rarely late for dinner, or at teatime, or for their walks together. They did not leave the table so hurriedly, particularly in the evening. None of this escaped Charlotte's notice; and from time to time she watched to see whether one might show more inclination to linger than the other, but she detected none. By and large both men had become more sociable. In their conversation, they seemed to consider what would interest Ottilie, and to adjust their discussions to the scope of her intelligence and knowledge. When they were talking or when reading aloud, they stopped when she left the room and waited for her to return. Their conversation became gentler and less reserved.

In response to all this kindness, Ottilie's wish to be helpful increased day by day. As she became familiar with the arrangements in the household, with its members and with their circumstances, she set to work more eagerly, and even learned quickly to guess the meaning of any expression, movement, half-uttered word, or sound. Her silent attentiveness never changed, nor did her quiet activity. Her every movement, sitting down, getting up, going, coming, fetching, carrying, and sitting down again—all was done without the slightest appearance of restlessness; it was merely a constant change, a perpetual pleasant movement. Indeed, they never heard her walk, so light was her step.

Ottilie's agreeable and obliging behavior was a constant pleasure to Charlotte. There was only one thing of which she did not approve; and one day she spoke to the girl frankly about it. "It is very polite and commendable to stoop down immediately when someone drops something and pick it up. With this gesture, as it were, we show that we feel ourselves obliged to that person; but, in society, we must be careful to whom we show such respect. I do not set up any rules for you about women. You are young. To your superiors and to older persons it is a duty; to those of your own age and class, it is politeness; to those who are younger than you are and to your inferiors, it is an act of kindness and helpfulness; but it is not proper for a young girl to be so eager to do such a service for a man."

"I shall try to rid myself of this bad habit," Ottilie replied, "but you will pardon it when I tell you how I came to adopt it. In our history class I was taught many things that I do not remember as well as I should; I did not realize then how useful they could be later on. Only a few incidents impressed me very much—this one, for example:

"When Charles I of England was facing his so-called 'judges,' the gold top of the stick he carried in his hand fell to the ground. Being used to having everyone do everything for him, he looked about, expecting that this time, too, someone would do him this little service. No one made a move; he himself bent down to pick up the fallen object. I thought this action so pitiful—whether rightly I do not know—that from that moment on I could not see anyone drop anything without bending down to pick it up. Because this is probably not always proper and because" she continued with a smile, "I cannot tell my story on every occasion, I shall be more careful in the future."

Meanwhile, all the useful work which the two men had planned went on without interruption. Every day they found fresh reasons for planning and undertaking something new.

One day while they were walking together through the village, they discussed their dissatisfaction with its backwardness, in so far as order and cleanliness were concerned, in comparison to other villages, where lack of space compelled the inhabitants to pay more attention to such matters.

"Do you remember, on our trip through Switzerland, how we wanted to improve a country estate by laying out a village located as this one is; not in the Swiss style, but with the Swiss order and cleanliness so conducive to a healthier way of living?" the Captain asked.

"It could be done here, for example," Eduard replied. "The hill runs down from the castle in a projecting spur, and the village lies opposite, more or less in a semicircle. All the villagers have tried to protect themselves against the brook which separates the two; some have used stones, some piles and some planks, but none of them has helped his neighbors by these expedients; indeed, they all interfere with each other. And the road is very bad; it runs uphill and down, through water and over the boulders. If all the villagers would cooperate, it should not require a great deal of financial help to build a semicircular dam, and raise the road behind it to the level of the houses. The space this would provide ought to promote cleanliness, and such large-scale planning would make all these petty and inadequate measures unnecessary."

"Let's try it," said the Captain, taking in the entire scene at one glance and quickly appraising its possibilities.

"I don't like to deal with townspeople and peasants unless I can actually give orders," Eduard said.

"You may be right," the Captain agreed. "I have had many annoying experiences on that score myself. How difficult it is for some people to weigh sacrifices against possible gains! How hard it is to desire the ends without despising the means! Many people, as a matter of fact, confuse the means with the end and enjoy the one but lose sight of the other. People set in to remedy evils at the point where they appear; nobody pays any attention to their actual source and origin. This is why it is so difficult to give advice and have it heeded, especially by the general run of men, who are quite reasonable in everyday matters but seldom see beyond tomorrow. And if, in a common arrangement, one person will gain and another lose, you never can persuade anybody to come to terms. Only absolute authority can further the common good."

While they stood and talked, a man approached them, to beg—although he looked more insolent than poor. Eduard, who disliked being interrupted and bothered, shouted at him, after several unsuccessful attempts to get rid of him by using a quieter tone. The fellow slouched away, grumbling and even talking back, claiming the rights of beggars to whom one might refuse alms but whom one should not insult, he being under the protection of God and of the authorities as much as any other man. All this upset Eduard greatly.

The Captain, in trying to calm him, said, "Let us take this incident as an occasion to extend our authority to almsgiving, as well. There is no doubt that we must practice charity; but it is better not to give alms personally, particularly not in our own neighborhood. At home we should be as moderate and sensible in our charity as in everything else. A generous gift attracts beggars instead of speeding them on their way. When we travel, we can allow ourselves the passing luxury of playing Fortuna in person, and throwing a surprisingly large gift to some poor man by the roadside. As a matter of fact, the village and the castle are very favorably located for a planned system of charity; it actually occurred to me some time ago. The inn is situated at one end of the village; at the other is the home of an honest old couple; at both places small sums of money should be deposited. Not the person entering the village but the person leaving it will get something; and as these two houses are also on the road leading up to the castle, everyone who intends to go up there can be directed to one place or the other."

"Come, let's settle that immediately," Eduard said. "The details can be arranged later."

They visited the innkeeper and the old couple, and found them agreeable to this plan.

While they walked back up to the castle, Eduard said, "I am perfectly aware that everything in this world depends upon a brilliant idea and a firm determination. You were a good judge of my wife's projects in the park; you also gave me a hint as to how these might be improved. I must confess that I told her about your advice eventually."

"I suspected that you did," the Captain replied, "and I did not approve of it. You have confused her completely; she has stopped all work up there and on this one point stubbornly refuses to talk to us; she has not invited us up to the summer house again, although she goes there herself sometimes with Ottilie."

"We ought not to let this interfere with our plans," Eduard said. "If I am convinced that a desirable idea can and should be carried out, I cannot rest until it is. Haven't we always been clever enough at turning the conversation as we wished? Tonight, for instance, let us get that book describing English parks, and the engravings that go with it. After we have looked at them for a while, we'll turn to your map of our estate. We'll first discuss it all theoretically as if we were just amusing ourselves; serious consideration of the matter will follow quite naturally."

As agreed, they took out the book and looked at the first drawings together: the basic plan of each English district, its geographical character and its original natural state; followed by the changes which cultivation and landscaping had brought about, to employ and improve inherent advantages. The transition to their own property, to their own region, and to the possible improvements they could make was now very easy. It was convenient to spread out the Captain's map as a basis for their discussion; but it was difficult to abandon altogether the plan by which Charlotte had originally begun the work. They devised, however, an easier ascent to the crest of the hill and also planned to build there a kind of lodge at the top of the slope and in front of a pretty little wood. This structure was to have a special relation to the castle, from the windows of which it would be visible, while the lodge itself would offer sweeping views of the castle and the park. The Captain, having planned and measured every detail with great care, now brought up the problem of the road to the village, the dam at the brook, and the raised road behind it. "Building that convenient path to the hilltop," he said, "will produce exactly the quantity of stone required for the dam. As soon as one project links up with another, both become less expensive and can be carried out more quickly."

"And now to my own part in the project," Charlotte said. "We will have to agree upon a definite sum of money; and, as soon as we know how much we will need, we can divide the sum into regular payments, at least monthly, if not, weekly. I have the keys to the cashbox; I shall pay the bills and keep the accounts."

"You evidently do not trust us," Eduard said.

"Not so much in an arbitrary matter," Charlotte replied. "We women know better than you how to keep such things in check."

Everything was settled; the work began at once. The Captain was always about, and Charlotte had daily evidence of the seriousness and firmness of his character. He learned to know her better as well; and it was easy for them to work together and to achieve results.

Work is like dancing: those who keep step become indispensable to each other, and a warm mutual sympathy is bound to result; Charlotte really liked the Captain after she knew him better. Indeed, she calmly allowed him to destroy a particularly lovely spot where a

bench stood, which did not fit into his plans; although she herself
had selected the site and arranged it with taste, she did not even feel
the slightest resentment.

Chapter Seven

Since Charlotte was busily engaged in her work with the Captain, it
was only natural that Eduard looked more frequently to Ottilie for
companionship. He had, in any case, been attracted to her by a quiet
and friendly feeling for some time past. She was helpful and polite to
everyone; but his vanity made him believe that she was more attentive
to him than to others. There was no question that she knew by now
exactly what food he preferred and how it should be prepared; how
much sugar he liked in his tea; many other such trifles did not
escape her attention. She was particularly careful to shut out drafts,
to which he was abnormally sensitive and about which he was often
at odds with his wife, who never had enough fresh air. Ottilie also
had a good knowledge of trees and flowers. She tried to accomplish
whatever he desired; she tried to prevent anything that might try his
patience. Soon she was as indispensable to him as a guardian angel;
and he became restless when she was not present. She seemed more
talkative and openhearted when they were alone together.

Even in maturity, Eduard had about him something of the child to
which Ottilie's youth responded eagerly. They both liked to talk
about the days when they had first seen each other; these memories
went back to the first beginnings of Eduard's love for Charlotte.
Ottilie said that she remembered them as the handsomest couple at
court; and, when Eduard expressed a doubt that her memory of her
earliest childhood could be so clear, she insisted that she remembered perfectly one particular moment, when he had come into the
room and she had hidden her face in Charlotte's lap—not from fear
but from childish surprise. She might have added that it was because
she had immediately liked him so much.

These conditions had brought to a standstill many things which
the two men had been accustomed to do together, and it became
again necessary for them to look into matters again, to make some
drafts and write letters. To attend to this business, they met at their
office, where they found the old clerk in involuntary idleness. They

set to work and soon had work for him, without realizing that they now left to him many things which they had once done themselves. The first draft which the Captain attempted was not successful; and it was the same with Eduard's first letter. They fretted for a while over a new idea and a new draft, until Eduard, who was not getting on at all, asked what time it was. The Captain had, evidently for the first time in many years, forgotten to wind his chronometer; and both friends seemed at least to feel, if not to realize, that they had begun to be indifferent to time.

While the two men had more or less relaxed in their work, the women's activity increased considerably. The life of an ordinary family revolving as it does around a given group of people and their pursuits, can generally, like a vessel, hold an unusual attachment or a growing passion; and a considerable period of time may pass before this new ingredient causes a noticeable fermentation and all runs foaming over the rim.

In the case of our friends, the effects of their growing mutual sympathies were most agreeable. Their hearts opened, and a feeling of kindliness sprang up. Each member of the group was happy and did not begrudge happiness to the others.

Such a situation lifts up the soul and expands the heart; and everything one does and undertakes faces toward the Infinite. Consequently, the friends were no longer inclined to stay much at home; and they extended their walks farther and farther. Eduard would hurry ahead with Ottilie, to lead the way and find new paths, while the Captain slowly followed with Charlotte, in serious conversation, frequently enjoying a newly discovered spot or some unexpected vista.

One day their walk led them from the gate at the right wing of the castle down to the village inn, then across the bridge toward the ponds. They walked along their shores as far as they usually followed the water; farther along, it was not possible to walk by the water's edge, because of the thickly wooded hills and, beyond them, impassable rocks. But Eduard, who had often gone hunting in this region, pushed on with Ottilie, along a grass-grown footpath, knowing well that an old water-mill, hidden between the rocks, could not be far distant. The little-used path soon came to an end, and they found themselves lost in the dense thicket, among the moss-grown boulders. But the churning sound of the mill wheel indicated that the place they were seeking was quite close at hand. They stepped out onto a projecting ledge and saw the quaint, old, black wooden building deep down below them, shaded on all sides by steep rocks and tall trees. Impulsively they decided to climb down over the moss and boulders. Eduard led the way, and when he looked back and saw Ottilie above him, stepping lightly—fearless, confident, and perfectly poised as she followed him from rock to rock—he thought he saw a celestial being hovering above him. When, at a difficult place, she grasped his outstretched hand, or even supported herself on his shoulder, he had to admit that she was most exquisitely feminine. He half wished that she might slip or stumble, so that he could catch her in his arms and press her to his heart. But for more than one reason he would not have done this under any circumstance; he would have been afraid to offend or hurt her.

His reason for this will soon be understood. Arriving at the mill, they sat down at a rustic table under the tall trees. They had sent the miller's wife for a glass of milk, and after the miller had welcomed them, they asked him to go and look for Charlotte and the Captain. Then Eduard began to speak, rather hesitantly: "I must ask you something, Ottilie; forgive me even if you should have to refuse my request. You have made it no secret—and why should you?—that you wear a miniature next to your heart. It is a portrait of your father, an excellent man whom you scarcely knew, and who deserves in every sense a place close to your heart, but forgive me if I suggest that the picture is much too large and awkward; the metal frame with its crystal gives me anxious moments whenever I see you lifting a child or carrying something in your arms; when the carriage sways, when we force our way through tangles of underbrush; or when we climb down the rocks, as we did just now. The possibility that some fall, or accident or other, might prove serious terrifies me. For my sake, remove the miniature from your person—not from your affection, not from your room. Treasure it in your heart; give it the place of honor, I beg of you; display it in your room—only do not wear it so close to your breast. Perhaps my anxiety is exaggerated, but I think it dangerous."

Ottilie sat silent and motionless while Eduard was speaking. Then, without haste, but also without hesitation, turning her eyes more toward Heaven than toward Eduard, she unclasped the chain, removed the miniature, pressed it against her forehead, and handed it to her friend with the words, "Do keep it for me until we reach home. I cannot give you a better proof of my gratitude for your kind concern."

Eduard did not dare to raise the picture to his lips; but he took her hand and pressed it to his eyes. They were the two most beautiful hands that had ever joined. He felt a weight lifted from his mind, as if a wall between Ottilie and himself had fallen.

With the miller as their guide, Charlotte and the Captain came down by an easier road. There was a general welcome and exchange of pleasantries; they, too, sat down and took some refreshment. No one wished to return the way they had come; and Eduard proposed to lead them by a path through the rocks, on the other side of the brook, where they could see the ponds again. The walking was not easy at first; they went through woods and thickets, and saw, down in the countryside, a great number of villages, large and small; dairy farms surrounded by green pastures and fertile fields; and, higher up, a farm snugly nestled in the woods. From the height which they had gradually ascended, they had a fine view in all directions of this rich terrain. Here they entered a pretty grove and, on leaving it, found themselves on the rock opposite the castle.

How delighted they were to have arrived there so unexpectedly! They had made a journey round a little world; they now stood on the site planned for the new building and looked once more at the windows of the castle.

They went down to the summer house, and, for the first time, all four of them sat down together in it. Nothing was more natural than for them all to express the wish that the rather difficult path they had followed today, should be laid out so that they could take a leisurely stroll along it with friends and guests. Each offered suggestions; and they estimated that the road which had taken them several hours to walk, could, if well constructed, bring them in no more than an hour from the castle and back again. But when they began to make plans for a bridge below the mill, where the brook ran into the ponds—a bridge which would shorten the walk and be an added ornament to the landscape—Charlotte gently stopped their inventive imaginings, reminding them of the expense involved in such an undertaking.

"That need not worry us!" Eduard exclaimed. "That pleasant little farm in the woods brings in very little rent; let's sell it and use the money for this project. The interest of well-invested capital will then add to the enjoyment of our delightful walks. As it is now, when we settle our accounts at the end of the year, the pitifully small income from that farm merely annoys us."

Even Charlotte, who was a thrifty housewife, could not say much against this plan. The whole matter of selling the farm had already been discussed. The Captain was for parceling out the land among the peasants of the forest; but Eduard wanted a shorter and simpler transaction. The present tenant, who already had made a first bid for the farm, should have it and pay for it in installments; and gradually, as the money came in, they would carry out the planned construction, step by step.

Such a reasonable and prudent arrangement was approved by all. In their imagination the friends saw the new paths winding along and all the charming retreats and lovely views they were hoping for.

In order to bring everything vividly to their minds in complete detail, they spread out the new map again that evening. Now once more they could follow with their eyes the road they had taken; and they wondered whether it could not be improved by relocating it here and there. All previous projects were again discussed and brought into line with their latest schemes. The site of the new building opposite the castle was again approved; and they decided that the circuit of paths leading up to it should end there.

Ottilie had not said one word the whole time, so that Eduard at last moved the map, which had been spread out before Charlotte, over to her, at the same time inviting her to give her opinion. When she still hesitated, he warmly encouraged her to speak out. "Nothing has been settled yet," he said. "We are still just making plans."

"I would build the lodge here," said Ottilie, indicating the highest level of the hill. "It is true that you cannot see the castle from there, since it is hidden by a little grove, but, to make up for that, you will be, as it were, in another and a new world, because the village with all its houses is also hidden. The view of the ponds, the mill, the hills and the mountains, and the country below is extremely beautiful; I noticed it as we came along."

"She is right!" exclaimed Eduard. "How could we have overlooked it! This is what you mean, isn't it, Ottilie?" he said. He took a pencil, and with bold strokes, drew an oblong on the crest of the hill.

It broke the Captain's heart to see his carefully and neatly drawn map defaced in this way; but, after a slight disapproving remark, he controlled himself and took up Ottilie's suggestion. "Ottilie is right," he said. "Don't we enjoy a long carriage ride just to get a cup of coffee or walk a long distance to eat fish which would not have tasted half so well at home? It is a change we seek—and unfamiliar things. Your ancestors exercised good judgment in building the castle on this site; here it is protected against the winds, and everything you need is close at hand. A building designed more for entertainment and recreation than as a residence, however, will be very appropriate on the height and will permit us to spend most agreeable hours there in summertime."

The more they discussed the plan, the better it seemed; and Eduard could not conceal his triumph that it had been Ottilie's idea. He was as proud as though it had been his own.

Chapter Eight

Early the next morning the Captain went up to examine the place they had chosen. He first made a rough sketch and, after all of them had confirmed their decision on the site, he completed a plan, with an estimate of costs and requirements. They began preparations immediately. Negotiations leading to the sale of the farm were taken up again. Both men found renewed energy for their activities.

The Captain reminded Eduard that it would be a courtesy—almost an obligation—to celebrate Charlotte's birthday with the laying of the cornerstone. It was not too difficult to overcome Eduard's former antipathy against such celebrations, for it suddenly occurred to him that then they could celebrate Ottilie's birthday, which came later, as well.

Charlotte took the whole project and everything it involved very seriously indeed, for she thought it important and almost hazardous; she was always busy with estimates, contracts, and payments. The friends saw less of each other during the day, and looked forward with much greater eagerness to their evening meetings.

Meanwhile Ottilie had become almost absolute mistress of the household. With her quiet and reliable ways, how could it have been otherwise! She was, moreover, by nature inclined rather toward the house and domestic affairs than toward social and outdoor life. Eduard soon noticed that she accompanied them on their walks only to be agreeable and that she stayed outdoors longer in the evening only because she thought it the proper thing to do; she sometimes even tried to find an excuse to go inside again because of some household task. He soon succeeded in arranging their excursions together so that they were home before sunset. He also resumed his former habit of reading poems aloud, preferring those which expressed a pure yet passionate love.

In the evening they usually gathered around a small table in their customary places: Charlotte on the sofa, Ottilie opposite her in a chair, the men completing the circle. Ottilie sat at the right of Eduard, who moved the lamp closer to her when he was reading. Then Ottilie would move a little closer to him and look into his book because she trusted her own eyes more than the lips of another; and Eduard would also move closer, so she could see more easily. He even paused frequently, longer than was necessary, in order not to turn the page before she had finished reading it.

This did not escape Charlotte and the Captain; and they often exchanged a smile over it; but both were really surprised by still another indication which, once, betrayed Ottilie's secret affection.

On one occasion, when boring visitors had spoiled the better part of an evening, Eduard suggested that they not retire quite yet. He felt in the mood to play his flute, which he had long neglected. Charlotte looked for the sonatas they usually played together; when she could not find them, Ottilie, after some hesitation, confessed that she had taken them to her room.

"Then you *can*—you *will*—accompany me at the piano?" cried Eduard, his eyes shining. "I think I can," Ottilie replied. She brought the music and sat down at the piano. Charlotte and the Captain were attentive and were surprised to note how perfectly Ottilie had learned her part but, still more, how well she adapted her accompaniment to Eduard's playing. "Adapt" is not quite the right word in this case. With Charlotte, everything had depended on her skill and her own free will to slow down in one part and accelerate the tempo in another, sometimes hesitating, sometimes racing ahead, to please her husband; but Ottilie, who had heard the couple play the sonata several times, seemed to have studied it entirely from the viewpoint of Eduard's rendition. She had made his shortcomings so much her own that they played in unison; although the tempo was quite wrong, the performance still sounded extremely harmonious and pleasant. The composer himself would have enjoyed hearing his work altered in such a mistaken but sincere way.

Charlotte and the Captain silently observed this strange and unprecedented performance with the emotion we often experience when we watch childish behavior we cannot approve because of its disquieting consequences, but which we cannot condemn, and sometimes even must envy. For between these two, as between Ottilie and Eduard, there was growing a tender affection which was perhaps even more dangerous since they were both more serious. more self-possessed, and more capable of controlling themselves. The Captain had already begun to feel that a strong attachment threatened to draw him irresistibly to Charlotte. He forced himself to avoid her and did not visit the new grounds at the hours she was accustomed to be there. He got up very early, gave his orders, and then retired to work in his wing of the castle. At first Charlotte thought this absence accidental and looked for him in all the places he might possibly be. But later she thought she understood his reasons, and her respect for him increased.

Although the Captain avoided being alone with Charlotte, he was no less eager to push forward the work on the paths, so that all would be ready for the grand celebration of her birthday. When he was constructing the path along the more gentle slope at the bottom, coming up from the rear of the village, he also had a crew of men building the upper part, while he pretended they were merely breaking stones; and he had arranged and timed everything so exactly that the two pathways would be joined on the eve of the birthday. The foundation for the new house on the hill had been started but not completed; and a fine cornerstone had been hewn out, with hollow spaces and a slab to cover them.

These overt activities and many small, covert schemes, as well as more or less repressed emotions, did not make for a very lively conversation when the four were together; so that Eduard, who felt that something was lacking, asked the Captain one evening to bring his violin and play while Charlotte accompanied him at the piano, to which the Captain readily agreed. To the great pleasure of themselves and their listeners, he and Charlotte played a difficult work with feeling, gusto, and ease. They promised to play together more often and to practice.

"They play better than we do, Ottilie!" Eduard said. "We will admire them; but we can have a good time, too!"

Chapter Nine

The birthday arrived, and everything was ready. The whole length of the built-up road was now safe from the waters of the brook behind its dam, as was the road past the church, which followed for a time the path Charlotte had laid out, and then, winding through the rocks, ran first below the summer house to the right and later, after curving upward, overlooked it to the left and gradually reached the crest of the hill.

Many guests had arrived for this festive day. Everyone went first to church, where the whole congregation was waiting, dressed in holiday best. After the service, all of them formed a procession, headed by the smaller boys, the young men, and the older men; then came the master and mistress of the castle with their guests and servants, with the little girls, maidens and married women following at the end.

Where the road rounded the curve, the Captain had arranged a seat in the rocks; and he asked Charlotte and her guests to stop here and rest. From this point they could see the whole length of the road, the group of men who walked ahead, and the women who were now passing. The weather was lovely; the entire picture very impressive. Charlotte was surprised and moved; she pressed the Captain's hand affectionately.

They and their guests followed the slowly ascending crowd which was forming a circle around the site of the new building. Eduard, his family and friends, and the most distinguished of the guests were invited to step down into the excavated space where the cornerstone, propped up on one side, lay ready. A mason, in holiday attire, his trowel in one hand, his hammer in the other, made a handsome speech in well-turned verse, which can only be inadequately rendered here in prose.

"Three things are very important in building a house," he began; "first, that it stand in the right place; second, that it be well founded; and, third, that it be well built. The first requirement is really the responsibility of the man who has the house built. Just as in the city the ruler and the community alone can decide where a house shall stand, so it is the privilege of the lord of the manor to say: Here I want my house and nowhere else!"

Eduard and Ottilie did not dare to exchange a glance, although they stood exactly opposite each other.

"The third requirement, the building of the house, is the concern of many crafts and trades; nearly all of them share in the work. But the second requirement, the laying of the foundation, is the mason's affair and, to speak quite frankly, the most important part of the whole undertaking. It is a serious matter, and our invitation to you is solemn, because this festive act takes place in the depths of the earth. Here, in this narrow space we have dug, you do us the honor of appearing as witness to an act of mystery. Soon we shall lower this well-hewn stone; and shortly this excavation, now adorned by lovely and distinguished guests, will no longer be accessible; it will be filled in.

"This stone, its corner a symbol of the right angle of the corner of the building, its rectangular shape a symbol of its regularity, and its horizontal and perpendicular position a symbol of the right angles of all the walls and partitions—this cornerstone might now be laid as it is without delay, since its own weight will keep it in place. Nevertheless, we shall use mortar to cement it; just as human beings, drawn to each other by natural inclinations, are better joined when the law binds them, stones, too, even though they are already shaped to fit, are better joined by a binding force. But since it is not becoming to be idle among busy people, you will surely not refuse to assist us here in our work."

With these words he gave his trowel to Charlotte, who threw mortar beneath the stone. Several others were invited to do likewise; and then the stone was put into place. After this Charlotte and the others in turn took the hammer and, with three taps, blessed the union of the stone with the earth.

"The work of the mason," the orator continued, "done openly

here, is almost always carried on in obscurity and is destined to remain in obscurity. The carefully constructed foundations will be covered when the ground around them is leveled, and nobody will be reminded of us not even by the testimony of the walls we build above ground. The work of the stone-cutter and the stone-carver is more conspicious; and we masons are even expected to approve that the plasterer completely effaces our handiwork with stucco and paint. Is it not important for the mason, therefore, even more than for other workmen, to turn out work that satisfies himself? Who has more reason to feel his own worth? After the house is built, the floors leveled and tiled, the outer walls adorned with ornaments, he can still discern, beneath all this later work the carefully and accurately joined stones of his masonry, to which the whole building owes its existence and support.

"But just as the man who has done an evil deed must live in fear lest it come to light some day, so the man who has done good in secret may expect to be rewarded openly. And by the same token, we declare this cornerstone to be a memorial stone as well. Here in these pockets of varying sizes hollowed out of the stone, objects will be preserved to bear witness of this act to later generations. These sealed metal cases contain handwritten documents; on these metal plates sundry memorable legends are graven; in these fine bottles we immure the choicest old wine with the date of its vintage; here also are coins of many kinds, minted this year; and all these are contributed by the generous master whose house we build. There is still room left; do some of the guests or spectators care to dedicate something to posterity?"

There was a pause, and the young orator looked around; but, as is so often the case on such occasions, no one was prepared, and everyone was taken by surprise. After a bit a jaunty young officer said, "If I am to contribute anything that is not as yet represented among these memorial objects, it will have to be a button or two from my uniform, and I believe these deserve to be handed down to posterity!" This was no sooner said than done. Soon others began to contribute. The women did not hesitate to drop in sidecombs, scent-bottles and other trinkets and jewelry. Only Ottilie still hesitated; she was preoccupied with watching the others until Eduard roused her. Then she unclasped from her neck the gold chain on which she had carried her father's picture and laid it down gently with the other jewelry; whereupon Eduard hastily ordered the cover to be placed on the cornerstone and sealed.

The young mason who had taken an active part in this procedure, resumed the rostrum and continued: "We lay this stone for eternity, as an earnest of a long happy life for the present and future owners of this house.

"But in committing these treasures to the earth so carefully, we emphasize the frailty of human existence! We are thinking that this tightly sealed cover may again be lifted, which could happen only if the whole house, as yet unbuilt, were destroyed.

"But just for that reason—because we are confident that it will be built—let us turn our thoughts from the future back to the present. After this celebration, let us resume our work at once, making ready for the other trades which will build on top of our foundations; so that the house will rise quickly to its completion, and the master of this house, his family and his guests may enjoy the view from windows yet to be provided. And now let us drink to their health and to that of all who are present!" With these words he emptied a fine crystal goblet at one draught and flung it into the air, wishing to express the fullness of his joy by breaking the glass used on this happy occasion. But this time fate would have it otherwise; the glass did not crash to the ground, though it was no miracle that saved it from destruction.

To speed the construction of the building, the opposite corner of the foundation had already been completely excavated; here the walls had been started and scaffolding built.

For today's ceremony boards had been laid across the scaffolding for a number of spectators to stand on; but mainly to accommodate the workmen. The glass flew in that direction and was caught by one of the men, who took this as an especially lucky sign for himself. He kept the glass in his own hands, but he let the bystanders look at it; and all could see the letters *E* and *O* worked into a graceful monogram; it was one of the glasses which had been made for Eduard as a child.

The workmen had now left the scaffolding, and the more agile guests climbed up to look about; they expressed themselves enthusiastically about the view. How true it is that we can discover so many new things from a point of vantage only a very little higher than the one we have been accustomed to. Deep in the countryside, several new villages came into view; one could also follow the silvery bends of the river; someone even insisted that he could see the spires of the city. On turning round, one saw, behind the wooded hills, the blue summits of a distant range of mountains rising into the sky; and the whole country immediately below could be taken in at a glance. "To make the view perfect, the three ponds should be made into one lake!" one of the guests exclaimed.

"That could well be done," the Captain said. "In earlier times they actually were one lake."

"But I should like to have you spare my grove of plane and poplar trees, which are so beautiful standing there by the middle pond," said Eduard. He turned to Ottilie, led her a few steps forward, and pointed downward. "Look; it was I who planted those trees."

"And how long ago was that?" asked Ottilie.

"They are just about your age," Eduard replied. "Yes, my dear child, I planted them when you were still a babe in arms."

The party returned to the castle. After dinner, they were invited for a walk through the village, to look at the new work that had been carried out there. At a suggestion from the Captain, the villagers had gathered in front of their houses. They did not stand in a row as if at attention but rather in natural family groups; some busy with work they usually did in the evening, others resting on the new benches. They had been urged to consider it a pleasant duty to appear at their best on Sundays and holidays, with a special emphasis on order and good behavior.

A congenial atmosphere, such as prevailed among these four friends, is always unpleasantly disturbed by the intrusion of a large number of people. They were much relieved to find themselves alone once more in the big hall. But their regained privacy was soon interrupted when a letter was delivered to Eduard, with the news that yet other guests would arrive on the following day.

"Just as we thought!" Eduard called to Charlotte. "The Count won't stay away; he is coming tomorrow."

"Then the Baroness is not too far away," Charlotte replied.

"You are right!" said Eduard. "She will also arrive tomorrow, from the other direction. Both ask us to put them up for a night, as they will leave together the following day!"

"Then we must begin preparations at once, Ottilie," Charlotte said.

"How do you want me to arrange things?", asked Ottilie.

Charlotte gave her some general directions, and Ottilie left the room.

The Captain inquired about the relationship of these two persons whom he knew only casually. Many years ago, these two had fallen madly in love with each other, although both were already married. The wrecking of two marriages had nearly led to a scandal. They resorted to divorce. The Baroness succeeded, but not so the Count. For the sake of appearance, they could not be seen together, but their relationship remained unchanged. Unable to be together in the city during the winter season, they made up for this in the summer, traveling together and visiting the same watering places. They were both a little older than Eduard and Charlotte, with whom they had become close friends at Court years ago. Eduard and Charlotte had remained loyal to the Count and the Baroness, although they did not approve of everything they did. This was the first time that Charlotte had found their visit particularly inconvenient; and if she had examined her reasons closely, she would have discovered that it was on account of Ottilie. She did not want the young girl to be exposed to this sort of informal relationship so early in life.

"They really might have stayed away a few days longer, until we had finished the business about the farm," Eduard said, just as Ottilie returned. "The draft of the deed of sale is ready, and I have one copy of it here; but the second is not yet done, and our old clerk is seriously ill." The Captain offered his assistance, and so did Charlotte, but there were objections to their helping.

"Please, let me do it!" cried Ottilie, eagerly.

"You will not be able to finish it in time," Charlotte said.

"I absolutely must have it early the day after tomorrow; and it is a long document," Eduard added.

"It *will* be ready!" Ottilie exclaimed and took the paper.

The next morning while they watched from an upstairs window for their guests, so that they would be on hand to greet them, Eduard said: "Who is that man on horseback riding so slowly up the road in our direction?" The Captain described him in some detail. "Yes, that is he," Eduard said; "the details which you can see better than I, correspond to what I can make out. It is Mittler! But why is Mittler, of all people, riding slowly, so slowly?" The rider came nearer, and indeed it was Mittler. They welcomed him cordially as he came slowly up the steps to the entrance.

"Why didn't you come yesterday?" Eduard called down to him.

"Noisy parties are not to my liking," Mittler replied. "Instead I have come now to celebrate yesterday's birthday quietly with you."

"Are you sure you can spare the time?" asked Eduard, laughing.

"For my visit you are indebted—if you consider yourselves indebted at all—to a thought that crossed my mind yesterday. I was happily spending several hours in a home where I had restored peace and happiness, when I heard of your birthday celebration. It is downright selfish, I said to myself, for you to insist on enjoying yourself only with people you have persuaded to live in concord. Why don't you go and enjoy yourself, for once, with friends who live peaceably and go on living peaceably? No sooner said than done! I made up my mind, and here I am!"

"Yesterday you would have found a large gathering here; today you will only find a small one," Charlotte said. "We are expecting the Count and the Baroness, who have already given you a great deal of trouble."

At these words the crotchety little man darted out of the circle of his welcoming friends, and looked for his hat and riding crop. "My unlucky star always rises whenever I try to relax and enjoy myself. Why don't I stick to my business? I never should have come here; and I certainly can't stay, for I shall never abide under the same roof with those two! And I warn you all—be careful! They bring nothing but trouble; their nature acts like a ferment that corrupts and contaminates everything it touches."

They tried to calm him, but without success. "He who attacks marriage," he exclaimed, "who undermines by word or by action this foundation of all moral society, is my enemy wherever I find him; and if I cannot defeat him, at least I shall have nothing to do with him. Marriage is the Alpha and Omega of all civilizaton. It makes the savage gentle; and the gentility of the most civilized finds its highest expression in marriage. It must be indissoluble because it brings with it such an abundance of happiness, that the occasional moments of unhappiness scarcely weigh in the balance. And why all this talk about unhappiness? It is the impatience that grips men from time to time which makes them indulge in a feeling of unhappiness. If you let time cure your impatience you will rejoice at finding this longstanding relationship still intact. There is no plausible reason for divorce. Life is brimming over with pleasure and pain; no married couple can calculate their debt to each other. It is an infinite debt and can only be paid in eternity. Marriage is a burden; I can well believe that, and so it should be. Are we not also married to our consciences; and do we not often wish to rid ourselves of them, because they are even more of a burden, than a husband or a wife could ever be?"

He continued to speak with great vehemence and would not have stopped had not the sound of the postilions' horn announced the arrival of the visitors, who, as if by previous arrangement, drove at the same moment into the castle yard from different directons. When their hosts hurried down to receive them, Mittler slipped away, ordered his horse brought to the inn, and left in a very black mood.

Chapter Ten

The guests were welcomed and escorted into the house. They were delighted to be back once more after so long a time in a place where they formerly had spent so many happy days. Eduard and Charlotte, too, were very glad to see them again. The Count as well as the Baroness had that sort of tall and handsome presence which is at its best not so much in youth as in middle life, when, as a compensation for youth's fresh energy, attractiveness is coupled with the ability to inspire confidence. They were very agreeable guests. Their easy way of accepting and shaping the events of their lives, their continued good spirits and evident freedom from any embarrassment, were immediately infectious; and with scrupulous good taste they never overstepped the bounds of decorum while they never seemed to feel the least constraint.

The effect on everyone could be immediately observed. The new arrivals, fresh from the great world, as their dress, their belongings, and everything about them showed, somehow contrasted with their friends' rural life and their hidden emotional state, a contrast which, however, faded in the exchange of old memories and new interests; and they all joined at once in an animated conversation.

But it was not long before they separated. The ladies retired to their own wing, where they found enough to keep them occupied: mutual confidences and the latest styles and patterns in morning robes and hats and such; while the men were busy looking at the new coaches, having the horses trotted out, and beginning at once to bargain and trade.

They did not meet again until dinner. Everyone had dressed, and again the newcomers showed to advantage. Everything they wore was new and rather unusual to their friends, but their way of wearing it made it natural and very becoming.

The conversation was lively and touched on a great variety of topics, for everything and nothing seems interesting in the company of such people. They all spoke French, so they could speak freely in front of the servants; with ease and a touch of malice they discussed great issues and issues not so great. The conversation had dealt with one particular subject for an undesirably long time, when Charlotte inquired about a childhood friend, and heard, with amazement, that she would soon get her divorce.

"It is distressing," Charlotte said, "suddenly to hear of misfortunes which have befallen acquaintances we thought comfortably settled, or that a dear friend we thought provided for is in difficulties and is forced to begin a new life—perhaps an insecure one."

"After all, my dear, it is our own fault if that sort of thing surprises us," the Count replied. "We rather indulge ourselves in imagining that human institutions, and particularly the institution of marriage, are extremely stable. The comedies which we see so often are misleading; they tempt our imagination away from the realities of the world. In a comedy we see marriage as an ultimate goal, reached only after surmounting obstacles which fill several acts; and, at the moment when this goal is achieved, the curtain falls and a momentary satisfaction warms our hearts. But it is quite different in life. The play goes on behind the scenes, and, when the curtain rises again, we would rather not see or hear any more of it."

"It cannot be as bad as that," said Charlotte, smiling. "We often see that people who have made their exit from this stage would very much like to reappear in a new role."

"There is nothing wrong with that," said the Count. "We always like to play a new part, and, knowing the world, we know that the difficulty, in a world which is ever changing, merely arises from the unchanging and unending character of marriage. One of my friends who generally shows his good humor by suggesting new laws, maintained that every marrige should be contracted only for five years. It is, he said, a fine, odd, and sacred number and a period just long enough in which to get to know each other, have a child or two, quarrel, and—the best part!—become reconciled again. He used to exclaim: How happy the first part of that period would be! Two or three years at least would be sheer bliss! After that, one of the partners would probably want to prolong the relationship, and the nearer the end of the five years came, the more amiable he or she would grow. The indifferent or even dissatisfied partner would gradually be reconciled and charmed, and both of them would forget that time was swiftly running out—just as we forget the passage of time in good company—and it would be a pleasant surprise when they realized, only after the term had expired, that they had tacitly extended it."

Charming and amusing as all this sounded—and it had a deeper moral significance which did not escape Charlotte—she was uneasy about the conversation because of Ottilie's presence. She was very well aware that nothing is more dangerous than too candid a discussion of an improper, or at least questionable, situation as though it were not at all unusual, taken for granted, and even praiseworthy; any attack on marriage certainly belonged in that category. In her tactful way she tried to turn the conversation to other subjects; but she was unsuccessful and was sorry now that Ottilie had arranged everything so well that there was no reason for her to leave the table. The quiet and observant girl gave her orders to the butler by a look and a nod; and everything went smoothly and without incident, although there were two new men in servants' livery who were still clumsy at waiting on table.

The Count did not understand Charlotte's covert suggestions and continued to express himself on the same subject. His conversation was not usually tiresome, but the whole matter weighed heavily on his mind; and his difficulties in obtaining a divorce from his wife had made him bitter about everything connected with marriage, even though, after all, he desired just that so passionately for himself and the Baroness.

"The same friend," he went on, "made another legal suggestion. A marriage should be declared indissoluble only if both parties, or at least one of them, had been married twice before, for such persons have conclusively demonstrated that they regard marriage as indispensable. Furthermore, their behavior in their previous marriages would be known, and so would their peculiarities, which actually cause more divorces than do bad dispositions. It is therefore necessary to make mutual investigation and to observe married as well as unmarried people closely, for no one knows how a marriage may turn out."

"That would, of course, make social life more interesting," said Eduard. "As it is now, as soon as we are married, nobody cares any longer about our virtues or our vices."

"Under such an arrangement," the Baroness said with a smile, "Our dear hosts, who already have passed the first two stages successfully, could be making their preparations for a third."

"They have been very lucky," said the Count. "In their case, death was willing to do what the law courts do only reluctantly."

"Let the dead rest!" said Charlotte, rather gravely.

"Why should we," the Count asked, "when we can speak of them with admiration? They were modest enough to be satisfied with a few years, in return for all the good they left behind."

"If only," said the Baroness, suppressing a sigh, "such cases did not require the sacrifice of our best years."

"Quite," the Count agreed. "It would be enough to drive one mad if it were not for the fact that, as a rule, very few things in life turn out as we hoped they might. Children do not fulfil expectations, and young people rarely do—and, if they do fulfil their early promise, the world does not keep its promises to them."

Charlotte, glad that the conversation had at last changed, replied gaily: "Well, after all, we have to get used to enjoying the good things of life as they come."

"Certainly," the Count again agreed. "You two have enjoyed some wonderful years. When I think of the time when you and Eduard were the most handsome couple at Court—nowadays there is nothing to compare with that brilliant time and those distinguished personalities. When you two danced together, all eyes followed you and paid you homage while you only saw each other!"

"So much has changed since then," Charlotte said, "that we can listen to such flattering words in all modesty."

"I admit that I was often privately inclined to blame Eduard for his lack of persistence," the Count continued, "for his unreasonable parents would probably have finally relented; and it is no small matter to regain ten years of one's youth."

"I must defend Eduard," interposed the Baroness. "Charlotte was not completely blameless, nor above occasional coquetry. Although she loved Eduard with all her heart and secretly thought of him as her future husband, I saw how often she worried the life out of him, so that he was easily rushed into an unfortunate decision to travel, to get away from her, to try to forget her."

Eduard nodded to the Baroness and seemed grateful for her defense.

"But I must say something in Charlotte's defense, too," the Baroness went on. "The man who was paying court to her then had long displayed his affection for her and when you knew him well, he was far more lovable than the rest of you want to admit."

"My dear," said the Count with a touch of spirit, "you should also confess that he was not wholly indifferent to you and that Charlotte had more to fear from you than from any other woman. I think it a very charming quality in women that they can be so steadfastly attached to one man and that no sort of separation suspends or banishes such an attachment."

"This charming quality may be even more frequent in men," the Baroness retorted. "In your case, at least, my dear, I have noticed that no one has more influence over you than a woman of whom you once were fond. I have seen you go to more trouble to oblige such a person than you ever would for your present friend."

"I take a reproach like that as a compliment," the Count replied. "And as for Charlotte's first husband—I disliked him simply because he separated two fine persons—a really predestined couple who, once they were married, would have had no reason to be afraid of those five years or to think of a second marriage, much less a third."

"We shall try to make up for what we missed," Charlotte said.

"Then you must stick to it," warned the Count. "Your first marriages were of the kind which is really the most objectionable," he continued, almost passionately. "Unfortunately, most marriages have something awkward about them, if you will forgive my putting it so strongly; they spoil the most delicate relationships, merely because of the gross assurance which at least one of the partners will exhibit. Everything becomes a matter of course; and two people seem to have come together only so that both can then go their own ways."

At this moment Charlotte, who was determined to stop this sort of talk once and for all, managed to change the subject completely.

They began a conversation about matters of general interest in which Eduard, Charlotte, and the Captain could join; and even Ottilie was asked for her opinion. They were in an excellent humor when dessert arrived, and the gaiety was greatly stimulated by the table decorations: a profusion of fruit in pretty baskets, and handsome bowls and vases filled with beautifully arranged flowers of all colors.

The changes in the park were also discussed, and, after dinner, they went out to look at them. Ottilie did not come with them; she said she had something to do in the house; but actually she sat down to go on with her copying. The Count fell into conversation with the Captain, and Charlotte later joined them. When they had reached the top of the hill, and the Captain had obligingly hurried back to fetch his map, the Count said to Charlotte, "I like this man very well indeed. He is well informed and has a logical mind. His work, also, seems to be well planned and systematic. Accomplishments of the sort he has achieved here would be very important in a larger field of action." Charlotte listened with secret delight to the Count's praise; she did not betray her feelings but merely agreed calmly and without elaboration. She was, however, completely taken aback when the Count continued: "I have met this man at just the right time. I know of a position which will suit him perfectly and make him happy. At the same time I can do one of my friends, a person of high rank, a great favor."

Charlotte was thunderstruck. The Count did not notice it, for women, used to controlling themselves at all times, maintain an apparent composure even in the most extraordinary circumstances. But she did not hear the Count's next remarks. "When I make up my mind about something, I always act quickly. My letter is already composed in my mind, and I am anxious to write it down. Please order me a mounted courier—I want to send the letter off tonight."

Charlotte's heart was torn by conflicting emotions. She was so overwhelmed by the Count's proposal and by her own reaction to it that she was unable to utter a single word. Fortunately, the Count went on talking about his plans for the Captain; and Charlotte saw their advantages only too clearly. Just then the Captain returned and unrolled his map before the Count. How different were her feelings as she looked at the friend she was soon to lose! She bowed slightly, turned, and hurried back to the summer house. Before she was halfway there a stream of tears gushed from her eyes; she rushed into the little hermitage and, sheltered by its four narrow walls, completely surrendered to a grief, a passion, a despair, which she would not have dreamed possible a few moments before.

Meanwhile Eduard had walked along the shores of the ponds with the Baroness. That astute lady, who evidently liked to know all about everything, soon noticed, when she put out her feelers, that Eduard could not stop singing Ottilie's praises. She drew him out gradually with apparently casual questions, and finally was quite convinced that this was no budding passion, but one already full-blown.

Married women, even though they may not like each other, are always tacit allies, particularly against young girls. Her worldly mind quickly foresaw the consequences of such an attachment as Eduard's. That very morning, in a conversation with Charlotte, she had expressed her disapproval of Ottilie's sojourn in the country, particularly because of the girl's quiet disposition. The Baroness had proposed taking Ottilie with her to the city; she had a friend there who spared no expense in the education of her daughter—an only child—and who was very eager to find a congenial companion for her, who would be treated like one of the family and enjoy the same advantages as her own child. Charlotte had promised to think the matter over.

But now, after this glimpse into Eduard's heart, the Baroness' suggestion changed into a firm resolution; and, as she made up her mind, she appeared to become even more sympathetic to Eduard's desires, for no one had more self-control than the Baroness. Self-control at crucial moments accustoms us to maintain outward composure on all occasions. When we have so much control over ourselves, we are inclined to extend it to others as an external compensation for all our inner privations.

This state of mind is usually connected with a secret enjoyment of the blindness of others who walk unsuspectingly into the trap. We enjoy not only our present success but, at the same time, the other person's future embarrassment. The Baroness, therefore, was malicious enough to invite Eduard to come with Charlotte to her estate at the vintage season; and when he asked whether they might bring Ottilie, she gave an answer which he could take to be affirmative, if he chose.

Eduard immediately began to exclaim about that wonderful region—the great river, the hills, rocks and vineyards, the ancient castles, the boating parties, the merrymaking when the grapes were gathered, the wine-pressing, and so on. In the innocence of his heart he exulted, anticipating the impression these scenes would make on Ottilie's fresh and receptive mind. At this moment they saw her coming toward them; and the Baroness quickly warned Eduard that he must not breathe a word about the plan for this autumn visit, for if we look forward to things with too much eagerness, they usually do not happen at all. Eduard promised, but he made her walk more quickly to meet Ottilie, and, when they were quite close, even hurried on ahead. His whole person expressed a warm happiness. He kissed Ottilie's hand and pressed into it a nosegay of wild flowers he had gathered on his walk. The Baroness felt something like bitterness in her heart as she watched. Although she could not approve of the improper side of this affection, she could not bear to see its sweet and pleasant side wasted on so simple and inexperienced a girl.

When they all sat down for supper, the whole atmosphere had changed. The Count, who had already written his letter and sent it off by messenger, had managed to have the Captain beside him at the table, and talked only with him, drawing him out without appearing impolite or inquisitive. The Baroness, at the Count's right, got little attention from him or from Eduard who, first because he was thirsty and then because he was excited, drank more wine than usual and chatted animatedly with Ottilie, whom he had asked to sit by his side. Charlotte, opposite them and next to the Captain, found it almost impossible to hide her emotion.

The Baroness had sufficient time to make her observations. She noticed that Charlotte was not at ease; and, since she herself was preoccupied with Eduard's relation to Ottilie, she was convinced that Charlotte was likewise worried and hurt by her husband's behavior; and she pondered how she could best gain her ends.

Even after supper the private conversations went on. The Count, who wanted to sound the Captain's mind thoroughly, had to resort to many roundabout methods to get what he wanted to know out of him, for the Captain was quiet, reserved and not at all vain. They walked up and down one side of the salon, while Eduard, animated by wine and hope, chattered gaily with Ottilie near a window.

Charlotte and the Baroness walked silently up and down the other side of the room. Their continued silence and aimless standing about eventually affected the others. The ladies retired to their rooms, and the men went to theirs in the other wing of the castle; the day seemed to have come to an end.

Chapter Eleven

Eduard accompanied the Count to his room and was easily persuaded to stay and talk for a little while. The Count indulged in reminiscences. He had a lively recollection of Charlotte's beauty, and spoke as a connoisseur in describing it. "A pretty foot is a great gift of Nature," he said. "Its graceful charm is imperishable. I watched her as she walked today, and I really felt tempted to kiss her shoe, and to revive a rather barbaric but touching custom of the Slavs, whose highest tribute to a woman they love and admire is to drink to her health from her shoe."

But a pretty foot was not the only object the two old friends praised. From these intimate reflections, they went back to recall old adventures and the difficulties Eduard and Charlotte had met with in those bygone days when they wished to see each other; what efforts they had made, what expedients they had devised to create an opportunity to assure each other of their love.

"Do you remember," said the Count, "how I stood by you as a staunch friend in a certain adventure when Their Highnesses visited their uncle, and we were all together in that big rambling castle? The day had passed with pomp and circumstances and we wanted at least part of the night for a quiet and intimate talk."

"You had made a mental note of the way to the suites of the ladies-in-waiting," said Eduard, "and we arrived safely in my ladylove's room."

"—Who cared more for decorum than for my personal pleasure and had kept a very ugly chaperone with her," sighed the Count, "so that I had a most disagreeable time, while you two enjoyed yourselves, exchanging affectionate looks and words."

"Only yesterday, when we had received word that you were coming, my wife and I reminded each other of that episode and particularly of our retreat," said Eduard. "We took the wrong corridor, and found ourselves in the anteroom where the guards were stationed. Since we knew the way from there, we thought it would be easy to cross the hall and elude the sentinel on duty as well as the other guards. Do you remember our surprise when we opened the door? The whole floor was littered with mattreses on which those giants were stretched out in rows, sleeping. The only man awake was the sentinel on duty; he eyed us with suspicion, but we calmly picked our way among the outstretched boots—reckless young daredevils that we were—and not one of the snoring Sons of Anak woke up."

"I had a mind to stumble, and sound the alarm," said the Count. "What a strange resurrection we would have witnessed!"

At this moment the clock of the castle struck twelve.

"Midnight!" said the Count, smiling. "It is the right hour. Now I must ask a favor of you, my dear fellow. Please guide me, as I once guided you, for I have promised the Baroness to pay her a late visit. During the day we have not had one minute to ourselves. It has been a long time since we have seen each other, and it is only natural that we should long for an hour for privacy. Show me the way; I shall certainly find my way back; in any case, there is no danger of my stumbling over somebody's boots."

"As your host, I'm glad to give you this proof of my friendship," Eduard replied; "but the three ladies are all in the same wing. For all we know, they may be still sitting together, and there is no telling what disturbance we may create."

"Don't worry: the Baroness expects me," the Count said. "At this hour she is most certainly in her room—and alone."

"It is quite easy, anyway," Eduard said, taking up a candle and lighting the Count down a private staircase which led into a long passage, at the end of which he opened a small door. They climbed a winding staircase to a narrow landing, where Eduard gave the candle to the Count and pointed to a concealed door on the right. It opened easily and swallowed up the Count, and Eduard was left in complete darkness.

Another door on the left led into Charlotte's bedroom. He heard voices and listened. Charlotte was talking to her maid: "Has Ottilie gone to bed?"

"No, Madam, she is still downstairs, writing."

"You may light the night lamp and go," said Charlotte. "It is late. I shall put out the candle myself, and I shan't need you any longer."

Eduard was delighted to hear that Ottilie was still at her copying. "She is doing something for me!" he thought proudly. He could almost see her sitting and writing as he stood quite alone here in the enveloping darkness; he imagined himself approaching her, saw her turn her head and look up at him. An irresistible desire to be close to her once more took hold of him. But from where he stood, there was no way down to the floor where she had her room. He was standing directly before his wife's door; a strange confusion of emotions came over him; he tried to turn the knob; he found the door locked and rapped gently. Charlotte did not hear him.

She was nervously walking up and down in the next room, repeating to herself again and again what she had turned over in her mind since she had heard the Count's unexpected suggestion. The figure of the Captain rose up before her. His presence still filled the house; he still enlivened their walks; but soon he would be gone, and nothing left but emptiness. She told herself all the things we can tell ourselves; she even anticipated, as we usually do, the cold comfort that time will heal even such wounds as these. But she dreaded the time needed to heal them, and she dreaded the deadly period when they would be healed.

At last she took refuge in tears, which eased her pain, for she rarely wept. She flung herself on the sofa and completely abandoned herself to her grief. All this time Eduard could not bring himself to move away from the door; he knocked again, and a third time, a little louder, so that Charlotte could hear it quite distinctly in the quiet of the night, and started in alarm. Her first thought was: It could be—it must be—the Captain! Her second: It could not be! She thought it was a delusion; but she had heard it; she hoped she had heard it; and she was afraid she had heard it. She returned to her bedroom and tiptoed to the locked door. She reproached herself for her fears; perhaps the Baroness needed something she told herself, and she called in a composed voice: "Is someone there?"

A hushed voice answered: "It is I."

"Who?" asked Charlotte, not recognizing the voice. For her the Captain was standing on the other side of the door. Now the voice was a little louder: "Eduard." She opened the door, and her husband stood before her. He greeted her with a humorous remark. She managed to answer in the same vein. Then he involved himself in mysterious explanations of his mysterious visit. "Well, let me confess that the real reason for my coming is: I made a vow to kiss your slipper tonight."

"It has been a long time since you thought of doing anything like that," said Charlotte.

"So much the worse," Eduard replied, "and so much the better." She sat down in a deep chair to conceal the lightness of her gown. He knelt down before her, and she could not prevent his kissing her slipper. When the slipper came off in his hand, he clasped her foot, and pressed it lovingly to his heart.

Charlotte was one of those temperate women, who even after marriage continue to behave in the modest manner of loving girls. She never sought to charm her husband; she scarcely encouraged desire; yet without coldness or austerity, she was always rather like an affectionate bride who feels a certain shyness even toward that which is sanctioned. Tonight Eduard found her doubly shy. She fervently wished that her husband would leave, for she kept envisioning the reproachful image of her friend. But her mood rather than repelling Eduard, attracted him all the more strongly. Her expression betrayed her emotions. She had been crying, and tears so unbecoming to weak persons, make those who are normally strong and composed so much the more attractive. Eduard was gentle, affectionate, insisting—he implored her to allow him to stay—he did not demand but, half-serious and half-laughing, tried to persuade her. At last, he simply blew out the candle.

And immediately, in the dim light of the night lamp, their passions and their imaginations asserted their rights over reality. It was Ottilie who was closed in Eduard's embrace; while the Captain's image—now clearly, now vaguely—hovered before Charlotte. The absent and the present, strangely interwoven, blended in their blissful ecstacy.

But the present will assert itself. They spent part of the night in playful small talk which was quite unrestrained as their hearts had no part in it. But when Eduard woke the next morning, at his wife's side, the day before him seemed ominous; and the sun seemed to illumine a crime. He stole away; and Charlotte found herself alone when she woke.

Chapter Twelve

When they all met again at breakfast, an acute observer would have been able to discern the innermost thoughts and emotions of each one of them from his or her behavior. The Count and the Baroness conducted themselves like a pair of happy lovers who, after a forced separation, have reassured each other of their mutual affection. Charlotte and Eduard, on the other hand, were almost embarrassed and conscience-stricken as they faced the Captain and Ottilie, for it is the nature of love to recognize no rights but its own; and all other rights vanish before it. Ottilie was as happy as a child; she was almost talkative. The Captain was in a serious mood. Things that had lain undisturbed, even dormant, in him for some time had been stirred up by his conversation with the count, and he had come to realize only too clearly that he was actually neglecting his vocation, wasting his time in idleness disguised as petty activity.

Almost immediately after the Count and the Baroness had left, other visitors arrived. They were quite welcome to Charlotte, who wished to escape from herself and to be diverted, but unwelcome to Eduard, who felt a redoubled desire to devote himself to Ottilie; unwelcome also to Ottilie, who had not yet finished her copy of the document which had to be ready early the next day. She therefore hurried to her room as soon as the last of the visitors had made a late departure.

It was now evening. Eduard, Charlotte, and the Captain walked part of the way with their visitors and saw them into their carriage. They then decided to walk on to the ponds. A boat, which Eduard had ordered at considerable expense from a distant place, had arrived; and they wanted to see if it handled easily.

The boat had been tied up by the shore of the middle pond, not far from a clump of old oak trees which figured in the landscaping plans for this spot. They intended to build a dock here and an elaborate stone seat which could serve as a landmark for people crossing the water.

"And where shall we build the landing on the other side?" Eduard asked. "Near my plane trees, I should think."

"They are a little too far to the right," the Captain replied. "If we can land further down, we shall be nearer the castle. But we must think it over."

The Captain was already standing in the stern of the boat and had taken one oar. Charlotte got in, and Eduard followed, taking the second oar; but as he was just about to shove off, he suddenly thought of Ottilie and realized that this boating trip would delay him and that there was no telling when he would get home! He made a quick decision, jumped back to the shore, passed the oar over to the Captain, and with a casual excuse hurried toward the castle.

When he arrived there, he was told that Ottilie had locked her door and was writing. Although it was agreeable to know that she was working in his behalf, he was most disappointed not to see her. His impatience increased from moment to moment. He paced up and down the big hall; he picked up this and that; but nothing held his interest for long. He wanted to see her, to see her alone, before Charlotte and the Captain returned. Night had fallen, and the candles were lighted. At last Ottilie came in, radiant with loveliness. The feeling that she had done something for her friend had given her a certain pride in herself. She laid the document and her copy on the table before Eduard. "Shall we check this together?" she asked, smiling. Eduard was at a loss for an answer. He looked at her; he looked at the copy. The first pages were meticulously written in a delicate feminine hand; but then her writing seemed to have changed, to have become less cramped and more flowing; and how surprised he was when he ran his eye over the last pages.

"For heaven's sake!" he exclaimed. "What's this? It's my own handwriting!" He looked at Ottilie and again at the written pages; the end, particularly, looked as though he had written it himself. Ottilie did not utter a word, but in her eyes was an expression of deep happiness. Eduard stretched out his arms. "You love me!" he cried out. "Ottilie, you love me!" And they were in each other's arms. It was impossible to tell who had embraced the other first.

From this moment the world was changed for Eduard. He was not the same, and life was not the same. They stood face to face; he held her hands. They lost themselves in each other's eyes and were on the point of embracing again when Charlotte entered with the Captain; both of them were apologizing for having been delayed so long. Eduard smiled to himself. "Oh, how much too early you did come!" he thought.

They sat down to supper and talked about the day's visitors.

Eduard, elated by love and happiness, had a good word to say for everyone—always kind and often favorable. Charlotte, who did not entirely agree with him, noticed his generous mood and chaffed him that he who usually made such biting comments after visitors had left was so mild and tolerant today.

Eduard exclaimed, with passionate sincerity, "If only you love one person with all your heart, everybody seems lovable."

Ottilie did not look up, and Charlotte looked straight ahead. Then the Captain took up the subject: "I think the same thing is true of our feelings of respect and admiration. Only after we have had a chance to experience such feelings in respect to one particular object do we learn to recognize what is really valuable in the world."

Charlotte retired to her room as early as she could, for she wished to abandon herself to the memory of everything that had happened tonight to her and the Captain.

When Eduard had jumped from the boat and shoved it off, leaving his wife and his friend to the mercies of the unstable element, Charlotte found herself face to face in the twilight with the man for whom she had secretly suffered so much, and who was now rowing the boat about easily with both oars. A deep sadness, such as she had seldom felt, overcame her. The boat's circling movement, the splash of the oars, the faint breeze rippling the mirror of the water, the rustle of the reeds, the last hovering flight of birds, the flickering of the stars and their reflections in the water—all this seemed unreal in the surrounding stillness. It seemed as though her friend were rowing her far away and would set her on shore somewhere and leave her there alone. Strange feelings stirred in her, but she could not weep.

Meanwhile the Captain was explaining to her his ideas for further improvements to the estate. He praised the boat, which handled easily with one person at the oars. He suggested that if she learned to row, she might find it very pleasant, at times, to float on the water alone—her own boatman and pilot.

When he said this, she was struck again by the threat of imminent separation from him. "Is he saying all this on purpose?" she wondered. "Does he know already, or did he just happen to say that, without realizing that his words seal my fate?" A deep melancholy descended on her, mixed with impatience. She asked him to pull to shore as soon as possible and return to the castle with her. It was the first time the Captain had been out on this pond, and, although he had taken some soundings of its depth, he was not familiar with all of its parts. Darkness fell quickly, and he set his course toward the spot near the footpath to the castle where he thought it would be easy to land. But he changed his mind when Charlotte repeatedly implored him, almost in a panic, to get her to the shore quickly. He approached it with vigorous strokes but unfortunately ran aground some distance out in the water. His efforts to pull the boat free were unsuccessful. What could he do? He had no choice but to step out into the water, which fortunately was shallow, and to carry Charlotte to dry land. He carried his precious burden easily, being strong and steady on his feet, so that she had no reason to be afraid; but she put her arms around his neck and clung to him anxiously. He held her firmly and pressed her close to him. He released her only after they had arrived at the grassy bank; he was moved and confused. She still clung to him; and he folded her in his arms again and kissed her. The next moment he was at her feet, pressing his lips to her hand and crying, "Charlotte, will you forgive me?"

The kiss, which came so unexpectedly from her friend and which she had almost returned, brought Charlotte to herself. She pressed his hand but did not help him to rise. Leaning forward, she laid her hand on his shoulder and said, "We cannot keep this moment from being a memorable one; but whether we shall be equal to it depends on us. You must leave, dear friend, and you shall leave. The Count has made plans for a better future for you. This makes me happy and sad. I didn't want to say anything until it was all decided; but this moment forces me to tell you my secret. I can forgive you—and forgive myself—only if we have the courage to change the situation, for it is not in our power to change our feelings." She drew him up and supported herself on his arm. They returned to the castle in silence.

Now Charlotte was standing in her bedroom, where she could not help feeling and remembering that she was Eduard's wife. In this inner conflict her character, strengthened by the many experiences of her life, came to her aid. She was accustomed to recognizing and controlling her feelings, and so she very nearly regained her usual composure without difficulty; indeed, she smiled when she thought of the previous night's surprising visit. But suddenly she was filled with a strange presentiment, a happy though tremulous agitation which was slowly transformed into quiet hope. Deeply moved, she fell on her knees and repeated the pledge she had given to Eduard before the altar. Consoling thoughts of friendship, affection, and resignation passed through her mind. She felt her old self once more. Overcome by a sweet drowsiness, she fell peacefully asleep.

Chapter Thirteen

Eduard, on the other hand, was in a quite different mood. He felt so little like sleeping that he did not even think of undressing. Again and again he kissed the copy of the document—at least the first pages, which were written in Ottilie's childish and timid hand. He hardly dared press his lips to the last pages, which he thought so strangely resembled his own hand. "If it were only a different document!" he thought to himself, but it was, all the same, a delightful assurance that his most fervent wish had been fulfilled. He would keep it and always carry it next to his heart, even though it would be sullied by the signature of a third person. The waning moon rose behind the wood. The warm night tempted Eduard to go out of doors. He strolled about, the most restless and happy of men. He walked through the gardens, and found them too confining; he ran across the fields, and found them too open. He was drawn back to the castle and stood under Ottilie's windows; he sat down on the steps of the terrace below. "Walls and locks divide us, but our hearts are not divided," he said to himself. "If she were standing here now, she would fall into my arms, and I into hers; and is not this certainty enough for us?" Around him all was quiet—not a breeze stirred. It was so still that in the ground beneath him he could hear the burrowing of busy animals, to whom night and day are alike. He was wrapped in happy dreams; at last he fell asleep and did not waken until the sun came up in all its splendor and scattered the early mists.

He was the first person awake on the whole estate. It seemed to him that the workmen should be already there. They finally arrived. He thought there should be more of them; the work planned for the day was too trifling for his eager desires. He insisted that more workmen be hired; it was promised and they arrived later in the day. But even this extra help was insufficient to carry out his projects quickly enough. He had lost interest in the work itself; what he wanted was to see it finished; and for whom? The paths should be smoothed, so that Ottilie could walk on them in comfort; and benches should be placed everywhere, so that Ottilie could rest. He also speeded up the work on the new building; the carpentry work was to be completed on Ottilie's birthday. There was no moderation in anything Eduard thought or did. The certainty of loving and of being loved in return banished all restraint. How changed everything seemed to him: all the rooms, all his surroundings. He no longer felt at home in his own house. He was completely absorbed in her—he had no other thought; his conscience was dumb. Everything that had been subdued in him burst forth, and his whole being rushed toward Ottilie.

The Captain watched this frantic activity and wished to avert unfortunate consequences. The exaggerated haste with which part of the new work was being done had upset the plans of the Captain, who had expected their gradual completion to occupy months of their quiet and friendly life together. He had concluded the sale of the farm; the first instalment had been paid and entrusted to Charlotte, as agreed. But even during the first week she had to be consistently firm, patient and orderly, for the sum set aside for the work would not last long at the present rate.

A great deal had been started, and still more had to be done. How could the Captain leave Charlotte in such a situation? They discussed the matter and came to the conclusion that it would be wisest to speed up work on the whole project, and, for that purpose, to borrow money which would be repaid by the instalment payments from the sale of the farm. This could be done with almost no loss by a transfer of the title deed. They would then have a freer hand and could get more done, since everything was now well under way; they had as many workmen as they needed; they could soon complete the entire project. Eduard gladly assented, since the plan coincided with his own wishes.

Meanwhile, deep in her heart Charlotte clung to her resolution, and her friend was staunch in his support of this spirit, but this only increased their intimacy. They talked frankly about Eduard's passion and discussed what they should do. Charlotte spent more time with Ottilie and observed her closely; but, the more she understood her own heart, the more deeply she understood Ottilie's heart. She saw no other way out; she must send her away.

It was fortunate that her daughter Luciane had excelled at school, because her great-aunt, on hearing this, decided to take her into her household permanently and bring her out into society. Ottilie could now go back to school; the Captain would leave for a better post; and everything would once more be as it had been a few months before, perhaps even better. Charlotte hoped soon to mend her relationship with Eduard, and she explained everything to herself so reasonably that she kept strengthening her delusion that a disturbed situation can be restored to its earlier tranquility—that what has been violently released can be suppressed again.

Eduard was acutely aware of the obstacles which were put in his way. He soon noticed the arrangements which kept Ottilie and him apart, so that it became difficult for him to speak to her alone, or even to approach her, except in the presence of others. He resented this and many other things as well. When he succeeded in exchanging a few words with Ottilie, he not only reassured her of his love but also complained to her about his wife and the Captain. He did not realize that his own unreasonable actions were about to exhaust their funds. He blamed Charlotte as well as the Captain for not keeping to their first agreement; but he forgot that he had consented to the second agreement and had, in fact, been the cause of it himself.

Hate is partial but love is even more so. Ottilie's attitude toward Charlotte and the Captain also changed. One day when Eduard complained about the Captain to Ottilie, saying that under the circumstances he did not act quite honestly, as a friend should, Ottilie thoughtlessly replied, "I have been displeased before when he was not quite honest with you. I once overheard him say to Charlotte, 'If only Eduard would spare us his wretched tootling; he'll never be a good flutist, and it is painful to listen to him.' You can imagine how this hurt me, for you know how I love to accompany you."

As soon as she had said this, some instinct told her that she should have held her tongue; but it was too late. Eduard's expression changed. Nothing had ever hurt him more; his weakest point had been attacked; he knew that he had cherished a childish kind of ambition, without wishing to make the slightest pretension. He expected his friends to be tolerant of the things which amused and pleased him. He forgot how unbearable it is for a listener to have his ear irritated by an amateurish performer. He was offended—furious—unforgiving. He felt himself absolved from any obligations of friendship.

His overmastering need to be with Ottilie, to see her, to whisper to her confidentially, became more urgent every day. He decided to write her, asking her to correspond with him in secret. The slip of paper on which he had written his brief request was lying on his desk, and the draft blew it off when his valet entered the room to dress his hair. The valet was in the habit of picking up any scrap of paper lying on the floor to test the heat of his curling iron. This time he got hold of Eduard's note, which he pinched quickly with the iron, singeing it. Eduard, seeing his error, snatched the note from him. He sat down a few minutes later to rewrite the message, but it did not sound as well the second time. He felt a little uneasy, even doubtful; but he overcame this feeling. He pressed the slip of paper into Ottilie's hand the first moment he could approach her.

Ottilie wasted no time in replying. He put her note in his waistcoat without reading it. The pocket of his short waistcoat, cut fashionably, was too shallow to hold it. It slipped out and fell to the floor without his noticing it. Charlotte saw it, picked it up, and after a quick glance gave it to him. "Here is something you have written down," she said; "you probably would not like to lose it."

He was puzzled. "Is she pretending?" he thought. "Did she read what was written on it, or did the similarity of the handwriting deceive her?" He hoped and believed that the latter was the case. It was a warning to him in a double sense; but he did not heed these accidental hints which some higher Being seems to give us. On the contrary, the further his passion drove him, the more intolerable did he find the restraint which he felt was forced upon him. He avoided the company of his friends. He hardened his heart, and, if it was necessary for him to be together with his wife and his friend, he could not recapture the pleasure he had once found in their company. He could not help feeling guilty about it, which, in turn annoyed him and he resorted to a kind of humor which, lacking affection, also lacked its usual charm.

In all these trials, Charlotte was sustained by her own integrity.

She did not relax her determination to renounce her affection for the Captain, however pure and noble she knew it to be.

And she was also sincerely anxious to help the others. She knew only too well that separation alone is not enough to heal such wounds. She made up her mind to speak frankly with the girl about the whole matter; but she could not bring herself to do it; the memory of her own conflict stood in her way. She tried to refer to the matter in general remarks; but again, these fitted her own situation—a situation she hesitated to discuss. Any hint she wished to give Ottilie touched her own heart. She wanted to warn her and felt that perhaps she herself was in need of some warning.

She merely tried to keep the two lovers apart as before, without saying anything; but she gained nothing by this. Gentle hints, which sometimes slipped out, had no effect on Ottilie, who had been assured by Eduard that Charlotte loved the Captain and that Charlotte herself wanted a divorce which he would try to arrange in the fairest possible manner.

Ottilie, confident in the feeling of her own innocence and seeing herself on the road to supreme happiness, lived for Eduard alone. Strengthened in goodness by her love for him, still happier in her work, more communicative with others than formerly, she felt herself in a heaven on earth.

And so all four continued their normal daily life, each in his own way, with or without reflection. Everything seemed to go on as usual, just as, in troublous times, when all hangs in the balance, everyone goes on living as though nothing at all could happen.

Chapter Fourteen

Meanwhile, a letter arrived from the Count, addressed to the Captain—two letters, actually: one with splendid promises for the future, which he could show his friends; the other with the definite offer of an immediate important position at Court, including the rank of Major, a good salary, and other advantages; but the Count requested him to keep this to himself for a while, as there happened to be reasons for secrecy. The Captain, therefore, told his friends only about the remote expectations and kept the imminent decision to himself.

He continued his present occupations with great zeal and quietly made the necessary preparations so that, even in his absence, all would go on without interruption. Now he, too, was eager to set a final date for the end of the work and wished that as much as possible should be ready for Ottilie's birthday; as a result the two friends really enjoyed working in agreement, although the agreement was tacit. Eduard was very pleased that more funds were available, because they had raised the money in advance, and that all the projects moved ahead rapidly.

The Captain would have liked to put an end to the plan of combining the three ponds into one large lake. The lower dam would have to be reinforced, and the middle ones demolished; and all this was, from more than one point of view, a large and precarious task. Both projects, however, interrelated as they were, had already been started. A young architect had arrived—a former pupil of the Captain—who was a very desirable addition, for he pushed the work ahead, partly by employing skilled laborers, partly by letting contracts, when possible. All this promised security and stability for the project. It also gave the Captain a feeling of quiet satisfaction to know that his own absence would not be so keenly felt. It had always been his principle not to abandon any work he had started before it was finished unless his position was satisfactorily filled by someone else. Indeed, he despised those who, in order to make their departure felt, leave everything in chaos, wishing, like uncivilized egotists, to wreck anything they are no longer allowed to work at.

And so everyone exerted himself to prepare for a splendid celebration of Ottilie's birthday, although no one ever mentioned it or even admitted it to himself. Charlotte, while not at all jealous, did not approve of a conspicuous celebration. Ottilie's youth, her circumstances of life, her relation to the family, did not qualify her to appear as the queen of such a day; nor did Eduard wish the date to be mentioned, since he wanted everything to happen spontaneously, to be a surprise and, of course, a delightful one.

For all these reasons, they tacitly agreed on the pretext of having the carpenters' festival at the new house on that day, without any mention of the birthday, which would enable them to invite their friends and the villagers for the occasion.

But Eduard's passion knew no bounds. His longing to call Ottilie his own was as immoderate as were his gifts and promises to her. Charlotte's suggestions about birthday presents for Ottilie seemed to him much too modest. He talked with his valet, who, taking care of Eduard's wardrobe, had connections with tradespeople and dealers in luxuries. This man knew what gifts would please and how they ought to be given, and immediately ordered a handsome, even elegant, red morocco traveling case, studded with brass nails, and filled it with gifts worthy of the case itself. The valet made another suggestion; there were some fireworks which had never been set off. It would be easy enough to add to them. Eduard took up this idea with great enthusiasm; and the valet promised to attend to everything and keep everything a secret.

As the day grew near, the Captain made arrangements with the constabulary for guards, a precaution he thought necessary whenever a crowd was attracted or called together. He had also taken precautions against the beggars and rowdies who are likely to be a nuisance at a festival.

Eduard and his confidant, on the other hand, busied themselves mostly with their fireworks. They planned to set them off near the middle pond under the tall oaks. The guests would stand on the opposite shore, under the plane trees, where, safely and conveniently, they would have a good view of the display, the reflections in the water, and the pieces set afloat on the water.

On another pretext, Eduard gave orders to have the ground under the plane trees cleared of underbrush, grass, and moss. Only then did the beauty of the trees, magnificent in height and spread, come into full view on the cleared ground. Eduard was delighted. "It must have been just about this time of year when I planted them. I wonder how long ago it was?" he pondered. As soon as he returned home, he got out the old diaries his father had kept so methodically, especially when he was at this country seat. Eduard's planting of the trees was probably not recorded, but he was sure to find another important family event, which he still remembered clearly as having happened on the same day. He skimmed through several volumes. Sure enough, the event *was* mentioned! But how amazed and happy Eduard was when he discovered a strange coincidence. The day and the year when he had planted the trees was the day and year of Ottilie's birth.

Chapter Fifteen

At last the radiant morning of the day Eduard had so eagerly awaited had come. Gradually the guests arrived. Invitations had been sent to the whole neighborhood, and many who had not been present at the laying of the cornerstone, but had heard how memorable that occasion had been, did not want to miss this second celebration.

Before they sat down to dinner, the carpenters marched into the courtyard to the music of a band. They carried a huge floral piece made of several wreaths of foliage and flowers, swinging loosely one above the other. The carpenters greeted the company and asked the ladies, in the traditional way, for silk handkerchiefs and ribbons to decorate their garland. While the guests had dinner in the castle, the procession went on its way with sounds of rejoicing; it lingered for a time in the village, where the women and girls also had to sacrifice many ribbons. It eventually arrived on the hill, accompanied by a large crowd which joined the one already waiting beside the half-finished lodge.

After dinner Charlotte detained her guests in the castle for a little while. She wanted to avoid a solemn and formal procession; therefore, they all arrived on the hill in separate groups walking slowly and without regard to distinctions of precedence. Charlotte lagged behind with Ottilie, but her strategem did not improve matters, for Ottilie turned out to be the last person to arrive on the scene, and it seemed as though the trumpets and drums had only been waiting for her and the festivities seemed to start immediately upon her arrival.

To cover its bare appearance the house had according to the Captain's directions been decorated with green branches and flowers; but, without the Captain's knowledge, Eduard had directed the architect to outline the date in flowers on the cornice. There was nothing really objectionable about that; but the Captain arrived just in time to prevent Ottilie's name from being displayed in bright colors on the gable as well. He cleverly managed to prevent this and have the flowery letters which had already been prepared put aside.

The wreath was raised and was visible far and wide. The gay scarves and ribbons fluttered merrily in the breeze, which also blew away the greater part of a speech. When the ceremony was over, the dancing began on a level space in front of the building enclosed by arbors made of branches.

A spruce young apprentice introduced a lively village girl to Eduard and asked Ottilie, who was standing next to Eduard, for a dance. The two couples were immediately followed by others, and soon Eduard changed partners, caught Ottilie, and danced the round with her. The younger guests mixed gaily with the villagers and workmen, while the older ones looked on.

Then, before everyone began to stroll about, it was agreed that all the guests should meet again at sunset under the plane trees. Eduard arrived there first and made all necessary arrangements with his valet, who, together with the man who had made the fireworks, was to attend to the aerial magic on the opposite shore.

These arrangements did not altogether please the Captain. He tried to have a word with Eduard concerning the expected crush of spectators; but his friend asked rather nervously that this part of the festivities be left to him.

A great crowd had already gathered on the dams, where the ground was uneven and unsafe, because the sod had been removed. The sun went down, and it grew darker. As they waited for complete darkness, the guests were served refreshments under the trees. Everybody thought it an incomparable spot, and anticipated with delight the view they would eventually have from here over a wide lake with a variety of scenery along its shores.

A perfectly calm evening with not the slightest breeze stirring promised success for the spectacle. But all at once loud and terrified cries were heard. Large sections of earth had broken off the dam, and several people had been plunged into the water. The ground had given way under the trampling and pushing of the rapidly increasing crowd. Everyone had tried to get the best point of vantage, and now no one could move forward or back.

All crowded forward, more to see what had happened than to help, as it was impossible to reach the unfortunate victims. With the assistance of a few resolute men, the Captain ran to the scene of the disaster and cleared the crowd off the dam onto the shore to make more room for those who were trying to help the people in the water. These were soon on dry land again, partly through assistance, partly through their own efforts, except for one boy whose violent struggles carried him far out into the water instead of back to the dam. His strength was visibly failing; and only now and then did a hand or a foot appear above the surface. The boat, unfortunately, was on the opposite shore, filled with fireworks; the unloading of these went slowly and help was delayed. The Captain came to a quick decision; everyone watched him throw off his outer clothing, and was inspired with confidence in his physical strength, but a cry went up from the crowd when they saw him jump into the water. All eyes followed the skillful swimmer who, in a short time, reached the boy and brought him, seemingly dead, to shore.

Meanwhile the boat had arrived, and the Captain stepped into it and asked those about him if everyone had been saved. The physician arrived and took care of the still unconscious boy. Charlotte had come over, and implored the Captain to think of himself—to go back to the castle and change his clothes. He hesitated, until he was assured that everyone had been saved. The people who told him that were sensible and reliable, and had helped him in the rescue.

When Charlotte saw the Captain going back to the castle, it suddenly occurred to her that such necessaries as wine and tea had been locked up, and that people are likely to get hold of the wrong thing on such occasions, in any case. She hurried past the rest of the guests, who were still standing under the plane trees in scattered groups, and found Eduard busy urging everyone to stay for a little while: he was about to give the signal for the beginning of the fireworks. Charlotte went up to him and begged him not to go on with an entertainment which would be out of place this moment and which no one would enjoy. She reminded him of their duty toward the boy and the one who had rescued him. "The doctor will manage all right," Eduard replied. "He has everything he needs, and we would only be in the way." Charlotte insisted and made a sign to Ottilie, who started to follow at once. But Eduard took her hand and protested: "This day shall not end in a hospital! I'll not have Ottilie playing the sister of mercy. The half-dead will be wakened without our help, and the living will rub themselves dry."

Charlotte did not answer and left. Some of the guests followed her; others stayed; finally, as no one wished to be the last, they all left. Eduard and Ottilie were now alone under the plane trees. He insisted on staying although Ottilie was uneasy and implored him to return with her to the castle. "No, Ottilie," he cried, "extraordinary things do not happen in an ordinary way. This startling incident tonight unites us all the more quickly. You are mine—I have said that to you so often and sworn it. Let's stop talking and promising; let it now be a fact!"

The boat crossed over from the other shore. The valet was in it, and asked with some embarrassment what should be done with the fireworks. "Set them off," Eduard called to him. "They were meant for you, Ottilie, and you alone shall see them. Let me sit beside you and share your pleasure!" He sat down by her side, without touching her.

Rockets rose roaring into the sky; cannonades thundered; star shells climbed high; firecrackers flashed like hissing serpents and exploded; pin wheels whirled—first separately, then in pairs, then in masses—blazing brighter and brighter, one after the other, and then merging. Eduard, his heart on fire as well, watched the fiery phantoms with eager and happy eyes. Ottilie, with her sensitive emotional disposition, was more frightened than delighted by this deafening and flashing rise and fall. Timidly she leaned against Eduard, who felt her nearness and confidence to be a pledge that she belonged to him completely. Hardly had the night closed around them once more, when the moon rose, lighting their way back to the castle. A man, his hat in his hand, stepped into their path and begged alms, claiming that he had been forgotten on this festive day. The moon shone full on his face, and Eduard recognized the insolent beggar he had met before. But in his present state of happiness, he could not possibly be angry with anyone. He had also completely forgotten that on this particular day begging had been forbidden. It did not take him long to search in his pocket and find a gold coin. He wanted to see everyone happy, for his own happiness seemed to be boundless.

In the castle, all had turned out well. With the help of the doctor's skill, the provision of everything he needed, and Charlotte's assistance, the boy had been restored to life. The guests had scattered, some to catch a glimpse of the fireworks from a distance, and some to return to their quiet homes after all the excitement.

After quickly changing his clothes, the Captain had also helped where he was needed. All was quiet again, and he was alone with Charlotte. With his characteristic kindness he now told her that he would be leaving very soon. She had gone through so much tonight that this disclosure made almost no impression on her. She had seen her friend risk his life and save the life of another without suffering any harm himself. She saw in these miraculous happenings a propitious omen for his future and felt that fate would be kind to him.

When Eduard returned with Ottilie, he was also told of the Captain's imminent departure. He suspected that Charlotte had known all about this for some time; but he was too preoccupied with himself and his own plans to resent it.

On the contrary, he listened with attention and pleasure to the description of the fine and honorable post which had been offered the Captain. His own secret desires raced ahead of all these changes. He already saw his friend married to Charlotte, and himself married to Ottilie. He could think of no finer gift he might have received on this festive day.

And how surprised Ottilie was when she entered her room and found on her table the handsome traveling case. She opened it at once. Everything in it was so beautifully packed and arranged that she did not dare to remove or even to touch anything. Muslin, batiste, silk, scarves, and lace vied with each other in their beauty, elegance, and costliness. Nor had jewelry been forgotten. Although she understood perfectly that it was intended to provide her with a more varied wardrobe, everything seemed to her so lavish and strange that she did not dare, even in her thoughts, to claim these things as her own.

Chapter Sixteen

On the following morning the Captain had disappeared, leaving behind a note for his friends filled with expressions of his gratitude. The night before, he and Charlotte had said a vague and almost wordless goodbye. She felt that it was a final separation and had resigned herself to it, for in the Count's second letter, which the Captain had at last given her to read, the prospect of a favorable marriage had also been touched upon; and, although the Captain had not stressed this point, Charlotte accepted the arrangement as settled and gave him up for good with a pure heart.

But she also felt that now she had a right to demand of others the same self-control which she had practiced herself; it had not been impossible for her, and it should not be impossible for them. In this mood she began to talk to her husband, and she was able to do this openly and confidently, because she was determined that the matter should be settled once and for all.

"Our friend has left us, and we are once again in our old situation," she said. "It is now entirely up to us whether or not we wish to return to the old state of things."

Eduard, who heard only what flattered his passion, thought that Charlotte's remark referred to the earlier period when she had been a widow and that in a veiled way she wished to give him some small hope for a separation. He therefore answered, with a smile, "Why not? The only important thing would be to come to an understanding."

But from Charlotte's answer he saw that he was mistaken. She said, "Now we have only to choose between two possibilities, both very desirable, to change Ottilie's situation as well. Either she can go back to school, since my daughter has left there and is staying with her great-aunt; or she can be received into a very good family where she will enjoy all the advantages of an education suitable to her station, together with an only daughter."

"But living with us so long in a congenial atmosphere has spoiled Ottilie, and leaving us will not be pleasant for her," Eduard replied, trying to hide his feelings.

"All of us have been spoiled; certainly you have," Charlotte replied. "We are now at a turning point, where we should stop and look back and think what would be best for all members of our little circle; and we should be willing to make some sacrifices."

"But I do not think it is fair to sacrifice Ottilie," Eduard argued, "and that is just what we would be doing if we banish her to live among strangers. The Captain was called away by his good fortune; we could see him leave with no qualms and even with pleasure. But who knows what Ottilie will have to face? And why such haste?"

"What you and I are going to face is quite clear," Charlotte replied with some emotion. Determined to speak her mind once and for all, she went on: "You love Ottilie, and every day you become more attached to her. Her affections, too, are centering more and more on you. Why not speak frankly of something which is clear and obvious at every moment? Should we not have enough foresight to ask ourselves how it will all end?"

"A precise answer to that question, of course, is impossible, but if we cannot be sure how things will turn out, the best decision is always to wait and see what the future will bring," Eduard said, trying to control himself.

"It takes no great wisdom to see the future clearly in our case," said Charlotte. "At least we know this much: both of us are too old to walk blindly into something we should not and must not do. There is no one to take care of us; we have to be our own friends and our own advisers. People expect us not to go to extremes; we can't afford to expose ourselves to criticism or ridicule."

"Can you blame me for having Ottilie's happiness at heart? Can't you understand that?" said Eduard, embarrassed for an answer to his wife's straightforward words. "And I do not mean her future happiness, which is quite beyond our calculation, but her present situation. Imagine for a moment, honestly and without deceiving yourself, Ottilie torn away for us and at the mercy of strangers; for my part I am not cruel enough to let her suffer such a change."

Charlotte clearly recognized the firm determination behind her husband's dissembling. For the first time she realized how far apart they had grown. Almost trembling, she cried, "Can Ottilie be happy if she comes between us, if she takes my husband from me, if she takes their father from his children?"

"I should think that our children are well taken care of," Eduard said, with a killing smile; but he added in a kindlier tone, "Why go to such extremes?"

"Extremes border on passion," Charlotte said. "While there is still time, do not reject my advice, but help me to help both of us. In uncertain situations, the person who sees most clearly ought to act and help. This time it is I! My dear, dearest Eduard, let me prevail! Can you expect me simply to give up my well-deserved happiness, my most precious rights—can you ask me to abandon *you?*"

"Who has asked you to?" Eduard answered, rather embarrassed.

"You have," Charlotte replied. "Is not your wish to keep Ottilie near you an acknowledgement of everything which must come of it? I do not wish to press the matter, but, if you cannot master yourself, you will at least not be able to deceive yourself much longer."

Eduard knew how right she was. It is a shock to hear in plain words what our heart has cherished secretly for a long time. Simply to change the subject for the moment Eduard said, "I do not even know what your plans exactly are."

"I intended to talk over the two possibilities with you. Each has its good points. In Ottilie's present stage of development, the school would be better for her. But when I think of her future, I see that the other situation promises more opportunities and a wider scope." Charlotte went on to tell her husband all the details of the two proposals, and then she summed up: "My own feeling is, that, for several reasons, the lady's household is preferable to the school, particularly because I should not like to encourage the affection, if not passion, which the young Tutor feels for Ottilie."

Eduard seemed to agree, but he did this only to gain time. When Charlotte, who wanted to come to a final decision, met with no pronounced opposition, she seized the opportunity to fix the date of Ottilie's departure; she had already made quiet preparations for Ottilie to leave a few days later.

Eduard was horrified. He believed himself betrayed and suspected behind his wife's affectionate words subtle plans to separate him forever from his happiness. On the surface he seemed to leave the whole matter to her; but in his heart his decision was already made. Only to get a breathing spell, and to prevent the threatening and unimaginable disaster of Ottilie's being sent away, he decided to leave home. He told Charlotte that he was going, but he was able to deceive her by explaining that he did not wish to be present when Ottilie left; that he did not even want to see her again. Charlotte, believing that she had won, encouraged him warmly. He ordered his horses, gave his valet the necessary instructions about packing and following him, and then, at the last moment, he sat down and wrote:

Eduard to Charlotte

"The misfortune which has befallen us, my dear, may be curable or it may not—I am sure of only one thing—if I am not to be driven to despair—I must gain some time for myself, and for all of us. Since I am making a sacrifice, I am entitled to require something in return. I am leaving my home, and I shall return only when there are prospects happier and more peaceful. Meanwhile, you are to remain in possession, but together with Ottilie. I want to be sure that she lives with you and not with strangers. Take care of her; treat her as you always have and even more affectionately, more gently. I promise you that I shall not try to get in touch with her without your knowledge. At least for a short time, please do not let me know how you are getting on; I shall assume the best; do the same about me. One promise only I implore you most fervently, most urgently to give me—not to make any attempt to send Ottilie away, into new surroundings. Once she is out of your castle, your park, and entrusted to strangers, she belongs to me, and I shall take her. But if you have any regard for my affection, my wishes, and my suffering, if you leave me to my illusions and hopes, I shall not resist a cure if it should offer itself. . . ."

The last phrase came from his pen, not from his heart. Indeed, when he saw it on paper, he began to weep bitterly. That he should ever renounce in the slightest, the happiness, or even the misery of loving Ottilie! For the first time he realized fully what he was doing: he was going away without knowing what his action might lead to. At least he would not see her again *now;* would he ever see her again? What assurance did he have of that? But the letter was written; the horses were ready at the door; and he was afraid that at any moment he might see her somewhere and be shaken in his resolution. He pulled himself together and reflected that it would, after all, be possible for him to return at any time and that his very absence might bring him closer to his heart's desire. On the other hand, he pictured Ottilie's being forced to leave if he were to stay. He sealed the letter, ran down the stairs, and mounted his horse.

As he rode past the village inn, he saw the beggar to whom he had been so generous the night before. The man was sitting outside under the trees, comfortably eating his dinner, but he rose and bowed to Eduard respectfully and almost reverentially. It was the figure that had stepped out in their path last night, as Eduard had walked arm in arm with Ottilie. He now reminded Eduard painfully of the happiest hour of his life. His agony increased, the consciousness of what he was leaving behind became unbearable; he turned to look at the beggar and cried, "You lucky fellow! You can still live on yesterday's alms, but I cannot live any longer on yesterday's happiness."

Chapter Seventeen

Ottilie went to the window when she heard someone riding off and was just in time to see Eduard's back. She thought it odd that he was leaving the house without having seen her or without having wished her "Good morning." She was uneasy and became more and more perturbed when Charlotte invited her for a long walk and talked about many things without ever mentioning her husband—apparently on purpose. When they returned to the castle it was a still greater shock to Ottilie to find the table only set for two.

We do not even like to lose apparently unimportant things to which we are accustomed; but the loss of something vitally important is actually painful. Eduard and the Captain were not with them. Charlotte, for the first time in months, had ordered the meal herself, and Ottilie almost felt herself supplanted. The two women sat opposite each other. Charlotte talked quite freely about the Captain's post and how unlikely they were to see him again soon. At the moment, Ottilie was able to comfort herself only with the belief that Eduard had ridden after his friend in order to keep him company part of the way.

But, when they left the table, they saw Eduard's traveling coach standing under the window; and when Charlotte, rather annoyed, asked who had given orders to bring it there, she was told that it had been the valet, who wished to load some things into it. It took all Ottilie's self-control to hide her astonishment and anguish.

The valet came in and asked for some small objects: his master's cup, a few silver spoons, and some other things, which Ottilie took to mean that a long journey and a prolonged absence had been planned. Charlotte simply dismissed the valet's request, saying that she did not understand what he was talking about, since he himself had everything which belonged to his master under lock and key. The shrewd fellow only wished to speak to Ottilie and was seeking a pretext to get her out of the room, so he made an excuse and persisted in his request, which Ottilie was quite willing to grant; but, since Charlotte refused, the valet was forced to leave, and the coach drove off.

It was a terrible moment for Ottiie. She understood nothing; she grasped nothing; she realized only that Eduard was parted from her for a long time. Charlotte knew how she felt and left her alone. It is impossible to describe Ottilie's agony or her tears; she suffered beyond measure. She prayed God to help her live through this one day; she lived through the day and the night, and, when she was able to think clearly once more, she felt she was a changed person.

She had not entirely recovered from the shock, nor was she resigned; but, having survived such a great loss, she still had something to fear. Her immediate anxiety, after she had collected herself, was: would she, too, be sent away, now that the men were gone? She did not know about Eduard's threats, which had insured her continuing to stay with Charlotte, but Charlotte's own behavior helped to calm her. Charlotte tried to keep the young girl occupied, and only rarely and reluctantly let her out of her sight. Although she knew how little words can accomplish in the face of a powerful passion, she also knew the power of reflection and reason; and therefore she talked with Ottilie about many subjects.

It was a great comfort to the girl, when Charlotte on one occasion casually but intentionally made the wise observation: "How grateful people are, when our calmness helps them through an emotional crisis," she said. "Let us cheerfully devote our energies to the projects the men have left unfinished. We can make the prospect of their return all the more pleasant, since our moderation will have preserved and improved the work that their violent and impatient natures might well have ruined."

"When you speak of moderation, dear aunt, I cannot help thinking of the lack of it in men, particularly in regard to wine," Ottilie replied. I have often been distressed and upset to see them, for hours on end, lose their clarity of judgment, their consideration for others, their charm and their good manners, when confusion and disaster threaten to spoil all the pleasure to be found in the company of cultivated men. It must have been the cause of many a rash decision!"

Charlotte agreed, but she did not continue the conversation, for she felt sure that Ottilie was simply thinking of Eduard again. Although he was not a habitual drinker, he took wine more often than was desirable when he was working or engaged in animated conversation, or in low spirits.

If Charlotte's remarks had reminded Ottilie of the two friends and of Eduard in particular, she was all the more surprised when Charlotte spoke of the Captain's impending marriage as something settled and generally known, which put an entirely different complexion on everything Eduard's earlier assurances had led her to imagine. All this made Ottilie keenly watchful of every remark, every allusion, every step and action of Charlotte's. Ottilie, without being aware of it, had grown wise, alert, and suspicious.

All this time Charlotte conscientiously looked after every detail in her domestic domain and went about her work with her usual efficiency, constantly urging Ottilie to participate in her activities. She resolutely economized in her household. On deeper reflection, as a matter of fact, she considered the emotional incident as almost providential. At the rate they had been spending money, they might easily have lost all sense of proportion; if they had not stopped and considered before it was too late, their ample fortune would have been depleted, if not dispersed by their extravagant life and diverse projects.

She did not interrupt the work in the park, and, indeed, went on with everything that might serve as a basis for future development, but that was all. She wanted some pleasurable occupation to be available for her husband on his return.

In all this work and planning she could not sufficiently praise the methods of the young Architect. In a short time the lake lay stretched before her eyes, and the new shores were turfed and planted in excellent taste. All the rough work on the new house was soon finished, and everything necessary had been done to protect it against wind and weather. She stopped the work at a point where it would be a pleasure to take it up again in the future. She was always calm and in good spirits; Ottilie was calm, too, but only on the surface. She watched everything only in search of indications of Eduard's return. She had no interest in anything but that.

For this reason she welcomed a plan to recruit a group of peasant boys and train them to keep the enlarged park always neat. This had earlier been Eduard's idea. A kind of bright uniform was made for the children, which they had to put on in the evening after having washed and cleaned themselves thoroughly. The uniforms were kept at the castle in the care of the most responsible and reliable of the boys. The Architect supervised the group; and in a very short time they all did their work quite efficiently. They were easy to train, and they performed their chores almost like a military exercise. When they marched along with their scrapers, garden shears, rakes, their small spades and hoes and brooms, while others marched behind with baskets for stones and weeds, and still others pulled along the heavy iron roller, it was a cheerful and pretty procession indeed, and the architect sketched a series of attractive poses and actions for the frieze of a garden pavilion. But to Ottilie it was only a kind of parade that would welcome the returning master of the castle.

This encouraged her to arrange something else of the same kind to receive him. For some time the girls of the village had been taught to sew, knit, spin, and engage in other forms of feminine industry. The gradual improvement in the cleanliness and beauty of the village had stimulated these domestic virtues. Ottilie had occainally lent a helping hand whenever she had time or felt so inclined. Now she began to work more consistently and systematically. But it is more difficult to form girls into corps than boys. She used her common sense, and, almost unconsciously, merely tried to inspire each girl with a feeling of devotion for her home, her parents, and her brothers and sisters. In a good many instances she was successful. She heard only complaints about one lively little girl, who, people said, was utterly useless and refused to do anything around the house. Ottilie did not have the heart to be angry with this child, who was always friendly and especially attached to her, walking with her and running after her, if permitted. In Ottilie's company the child was helpful, gay, and never tired. The devotion to a lovely mistress seemed to be all she needed. At first Ottilie tolerated her companionship; later she became attached to her, at last they became inseparable; and Nanni accompanied her mistress wherever she went.

Ottilie frequently visited the garden and was pleased to see how everything thrived and grew. The season of berries and cherries was almost over; but Nanni in particular feasted on the last late fruit. All the other trees promised a rich crop in autumn; and the gardener constantly talked about his master and wished to see him at home again. Ottilie loved to listen to the good old man. He was an expert in his profession and could not stop talking to her of Eduard.

When Ottilie showed her delight that the shoots which had been grafted in the spring had developed so well, the gardener said doubtfully: "I only hope that my good master will be pleased with the results. If he were here this autumn, he could see what wonderful fruit we are going to get from the trees in the old park which our late master, his father, planted. The present nurserymen are not as reliable as the Carthusian monks used to be. In the catalogues we find, of course, only the most respectable firms. We buy from them their shoots, graft them, but in the end, when the trees bear fruit, we find our orchards full of trees which were not worth all that trouble."

Whenever this faithful servant met Ottilie, he asked her if his master were coming back and when. And if Ottilie could not give him any information, the old man let her feel by his behavior, and by his barely concealed sadness, that he thought she did not trust him. The feeling of being in the dark herself, which such occasions emphasized, was unbearably painful. And yet she could never stay away from these borders and flowerbeds. What she and Eduard had sown and planted together was now in full bloom. The flowers hardly needed any special care, but Nanni was always willing to water them. With what emotions did Ottilie look at the late flowers that were just beginning to bud. Their brilliant abundance was intended to decorate the celebration of Eduard's next birthday, to express her own love and gratitude. Sometimes she tried to imagine this birthday as a gala day; but her hope often faded. Doubt and anxiety always haunted the poor girl.

A genuine and candid understanding between Charlotte and herself could, perhaps, never be completely restored. The situations of the two women were, of course, very different. If it had been possible to return to the old state of things, and restore their life to normal, Charlotte would have been happy for the present and hopeful for the future, but for Ottilie all would have been lost. We may say *all*, because with Eduard she had found real life and happiness for the first time, and in her present condition she felt an emptiness so complete that she could never have conceived of it. A heart which longs for love may feel that it lacks something; but a heart that has lost love is desolate. Thus longing changes into disappointment and impatience, and a woman's heart, used to waiting and hoping, seeks a new sphere, wishing to do something, to attempt something for its own happiness.

Ottilie had not given Eduard up. How could she, even though Charlotte, against her inner convictions, was wise enough to take it silently for granted that a friendly and calm relationship would be possible between her husband and Ottilie? How often at night, behind her locked door, did the girl kneel before the open traveling case, absorbed in contemplation of the birthday presents she had never touched! She had never used this cloth, never cut it or sewn a stitch! How often did the young girl hurry out of the house at sunrise—she who formerly found all her happiness indoors. She now felt a desire to be out in the open, in the countryside, which never had had any attraction for her. She did not even like to stay long on dry land but would jump into the boat and row out to the middle of the lake. There she would take out a book of travel and let herself be rocked by the rippling waves, reading and dreaming that she was in a far country where she always found her friend—forever close to his heart, as he was to hers.

Chapter Eighteen

It can be imagined that Mittler, about whose odd and busy career we already know, was very eager to show his friendship and exercise his skill in this particular case. He had been informed of the crisis in the life of his friends, although neither of them had as yet asked for his help. He thought it advisable, however, to wait for an opportunity, as he well knew that it is more difficult to help educated people in their moral entanglements than the uneducated. He therefore decided to leave them alone for a while; but presently he could not bear to wait any longer, and hurried to see Eduard after he had tracked him down.

His route took him to a pleasant valley with a bottom of green, richly-wooded meadow, through which a purling brook twisted and sped. Fertile fields and rich orchards covered the whole extent of the gently sloping hills. The villages were not too close to one another, and the whole landscape had a peaceful character. Although it would not have attracted a painter, every part of it seemed to offer pleasant living.

At last Mittler came upon a well-kept farm with a neat and unpretentious farmhouse, surrounded by gardens. He suspected that this was Eduard's refuge, and he was right.

Eduard in his seclusion had completely abandoned himself to his passion, while turning over in his mind innumerable schemes and cherishing all sorts of hopes. He could not deny that he longed to see Ottilie here, that he would like to bring her to this place or to tempt her to come; he also permitted himself other seemly or unseemly thoughts. He lost himself in all sorts of speculations. If he could not make her his own, if she could not be legally his, he would present her with this farm. Here she could live quietly and independently; here she would be happy, and—to such extremes did his self-torturing imagination sometimes carry him—she might even be happy with another man.

So the days passed for him, in an eternal conflict between hope and suffering, tears and happiness; among plans, preparations, and despair. He was not surprised to see Mittler. He had expected him all along and was almost glad when he arrived. If Charlotte had sent him, Eduard was prepared for excuses and postponements as well as more definite proposals; but, if Mittler was bringing him news from Ottilie at last, he would welcome him as a messenger from Heaven.

Eduard was, therefore, rather upset and annoyed when Mittler told him that he did not come from the castle, but on his own impulse. Eduard promptly lost interest, and at first the conversation lagged. But Mittler knew only too well that a person in love wants nothing more than to pour his feelings into the ear of a friend. After a little casual conversation, therefore, he allowed himself for once to drop his usual role and to play the confidant instead of the mediator.

Later, when he gently reproached Eduard for having buried himself in this solitude, his friend replied, "Oh, I do not know how I could spend my time more agreeably! I am always thinking of her; I am always close to her. I have the invaluable advantage of being able to picture in my mind where Ottilie is at any given moment; where she is going, where she is standing, where she is resting. I see her before me, moving and working as usual, doing and planning this or that; always something, of course, principally to make *me* happy. But that is not all: how could I be happy far from her! So then I begin to imagine what Ottilie could do to get in touch with me; I write loving and confiding letters from her to me; I answer them and keep both letters together. I have promised not to take any steps to communicate with her, and I shall keep my promise. But what has *she* promised that keeps her from turning to me? Was Charlotte cruel enough to demand a sworn promise from her that she would not write or send me one word about herself? It would be only natural, and it is very likely what happened; but still I think it outrageous; it is unbearable. If Ottilie loves me, as I believe she does, as I know she does, why doesn't she make up her mind, why doesn't she have the courage to run away and throw herself into my arms?

She ought to do it; I sometimes think she might do it. If I hear the slightest noise in the hall, I look toward the door. I think—I hope—she must be coming. Alas, just as the possible is impossible, I imagine that the impossible could become possible. When I wake up at night and see the flickering lamp fill the room with shadows, I expect her image, her spirit, a breath of her presence, to float past me, approach me, and touch me for one brief moment—to give me some kind of assurance that she thinks of me, that she is mine. There is only one thing left to make me happy. When I saw her constantly, I never dreamed of her; but now that I am far away from her, we are together in my dreams. Strangely enough, only since I have met other attractive people in this neighborhood, she seems to want to say to me in all my dreams, 'Look about you! You will not find anyone more beautiful or more lovely than me.' And so her image slips into all my dreams. Everything that happened to us runs together. Sometimes we sign a contract together: there is her handwriting and mine, her signature and mine; each blots out the other; both intertwine. These delightful ephemeral fantasies are not without pain. Sometimes she does something inconsistent with the pure conception I have of her; only then do I feel how much I love her, for I suffer indescribable agonies. Sometimes she teases and torments me, which is quite unlike her; but then the image changes; her lovely, round, angelic face becomes drawn; it is a different person. But I still feel tortured, unsatisfied, and exhausted.

"Do not smile, my dear Mittler; or do smile if you like. I am not ashamed of my attachment, my foolish and mad passion, if you choose to call it that. Indeed, I have never loved before; only now do I feel what it means. Up to now, everything in my life has been only a prelude, an anticipation—a pastime—time wasted—until now that I have met her and loved her; loved her alone with all my heart and soul. Some people have accused me, not exactly to my face but certainly behind my back, of being a dilettante in most things. This may be true, but before this I had not found anything in which I could prove myself a master. I should like to meet the man who excels me in the art of loving. True, it is a miserable, sorrowful, and tearful gift, but for me it is so natural, so instinctive, that I do not think I can ever part with it."

This impassioned and frank unburdening of his heart relieved Eduard greatly; but he had also suddenly comprehended his strange condition fully; so that, overwhelmed by a terrible inner conflict, he burst into tears, which flowed all the more freely because his heart was softened by his confession to his friend.

Eduard's violent and passionate outburst diverted Mittler from his purpose in coming, and made it even harder for him to suppress his own quick temperament and stubborn common sense; and he expressed his disapproval frankly and without mincing words. He advised Eduard to pull himself together and to realize what he owed to himself as a man; he should not forget that it does a man the greatest credit when he can control his feelings in misfortune, when he can suffer pain with equanimity and dignity; he will be respected, admired, and held up as an example.

To Eduard in his agitation, racked by the most distressing emotions, words like these could only sound hollow and meaningless. "For the man who is happy and untroubled, it is easy to talk in this way," he snapped back, "but he would be ashamed if he knew how unbearable he sounds to the person who is suffering. The stubborn optimist who demands infinite patience refuses to acknowledge the existence of infinite agony. There are cases—yes, there are—when consolation is an offense, and despair a duty! Even a noble Greek who well knew how to portray heroic characters did not disdain to let his heroes weep when they suffered such agony. He said: Noble are the men who can weep. Leave me alone—you who have a dry heart and dry eyes! I curse the happy for whom the unhappy is not only a spectacle. They wish him to act nobly even in the cruelest situation, when he is in physical and spiritual distress, if he is to win their applause; and if they are to applaud him at his exit, he should die before their eyes with the proud dignity of a gladiator. My dear Mittler, I thank you for your visit, but you would do me a great favor if you would take a walk around the garden and look at the countryside. We'll meet later again. I shall try to quiet down and become more like you."

Mittler preferred to change his tactics rather than to break off a conversation it would be difficult to take up again. Eduard also was quite ready to go on talking, for their conversation was tending toward the point he wanted to discuss.

"There is no question that brooding and arguing over a problem leads nowhere," Eduard said; "but, while we were talking, I understood myself for the first time and realized clearly what decision I should reach and have reached. I see my present and my future life before me; the only alternatives are misery or happiness. Dearest friend, try to bring about a separation which is necessary, which already exists; persuade Charlotte to consent. I shall not tell you now the reason why I believe she will. Go to her, my dear man, and bring us all peace and make us happy."

Mittler was taken aback. Eduard continued, "My fate and Ottilie's are inseparable, and we shall not be destroyed. Do you see this glass? Our initials are engraved on it. At a merry celebration some gay fellow flung it into the air so that no one would drink out of it again. It was expected to shatter on the rocky ground, but someone caught it. I paid a high price for it and use it daily, to convince myself every day that all human relations predestined by Fate, are indestructible."

Mittler wailed, "The patience I must have with my friends! Now you bring in superstition—of all things—the most hateful and harmful of all human stupidities. We play with prophecies, premonitions, and dreams in order to give everyday life some significance. But as soon as life itself becomes significant, when everything about us begins to heave and roar, then the gathering storm becomes all the more terrifying because of these ghosts."

"In the uncertainties of my life, suspended between hope and fear, leave my poor heart at least a guiding star to which I can turn, even if I cannot steer by it," Eduard exclaimed.

"There is nothing wrong with that," Mittler replied. "If only I could see some logic in all this—but I have always found that nobody pays attention to warning symptoms. People heed only flattering and promising signs and portents and believe firmly in them."

Mittler had allowed this conversation to tempt him off into dark regions where he felt more and more uncomfortable the longer he remained in them, so that he was now more than willing to comply with Eduard's urgent wish that he should go to see Charlotte. What else could he say to Eduard now? The best he could do at the moment was to gain time and ascertain how the two women felt about the situation, which accorded with his own inclinations.

He hastened to Charlotte, whom he found calm and cheerful, as usual. She was quite ready to tell him about everything that had happened; Eduard's conversation had not really told him anything except the effect of events on Eduard. Mittler approached the matter most cautiously and could not bring himself to mention the word "divorce" even in passing. He was, therefore, surprised, amazed, and, for his part, delighted when at last Charlotte said to him, after a series of depressing disclosures: "I hope and firmly believe that all this will pass and that Eduard will come back to me. "How could it be otherwise, since you find me expecting?"

"Do I understand you correctly?" Mittler interjected.

"Perfectly," Charlotte answered.

"A thousand blessings on this news!" he cried, striking his palm with his fist. "I know the force of this argument on a man's heart. How many marriages have I seen hastened, strengthened, or restored by it! Such a happy expectation has greater force than a thousand words; it is indeed the best expectation we can have. But as for me," he continued, "I should have every reason in the world to be annoyed, for I see that this case will not flatter my vanity. My service in your case will not be appreciated. I feel like a physician—a friend of mine—who was always successful when he treated the poor out of Christian charity but was seldom able to cure a rich patient ready to pay a large fee. Fortunately, here, things will take care of themselves, whereas my efforts—my attempts to persuade—would have been unsuccessful."

Charlotte then asked him to give Eduard the news, to take a letter from her to him, and to see what could be done. But he refused. "Everything has been done already," he exclaimed. "Write your letter; any messenger will do! I must go where I am needed more. I shall come back only to wish you happiness; I shall return for the christening."

Charlotte was again disappointed in Mittler, as she had often been before. His impetuous nature accomplished much good; but his rashness led to many failures. No one was more prone to act on impulse.

Charlotte's messenger found Eduard, who received him almost with trepidation. The letter might well contain a "No" instead of a "Yes." For a long time he hesitated to open it; and he was speechless after he had read the note—almost stunned by the passage with which it ended:

"Do you remember those hours of the night when you visited your wife like a lover in quest of adventure, when you drew her irresistibly to your heart, and closed her in your arms like a beloved, like a bride? Let us revere this strange accident as an act of Providence, which provided a new bond for our relationship at a moment when the happiness of our lives was threatening to dissolve and vanish."

It would be difficult to describe the tumult of emotions which filled Eduard's soul. In such a crisis old habits and old inclinations are again revived to kill time and fill the emptiness of life. Hunting and wars are always convenient escapes for a nobleman. Eduard longed for some external danger to counteract the inner one. He longed for death, for his life threatened to become unbearable; it even comforted him to think that he would not be long in this world and that by his very departure from it he could make his loved ones and his friends happy. No one dissuaded him, since he kept his plans a secret from everyone. When he had observed all the necessary formalities for making his last will and testament, he was very happy that he could transfer the ownership of his farm to Ottilie. He made provision for Charlotte, for the unborn child, for the Captain, and for all his servants. The resumption of hostilities forwarded his plan. In his youth military incompetence had greatly annoyed him, and he had left the service for that reason. Now he was delighted at the prospect of serving under a commander with whom he knew that death would be likely and victory certain.

When Ottilie was told of Charlotte's secret, she was just as stunned as Eduard had been, and even more so. She withdrew into herself completely. There was nothing for her to say. She could not hope and must not wish. Her diary alone will allow us a glimpse into her heart; and we intend to quote some passages from it later.

Part Two

Chapter Nineteen

In ordinary life we are often confronted with something which, in an epic poem, we are accustomed to admire as a poetic device, namely, that after the principal characters have left the scene or have withdrawn into inactivity, a second and even a third person, until then hardly noticed, comes forward at once to fill their places. These persons, as they display their whole activity, then seem to us also worthy of our attention, our sympathy and even of our praise and admiration.

So it was with the young Architect, who, after the Captain's and Eduard's departure, became from day to day a more important figure. The direction of a number of plans and their execution now depended entirely on him; and he proved himself exact, reasonable and energetic in everything, as well as useful to the ladies on many occasions. He was also inventive in entertaining them during their leisure hours, when time hung heavy on their hands. His whole appearance was of a kind that gives confidence and arouses sympathy. He was a young man in the true sense of the word—handsomely built, slim, perhaps a little too tall; modest without being timid, and natural without being forward. He took upon himself any work or duty; and since he was very good at accounts, the household soon held no secrets for him, and his good influence was felt everywhere. He usually received strangers who came to the castle, and was clever at either refusing an unexpected visitor, or at least warning the two women in time, so that the visit caused them no inconvenience.

One day a young lawyer gave them some trouble. He had been sent by a neighboring nobleman, to confer about a matter which, though of no particular importance, yet touched a special chord in Charlotte's heart. We must mention this incident because it set in motion several other matters which otherwise might not have come up for some time.

This incident concerned the change Charlotte had made in the churchyard. All the gravestones had been removed from their places and ranged along the walls and around the foundation of the church. The remaining space had been levelled; and with the exception of a broad path that led up to the church and beyond it to a little gate, all the rest had been sown with different kinds of clover, which was now a lovely green and in flower. New graves were planned to start in a certain order from the farther end; but these plots were to be kept level and also sown with clover. No one could deny that this arrangement offered a pleasant and dignified sight to churchgoers on Sundays and holidays. Even the aged clergyman, although attached to old customs and at first not too pleased with the new grouping, now enjoyed it all and took his rest, like Philemon with his Baucis, under the old linden trees at his back door, seeing before him, not irregular mounds and hillocks, but a lovely colorful carpet, which would, moreover, be a profit to his household; for Charlotte had secured the produce of this place for the benefit of the parsonage.

But in spite of all this, several members of the congregation had for some time disapproved of the fact that the markings of the plots where their forefathers rested had been removed, and that their memory had, as it were, been obliterated by this action. For although the well-preserved gravestones indicated *who* had been buried, they did not say *where*; and this *where* was, as many maintained, really the thing that mattered.

This opinion was shared by a family in the nieghborhood who, several years before, had reserved for themselves by contract a plot in this general place of rest, and in exchange had made a small endowment to the church. Now they had sent the young lawyer to announce that they cancelled this endowment, and would stop further payments, because the stipulation under which things had been done until now, had been eliminated by one party, in spite of all warnings and objections. Charlotte, who was the originator of these changes, wished to speak personally to the young lawyer who now presented, fervently but not too impolitely, his own and his client's reasons, thereby giving his audience food for some serious thoughts.

After a few introductory words, in which he gave a sound justification for his intrusion, the lawyer said: "You see what great importance the lowest and the highest attach to the marking of a spot that has received members of their families. The poorest farmer who buries his child feels a kind of comfort when he places a flimsy wooden cross on its grave, and hangs a wreath over it, in order to keep memory alive as long as his grief is alive; even if such a memorial is finally effaced by Time along with the mourner's grief. Well-to-do people change these crosses of wood to iron, and they fasten and protect them in many ways that may promise durability for at least some years. But because these crosses, too, will in the end collapse and lose their lustre, the wealthy are eager to set up a memorial of stone which promises to last for generations to come and can be renovated and restored by their descendants. It is not the stone which attracts us but that what lies beneath and has been received by the earth. It is not only a question of the monument, but also of the person; not only of a memory of the past but also of the present. The beloved departed is much closer to us when we see the mound before us—the mound rather than the monument, which is in itself of small significance. But around a grave as around a memorial husband or wife, relatives and friends are meant to gather after the dead have passed away; and the living should also have the right to keep off and turn away any strangers or ill-disposed people from the side of the beloved person who sleeps there. For all these reasons, therefore, I think my client is perfectly right in withdrawing the endowment; and it is a fair enough act, because the members of his family have been so offended that they can never be compensated. They are deprived of the bittersweet feeling that it is possible for them to bring their tributes to their dead; and they are also deprived of the fond hope of resting at some later day by their sides."

"The whole matter is not important enough to provoke a lawsuit," Charlotte replied. "I regret so little what I have done, that I am willing to indemnify the church for its loss. But I must tell you quite frankly that your arguments have not convinced me. The pure feeling of a final, universal equality, at least after death, seems to me a greater comfort than this obstinate, rigid persistence upon our personalities, our attachments and the circumstances of our life. And what is your opinion?" she asked, turning to the Architect.

"In such an issue, I should prefer not to argue nor to have my own notions influence the decision. Allow me modestly to mention something which pertains to my own art and therefore to my own point of view. We are no longer fortunate enough to be able to press to our hearts an urn with the ashes of our beloved, nor are we nowadays either rich or naïve enough to expect that we can preserve beloved remains from decay in large, elaborately ornamented sarcophagi. We are also no longer allowed to appropriate a place in a church for ourselves and our families but are banished into the open. For all these reasons we may, I think, approve of the ways and means Your Ladyship has introduced here. When the members of a congregation lie buried in one cemetery, they rest together as families, and if it is our destiny to be received one day by the earth, I do not think anything could be more natural than to level the mounds. They were, in any case, raised for a short while and will gradually disappear again; so that the covering now borne by all will be lighter for each."

"Do you mean to say that everything should pass away without a sign to evoke a memory?" Ottilie asked, in wonder.

"By no means!" the Architect continued. "We should not give up the memorial itself, only its position. The architect and the sculptor are extremely anxious for men to demand enduring evidence of their lives from them, from their art, from their handicraft. That is why I should like to see well-designed and well-executed monuments, not standing by themselves or scattered here and there at random, but set up together in a place which promises permanence for them. Since even the good and the great have renounced the privilege of being laid to rest in churches, we should at least set up monuments and hang up tablets with inscriptions in the churches or in beautiful arcades surrounding the cemeteries. Thousands of forms exist, which might be taken as patterns for these, and there are thousands of ornaments with which they might be adorned."

"If the artists are really so rich in models, please tell me why we never see anything but a mediocre obelisk, a broken column and an urn," Charlotte challenged him, "Instead of the thousands of forms which you boast of, I have never seen anything but a thousand repetitions of the same thing."

"That is perhaps the case in our country but not everywhere," the Architect replied, "and a difficult problem probably always exists between intention and proper application. Especially in a case like this, the great difficulty lies in trying to enliven a melancholy subject and not to render unpleasant an unpleasant one. Regarding the designs for monuments of all sorts, I have collected many of these and will show them to you on occasion. But I believe that the best memorial for a man is his portrait. More than anything else it gives an idea of what he was; it is the best text to all that can be said about him in a few or many words; but it should be done only in his best years, and this is usually neglected. While people are still alive, no one thinks of preserving their human forms, and if it *is* done, it is mostly done inefficiently. Sometimes a cast is taken in a hurry after a person's death; and such a death mask is set up on a pedestal and called a portrait bust. How rarely has an artist the skill to make it completely lifelike!"

"Perhaps without intention and purpose you have turned the scales of this discussion entirely in my favor," Charlotte remarked. "The portrait of a person is, without any doubt, quite independent;. in whatever place it stands, it stands by itself and need not necessarily mark the burial place proper. But I have to confess to a strange sort of emotional aversion to portrait busts. They always seem to me like a silent reproach; they point toward something far away and passed away, and remind me how difficult it is really to be just to the present. If we recall how many people we have seen and known, and confess to ourselves how little we have meant to them, how little they have meant to us—what must then be our feelings! We meet a man of genius without talking with him, a scholar without trying to learn from him, a widely-traveled person without broadening our knowledge, a person full of love without showing him any kindness.

"Unfortunately, this does not happen with casual encounters only. Societies and families behave in the same way toward their dearest members, cities toward their most deserving citizens, peoples toward their best sovereigns, nations toward their most distinguished men.

"I once heard someone ask: Why has everyone good words only for the dead, while there is always some caution in the case of the living? The answer was: because we have nothing to fear from the former, whereas it is still possible that we may meet the latter. Our concern for the memory of the others is often insincere and for the greater part only a selfish game; but we should be absolutely serious in keeping our relations with those who are still living always cordial and active."

Chapter Twenty

Stimulated by this incident and by the discussion arising from it, they went the following day to the churchyard, where the Architect made several happy suggestions. But the church itself was also to be entrusted to his care—a building which had aroused his interest from the moment of his arrival.

This church, built in the early German style, had been standing here for many centuries; its proportions were good, and its ornaments remarkable. One could clearly see that the master-builder of a monastery in the neighborhood had left, on this smaller building, authentic traces of his judgment and taste. It still made a solemn and peaceful impression on the observer, although the new arrangements for a Protestant service had deprived the interior of some of its calm and grandeur.

It was not difficult for the Architect to ask for, and to receive, from Charlotte, a small sum of money which he intended to use for the restoration in the old tradition, of the exterior as well as of the interior of the church and bring it into harmony with the "resurrection field" in front of it. He possessed considerable manual skill; and some men who were still busy at the new lodge could be kept on until this pious task was also finished.

They could now begin to make a thorough examination of the whole building with all its grounds and annexes; and in the course of this the Architect discovered, to his great surprise and delight, an almost forgotten little side-chapel of still more ingenious and balanced proportions, with still more beautiful and carefully worked out ornaments. This chapel also contained many carved and painted remnants of that earlier service which had marked the different church festivals with various vessels and vestments, and had celebrated each in its traditional way.

It seemed impossible to the Architect not to include the chapel in his project; and he decided to restore this narrow space with particular care, as a monument of earlier times and of their taste. He already imagined how he would like to see the empty wall spaces decorated, and looked eagerly forward to practicing there his talent for painting. But for the time being he kept this a secret from the others.

Before he began his restoration, he showed the two women, as he had promised, different reproductions and designs of ancient monuments for the dead, of urns and other objects to the same purpose. When the conversation turned upon the primitive *tumuli* of the Northern peoples, he also showed them his collection of various weapons and tools found in these places. He kept everything very neatly, and easily to be carried, in drawers and compartments, on partitioned and cloth-covered trays, so that, by the way he treated them, these grim old things appeared almost like precious trinkets. It was a pleasure to look at them, as though one were looking into the boxes of a dealer in jewels.

Since he had begun this display of his treasures, which formed an entertainment for the two lonely women, he got into the habit of producing every evening another part of his collection: objects mostly of German origin. Among these were thin mediaeval plates of silver, large silver coins, seals, and other things of this nature. All these objects directed the imagination toward ancient times; and as he finally illustrated his talks with the first examples of the art of printing, with wood-cuts and the earliest copper-plate prints; and as the church, developed from day to day, in decoration and color, in the spirit of the same age,—the question quite naturally arose: Were they actually living in modern times? Was it not a dream that they were surrounded by quite different habits, customs, modes of life and ideas?

After such preparation, a large portfolio which he finally produced made the strongest impression on them. It contained for the most part mere outlines of figures, but these had been traced from the original pictures, and therefore had completely preserved their ancient character—and how charming this character was, in the eyes of the spectators! All the figures breathed a perfect purity of heart; all were, if not noble, certainly full of goodness. Serene composure, willing recognition of a Divine Being above us, silent devotion full of love and hope, were expressed on their faces and in their gestures.

The bald-headed ancient, the boy with his profusion of curls, the buoyant youth, and the serious man; the Saint transfigured, the angel hovering in the air,—all seemed to be in a state of heavenly bliss, happy in an innocent, contented, pious expectation. The most ordinary scenes had a touch of heavenly beauty; and every being seemed to be worthy of a part in the divine service. Most people, very likely, look with yearning toward such a realm, in the way we look back toward a vanished Golden Age, a paradise lost. Ottilie was perhaps the only one who felt at home in that world.

After all this, who could have rejected the Architect's offer to paint the wall spaces between the pointed arches of the chapel in the manner of the original pictures—murals he wished to leave as his own memorial in a place where he had spent such happy days. He said this with a touch of sadness, for he knew that, as matters stood, his stay in this delightful company could not last forever: it might very soon come to an end.

Although not very much happened during these days, there was always occasion for serious conversations. We take this opportunity to set down some of the comments, written by Ottilie in her diary; and we cannot find a more suitable transition than a comparison which struck us as we were looking through her moving pages.

There is a curious custom in the British Navy: all the cordage of the Royal Fleet, whether heavy or light, is twisted so that a red thread runs through whole ropes, by which even the smallest piece can be recognized as Crown property.

In the same way a thread of love and deep attachment seems to run through Ottilie's diary, connecting everything she writes, and giving it a distinctive character. Because of this thread, the young girl's comments, observations and quotations bear a special mark, and convey a particular meaning. Each passage we have selected and recorded is definite proof of this.

From Ottilie's Diary

That we shall some day rest by the side of those we love, is the most comforting thought we can have, when we think about the Here-after. "To be gathered to our fathers"—are extremely heart-warming words.

So many different kinds of monuments and memorials exist, which bring those who have died, and friends who have left us, closer to our hearts. But nothing is as significant as a portrait. To talk to the picture of a person dear to us, though it may not be a good likeness, is as delightful as an occasional quarrel with a friend. We have the pleasant impression of being two who still cannot be separated.

Sometimes we speak to a person who is in our presence, as though we would speak to a picture. It is not necessary that he should speak to us or look at us or pay us any attention: it is *we* who look at him and deeply feel our relation with him, which may become even closer, without any action on his part, without his even being aware of it, since for us he is nothing but a picture.

We are never satisfied with the portraits of people we know. I have therefore always felt sorry for portrait-painters. Though we rarely expect from anyone the impossible, we expect it from them. They are supposed to include in their portraits everyone's relation to the orginal, whether it be sympathy or antipathy, and to paint him not only as *they* see him but as everyone else does. I am not surprised that such artists become, little by little, stubborn, indifferent and intractable. This would not matter so much, if it did not frequently deprive us of the portraits of many persons, dear to us.

It is certainly true, and borne out by the Architect's collection of weapons and tools, once buried with the dead under high mounds of earth or stones, that man's careful provisions for the preservation of his personality after death, are entirely useless. And how inconsistent we are! The Architect admits having himself opened such burial mounds of forebears, yet he keeps on occupying himself with monuments for their descendants.

But why should we be so critical? Is perhaps all we do done for eternity? Do we not put on our clothes in the morning, only to take them off in the evening? Do we not travel in order to come back again? And why should we not wish to rest by the side of our families and friends, though it may be only for a century?

When we see the many sunken tombstones, worn by the footsteps of churchgoers, and the churches, collapsed over their own memorial—tablets for the dead—life after death seems to us, indeed, a second life which man enters in the form of the portrait and the inscription, in which he exists longer than in his actual life-span. But this memorial, this second existence, will also be effaced—sooner or later. Time does not relinquish its rights, either over human beings or over monuments.

Chapter Twenty-One

Because it affords us so much pleasure to occupy ourselves even with something we can do only imperfectly, we should not perhaps blame the dilettante for dabbling in an art he will never master; nor should we blame the artist who feels inclined to trespass, beyond the boundary of his own field, on a neighboring one.

With these tolerant feelings we shall watch the Architect's preparations in the chapel: he mixed the colors, took the measurements and designed the preliminary cartoons. He made no claim to originality, but kept strictly to his sketches. His only concern was the skilfull composition of the seated or floating figures and their decorative effect within the given space. Scaffolding was set up, and the work moved forward. As soon as something definite could be seen, he no longer objected when Charlotte and Ottilie came over to look at his work. The lifelike faces of the angels, their robes billowing against a background of celestial blue, delighted them, and the serene composure of their devotion touched their hearts and filled their minds with peace.

They joined the artist on the scaffolding; and soon as Ottilie saw how easily and with how little effort the work proceeded in just the manner it had been planned—everything she had learned in school came back to her, and she understood its meaning. She took up a brush and some paint, and, after a few directions, touched in a richly folded drapery with accuracy and taste. Charlotte, who was always happy when she saw Ottilie busy or in some other way diverted, left the pair to their painting and went home alone, to follow the train of her thoughts and to work out on her own all the deliberations and worries which she could not confide to any other person.

When ordinary people are moved to strong emotions of passion and anxiety by common daily predicaments, we may smile indulgently, but we look with awed admiration on a mind which carries the seed of a great destiny, are forced to wait for the development of this seed, and must not and cannot hasten the good or the evil, the happiness or the misery, which is destined to come from it.

Eduard had sent an answer to Charlotte by the same messenger she had dispatched to him in his seclusion. His words had been kind and sympathetic, but at the same time more calm and grave than intimate and affectionate. Shortly afterward, Eduard disappeared, and Charlotte had not been able to obtain any news from him until, quite by accident, she saw his name in the newspaper, where he was mentioned with honor among those who had distinguished themselves in an important military engagement. She now knew where he had gone and that he had escaped great danger. But she was also convinced that he would expose himself to still greater danger, and she understood only too well that it would be impossible to restrain him from extreme action. She carried this constant anxiety in her thoughts, and no matter how she might look at it, she could find no comfort.

Ottilie had not the slightest suspicion of all this—she had become very much interested in her work in the chapel and had easily obtained Charlotte's permission to continue painting there regularly. The work was progressing rapidly, and soon the azure sky was filled with suitable figures. Through continued practice Ottilie and the Architect worked with more independence on the later pictures, which were distinctly better than the first. The faces, which had been left to the Architect, increasingly revealed a very peculiar quality: they all began to resemble Ottilie. To be so close to her had obviously made so strong an impression on the young man, who had not yet formed a preference for any one natural or artistic facial type, that on the way from his eye to his hand, nothing was lost—eventually, both worked together in perfect accord. One of the last little countenances he painted was a perfect likeness—it seemed that Ottilie herself looked down from the heavenly spaces.

The vaulting was finished; the walls were to be left undecorated and only painted a lighter umber tint; the slender pillars and the ingeniously carved ornaments were to be contrasted in a darker shade. But since, in such cases, one thing leads to another, they decided at the last moment to add festoons of flowers and fruit, to unite, as it were, heaven and earth. Here Ottilie was in her element.

The gardens supplied them with the loveliest motifs; and although the wreaths turned out to be very luxuriant, all was completed much earlier than it had been planned.

But everything else still looked very untidy and unfinished. The scaffolding had been piled up helter-skelter, planks thrown one on top of the other; the uneven floor looked worse than ever because of the paint they had dropped on it. The Architect now asked the two ladies for a week's time and for their promise not to enter the chapel until then. One fine evening he finally invited them both to go and see for themselves: he himself did not wish to accompany them and left immediately.

"Whatever surprise he may have in store for us, I am not, at the moment, in a mood to go see it," Charlotte said, after the young man's departure. "You won't mind going alone and telling me all about it later? I am sure he has created something beautiful. I shall enjoy it first in your description and then, with much greater pleasure, in reality."

Ottilie, who was well aware that Charlotte was now in many respects very careful—she avoided anything that might upset her and in particular disliked being surprised—started out at once. She looked, instinctively, for the Architect but could not see him anywhere—he was possibly hiding. The church was finished, cleaned and consecrated earlier. It was open and she entered. She stepped to the chapel door; its heavy bronze weight opened easily, and she was surprised by the unexpected sight of the familiar place.

A solemn many-colored light fell through the symmetrical panes of the one high stained-glass window. The whole space had taken on an unfamiliar quality and induced a peculiar mood. The beauty of the vaulting and the walls was heightened by the decorative design of the floor, paved with specially shaped bricks which were joined by mortar to form a beautiful pattern. These bricks as well as the stained-glass panes had been secretly assembled by the Architect and then been put together in a very short time. He had also looked about for seats. Among the ecclesiastical antiques, mentioned before, he had found some exquisitely carved chancel stalls and had arranged them along the walls.

Ottilie was delighted to see these familiar pieces now forming an unfamiliar whole. She stopped here and there and walked up and down, examining and re-examining everything; at last she sat down in one of the seats; looking above and around her, it almost seemed to her that she existed and yet did not exist; that she felt and did not feel—as if all this might vanish before her eyes and she might vanish too. Only when the sun left the window through which it had shone so brightly, did Ottilie waken from her dream and hurry back to the castle.

The fact did not escape her that his surprise had occurred at a strange moment. It was the eve of Eduard's birthday. How differently had she hoped to celebrate it—how she had wished to decorate everything for this occasion! But now the wealth of autumn flowers stood ungathered. The sunflowers still turned their disks to the sky; the asters looked about them with their quiet modesty, and the only flowers which had been made into wreaths had served as models for the decoration of a place, which, if it were not to remain merely an artist's whim but was to be used for any true purpose, seemed appropriately only for a family tomb.

She could not help remembering the noisy festivities with which Eduard had celebrated her own birthday; and she recalled the events at the newly finished house, under whose roof they had hoped to spend many hours. The fireworks flashed and sputtered again before her eyes—the lonelier she was, the more vividly she saw everything in her imagination but she also felt a deeper loneliness. She no longer leaned on his arm; and she had lost all hope ever to be thus supported again.

From Ottilie's Diary

I must make a note of a remark made by the young artist: we observe quite distinctly in the case of the craftsman as well as of the creative artist, that man is least able to appropriate to himself what is truly his own. His works utterly desert him, as birds desert the nest in which they have been hatched.

In this connection, the architect's fate is the strangest of all fates. How often does he give his intelligence and his entire devotion to the creation of buildings from which he is excluded! The halls of royal palaces owe their magnificence to him, but he does not enjoy them in their full splendor. In places of worship he draws a line between himself and the Holy of Holies: he is no longer allowed to ascend the steps which he has built for the heart-stirring celebration—like the goldsmith who only from a distance worships the monstrance whose enamel and precious stones he has set together. It is to the rich man that the masterbuilder gives, together with the key of the palace, all the luxury and opulence he will never enjoy. Is it not obvious that in this way his art will gradually withdraw from the artist, when his work, like a child who is well provided for, need no longer fall back on its father? And how much had art to do for its own advancement in the days when it was destined to work almost entirely in the public interest, with matters which belonged to all and consequently to the artist as well!

One conception of the ancients is solemn and almost frightening. They imagined their ancestors sitting in huge caves in a circle on thrones, in silent communication. When a newcomer entered, they rose and bowed their heads to welcome him, if he deserved it. Yesterday, when I was sitting in the chapel in my carved seat and saw opposite me other seats arranged in a circle, I remembered this, and it was a comforting and happy thought. Why can you not remain here? I said to myself,—remain here, quiet and lost in your thoughts for a long, long time, until your friends arrive at last and you will rise, and with a friendly gesture direct them to their places. The stained-glass panes transform the day into somber twilight; someone should donate an everburning lamp, so that here even the night would not be complete darkness.

We may imagine ourselves in any situation we like, but we always think of ourselves as *seeing*. I believe that the reason man dreams is because he should not stop seeing. Some day perhaps the inner light will shine forth from us, and then we shall need no other light.

The year moves toward its end like a sound toward silence. The wind sweeps over the stubble, and there is nothing for it to stir. Only the red berries of those slender trees seem to wish to remind us of gaiety; just as the rhythmic beat of the thresher's flail reminds us how much nourishment and life lie concealed in the sickled ear.

Chapter Twenty-Two

These incidents had filled Ottilie with a sense of instability and impermanence, and it was therefore a strange and unexpected shock to hear the news, which could no longer be kept a secret from her, that Eduard had exposed himself to the chances of war. Unfortunately, none of the possibilities involved escaped her; but, fortunately, we can absorb disastrous news only up to a certain point—anything beyond that destroys us or leaves us indifferent. There are situations in which hope and fear become one, cancel each other out, and are lost in dull apathy. How could we, otherwise, bear knowing that our distant loved ones are in continual danger, and yet go on as usual with our everyday life? It was therefore as though a benevolent spirit was caring for Ottilie by introducing into this quiet atmosphere, in which she seemed alone and inactive, a sudden flood of visitors, these gave her enough work to do, and at the same time drew her out of her seclusion and restored to her an awareness of her own strength.

Hardly had Luciane, Charlotte's daughter, left school to come out in society, to find herself surrounded by friends and admirers in her great-aunt's house, when her pleasing disposition found favor in the eyes of a very rich young man, who fell violently in love with her and wished to marry her. His large fortune gave him a right to own the best of everything, and he seemed to have everything except a perfect wife whom the whole world would envy him.

This domestic event had already kept Charlotte busy for some time; she devoted to it all her attention and all her correspondence, with the exception of the letters written to obtain more detailed information concerning Eduard. This was also the reason why Ottilie had been lately left to herself more than usual. Although the young girl knew about Luciane's expected arrival and had made the most necessary preparations, no one expected the visit so soon. Charlotte was about to write another letter to settle some details and to suggest a definite date, when the storm suddenly broke over the castle and over Ottilie's head.

The ladies' maids, the valets, and the *brancards* with trunks and boxes were the first to arrive, and even then it seemed as though two or three families were already in the house; but only now did the guests themselves arrive: Luciane with her great-aunt, some friends, and her fiancé, who had brought along a group of his own friends. The hall was littered with bags, portmanteaus, and all sorts of leather cases. It took some time to sort out all the smaller boxes. More luggage was brought in and moved about. In addition, it began to rain, causing much inconvenience. Ottilie met all this tumult and confusion with complete calm, and her cheerful efficiency was shown to advantage. In the shortest possible time she had arranged, and disposed of, everything. Everyone had been shown to a room, and felt well taken care of.

The moment came when everybody wished to rest after the tiring journey. Luciane's fiancé wanted to talk with his future mother-in-law, to assure her of his affection and good will; but Luciane herself would not rest. For the first time she had experienced the joy of riding horseback, and her fiancé had excellent horses which she wished to try without delay. Wind and weather, rain or storm, did not matter; the one thing in life that did seem to matter was first to get soaking wet and then dry again. When she felt in a mood for walking, she did not care how she was dressed or what shoes she wore; she had to inspect the new grounds of which she had heard so much. What she could not do on horseback, she did on foot—but always running. In a very short time she had seen everything and — criticized everything. She had such a quick temper that it was not easy to contradict her. The other guests had a great deal to bear, most of all her maids, who were continually washing, pressing, ripping things up, and sewing them together again.

As soon as she had finished exploring the castle and its immediate surroundings, she felt it her duty to make calls on all the neighbors. Since she and her friends rode and drove very fast, the area of neighborhood was extended on all sides. The castle was soon swamped with people returning the visits; and, in order that hosts and guests should not miss one another, special days were agreed upon when the hosts would stay at home.

While Charlotte tried to settle the financial arrangements with her aunt and the fiancé's agent, and Ottilie was busy with the servants, taking care that nothing was lacking for so many, and setting hunters and gardeners, fishermen and shopkeepers in motion, Luciane was behaving like the blazing heart of a comet which drags a long tail in its wake. The ordinary entertainment offered to visitors soon became boring to her taste. Even the oldest persons, peacefully sitting at their card-tables, were not safe frm her restlessness. Anyone who could still move a limb—and who could resist moving when coaxed by her charming insistence?—had to join her, if not to dance, then to play at forfeits and puzzles. But although all these games, particularly the redeeming of forfeits, were calculated for her own personal interest, no one, on the other hand (particularly no man, of any sort) ever went entirely unrewarded; and she was even successful in winning over to her some elderly distinguished persons, when she discovered the dates of their birthdays or name days and then celebrated these with special courtesy. On every such occasion, her personal skill in showing kindness to all was very useful, since she gave every single person to believe that he was the most favored: a weakness of which even the oldest man among the guests conspicuously proved himself guilty.

If it seemed to be her firm determination to conquer every man of importance,—or rank, character, fame or of whatever repute; to defeat wisdom and moderation and even to cause the sedate to forgive her wild, strange ways—the younger people were by no means losers in all this; each one received his share, his day and his hour, when she would deliberately set out to delight and captivate him. It could be expected that she would soon single out the Architect,—who, however, looking innocently from under his long dark hair, stood quite unmoved, at a quiet distance, and answered all her questions briefly and sensibly, without seeming to show the least inclination to go any farther; so that one day she decided,—half in anger and half in cunning—to make him that day's hero, and to win him over to her court of admirers by a trick.

Not unintentionally had she brought so much luggage with her, and had even sent for more. She had provided an endless array of dresses for herself since she liked to change three or four times a day from an ordinary gown to something more elegant—and this went on from morning to night. But in between she now and then appeared in actual fancy-dress—as a peasant-woman or a fisherman's wife; as a good fairy or a flower-girl. She was not even afraid of disguising herself as an old woman, if only to show her young, fresh face framed in a cowl; and she mixed so much of the actual with the fantastic that one might have thought one's self to be related directly, or by marriage to a nymph of the river Saale.

But her principal purpose for all these costumes was their use in pantomimes and dances, in which she was very good at expressing different characters. One of her admirers had arranged with her to accompany her performance with incidental music on the piano. They needed only to exchange a few words of explanation to understand each other at once.

One day, during an intermission of a gay ball, Luciane was asked for such a performance. The question seemed to come on the spur of the moment; but she herself earlier had secretly dropped a hint. Now she pretended to be embarrassed and taken by surprise; and she was also for a time reluctant, which was quite unlike her. She seemed undecided, wished the others to choose her role, and asked for a theme, as an improviser does, until at last her accompanist, with whom she had very likely arranged everything beforehand, sat down at the piano and, beginning to play a funeral march, asked her to do the *Artemisia,* which she had studied so admirably. She let herself be persuaded, and, after a short absence, again appeared as the royal widow carrying an urn in her arms and walking with measured steps to the tender and mournful sound of the funeral march. Behind her, a large blackboard was carried in, together with a well-sharpened stick of chalk fastened in a golden drawing-pen holder.

One of her admirers and aides, into whose ear she whispered, approached the Architect and asked—or rather, forced—him, while pushing him toward her, to draw, as a masterbuilder would, the tomb of Mausolus; adding that he should not consider himself by any means a supernumerary, but one of the actual performers. The Architect who, in his black tight-fitting modern civilian dress formed an odd contrast to all Luciane's gauze, crêpe, fringes, jet, tassels and crowns, looked very embarrassed at first, but soon regained his composure; still, it was a strange sight! With the greatest seriousness, he took his stand in front of the blackboard, which was supported by two pages, and slowly and carefully executed a drawing of a tomb which, although more appropriate for a king of the Langobards than for one of Caria, had such beautiful proportions, was so serious in all its detail and so ingenious in its ornaments, that everyone present watched the drawing grow with delight; and all were full of admiration when it was finished.

All this time the Architect had almost never looked in the direction of the Queen, but had given his whole attention to his task. When he finally bowed to her, to indicate that he believed he had carried out her orders, she offered him the urn, suggesting her wish to see it portrayed on the top of the tomb. He did this, although unwillingly, since it did not fit into the character of the rest. Luciane was now at last satisfied; it had certainly not been her intention to have him do a meticulous drawing. If he had done a hasty sketch in a few strokes, something approximately resembling a monument, and had occupied himself with her for the remainder of the time, it would have been much more to her liking. His behavior had made matters very difficult for her; she tried to vary somehow the expression of her grief, her commands and suggestions as well as her approval of the growing design, and even—in order to focus his attention on her—almost pushed him about. He, in turn, behaved so stiffly that she had to shift the urn much too fequently, pressing it to her heart and gazing up to heaven. Since a performance of this sort is bound to demand ever increasing intensity, she soon resembled a widow of Ephesus rather than a queen of Caria. For all these reasons the entertainment lasted much too long; the pianist, who had been very patient, was at a loss into what key he should modulate. He thanked God when he saw the urn standing on top of the pyramid, and involuntarily, just when the queen was on the point of expressing her gratitude, struck up a merry tune. This changed the whole character of the performance but cheered up the party, which at once divided into two groups—one expressing their delight and admiration to the lady for her excellent acting, the other showing the Architect their appreciation of his fine and artistic delineation.

The fiancé was particularly enthusiastic. "I am sorry that your drawing is so impermanent," he said. "Won't you at least allow me to have it brought to my room, so I can discuss it with you later?"

"If you are interested, I can show you elaborate drawings of monuments and buildings of that kind compared to which this is only a casual and imperfect sketch," the Architect replied.

Ottilie was standing not far away and now came nearer. "Don't forget to show your collection to the Baron," she said. "He is a friend of art and antiquity, and I wish you two would become better acquainted with one another."

Luciane swept up and asked;: "What are you talking about?"

"Of a collection of works of art which this gentleman possesses and will show us some time," the Baron answered.

"Go and get it immediately," Luciane exclaimed. "You *will* bring it at once, won't you?" she added, touching him kindly with both hands.

"I do not think that this is the right moment," he replied.

"What! You refuse to obey the orders of your queen?" Luciane cried in a commanding tone. Then she began to coax him like a child.

"Don't be stubborn!" Ottilie said in a low voice.

The Architect left them with a slight inclination of his head, neither "yes" nor "no."

He had hardly gone when Luciane began to chase through the room with her greyhound. "Alas! How unhappy I am," she exclaimed, brushing against her mother by accident. "I did not bring my monkey with me; everyone advised against it; it is only the laziness of my servants that deprives me of my fun. But I am going to have it brought here—I shall send someone to fetch it. It would even cheer me up to see his picture. I must have his portrait done, and I'll never again let it leave my side."

"I can perhaps cheer you by sending to our library for a whole volume filled with the most extraordinary pictures of monkeys," Charlotte said. Luciane shrieked with joy, and the large folio was brought. The sight of these hideous creatures, resembling men and, as drawn by the artist, exaggeratedly so, gave Luciane the greatest pleasure. But she was particularly happy in discovering in every single animal a resemblance to a person known to her. "Does he not look like my uncle?" she cried, mercilessly "and this one like M . . . our dealer in trinkets, and that one so like Parson S . . .; but this one is really the very image of Mr. So-and-So. After all, monkeys are the true 'Dandies,' and it is difficult to understand why they are excluded from good society."

All this was said in the presence of the best society; but no one resented it. Everyone was so used to allow her charm all possible liberty that they finally permitted her naughtiness, too.

Meanwhile Ottilie talked with Luciane's fiancé. She hoped that the Architect would return and, with his more serious and tasteful collection, rescue the company from this disgraceful fuss about monkeys. With this expectation in mind she talked to the Baron and told him more about the collection. But the Architect did not at once return; and when he at last appeared, he lost himself among the guests. He had not brought anything with him, and behaved as though no one had ever asked him for anything. Ottilie was for a few moments—how shall we describe it?—annoyed, angry, hurt; she had spoken kindly to him and she had also wished to give the Baron a pleasant hour, since she felt that, in spite of his deep love for Luciane, he quite evidently suffered because of her extravagant behavior.

The monkeys had to make way for supper. Social games, even more dancing, and finally a bored sitting about, and several attempts to stimulate an almost exhausted desire for pleasure, dragged out this time, as usual, until long past midnight. For it had already become a habit with Luciane never to get out of bed in the morning and never to get into it at night.

During these weeks Ottilie rarely recorded actual events in her diary; but she wrote down, more frequently, maxims and aphorisms which either referred to life or were taken from it. Since the greater part of these are probably not her own thoughts, it is likely that someone had given her a book, from which she copied those which corresponded to her feelings. But many of her own thoughts, related to the deep experiences of her heart, will easily be recognized by the red thread.

From Ottilie's Diary

We love to look into the future, because we should dearly like, by our silent wishing, to guide in our own favor the Undetermined that wavers there.

In a large gathering of people the thought seldom leaves us, that Chance, which brings so many together, may also lead our friends here.

However secluded we may live, sooner or later, and before we realize it, we become either debtors or creditors.

Whenever we meet a person who owes us a debt of gratitude, we instantly remember it. But how often do we meet someone, to whom *we* are indebted, without remembering it.

To communicate our thoughts to others is nature; to assimilate what is communicated to us, with understanding, is culture.

No one would talk much in society, if he knew how often he misunderstands others.

When we repeat what we have heard others say, we change a good deal; no doubt only because we did not really understand everything, to begin with.

He who talks alone and at length before others without flattering his audience, arouses antipathy.

Every word that is spoken provokes its contrary.

Both contradiction and flattery make poor conversation.

The most agreeable societies are those, governed by an easy mutual regard of their members.

Nothing reveals people's character more than their reaction to what they consider laughable.

The ridiculous arises from a moral contrast, by which, in a harmless way, two matters become connected in our mind.

The natural man often laughs, when there is no reason for it. Whatever stimulates him, it is his inner well-being that comes to the surface.

The reasoning man considers almost anything ridiculous; the reasonable man almost nothing.

An elderly man was sharply criticized for continuing to pay court to young women. "It is the only way to keep young," he replied, "and that is certainly everybody's desire."

We can bear being criticized for our faults, and even bear to be punished and to suffer on their account; but we become impatient, when we are expected to give them up.

Some faults are necessary to the life of the individual. We would be sorry if old friends gave up certain peculiarities.

People say "He will die soon," when someone acts in a way that is not characteristic of him.

What kind of faults are we permitted to keep, even to indulge in? Those which flatter rather than hurt others.

Passions are weaknesses or virtues, but intensified.

Our passions are true phoenixes. As soon as the old bird consumes itself, a new one rises at once from the ashes.

Great passions are incurable diseases. What might cure them, makes them all the more dangerous.

Passion becomes ennobled and calmed by confession. Nowhere is a middle course more desirable than in the choice of what we confide to, or conceal from, those we love.

Chapter Twenty-Three

And so the intoxication of living kept driving Luciane ever deeper into the vortex of social amusements. Her court of admirers daily increased, partly because her drive animated and attracted many; partly because she knew how to attach others to herself by her acts of kindness and her generosity. She was indeed generous to a high degree; and since her great-aunt's affection and her fiancé's love had flooded her so suddenly with so much that was beautiful and precious, it seemed as if nothing she possessed really belonged to her, and as if she did not know the value of the objects which accumulated around her. Therefore she never for a moment hesitated to take from her shoulders an expensive shawl and wrap it around a young woman who, in her opinion, was poorly dressed compared to others; and she did this, moreover, in such a droll and clever way that no one could refuse a gift, because of the way it was given. One of her followers always carried with him a sum of money, and had been instructed to inquire, in whatever place they stopped, after the most sick and the oldest persons, and to relieve their situation at least temporarily. In this way she made herself a great reputation in this part of the country; but this practice was also sometimes a great nuisance, since far too many needy persons were attracted to her.

Nothing increased her popularity more than her extraordinary and unwavering kindness to an unhappy young man who had given up all social life because he, otherwise handsome and well built, had lost his right hand, although with honor, in action. This disability had made him so melancholy, and the fact that each new acquaintance had to be told the story of his accident was so annoying, that he preferred to hide himself, devoting all his time to reading and studying, and not wanting to have anything to do with society.

Luciane had, of course heard of this young man. She did not rest, until he came first to small parties, then to larger ones, and finally to the largest. She paid more attention to him than to anyone else; and because of her eagerness to help him and her determination to compensate him for his loss, she even succeeded in making it valuable to him. At dinner she made him sit next to her and cut up his food for him, so that he needed only to use his fork. If he had to give up his place to older people or persons of higher rank, she extended her attention across the entire table, and the servants had to run and render him the services of which his distance from her deprived him. Finally she encouraged him to learn to write with his left hand; he had to address all his attempts to her, so that she was, far or near, constantly in touch with him. The young man did not know what had happened to him, and from this time on really started a new life.

One would have imagined that Luciane's fiancé might not have been pleased with such behavior, but just the opposite was true. He thought it much to her credit that she took all this trouble; he was not worried, since he knew her almost exaggerated fear of being entangled in anything in the least risky. She wanted to handle everyone according to her mood; at one time or another everyone was in danger of being pushed or pulled about, or otherwise teased by her; but no one was allowed to do the same with her—no one dared to touch her if she was unwilling; no one could take the slightest liberties with her in return for those she herself had taken. In this way she kept the others within the strictest bounds of proper behavior, whereas she herself seemed to trespass continually upon this propriety.

One might really have believed that it was a matter of principle with her to expose herself equally to praise and to blame, to affection and to dislike. For, although she tried in all sorts of ways to win people, she offended them at the same time by her sharp tongue which spared no one. After her visits to near-by castles and country houses, where the kindest hospitality had been shown to her and her guests, she would make the most reckless comments, which indicated that she saw all human relationships and conditions from a ridiculous angle only. There were, for example, the three brothers, who from sheer politeness as to who should marry first, had been overtaken by old age; there was the little young wife with the big old husband; and there was the jolly little man and the clumsy giantess. In one of the houses they had at every step stumbled over a child; another never seemed to be crowded—even with a host of guests— because there were no children at all. Old husbands should hurry to get themselves quickly buried, to give people an opportunity to laugh, since there were no legitimate heirs. Young couples should travel, because keeping house did not become them. She even treated objects in the same way as persons—house, furniture, the various articles of a dinner service. The wall decoration of a room provoked her in particular to merry remarks. From the oldest tapestry to the latest wallpaper, from the most venerable family portrait to the most frivolous new copper-plate engraving—they all had to suffer, pulled to pieces, as it were, by her sarcastic remarks; and it was almost a miracle, that for five miles around, anything continued to exist at all.

Her tendency always to be negative was not really malicious; usually she was prompted by an egotistic love of mischief; but true bitterness had developed in her relationship with Ottilie. She looked down with contempt on the younger girl's quiet, consistent activity, which was noticed and admired by all; and when Ottilie's great interest in the gardens and her good care of them and of the hothouses was mentioned one day, Luciane ridiculed it, pretending to be surprised—although it was now the depth of winter—that she could see neither flowers nor fruit. She also ordered from this time on so much green stuff, so many branches, even those in bud, for the daily decoration of the rooms and of the dinner table that Ottilie and the gardener were extremely distressed to see their hopes for the coming year, and perhaps longer, destroyed.

Luciane also begrudged Ottilie the quiet round of her domestic life in which she moved with so much ease. She forced her to join excursions and sleigh rides and to attend the balls which were arranged in the neighborhood; she was not supposed to mind the snow or the cold or the heavy night storms because, after all, other people did not die of such things. The delicate girl suffered under the strain, and Luciane gained nothing from all this; for although Ottilie was always very simply dressed, she was always—or so at least the men seemed to think—the most beautiful. Her gentle charm gathered all the men around her, whether she was in the foreground or in the background. Even Luciane's fiancé often talked with her, especially because he wanted her advice and assistance in a matter which occupied his mind.

He had come to know the Architect better, and, looking at his collection, had talked to him about its history. On other occasions, particularly when he saw the chapel, he had learned to appreciate the young man's talent. The Baron was young and wealthy; he was himself a collector and he wished to build; but, although his love for the arts was strong, his technical knowledge was limited. He now thought he had found in the Architect the man who could help him attain more than one purpose at the same time. He had told Luciane of his intention, and she had applauded it, delighted with the proposal, more, perhaps, because she hoped she could take the young man away from Ottilie—for she believed she had detected in him signs of a fondness for her—than because she wished to use his talents properly. Although he had proved very useful at her improvised entertainments and had made many intelligent suggestions, she always believed that she herself could do things better; and as her own inventions were for the most part very primitive, the skill of a clever valet would have served her as well as that of a superior artist. Her imagination was not capable of much more than an altar on which something could be sacrificed, or a wreath to crown some head (whether living or of plaster) on the occasions of a birthday or other day of honor.

Ottilie was best able to give the Baron the desired information, when he asked her about the position of the Architect at the castle. She knew that Charlotte had already taken steps to find him a new position. If the visitors had not arrived, the young man would have left immediately after finishing his work in the chapel, for during the winter all construction work would necessarily come to a standstill. It was therefore very desirable for him to find employment with a new patron.

Ottilie's personal relationship to the Architect was entirely innocent and natural. She had always keenly enjoyed his pleasant and active presence like that of an older brother. Her feeling for him remained on the quiet dispassionate level of a family relationship, for there was room in her heart for Eduard alone: it was filled to the brim with her love for him, and only the Deity that pervades all things could share her heart with him.

As winter advanced, the weather became inclement, and the roads more impassable; and the charm of spending the shortened days in congenial company increased. After brief periods of quiet, a tide of visitors would, now and then, flood the house again. Officers from distance garrisons were drawn to the castle; the educated among them were a welcome addition, while the ruder ones were frequently a nuisance. There was also no lack of civilians, and—quite unexpectedly—the Count and the Baroness arrived together one day.

Their visit created for the first time a real Court atmosphere. The men of rank and distinction formed a circle around the Count, and the ladies paid due homage to the Baroness. No one was surprised to see the couple together in such high spirits, for they now learned that the Count's wife had died and that the new marriage would take place as soon as propriety permitted. Ottilie thought of their first visit and remembered every word that had then been said about marriage and divorce, about uniting and separating—about hope, expectation, renunciation and resignation. Both these persons, at that time facing a hopeless future, were now standing before her, close to their hoped-for happiness; and an involuntary sigh escaped her.

No sooner had Luciane heard that the Count was fond of music than she made arrangements for a concert, at which she planned to sing and to accompany herself on the guitar. This soon took place. She did not play the instrument badly and she had a pleasing voice; but it was impossible to understand the words, as is so often the case when a German beauty sings to the accompaniment of a guitar. However, everyone assured her that she had sung most expressively, and she could be satisfied with the loud applause. But now a strange mishap occured. Among the listeners was a poet on whom Luciane wished to make a special impression, because she wanted him to dedicate some of his poems to her. With this in mind, she had sung many songs to which he had written words. He was polite to her as everyone else was; but she had hoped for more. She threw out a few hints but received no response. Impatiently, she sent at last one of her admirers to ask him if he had not been delighted to hear his wonderful poems sung so wonderfully. "My poems?" the poet asked in amazement, and added, "I am sorry, sir, but I heard nothing but vowels, and even those not always. But, of course, I feel bound to express my gratitude for such kind intention!" Luciane's messenger said nothing, and kept his secret. The poet tried to extricate himself from this embarrassing situation by means of a few well-turned compliments. Luciane now openly showed her desire to have something written especially for her. If it would not have been too malicious, the poet might really have presented her with the alphabet, so that she could have made for herself any eulogy she liked, to any existing tune. But this incident was not to be without humiliation for her. A short time afterward she heard that that same evening the poet had written a very lovely poem to one of Ottilie's favorite tunes—a poem that was more than a complimentary gift.

Like all people of her kind, who can never discriminate between something that becomes them and something that does not, Luciane now decided to try her luck at recitation. She had a good memory, but her declamation was not very intelligent, being vehement without passion. She recited ballads, stories and the usual pieces in a performer's repertory. But she had fallen into the unfortunate habit of accompanying her recitations with gestures, thereby confusing more than blending in an unpleasant way the purely epic or lyric style with the dramatic.

The Count, who was an intelligent man, very soon saw through the whole company—their dispositions, passions, and their amusements; and, fortunately or unfortunately, suggested to Luciane a new kind of performance, extremely suitable to her personality. "I see here so many handsome people who are certainly capable of imitating picturesque poses and movements," he said. "Have you really never tried to represent well-known paintings? Such imitation, although it requires much careful preparation, produces, on the other hand, an unbelievably charming effect."

Luciane quickly saw that this would be completely in her own field. Her beautiful stature, her full figure, her regular yet expressive features, her light-brown braided hair, her slender neck—all these were really made for a painting. And had she only known that she was more beautiful when she stood still than when she moved (since in this latter case something ungraceful inadvertently spoiled the effect) she would have devoted herself with still more eagerness to this kind of natural plastic art.

They now searched for prints of famous paintings, and selected for the first *tableau vivant* the *Belisarius* of Van Dyck. A tall, well-built man in his middle years was picked to represent the seated blind general; the Architect would be the sympathetic soldier, standing sadly before him—a figure he in fact somewhat resembled. Luciane, almost modestly, had chosen the part of the young woman in the background, who counts generous alms for a purse into the palm of her hand, while an old woman seems to try to prevent her, and to point out that she is giving too much. Another woman, who actually hands Belisarius alms, had not been forgotten.

With this picture and others as well, they occupied themselves very seriously. The Count made a few suggestions to the Architect about the style of the settings, and the latter at once set up a kind of stage and made all the necessary arrangements for the lighting. They were already deeply involved in these preparations before they became aware that such an undertaking requires considerable expenditure; and that here in the country, in the middle of winter, it would be very difficult to procure many things that they needed. Therefore, to prevent any delay, Luciane had almost all her dresses cut to pieces to supply material for the different costumes which the painters had rather arbitrarily designed.

The evening came, and the performance took place in the presence of a large audience and met with general applause. Music of a characteristic kind raised the highest expectations. The curtain rose on *Belisarius*. The figures were so perfect, the colors so successfully distributed, the lighting so ingenious, that all seemed transported into another world, except that realism instead of illusion produced a kind of uneasiness.

The curtain fell, and was raised more than once by general request. A musical interlude kept the company diverted, since it had been planned to surprise them with a picture of an even higher order. This was the well-known painting by Poussin: *Ahasuerus and Esther*. This time Luciane had chosen a better part for herself. As the queen, who has fallen into a swoon, she displayed all her charms; and she had cleverly selected, as the maids who surrounded and supported her, only pretty and well-shaped figures. But among them no one was the slightest match to hers. From this picture as from the others, Ottilie remained excluded. They had selected, to sit on the golden throne as the Zeus-like king, the most vigorous and handsome man of the party, so that this tableau was really perfect and beyond comparison.

For the third picture they had chosen the so-called *Paternal Warning*, by Ter Borch; and who does not know Wille's magnificent copper engraving of this painting? A noble knight sits, with crossed feet, evidently severely lecturing his daughter, who faces him. A superb figure in a white satin dress with rich folds, she can only be seen from the back; but her whole posture seems to indicate that she is controlling herself. The expression and gesture of her father tells us, however, that his reproof is not too violent or humiliating; and the mother seems to hide a slight embarrassment while she gazes into the glass of wine she is about to sip.

This was an opportunity for Luciane to appear in her highest brilliance. Her braided hair, the shape of her head and of her neck and shoulders were perfectly beautiful—and the waist, which in women's modern dresses modelled on classical patterns, is hardly visible, in her case was very shapely, slim and graceful, and showed much to advantage in the medieval costume. The Architect had taken special care to dispose the rich folds of the white satin in the most artistic naturalness, so that this living reproduction without any question exceeded the original by far, and excited general delight. There was no end of requests for a repetition of the performance; and the entirely natural wish to see the face of the beautiful girl, after having seen her back for so long, became so urgent that general applause broke out when a witty fellow impatiently shouted the words which we sometimes write at the end of a page: *"Tournez, s'il vous plaît!"* But the performers knew their advantage too well, and had grasped so perfectly the idea of these artistic illusions that they did not yield to the general challenge. The evidently embarrassed daughter did not make a move, and did not allow the audience to see the expression of her face; the father remained seated and kept to his admonishing gesture; and the mother removed neither her nose nor her eyes from the transparent glass in which the wine never diminished although she seemed to drink. It is not necessary to describe the other pictures: small night-pieces, chosen from Dutch tavern-, fair-, and market-scenes.

The Count and the Baroness again left, promising to return in the first happy weeks of their approaching marriage; and now Charlotte hoped to get rid of the rest of the party, too, after the strain of the last two months. She was certain of her daughter's future happiness, as soon as the first emotional excitement of her engaged state had subsided; for Luciane's fiancé considered himself the happiest man in the world. Although his fortune was large and his character sensible, he seemed to feel strangely flattered to become the privileged husband of a woman whom the whole world must find lovely. In a peculiar way he related everything to her; and only through her related things to himself. Therefore he had always a bad moment when any newcomer did not instantly give her his whole attention and (as often happened in the case of older people), because of his fine qualities—turned to give some attention to him—without taking special notice of her.

The business with the Architect was soon settled. He was supposed to follow the Baron on New Year's Day, and spend the carnival season with him in the city, where Luciane promised herself the most heavenly time because of a repetition of the beautifully studied *tableaux vivants,* as well as of a hundred other matters; and all the more since her great-aunt and her fiancé seemed to think little of any necessary expense incurred to keep her amused.

The hour of departure drew near; but this could not possibly happen in any ordinary way. Someone remarked rather audibly and in fun, that the guests would soon have eaten up Charlotte's provisions for the winter. The nobleman who had taken the part of *Belisarius,* a rich man, completely swept away by Luciane's charm, which he had long been admiring, thoughtlessly exclaimed: "Why not then act in the Polish fashion? *You* come now to *my* house and eat me out of house and home; and then we shall go on and make the round of the countryside." No sooner said than done. Luciane enthusiastically agreed. The next day they all packed their things, and the swarm invaded another estate. Here there was also ample room, but less comfort and accommodations. All this created many unsuitable situations, which only contributed to Luciane's happiness. Life became every day more disorderly and wilder. Hunting parties with beaters through the deepest snow, and whatever other inconvenient sport could be invented, were arranged. Neither men nor women were allowed to excuse themselves on any account; and in this manner they roamed about, hunting and riding in sleighs with great clamor, from one estate to another, until they finally arrived at the capital, where news and gossip about amusements at Court and in the city gave their imaginations another direction, and Luciane with all her following (her great-aunt having gone home some time before) was irresistibly drawn into a new sphere of life.

From Ottilie's Diary

In society we accept everyone as he appears to be, but he must appear to be something. We tolerate difficult people more easily than insignificant ones.

Anything can be imposed upon society except those matters which have consequences.

We never learn to know people by letting them come to us; we must go to them in order to find out how matters stand.

It seems to me a rather natural trait to find fault with guests and to criticize them after they have left, though not always charitably; for we have, so to speak, a right to measure them by our own standards. On such occasions even sensible and impartial persons are likely to be extremely censorious.

But when we have stayed in the homes of others and have seen our hosts in their own surroundings, have watched their habits and the way they adapt or do not adapt themselves to the necessary and inevitable circumstances of their lives—we would show a want of understanding, or even malice, if we found ridiculous that which is worthy of our respect in more than one sense.

We should gain, by what we call good behavior and polite manners, something which is otherwise gained only by force, and perhaps not even by force.

To move in the society of women creates good manners.

How can the character, the particular personality of a man survive the conventions of well-bred behavior? Good manners should enhance personality. We desire the unusual, but it should not be embarrassing.

The educated soldier possesses the greatest advantages in life in general and in society in particular.

Crude soldiers do not, at least, behave out of character; and since good nature is usually concealed behind their strength, it is possible to get along with them, if necessary.

There is no greater nuisance than an ill-mannered civilian. We have a right to expect a certain refinement from a person who is not engaged in rough action.

When we are living with people who have a fine sense of propriety, we are alarmed if something improper occurs in their presence. I always suffer with and for Charlotte when someone rocks back and forth in his chair, a habit which she loathes.

No man would ever dare to enter a drawing-room with glasses perched on his nose, if he realized that women instantly lose any desire both to look at and to talk to him.

Familiarity is always ridiculous when it should be deference. No man would put down his hat immediately, after having paid his respects, if he knew how ridiculous it looks.

Any outward sign of politeness is founded on a deeper moral

reason. True education should give us the outward sign and its underlying reason, at the same time.

Behavior is a mirror which reflects the image of everyone.

There is a politeness of heart which is akin to love. The most natural politeness which we outwardly show, springs from this inner source.

Voluntary dependence is the most beautiful condition of life, and how could it possibly exist without love?

We are never so far from our wishes as when we imagine that we possess what we wished.

No one is a greater slave than he who imagines himself free when he is not free.

We have only to declare ourselves free, instantly to feel bound. If we have the courage to declare ourselves bound, we feel that we are free.

Against the superiority of another person there is no other remedy but love.

It is shocking to see a superior man surrounded by fools who plume themselves on his friendship.

It is said that "no man is a hero to his valet," the meaning being that a hero can only be recognized by another hero. The valet, however, is, no doubt, capable of recognizing his own equal.

There is no greater consolation for mediocrity than the knowledge that a genuis is not immortal.

The greatest human beings are always connected to their own century by some weakness.

We usually consider people more dangerous than they are.

The fools and the wise are equally harmless. It is the half-fools and the half-wise who are very dangerous.

Art is at once the surest escape from the world and the surest link with the world.

Even in moments of extreme happiness or of extreme misery we need the artist.

The concern of art is the Difficult and the Good.

To see the Difficult treated, as it were, without effort, gives us an idea of what is impossible.

Difficulties increase, the nearer we come to the goal.

To sow is not as difficult as to reap.

Chapter Twenty-Four

Charlotte was in some way compensated for the turmoil this visit had created, by having obtained a deeper insight into her daughter's nature—in this her knowledge of the world gave her much help. It was not the first time she had come face to face with such a peculiar character, although she had never come across one quite so fully developed. Yet her own experience had taught her that people like her daughter, once they have been educated by life, by various experiences and by their environment, can mature and become perfectly agreeable and charming human beings; they become less self-centered, and their haphazard activities find a definite direction. Charlotte, being her mother, could be more lenient toward Luciane's eccentricities which were perhaps unpleasant to others; for parents are justified in being hopeful, where strangers only expect gratification or, at least no annoyance.

But after her daughter's departure, she suffered a strange and unexpected shock: people spoke indignantly of Luciane, not so much because of her faults, but because of certain traits in her behavior which might have been thought praiseworthy. She had apparently made it a rule not only to be merry with the merry but also to be sad with the sad; and giving full sway to a spirit of contradiction, to put sometimes the merry into a bad humor and make the sad cheerful. In every family she inquired at once about the sick or the infirm who could not appear in society. She visited them in their rooms, played the doctor and urged on each of them drastic medications which she always carried in her own traveling medicine chest. Such treatments, naturally, either succeeded or failed, as good or bad luck would have it. She was almost cruel in the exercise of her charity and never listened to advice, being utterly convinced that what she did was right. But in one attempt in the moral field she failed completely, and it was this case which gave Charlotte grave concern, because it had serious consequences, and everybody talked about it. She heard of it only after Luciane had left; and Ottilie, who had been at the party in question, had to tell her the story in all its details.

One of the daughters of a respected family had been so unfortunate as to have caused the death of one of her younger sisters, and she had never been able to recover from the shock. Ever since the day of the tragedy, she had kept to her room. She could bear to see members of her family only if they visited her one at a time, because, if several of them came together, she immediately suspected them of discussing her and her condition. To each of them singly she would speak reasonably enough and would converse with that person for hours.

Luciane had heard about all this and at once made up her mind that she would visit the house, work, as it were, a miracle and lead the girl back into the world. She behaved on this occasion with more caution than usual and succeeded in getting to see the depressed girl alone, whose confidence she apparently gained by playing the guitar for her. Only in the last stage of her plan did she make a fatal mistake; because she longed to create a sensation and thought her patient prepared, one evening she suddenly led the lovely pale child into a gay and brilliant group of visitors. Even this might have perhaps been successful, had not the guests themselves, out of curiosity and apprehension, behaved very unwisely. They crowded around the invalid and then drew back again and confused and agitated her by putting their heads together and whispering. To the girl's sensitive nerves this was unbearable. She screamed and ran away, as though something horrible pursued her. Frightened, the guests also fled in all directions, and Ottilie carried, with the help of others, the poor creature, who had fainted, back to her room.

Luciane had meanwhile severly lectured the group—as she was likely to do—without being in the least aware that she alone was to blame. She never learned from this or her many other mistakes to refrain from this kind of experiment.

The condition of the sick girl had become worse since that evening, and her mental disturbance had increased so seriously that her parents could no longer keep the poor child at home but had to commit her to an institution. Charlotte could only try, by being particularly tactful toward the family, to soothe, to a certain degree, the grief her own daughter had caused them. The whole incident had made a deep impression on Ottilie, who felt sorry for the unfortunate girl, especially since she was convinced—as she said frankly to Charlotte—that with careful treatment she might have been cured.

Since we usually talk more of unpleasant events in the past than of past pleasures, Ottilie and the Architect finally came to discuss a slight misunderstanding between them. It concerned the evening when Ottilie had been puzzled by the Architect's refusal to show his collection, although she had begged him to. His bland refusal had left a slight sting in her heart ever since: why, she did not herself know. Her feeling was perhaps justified: whatever a young woman like Ottilie requests, a younger man like the Architect should not refuse. But now, when she, somewhat reprovingly, brought up the subject, his excuses were quite plausible.

"If you knew how rudely even educated people handle the most valuable works of art, you would forgive me when I do not wish to show my pieces to a large crowd," he pleaded. "No one seems to know that a medal must be held by the rim; people finger the most beautiful raised lettering, the cleanest surface, and rub the most precious pieces between thumb and forefinger, as though this were a test suitable for objects of art. Without even considering that a large sheet of paper should be held with both hands, they seize with one hand an invaluable copper-plate engraving or an irreplacable drawing, just as any foolish politician might take hold of a newspaper to indicate beforehand his opinion of world events by his crumpling of the pages. No one realizes that if only twenty persons should handle an object of art in this way, the twenty-first would not have much to look at."

"Have *I* not sometimes given you reason for worry, too?" Ottilie asked. "Have *I* perhaps occasionally harmed your treasures without realizing it?"

"Never," the Architect replied. "Never! That would be impossible for you! You do the right thing instinctively."

"In any case," said Ottilie, "it might not be a bad idea, if in a future edition of the Laws of Etiquette—after the chapters, entitled 'Rules on How To Behave When Eating and Drinking in Good Society"—a very detailed chapter should be inserted on 'How To Behave in Private Art Collections and Museums.' "

"It would certainly encourage curators and private collectors to show their rarities more readily," the Architect agreed.

Ottilie had long since forgiven him; but when she saw him so deeply concerned about her reproof and heard him again and again reassure her how much he enjoyed letting people see his things, how he liked to do everything his friends wished—she knew that she had hurt his feelings and felt that she was in his debt. Therefore she could not flatly refuse something he asked of her after this talk; although she was not quite sure how she could conscientiously do what he wished.

This is what he had asked: he was hurt that, because of Luciane's jealousy, Ottilie had been excluded from the *tableaux vivants* and he had deeply regretted that Charlotte, because of her delicate condition, had been able only occasionally to attend this brilliant part of the entertainment. He did not wish to leave without having given additional proof of his gratitude by arranging (in honor of one of his friends and for the entertainment of the other) a performance, far more lovely than anything that had been done. Unknown to himself, he was probably moved by another secret impulse as well. It almost broke his heart to leave this house and this family, and it seemed impossible to him that a time should come when he would no longer see Ottilie's eyes, her calm and friendly look, which alone had sustained him during these last weeks.

The Christmas holidays were at hand, and it suddenly occurred to him that these "living pictures" had developed from the Nativity Groups, which pious folks made at this holy season to express their adoration of the Divine Mother and her Child, showing how these two were venerated in their apparent lowliness, first by shepherds and then by kings.

He had a perfectly clear vision of the execution of such a living picture: a handsome, lively baby boy would be found, and there would be no want of shepherds and shepherdesses. But without Ottilie the whole picture was impossible. He had exalted her to the character of the Mother of God, and there was no question in his mind that should she refuse, the whole undertaking would come to nothing. Ottilie, half-embarrassed at his request, asked him to speak to Charlotte, who was happy to give her permission. She also succeeded in persuading Ottilie to lay aside her hesitation in assuming so sacred a character. The Architect worked day and night in order to make everything ready by Christmas Eve.

He literally worked day and night. His personal needs had always been few, and Ottilie's presence seemed to be food and drink to him. When he was working for her, he did not sleep; when he was in her presence, he felt neither hunger nor thirst. Consequently, everything was ready on the Holy Eve. He had managed to bring together a small orchestra of wind instruments, which played an overture to create the desired atmosphere. When the curtain rose, Charlotte was completed taken by surprise. She had seen the picture reproduced so often that she had hardly expected to be impressed by it now. But here reality seemed to give it a special quality. The stage was not merely dim but dark as night, yet every detail in the center could be seen clearly. It had been the artist's excellent idea that all light should radiate from the Child and he had achieved this by a clever trick of lighting; the mechanism was hidden by the figures in the foreground who were in shadow, illuminated only by lights on the side. Happy girls and boys stood about, their ruddy faces sharply lit from below. There were angels, too, whose inner light paled beside that of the Divine Child; their ethereal bodies seemed solid and bereft of radiance in the presence of the Word made Flesh.

Fortunately, the baby had fallen asleep in a graceful position, so that nothing distracted the onlookers from their contemplation of the mother, who, with infinitely gentle grace, lifted a veil to reveal her hidden treasure. The picture seemed to have been caught just at this moment. Blinded by the radiance and overcome by awe, the surrounding group seemed to have just turned away their dazzled eyes; but their furtive gaze was directed toward the Child with expressions of wonder and joy. Rapture and adoration showed particularly clearly on the faces of some of the elderly figures.

Ottilie's whole appearance, her gesture, the expression of her face and eyes surpassed anything ever conveyed by a painter. Any connoisseur of art, seeing this spectacle, would have feared that some detail might change; and he would have doubted whether anything could ever give him such enjoyment again. Unfortunately, no one present was capable of grasping the complete effect. Only the Architect who, as a tall, slender shepherd, peered from the side over the heads of the kneeling figures, had, to some degree, an impression of the whole; and even he, standing where he was, was not afforded a complete view. And who could describe in words the expression on the face of the Queen of Heaven? Pure humility and a winning modesty at the great and undeserved honor bestowed on her, as well as an immeasurable happiness, showed in her face, expressing not only her own emotion but also a profound understanding of the role that she enacted.

Charlotte was extremely happy to see this beautiful picture, and the Child in particular moved her deeply. Tears welled into her eyes, and she imagined herself most vividly in the near future holding so dear a babe in her own arms.

The curtain fell, partly in order to let the actors relax a little, partly to change the tableau. The artist had planned to transform this first scene of night and lowliness into one of day and glory; and to this end had prepared a dazzling flood of light from all sides, which was to be lit during the intermission. Ottilie, in her half-theatrical pose, had felt until now quite unembarrassed knowing that no other spectators, with the exception of Charlotte and a few members of the household, were present at this religious spectacle. She was, therefore, somewhat taken aback when, during the inter-mission, she heard that a stranger had arrived in the hall and had been kindly welcomed by Charlotte. No one could tell her who he was. She put the matter out of her mind, because she did not wish to make a disturbance. The candles and lamps burned brightly, and she was surrounded by a perfect blaze of light. The curtain rose, and the scene presented a startling spectacle: all was bright, and, instead of shadows, colors distributed with great skill, gave a soft and subdued effect. Looking out from under her long eyelahses, Ottilie saw the figure of a man sitting next to Charlotte. She did not recognize him but she thought the voice was that of her tutor at school. A strange emotion ran through her. How many things had happened since she last had heard the voice of her faithful teacher! Like a forked flash of lightning, a whole chain of her pleasures and unhappiness passed rapidly before her mind, together with the questions: Can you tell him everything and confess everything to him? And how little do you deserve to appear before him in the guise of this holy figure? How strange he must feel to see you in this costume? With incredible swiftness emotion and reflection strug-gled in her heart. Her eyes filled with tears, while she forced herself to remain motionless. With great relief she felt the baby move; and the Architect had to give the sign for the lowering of the curtain. If a painful feeling of being unable to hurry and welcome a dear friend had, during the last moments, been added to Ottilie's other emo-tions, she now felt even more embarrassed. Should she meet him in this unusual costume? Should she change it? She did not hesitate for long; she changed her dress, trying, at the same time, to get control of herself and to calm her emotion. But she regained her usual poise only when she went to welcome their guest, dressed as usual.

Chapter Twenty-five

Since the Architect wished a pleasant time for his kind friends, the thought of their having such good company in the person of the deserving tutor was very agreeable to him, particularly as he himself had now really to think of leaving. But when he thought of his friends' special kindness to him, he could not help being a little distressed to see himself so quickly and (as he thought in his modesty) so well and even completely replaced. Formerly he had always hesitated; but now something urged him to leave, for he did not wish to see with his own eyes what he could not prevent from happening, after he had gone.

To the great relief of his low spirits, the ladies, at the very last moment, made him the present of a vest which he had seen both of them knitting over a long period; and he had secretly envied the fortunate unknown to whom it would one day belong. Such a gift is most enjoyed by a man who loves or admires the giver, because, as he remembers the never-tiring play of lovely fingers, he cannot help flattering himself that, at such long-lasting work, the heart as well cannot have remained entirely unsympathetic.

Now the two women were hostesses to a new young man for whom they had the kindest feelings and whom they wished to put at ease in their company while he stayed with them. All women have their own inner, unchangeable interests to which nothing in the world can make them disloyal; in their outward social relationships, however, they allow themselves, gladly and easily, to be influenced by the man with whom they are for the moment occupied; and in this way, by refusing as well as responding, by persisting and by yielding, they are actually in command, and no man in the civilized world dares to refuse them obedience.

While the Architect, following his own wishes and his inclination, had exercised and proved his talents for his friends' entertainment and their purposes; while occupation and conversation had been conducted in this spirit and to this end—the presence of the Tutor soon created an entirely different mode of life. His great gift was to talk well, and in conversation to discuss all sorts of human problems, particularly those concerning the education of young people. Accordingly, a rather distinct contrast to their previous way of life made itself felt, the more so, because the Tutor did not entirely approve of the interests which had for so long kept them occupied almost exclusively.

He did not once mention the *tableau vivant* he had seen when he arrived. But when, with great satisfaction, they showed him the church, the chapel and everything in it, he could not hold back his views. "As for me," he said, "all this imitating and mixing of the Sacred and the Sensuous does not please me at all. Nor do I like the consecration and decoration of places, set apart for the specific purpose of creating and sustaining a feeling of piety. No environment, not even the lowliest, should disturb in us that sense of the Divine which can be with us everywhere and can consecrate any place into a temple. I like to see a religious service conducted in the same hall where people usually take their meals, have their social gatherings or enjoy themselves with games and dancing. The highest and the best in man cannot be given form, and we should beware of giving it any form except that of noble action."

Charlotte, who already knew something about his general way of thinking and who was soon to probe it more thoroughly, at once assigned to him a task in his own field. She had her little gardeners, whom the Architect had just passed in review before his departure, march up to the great hall: they looked very attractive in their clean gray uniforms, with their rhythmic movements and their natural liveliness. The Tutor examined them after his fashion; and, by his many questions and his way of putting them, he soon found out something about the disposition and the aptitude of each child. At the same time he subtly instructed them and gave them a good many new suggestions; and all this in less than an hour.

"How do you manage it?" Charlotte asked, when the boys had marched off. "I listened very attentively. Only familiar things were mentioned, yet I would not know how to introduce these subjects into a discussion so systematically and in such a short time."

"Perhaps we should never reveal the tricks of our trade," the Tutor replied. "But I can tell you a simple principle that will help you to achieve these results and a great many more. Take up any topic, any subject, any idea; stick to it, make yourself thoroughly acquainted with it in every detail—and it will be easy for you to discover, as you talk with a group of children, how much of it they understand and what you may still have to develop and to impart. Their answers to your questions may be very unsatisfactory and may wander far from the subject; but if your questions in return bring the children's attention back to the subject, and if you do not allow yourself to be diverted from your own viewpoint, the children will eventually think, understand, and grasp, what you want them to learn and precisely in the way you want them to learn it. A teacher makes a most serious mistake when he allows himself to be drawn away from the subject by his pupils or if he is unable to keep steadily to the point he is discussing. Try this sometime; it will give you great pleasure."

"This sounds very sensible," Charlotte said. "I can see that the best method of teaching is the very opposite of the way we must behave in life. In society we are told never to stay too long on one subject; whereas in teaching the first commandment is to avoid any distraction."

"Variety without distraction would be the finest motto for both teaching and life, if only this highly commendable balance were so easy to keep," answered the Tutor. He was about to say more when Charlotte called him to look again at the boys, whose merry procession was just then moving across the castle courtyard. He expressed satisfaction that the children were kept in uniform. "Men should wear uniforms from early youth," he said; "they must accustom themselves to act in unison, to lose themselves among their fellowmen, to obey as a unit, and to work for the good of the whole. Moreover, any kind of uniform develops a martial spirit and a strictly disciplined deportment. Boys are, in any case, born soldiers; watch them playing war-like and competitive games, storming and scaling walls!"

"Then you will not blame me for *not* dressing all my girls alike," said Ottilie. "When I introduce them to you, I hope to delight you with a gay and colorful group."

"I quite approve of that," the Tutor replied. "Women should wear all sorts of dresses; and each should follow her own taste in her own style, so that she may discover what is really becoming and suitable to her. There is still more important reason for all this: namely— that it is women's lot to be on their own and to act alone all their lives."

"That seems to me a paradox" Charlotte protested. "Surely we are almost never alone."

"Oh, but you are," the Tutor replied, "at least in respect to other women. Think of any women—when she is in love, when a bride, wife, housewife or mother—she is always quite alone and wants to be alone. The same thing is true even of a vain woman. Each woman excludes all others. That is natural, for every woman is called upon to perform all the tasks which comprise the whole womankind. It is entirely different with men. A man needs another man; he would even create a second man for himself if no other existed. But a woman could go on living for ever and ever without even dreaming of creating a being like herself."

"If truth is formulated only in a peculiar manner, the oddest things will in the end seem true," Charlotte said. "Even though bearing in mind the most valuable of your remarks, we women, as women, will nevertheless stick together and work together with other women, in order not to give men too great an advantage over us. I hope you won't begrudge us the small malicious satisfaction we must feel, if, in the future, we should see that the gentlemen, too, are sometimes not getting along too well with one another."

The Tutor now closely examined the way in which Ottilie treated her little pupils, and expressed his definite approval. "You are quite right in educating these children for immediate usefulness," he said. "Cleanliness will make them enjoy keeping themselves clean, and much is gained if they are encouraged to do what they are doing with cheerfulness and self-confidence."

To his great satisfaction he found that nothing was done for form's sake only, or for mere outward show; everything was rather done for spiritual profit and the indispensable needs. "The whole business of education could be summed up in such a few words, if only people had ears to hear!" he exclaimed.

"Wouldn't you like to try my ears?" Ottilie asked, friendly and interested.

"Yes, I would," he replied. "But you must not give away my secret. Boys should be taught to be servants, and girls to be mothers—and all would be right with the world."

"To be mothers?" asked Ottilie. "I suppose, women would readily agree to that, for they must always prepare themselves, if not to become mothers, at least to take care of children. But I suspect that our young men would think themselves too good to *serve*. You can easily see for yourself that every one of them considers himself much more capable of being a master."

"For that very reason we shall not say anything about this to them," the Tutor replied. "We begin by flattering ourselves with high hopes but life does not flatter us. How may people would voluntarily choose that which in the long run they are forced to do? But let us disregard these observations which do not really concern us here. I think you are very fortunate in being able to apply the right method with your pupils. When your youngest girls carry their dolls about and stitch together a few little rags for them; when the older sisters take care of the younger, and each member of the household serves and helps the others, the next step in life will not be so difficult; and such girls will find in their husbands' homes what they left in their parents'. But on a higher level of society the problem is very complicated. We have to consider much more highly developed, more delicate, refined, and differentiated social conditions. We teachers must, therefore, give our pupils an education designed for the world they live in. This sort of education is necessary and essential and it may be valuable if we do not go too far with it. For, while planning to extend the education of our pupils we may easily become too vague and lose sight of their specific spiritual requirements. This is the problem which educators are apt to miss, or may solve only inadequately. I am concerned about many of the things we teach our pupils at the boarding school, because experience tells me that these will very likely be of small use in their future lives. So much is at once discarded, so much forgotten, as soon as a girl finds herself in the position of housewife or mother! But since I have devoted myself to this work, I must cling to the modest hope that some day, together with a faithful companion who will assist me, I may succeed in fully developing in my pupils what they really need when they leave for their own sphere of activity and are independent. Perhaps I may then be able to say to myself, 'In this sense their education is completed.' Of course, another sort of education immediately follows, and another and another, almost every year of our lives, forced upon us, if not by ourselves, then by circumstance."

How true these remarks seemed to Ottilie! She had learned so much during the past year through her unforeseen passion, and how many trials awaited her when she looked into the imminent future!

The young man had deliberately mentioned an assistant—a wife—for, in all modesty, he could not keep himself from hinting vaguely at his intentions. Several circumstances and occurrences had encouraged him to move a little closer to his goal during this visit.

The headmistress of the school was already advanced in years and had for some time been looking about among the members of her staff, men as well as women, for someone to be her associate. She had finally offered this post to the Tutor, who merited her highest confidence. He would share the management of the institution with her, work for it as if it were his own, and after her death, as her heir, become its sole proprietor. The principal condition seemed to be that he find a congenial wife. A vision of Ottilie was always before him; he was somewhat hesitant, but there were certain favorable circumstances which made him hopeful. Luciane had left the school, and Ottilie would be free to come back. There had been some rumors concerning her relation to Eduard, but, as in similar cases, the whole matter was not taken too seriously; this incident might even contribute to Ottilie's return. Nothing, however, would have been decided and no definite step would have been taken if unexpected visitors had not once more brought the matter to a head. After all, the appearance of exceptional people in any circle is never without some consequence.

The Count and the Baroness were often consulted about the value of different schools, since everyone has to face the problem of his children's education; they had, therefore, decided to inspect this particular school which had such an excellent reputation—an inspection which they could now undertake together because of their changed circumstances. But the Baroness had still another purpose in mind. During her last visit with Charlotte they had discussed Eduard and Ottilie in detail. She had insisted repeatedly that Ottilie should be sent away, and had tried to encourage Charlotte, who still feared Eduard's threats. They had also talked of ways and means, and, when the school was mentioned, and the Baroness learned of the Tutor's attachment for Ottilie, she was all the more determined to visit the place.

She and the Count arrived at the school, met the Tutor, inspected the establishment and mentioned Ottilie. The Count was always glad to speak of her, since he had learned to know her better during their recent visit. Ottilie had approached him and had even been attracted by him, for she thought she found in his interesting conversation something which had until now been entirely unknown to her. When she was with Eduard the world was forgotten, while in the presence of the Count, the world seemed desirable for the first time. Any attraction is reciprocal. The Count became very fond of Ottilie and liked to think of her as a daughter. Once again she stood in the way of the Baroness, and now even more so than at first. Who knows what the Baroness would have plotted against the girl in times more violently passionate than our own. Now, she would be satisfied to find her a husband and so remove a danger to married women.

She urged the Tutor, therefore, unobtrusively but effectively, to arrange a little excursion to the castle where he should take steps to realize his plans and desires, which he had not kept secret from the Baroness.

With full approval of the headmistress, he started on his journey, his mind filled with the happiest expectations. He knew that Ottilie did not dislike him, and, although there was some disproportion in their social status, this would not count too much, considering the liberal views of the period. The Baroness had, moreover, given him to understand that Ottilie would always be without a fortune. To be related to a rich family is said to be no help to anyone; even persons of immense wealth have serious scruples against deducting any considerable sum from the inheritance of those who seem to have an indisputable right to it, because of a closer relationship. Strangely enough, a man rarely uses his great privilege to dispose of his property after his death, for the benefit of those who are actually closest to his heart; apparently out of respect for tradition he bequeaths it only to those who would become the heirs of his fortune in any case, even if he made no will.

While the Tutor was on his journey, he felt himself on a completely equal footing with Ottilie. The kind welcome at the castle also raised his hopes. It is true that he found Ottilie not quite so open with him as formerly; but she was also more mature, more cultivated, and perhaps more communicative in general than she had been when he knew her before. Like a close friend, he enjoyed confidence about many matters, particularly those that concerned his profession. But when he wished to approach the real purpose of his visit, a certain shyness always held him back.

Charlotte once offered him an opportunity when she said to him, in Ottilie's presence, "Well, now that you have seen almost every-thing that is developing within my little realm, what do you think of Ottilie? You may speak frankly before her."

The Tutor replied with great understanding and quiet objec-tiveness that he had found Ottilie very much changed to her advan-tage; that she behaved with more ease, expressed herself more freely, and showed greater understanding of the ways of the world; all of which appeared in her actions more than in her words; but that he still believed that it might be very useful to her if she returned to the school for a short period, in order to learn, thoroughly and system-atically, the lessons that the world was teaching her only in frag-ments, fragments more confusing than satisfying, and sometimes almost too late. He did not wish to go too much into detail, he said: Ottilie herself would remember that she had suddenly been taken out of a systematic course of instruction.

Ottilie would not deny this; but she could not reveal her feelings on hearing these words, for she was hardly able to explain them to herself. Nothing in the world seemed unsystematic to her when she thought of the man she loved; and she could not understand how—without him—anything could make sense at all.

Charlotte's reply to the suggestion was wise and kind. She said that both she and Ottilie had for a long time wished for Ottilie's return to school. But now the presence of such a dear friend and helper had become indispensable to her; she would not, however, later put any obstacle in Ottilie's way if it was then still her wish to go back to school long enough to finish the work she had begun and to complete any courses which she had not finished, when she left.

The Tutor received this suggestion with a very happy heart. Ottilie did not dare to object, but she shuddered at the mere thought of having to leave. Charlotte's only concern was to gain time. She hoped that when Eduard returned he would find himself a happy father and would become his old self again. She was convinced that all would be forgotten and that, in one way or another, something could be done for Ottilie as well.

After an important conversation which gives all participants much food for thought, a lull, resembling a general embarrassment, usually sets in. They walked up and down the salon. The Tutor leafed through some books and finally came upon the folio which was still lying where Luciane had left it. When he saw that it contained only pictures of monkeys, he clapped it shut at once. This little incident may have given rise to a conversation, traces of which we find in Ottilie's diary.

From Ottilie's Diary

It is incomprehensible that people can have the heart to draw hideous monkeys with so much care. We already lower ourselves when we look at monkeys simply as animals; but we become really vicious when we yield to the temptation to try and discover people we know behind these animal masks.

It is a sign of perversity when people delight in looking at caricatures and grotesques. I am grateful to my Tutor that I was never tortured with the study of natural history: I always had an uneasy feeling about worms and beetles.

Today he confessed that he felt the same. We should not know anything of nature but what is alive and actually around us, he said. With the trees in our gardens, whether in flower, in leaf or in fruit, with any bush we pass, any blade of grass we step on, we have a true relationship; they are all our true fellow-creatures. The birds, hopping up and down on our branches and singing among our leaves belong to us; they have spoken to us since our childhood and we have learned to understand their language. Is it not true that any strange creature, torn from its natural habitat, makes a certain frightening impression on us which can only be dulled by habit? Indeed, a colorful and noisy background is needed for us to put up with monkeys, parrots and blackamoors.

When I have been seized sometimes by a mood of curiosity about such exotic things, I have envied travelers who see all these marvels together with others in their natural everyday pattern of life. But the traveler, too, will become a different man. No one walks under palmtrees with impunity, and I am sure that one's outlook will change in a country where elephants and tigers are at home.

We admire only that naturalist who knows how to describe and depict for us the strangest and most unusual objects in their proper locality and environment. How I should like to hear only once Humboldt talk.

A cabinet of natural curiosities must look to us like an Egyptian burial place, where the various nature-gods and animal-gods stand about mummified. It is perhaps fitting for a priestly class to occupy itself with these matters in a twilight of mystery; but they should not be introduced into general education, especially since they may easily displace something more familiar and of greater value.

A teacher who can rouse in us enthusiasm for a single good deed, for a single good poem, accomplishes more than the teacher who crams our minds with the names and characteristics of series after series of inferior natural forms; for the only result of this cramming will be something we know in any case: that the human form is the only superior form, created in the image of God.

The individual may be free to occupy himself with whatever attracts him, pleases him, or seems useful to him; but the proper study of mankind is man.

Chapter Twenty-six

Very few people care to occupy themselves with the immediate past. Either we are forcibly bound to the present, or we lose ourselves in the remote past and try to recall and restore as much as possible of what is gone irrevocably. Even in great and wealthy families who owe so much to their ancestors, we generally find that everyone remembers his grandfather better than his father.

These thoughts arose in the Tutor's mind as he walked, on one of those lovely days when the departing winter pretends to be spring, through the extensive older part of the park, admiring the avenues of tall linden trees and the formal grounds, laid out by Eduard's father. Everything had, remarkably enough, turned out as the man who planted had intended; and now, when the time had come to appreciate and enjoy, no one ever talked of the formal grounds: they were very rarely looked at. All interest and expenditure had now been turned in another direction: into the open country and toward freer vistas. On his return, the Tutor commented on this fact, and Charlotte did not resent it. "While life is carrying us along with it," she said, "we imagine that we act from our own motives and choose what we do and what we enjoy; but, if we look more closely we will find that we are actually compelled to carry out the ideas and tendencies of our time."

"That is true," the Tutor replied. "Who, after all, can resist the force of the tendencies of his period? Time moves on, and with it opinions, ideas, prejudices and fashions. If the early years of a young man fall in a period of transition, we can be sure that he will have nothing in common with his father. If the father lived in a period which tended toward acquiring a good deal, toward protecting this property, restricting and confining it, and in the sequestration from the world securing its full enjoyment—the son will be inclined to expand, to communicate, to extend and to open up what was closed."

"Whole periods resemble this father and son you have described," Charlotte agreed. "It is hardly possible for us to conceive of that remote period when every small town had to have its walls and moats; when the nobleman still built his manor in the middle of a swamp, and the smallest castles could be entered only by a drawbridge. Nowadays even larger towns pull down their walls; the moats of castles are filled in; towns are nothing more than large open places, and when we travel, we can see all this, and might almost believe that universal peace has been established and that the Golden Age is near at hand. No one nowadays feels comfortable in a garden which is not like open country; nothing must remind us of art and constraint; we wish to breathe with absolute freedom and feel unconfined. Do you really think that we could return from this condition into another, older one?"

"Why not?" the Tutor answered. "Every condition has its difficulties, the restricted as well as the unrestricted. The latter state presupposes abundance and leads to extravagance. Let us stick to your very striking example. As soon as want reappears, self-restriction is at once re-instituted. People who must make use of their land, begin to raise walls around their gardens in order to protect their produce. Gradually a new outlook develops. Considerations of usefulness once more gain the upper hand, and even the rich landowner finally comes to the conclusion that he too should make use of all his acres. Believe me, it is quite possible that your son will neglect all the new grounds you have laid out and will again retire behind the austere walls and under the tall linden trees of his grandfather."

It gave Charlotte a secret pleasure to hear the Tutor predict that her child would be a son, and so she forgave him his somewhat unkind prophecy concerning the future of her beloved and lovely park. She said very amiably: "Neither of us is yet old enough to have seen a recurrence of this opposition of one generation to another; but when I remember my early youth, and the complaints I heard from elderly people, and then think of the subsequent changes in city and country, I cannot contradict you. But should it not be possible to bring about an understanding between father and son, between parents and children? You have been kind enough to predict a son for me; is it necessary that he should oppose his father? Why should he destroy what his parents have built, instead of completing it, and, if he continues the work in the same spirit, even improving it?"

"There is, of course, a sensible remedy which people only too seldom apply," the Tutor replied. "A father should make his son a partner; he should let him help with the building and planting and allow him some of the harmless whims that he allows himself. One activity may be woven into another; but they cannot be merely pieced together. A young shoot can easily and willingly be grafted onto an old trunk to which a grown branch can no longer be joined."

The Tutor was glad, that just when he was obliged to leave, he had been able to say quite accidentally, something agreeable to Charlotte, and so had confirmed her good opinion of him. He had already been away from home too long; but he had always hesitated to return, until the moment when he fully realized that he could not expect any decision concerning Ottilie before Charlotte had given birth to her child—an event which was imminent. He therefore submitted to circumstances and, still nursing his hopes and prospects, returned to the school.

Charlotte's hour drew near, and she kept more to her rooms. The women who had gathered around her were almost her only company. Ottilie looked after the household, but she could barely keep her mind on what she was doing. Although she had given up all hope for herself, she was anxious to do everything possible for Charlotte, for the child, and for Eduard, even if she could not imagine how this would be possible. Nothing could save her from utter despair but the daily performance of her duties.

A son was safely born to Charlotte, and all the women insisted that he was the very image of his father. Ottilie alone, when she went to wish Charlotte happiness and to welcome the child affectionately, did not think so. Even during the preliminaries to her daughter's marriage Charlotte had keenly felt the absence of her husband. Now the father was not to be present at the birth of his son; he would not choose the name which the child should bear.

The first of all the friends who came to wish Charlotte happiness was Mittler; he had posted messengers all over the neighborhood to bring him the news of the event at once. He arrived in an excellent mood and could barely, in Ottilie's presence, hide his triumph. But when he was alone with Charlotte, he expressed his satisfaction at the top of his voice, and was just the right man to remove all difficulties and brush away all momentary obstacles. The christening should not be delayed longer than was necessary. The old clergyman—already with one foot in the grave—would, with his blessings, bind the past to the future. The name of the child should be Otto: he could not possibly be given any other name than that of his father and of their friend.

It was the determined insistence of Mittler that brushed aside the hundreds of scruples: the opposition, hesitation, indecision; the "knowing better" and "having a better idea," the wavering and constant shifting of opinions; for on such occasions one scruple removed usually breeds more and more new ones; and when we try not to offend anyone, we are sure to hurt someone.

Mittler took care of all the letters announcing the birth, and of those to the godparents. He wished them to be written and sent off at once, for he was very eager to let the often ill-disposed and ill-judging world know of the happy event which was, in his opinion, so important for the family. And he was right, because the previous passionate vibrations had not escaped the attention of a public which is at all times convinced that whatever happens, happens only to provide them with food for gossip.

The ceremony of baptism was to be dignified but short and in private. Ottilie and Mittler were to hold the child as sponsors. The old clergyman, supported by the sexton, approached with slow steps. The prayer was said, and the child placed in Ottilie's arms; but when she looked down at it with affection, it opened its eyes. She was shocked; she seemed to look into her own eyes. The likeness would have startled anyone. Mittler, who was the next to hold the child was startled, too, when he saw in the child's features a striking resemblance to the Captain. He had never met with the like before.

The weakness of the old clergyman had prevented him from conducting the ceremony with more than the customary liturgy. Mittler, however, filled with the spirit of the occasion, remembered his former ministerial function; he had a curious tendency to imagine, on any occasion, how *he* would speak and what *he* would say. On this occasion he could control himself all the less, as he was surrounded by only a small group, all of whom were his friends. So he began, toward the end of the service, to put himself, with perfect ease, in the place of the clergyman and, in a spirited speech, to hold forth on his duties as godfather and his hopes for the child; and he dwelt all the longer on the subject when he thought he read approval in Charlotte's happy face.

The fact that the old clergyman longed to sit down escaped the vigorous orator who suspected still less that he was on the point of causing a serious accident. After having impressively described the relation of each person present to the child, thereby putting Ottilie's composure to a severe test, he turned to the aged man with the words: "And you, my venerable patriarch, you can now say with Simeon: Lord, now lettest thou thy servant depart in peace, for mine eyes have seen the savior of this house."

He was in full swing, and was winding up his speech very brilliantly, when he noticed that the old clergyman to whom he held up the child, first seemed to incline a little toward it, but then suddenly sank back. Barely prevented from falling, he was carried to an armchair; but, in spite of instant assistance given him, he was found to be dead.

To experience so immediately birth and death, coffin and cradle, not only to imagine them but to see these tremendous contrasts with their own eyes was a difficult trial for those present, particularly since they had been completely taken by surprise. Ottilie alone contemplated with a kind of envy the sleeping old man, whose sympathetic face still showed its expression of kindliness. The life of her soul had been destroyed; why should her body be kept alive?

Although the sad events of these days now frequently directed her thoughts toward the transitoriness of all things human, toward separation and loss, she was given the comfort of strange nightly visions which, by reassuring her that the man she loved was still alive, gave her own life security and new strength. When she lay down at night, and was still suspended between sleeping and waking, she seemed to be looking into a perfectly clear and softly lighted space. There she could see Eduard quite distinctly, not dressed as she had formerly seen him, but in military uniform, and each time in a new attitude and always perfectly natural and plausible: standing, walking, lying down, or riding. The figure, accurate to the smallest detail, moved easily before her eyes without any effort on her part, without her willing it, and without strain to her imagination. Sometimes she saw him surrounded by something in motion, something darker than the light background. But she could hardly recognize the shadowy figures which now seemed to her to be human, now like horses or like trees or mountains. Usually she fell asleep while the vision was still there, and, when she woke again in the morning, after a restful night, she felt refreshed and comforted, thoroughly convinced that Eduard was alive and that their close relationship was unbroken.

Chapter Twenty-seven

Spring had come—later but also more quickly and delightfully than usual. In the garden Ottilie could now gather the fruits of her careful labor: everything was thriving and came to leaf and flower; everything that had been nursed in the greenhouses and hotbeds now burst forth at once in the open air; and all the care and work that still had to be done was not merely a labor of hope, as before, but produced enjoyable and immediate results.

Ottilie had to comfort the gardener for the many gaps among the potted plants, caused by Luciane's rash behavior, and for the destroyed symmetry of more than one tree top. She tried to console him by saying that all would soon be as it was before; but he was much too sensitive and had too severe a conception of his profession to be comforted easily by well-meant arguments. A gardener should not be distracted by any other interests, just as the quiet course which a plant follows to its lasting or passing perfection should not be interrupted. A plant is like a stubborn person from whom we can obtain anything if we handle him in the right manner. Quiet observation and consistency in doing precisely what must be done in any season and at every hour, are probably required of no one more than of a gardener.

All these qualities the good man possessed to a high degree, and for this reason Ottilie liked to work with him; but for some time past he had not been able to practice his true talent as he pleased. He was an expert at any kind of fruit and vegetable gardening—it is difficult to be successful in both—and was also capable of doing all that was required in an old-fashioned flowergarden; but, although he might have challenged Nature herself in his management of the orangery, the flower bulbs, the potted carnations and auriculas, he was unfamiliar with the new varieties of ornamental shrubs and the flowers now in fashion, and felt a kind of grumbling awe before the infinite field of botany, lately opened up, with all its humming foreign names. Everything his master and mistress had ordered last year he considered a useless expense and a waste, the more so, because he saw many expensive plants die out, and because he was not on particularly good terms with the plant-dealers who, he believed did not serve him with sufficient honesty.

After a number of his own experiments he had developed a sort of system in which Ottilie strongly encouraged him, since it was basically related to the return of Eduard, whose absence was, in this case as in many others, daily felt as a disadvantage.

While the plants were gradually developing more and more roots and were putting forth new shoots, Ottilie felt herself becoming increasingly attracted to the green-houses. It was now exactly a year since she had come here as a stranger, a person of no importance. How much she had gained for herself in that time! But, alas, how much had she also lost! She had never before been so rich and so poor. These feelings of gain and of loss alternated in her heart from one moment to another, and even intersected deeply, so that her only resource was, to take up with interest, and almost with passion, the next thing that had to be done.

That she was inclined to take particular care of everything dear to Eduard was only natural; and it was also natural that she hoped he would soon return and personally and gratefully note the thoughtful services she had rendered her absent friend.

But she also set herself another task in his behalf. She primarily took charge of his child, whose exclusive nurse she could become quite easily, for it had been decided that a wet nurse would not be engaged but that the child should be brought up on milk and water. Since the little boy was supposed to be mostly out of doors in this beautiful season, Ottilie loved to take him out in her arms into the fresh air, and to carry the innocently sleeping little creature about among the flowers and blossoms which would one day smile in such a friendly way upon his childhood; among the young shrubs and plants which seemed destined, by their youth, to grow up with him. When she looked about her, she realized what a great and rich life this child could expect: very nearly everything, as far as the eye could see, would one day belong to him. How desirable, it would be, therefor, that he should also grow up under the eyes of his father and mother, confirming their restored and happy union!

Ottilie felt all this so deeply that she imagined it as a definite reality and completely left herself out of the picture. Under this unclouded sky, in this bright sunshine, it became suddenly quite clear to her that her own love ought to become entirely unselfish in order to perfect itself. There were even moments when she believed that she had already reached this height. She wished only the happiness of her friend; she believed herself capable of renouncing him, even of never seeing him again, if she could only know that he was happy. About one point, however, she was firm: she would never belong to another man.

They had taken care that the autumn would be as glorious as the spring. All the so-called estival plants, that do not cease flowering in autumn and even boldly challenge the frost—asters in particular—had been sown in great numbers and in a variety of colors, and planted now everywhere, would later form a starry heaven on earth.

From Ottilie's Diary

We like to record in our diaries any fine thought we have read, or anything striking we have heard. If we would also take the trouble to copy out unusual observations, original ideas, casual intelligent remarks from our friends' letters, we would become very rich. We keep letters and never read them again; one day we destroy them out of discretion, and in this way the most beautiful and direct breath of life vanishes irretrievably, for us and for others. I intend to make up in future for this negligence.

Once more the yearly fairy-tale repeats itself. We have now, thank Heaven, reached its most charming chapter. Violets and lilies-of-the-valley are, as it were, its headings and its vignettes. We are always pleasantly impressed when, opening the book of life, we again come upon these pages.

We are cross with the poor, particularly with children, who idle along the roads, begging. Why do we not notice that, as soon as there is something for them to do, they will start to work at once? Hardly has Nature displayed her bountiful riches when the children eagerly set up in business. Not one of them begs any longer. They hold out to you a bunch of flowers, picked before you have wakened from your sleep, and their pleading look is as sweet as the offered gift. No one ever looks miserable, when he feels that he has a right to ask something from us.

Why is a year sometimes so short and at other times so long; why does it seem so short as it passes and in our memory so long! This I feel about the past year, and nowhere so acutely than in the garden, where I see the transitory interfuse with the lasting. And yet— nothing is so ephemeral that it does not leave behind some trace and something of its own kind.

We can put up with the winter, too. We imagine that we are less confined when the trees stand before us so ghostly and so transparent. They are nothing and they hide nothing. But as soon as buds and blossoms appear, we become impatient to see the full foliage, the landscape shaping itself and the tree advancing upon us in its full form.

Anything perfect in its kind must transcend its kind; it must become something different, something incomparable. In some of its notes the nightingale is still a bird; but then it transcends its own kind and seems to intimate to all feathered creatures what singing really is.

Life without love, without the presence of the beloved, is only a bad *comédie à tiroir*. We pull out one drawer after another, push it quickly back and hastily try the next one. Whatever good or of importance may occur, has little connected meaning. Everywhere we have to begin all over again and everywhere we should like to end.

Chapter Twenty-eight

Charlotte herself was well and very happy. She delighted in her healthy boy, whose physical development gave great promise, and occupied her eye, mind and heart every hour of the day. He formed for her a new link between herself, the world and the estate. Her old activity again stirred in her; she saw how much she had accomplished in the past year, and felt happy concerning everything she had done. Moved by a strange impulse, she walked up to the summer-house with Ottilie and the child; and when she laid her son down on the little table, as upon a domestic altar, and saw the two empty seats, she remembered past times, and new hopes rose in her heart, for herself and for Ottilie.

Young women perhaps look modestly at this or that young man, asking themselves secretly if they would like him for a husband; but the person who has a daughter, or is the guardian of a girl, surveys a wider circle. This was what Charlotte did at this moment, and a marriage between the Captain and Ottilie did not seem impossible to her when she thought how they had sat side by side, once before, in this little summer-house. It had not remained unknown to her that the prospect of an advantageous marriage for the Captain had come to nothing.

They climbed farther up the hill, Ottilie carrying the child. Charlotte was absorbed in all kinds of reflections. Even on dry land shipwrecks can occur—to recover from them as quickly as possible, and to restore a former condition is wise and praiseworthy, for life calculates only gain or loss. Who has not made plans, to be interrupted in them! How often one turns into a road, only to find it impassable and to lose it again! How often is our attention turned away from a goal we had eagerly in view, only because we wish to attain a higher one! A traveler may be extremely vexed when a wheel of his coach breaks on the journey; but this unpleasant accident may lead to his making the most charming acquaintances and to his forming connections which will influence his whole life. Fate grants our wishes, but only in its own way, in order to give us something more than our wishes.

These, and similar thoughts, occupied Charlotte while she walked up to the new building on the crest of the hill; and up here, all her thoughts proved right. The view was now much lovelier than they could have foreseen. Obstructions on all sides had been removed; all the important features of the landscape, all that Nature and Time had done for it, now appeared in clear relief to the eye; and the new groups of trees and shrubs planted to fill in several gaps and to connect the separate parts in an agreeable way, were beginning to show green.

The house itself was almost ready to be occupied; and the view—particularly from the upper rooms—offered great variety. The longer they looked about, the more beauty they discovered. What superb effects would the changing of the different hours of the day, and sun and moon, create here! To live in this house seemed highly desirable; and Charlotte's delight in building and creating was again quickly aroused when she discovered that all the rough work had been finished. A carpenter, a paper-hanger, a resourceful painter who could manage a few stencils and a little gilding, were all that was needed, and in a very short time the building was habitable. Kitchen and cellar were quickly stocked, for, being so far away from the castle, they had to be provided with all essentials. Now the two women and the child lived upon the hill, and from this new residence, as from a new center, they discovered unexpected walks. They also greatly enjoyed in this higher altitude the fresh air and the lovely weather.

Ottilie's favorite walk, which she sometimes took alone and at other times with the child, led her, along an easy footpath, down to the plane trees, and from there to the point where one of the boats was moored that people used to cross the water. She enjoyed rowing, but she never took the child because Charlotte would have been uneasy about it. Ottilie also never missed her daily visit to the gardener in the park; she always showed special interest in his care of the many cuttings which he had been nursing in the hothouse but which were now set out in the open.

During this lovely season, Charlotte was much pleased by the visit of an Englishman who had met Eduard abroad, and was now curious to see the beautiful park, about which he had heard so many enthusiastic reports. He brought a letter of introduction from the Count and introduced to them his traveling companion, a quiet and very likeable man. While he walked about the countryside in the company of Charlotte and Ottilie, or with gardeners and hunters, frequently with his friend, and now and then alone, it could be gathered from his comments that he was a great lover and connoisseur of such 'landscape gardens,' and that he himself must have laid out some of the same type. Although no longer young, he showed a warm interest in everything that makes life more beautiful or lends it distinction.

In his company the two women for the first time fully enjoyed everything about them. His trained eyes took in every effect freshly, and he was all the more delighted with the improvements, since he had never seen the place before and could hardly distinguish between the natural and the artificial.

It might even be said that through his comments the park became actually richer and more beautiful. He was able to anticipate the future effect of the new and growing groups of trees. Not one spot where he thought a beautiful effect might be better set off or a new beauty created, escaped his notice. Here, he would point out a spring which, if cleaned out, might become the ornamental center of a whole group of shrubs; there, a grotto that only needed to be cleared and widened to form an attractive place to sit and rest; they needed to cut down only a few trees in order to obtain from this point a prospect of magnificently towering rocks. He considered the owners of all this very fortunate indeed; there was still much left for them to develop, and he urged them not to do anything hurriedly but to keep alive for themselves, for years to come, the pleasure of creating and arranging.

Apart from the hours they all spent together, their visitor was hardly noticeable; for the greater part of the day he was occupied in catching the picturesque views of the park in his portable *camera obscura* and in making drawings from these, in order to bring home from his travels mementos for himself and for others. He had done this for many years in all the remarkable places he had visited and had compiled a most pleasurable and interesting collection. He showed the ladies a large portfolio he had brought with him; and entertained them equally with the pictures and with his descriptions. There in their solitude, they enjoyed traveling so comfortably all over the world—seeing pass before their eyes shores and harbors, mountains, lakes and rivers, cities, castles and many other places which have a name in history.

Each of the two women had her special interest. Charlotte's was a more general one, in places which were historically remarkable; whereas Ottilie's attention was primarily arrested by the parts of the world of which Eduard had often spoken, where he had liked to stay, and to which he had frequently returned. For everyone, certain local features exist—far or near—which attract him according to his character, and which he considers particularly endearing and exciting, because of the first impression they have made on him, because of certain associations, or because of habit.

Ottilie, therefore, asked Lord . . . which one of all these places he had liked best; and where he would live, if he had the choice. He then showed her more than one lovely part of the world, and told her kindly, in his slow peculiarly accentuated French, what had happened to him here or there, to make him love and admire that locality.

But he answered her question as to where he usually lived, and where he best liked to return, very frankly, although in a way which was rather unexpected for his listeners.

"I am now quite accustomed to feel at home everywhere; and I think that nothing is more convenient than to let others build and plant and keep house for me. I have no longing to return to my own estates, partly from political reasons, but mainly, because my son, for whom I really planned and arranged everything—and to whom I hoped to transfer all, and with whom I hoped to enjoy everything for still a little while—has no interest in the property, but has gone to India like many others—where he thinks he can make better use of his life; but perhaps will only waste it.

"It is true that we make much too elaborate preparations for life. Instead of beginning at once to live happily, in moderate conditions, we forever expand, and thereby make our lives more and more uncomfortable. Who now enjoys my house, my park, my gardens? Not I, not even my family: but strangers, curious visitors, or restless travelers.

"Even with considerable means, we are always only half at home and particularly so in the country, where we miss many things we have become used to in the city. The book we are most anxious to read is not at hand; and just what we needed most has been forgotten. We always settle down in order to leave again; and if we do not leave of our own free will, or from a purposeless whim, we are forced by circumstances, passions, accidental events, necessity, or whatnot."

Lord . . . did not suspect how deeply the two women were touched by these general reflections. How often do we all run a risk, when we make such casual statements, even in the presence of persons whose circumstances are well known to us! Charlotte was quite used to such occasional thoughtless words, which wounded, even when they came from kindly-feeling and well-meaning people; but she knew the world so well that it did not shock her particularly when someone forced her—thoughtlessly and carelessly—to direct her attention to this or that unpleasant facet of life. Ottilie, however, who was still in her half-conscious youth, who felt more than she saw, and who was allowed, even bound, to turn her eyes away from what she neither should nor wished to know—Ottilie was thrown into the most anguished state of mind by these careless words, for they tore a graceful veil rudely from her eyes; and it seemed to her as if everything which had been done all this time for this house and this home, for garden and park, and for all the environs, was actually in vain, because he to whom it all belonged did not enjoy it; because he, too, like their present guest, had been driven out by those dearest and closest to him, to wander about all over the world; and was, moreover, driven into the most dangerous situation. She was accustomed to listen and keep silent; but on this occasion she found herself in a most difficult position, which only became more so when the foreign visitor continued, in his cheerful circumspect manner: "I believe I am now on the right road, since I consider myself at all times as a traveler who renounces much in order to enjoy much. I am now used to constant change; it has even become necessary to me, in the same way as we are always waiting, at the opera, for a new stage-setting, since there have already been so many. I know what to expect from the best inns, and what from the worst; they may be as good or as bad as they come, but, at least, I can always expect something new, and in the long run everything comes to much the same thing—whether we depend upon a necessary habit or entirely upon the caprice of change. Now I need no longer to worry that something cannot be found or is lost, that the room in which I am used to living is uninhabitable because of repairs, that my favorite cup is broken and that for a long time nothing will taste good from another cup. I am spared all this, and, should the house start to burn over my head, my servants would quickly pack my things, we would drive out of the inn yard, leave the town, and look for another lodging. When I consider these advantages and reckon up my expenses at the end of the year, I find that I have not spent more money than it would have cost me to live at home.

While he went on with his description, Ottilie saw only Eduard before her: marching along rough roads, in discomfort and hardship, encamped in open fields, exposed to danger and misery. Homeless and friendless in this hazardous life of constant change, he would have become used to throwing everything away, in order to have nothing to lose. Fortunately the friends separated for a short time, and Ottilie had an opportunity to be alone and to cry her heart out. Never had her silent suffering overwhelmed her more desperately than in this sudden realization which she tried to make even clearer to herself, as we do when we torture ourselves in a situation by which we are already tortured.

Eduard's present condition seemed to her so miserable and pitiful that she decided to do everything in her power to bring about his reunion with Charlotte; to hide her own pain and love, in some quiet place, and to deceive them by any kind of activity.

Lord . . .'s companion, a sensible and quiet man, but a keen observer, had meanwhile noticed the blunder his friend had made in the conversation, and had drawn his attention to the similarity of the circumstances. Lord . . . had not known any particulars about the situation in this family, but his friend—who, on his travels was, in fact, in nothing more interested than in strange occurrences, caused by natural or accidental relationships, by the conflict between the lawful and the uncontrollable, between feeling and reason, between passion and prejudice—had some time previously (and especially while staying here at the castle) informed himself of everything that had happened, and of the present state of affairs.

Lord . . . was sorry, but he did not feel embarrassed. "We should always have to hold our tongues in society if we wished nothing of this sort to occur; for not only meaningful remarks but also the most trivial pronouncements may upset the feelings of those present," he said. "We shall set things right this evening and avoid all general talk. Do tell us some of the many pleasant and remarkable anecdotes, with which you have, on your travels, enriched your portfolio as well as your memory."

But even with the best intentions the two strangers did not succeed in amusing their friends with an apparently harmless entertainment. For after Lord . . .'s companion had told various strange, remarkable, gay, moving or terrifying stories, which arrested their attention and frequently held them in suspense, he thought of concluding with an unusual though less exciting incident. He did not suspect how deeply it would affect one of his listeners.

The Amazing Young Neighbors Novella

"Two young persons of good family, living near one another, grew up together in the pleasant expectation of one day becoming husband and wife; and the parents of both looked forward with happiness to their future marriage. But it soon became quite evident that their plan would probably come to nothing, because a strange antipathy between the two young people, who were both of excellent character, manifested itself very distinctly. Perhaps they were too much alike. The minds of both were directed toward their respective interests; they were determined in their desires and firm in their resolves; each was loved and admired by his or her playfellows; but they were always antagonists when together. Each was constructive but destructive in the other's company; wherever they met, they were not competitors for one goal but fighters with only one purpose in mind. They were both, on the whole, good-natured and amiable, and hostile or even malicious only in their relations to each other.

"This curious attitude revealed itself early in their childhood games; it increased with their years. Once, when the boys played at war and divided into battling factions, the girl, defiant and courageous, placed herself at the head of one of the armies and fought against the other with such vehemence and spirit, that the other side would have been disgracefully put to flight, if her own personal enemy had not held out bravely, finally disarmed his opponent, and taken her prisoner. But even then she defended herself so furiously that, in order to save his eyes without doing her any harm, he had to snatch off his silk scarf and tie the hands of his antagonist behind her back.

"This she never forgave him. Indeed, as time went on, she made so many secret attempts and plans to do him harm that his parents, and her own, who had been watching these strange passions for a long time, came to an agreement and decided to separate the two hostile children and to give up their own precious hopes.

"The boy soon distinguished himself in his new circumstances. Any instruction had splendid results. Following the wishes of those who were interested in him, and his own inclination, he decided to become a professional soldier. He was loved and respected everywhere. His excellent character always made him work for the benefit and well-being of others; and deep in his heart, he was very happy, if scarcely conscious of the fact, that he was rid of the one and only adversary whom nature had destined for him.

"The girl, on the other hand, suddenly reached a very different stage. Her age, her growing maturity, and a certain instinct made her avoid the wild boys' games in which she had formerly participated. She seemed, however, to miss something; nothing around her was worth exciting her hatred; and she had not yet found anyone worthy of her affection.

"A young man, older than her former neighbor and enemy, of rank, fortune, and distinction, well liked in society and fascinating to women, now turned all his affection toward her. It was the first time that a friend, a lover, a suitor, had wooed her seriously. The preference he gave her before so many others who were older, more educated, more brilliant, and of higher station than herself, gratified her exceedingly. His continual attention, without insistence, his loyal aid in various unpleasant circumstances, his quiet and patient courtship—concerning which he had informed her parents, as she herself was indeed still very young—all this made her think favorably of him; and habit, as well as the fact that their relationship was now taken for granted by everyone, contributed to this feeling. She was so often called his fiancée that at last she herself believed she was; and neither she nor anyone else thought that a test might be necessary before she exchanged rings with the man who for such a long time had been considered her betrothed.

"The quiet course which their friendship had been following was not quickened by the final, formal engagement. Both partners allowed matters to go on as before; they were happy to be together and planned to enjoy to the end this fine season which should be the spring of their future and more serious life.

"Meanwhile the neighbors' son had completed his studies with distinction. He had climbed to a well-deserved rung in his career and now came home on leave to visit his family. He saw his lovely neighbor again and found himself in a perfectly natural though rather peculiar situation. For some time her heart had known only the kindly feelings of domestic happiness which befit a future bride; she was in harmony with everything around her; she believed herself to be happy, and in a certain sense she was happy. Now, for the first time in years she was again confronted with something: she could not hate it, for she was no longer capable of hatred. Her childish animosity, which had actually been only a vague recognition of an inner value, now expressed itself in a happy surprise, an amiable admission, and a half-willing, half-reluctant attraction. And all this was mutual. Their long separation gave them occasion for prolonged talks. Both had matured, even their childish and absurd behavior of years before now amused them when they exchanged memories, and it seemed as if the least they could do was to make up for that teasing hatred by a mutual friendliness and consideration—it was as if these vehement misunderstandings of earlier days now required implicit understanding as compensation.

"On the youth's side, everything remained within reasonable and desirable limits. His profession, his circumstances, and his ambition occupied him so completely that he accepted the friendly behavior of the betrothed young girl quite naturally, as a gratifying gift, without assuming that it had any consequences for himself, or begrudging the fiancé his bride; he was, by the way, on very good terms with him.

"But with her it was quite different. She felt as though she had wakened from a dream. The struggle with her young neighbor had been her first passion; and that struggle had been, after all, nothing but a violent, almost innate affection in the form of opposition. When she now tried to remember, it seemed to her that she had always loved him. She smiled when she thought of her hostile pursuit with weapons in her hands; she recalled her most pleasurable sensation when he had disarmed her; she imagined having felt bliss when he bound her; and all her schemes to harm and to annoy him, now seemed to her to have been only an innocent means of attracting his attention. She loathed their separation; she bewailed the sleep into which she had fallen; she cursed the languid dreamy habit which had made her accept such an unremarkable man as her fiancé; she was changed—changed, in a double sense, to the past and for the future, as one might say.

"If anyone could have looked into her heart and entered into her feelings, he would not have blamed her; but she kept everything a secret. Her fiancé could not be favorably compared to the neighbor when they were seen side by side. Although no one could deny a certain feeling of trust to the one, the other inspired complete confidence; if one liked to meet the first, everyone wished the second as a friend: and if one had imagined occasions that demanded energy and resolution, one might have had a slight doubt concerning the fiancé, while the neighbor's son inspired a feeling of complete security. For these fine shades of character, women possess an inborn and particular instinct, and they have reason as well as opportunity to train this gift.

"The more the girl indulged in her secret emotions, the less people found an opportunity to say anything in favor of her fiancé or to remind her what her circumstances and her duty seemed to advise and require. Her loving heart continued to indulge its partiality. On one side, she was indissolubly bound by social standards, by her family, her fiancé, and her own pledge; the ambitious young man, on the other, made no secret whatever concerning his own plans and prospects and behaved toward her like a faithful but not even particularly affectionate brother. When at last he spoke of his imminent departure, her former childish spirit seemed to be roused in all its malice and violence, angry and ready to function now even more effectively and perversely. She decided to die, in order to punish the youth she had once hated and now so passionately loved, for his indifference; and, as she could not possess him, at least to be forever united with his memory and his remorse. He was never to rid himself of her dead image, nor ever to cease reproaching himself that he had not recognized, not fathomed nor treasured her feelings.

"This strange madness did not leave her for one moment. She kept it hidden under many disguises; and, although people may have thought her queer, no one was perspicacious or wise enough to discover the actual root of her queerness.

"Meanwhile, friends, relatives, and acquaintances had exhausted themselves in arranging all sorts of festivities. Hardly a day passed without their organizing something new and unexpected. There was almost no beautiful site in the neighborhood which was not decorated and arranged for the reception of many merry guests. Our young visitor, too, wishing to do his best before he left, invited the young couple with a small family group for an excursion by boat.

They boarded a handsome prettily decorated yacht, one of those elegant boats with a dining saloon and a few cabins which transfer the conveniences of the land to the water.

"They glided along the river to the sound of music; during the hot hours of the day the company assembled in the cabins below deck and amused themselves with games of skill and chance. Their young host, who could never remain inactive, had taken charge of the wheel, in order to relieve the old master of the vessel, who had fallen asleep at his side. Just at this moment the wary young man needed all his presence of mind, since the boat was nearing a place where two islands narrowed the channel and where their shallow gravelly banks stretching out, first on one side and then on the other, made navigation dangerous. The cautious and sharpsighted helmsman was almost tempted to waken the captain; but he thought he could manage by himself; and took his course toward the narrows. Just then his lovely enemy appeared on deck, a wreath of flowers in her hair. She took off the wreath and flung it to her friend at the wheel. 'Take this as a memento,' she called out.

" 'Don't disturb me!' he exclaimed, catching the wreath, 'I need all my strength and attention.'

" 'I shall not disturb you any longer,' she cried. 'You will never see me again.' With these words she ran toward the bow of the boat and jumped into the water. Several voices shouted 'Save her, save her—she is drowning!' The young man found himself in a most terrible situation. The old skipper woke up and tried to take the wheel at the young man's command; but it was too late; the boat ran aground, and the young man, throwing off his heavier clothes, plunged into the river and swam toward his lovely enemy.

"Water is a friendly element for a person who is familiar with it and knows how to deal with it. The stream carried him easily, and the skillful swimmer mastered it. Soon he had caught up with the girl, who had been carried away by the current; he clutched her and was successful in lifting and carrying her. Both were now swept away by the force of the stream, until the islands and shoals were far behind them and the river was again broad and quiet. Only now did the young man survey matters clearly; after the first immediate danger he had acted quite mechanically and without conscious thought. He raised his head high and swam with all his energy toward a shallow bushy place where the land projected conveniently into the river, and he could carry his lovely prize onto dry land. There seemed to be not a breath of life in her. He was desperate, but, looking about, he discovered a path running through the underbrush. He took up his precious burden and soon caught sight of a solitary house, and found kind people, a young married couple. The emergency needed no long explanation. What he asked for was instantly brought. Soon a bright fire was blazing, and woolen blankets were spread on a couch; furs, pelts, and other warm coverings were quickly accumulated. Their wish to save a human being overcame any other consideration. Nothing was neglected which might call life back to the beautiful, half-rigid, naked body. They succeeded in reviving her. She opened her eyes, saw her friend, and flung her arms around him. She held him for a long time; and then, tears gushed from her eyes and completed her recovery. "Are you going to leave me now, that I have found you?" she cried.

" 'Never!' he exclaimed; 'Never!' But he hardly knew what he said or did. 'But be careful now!' he added. 'Think of yourself, for your sake and mine.'

"She suddenly became conscious of herself and only now noticed the state she was in. But she could not feel ashamed in the presence of the man she loved, the man who had saved her life. She let him go to attend to himself: his clothes were still wet and dripping.

"The other young couple consulted with one another; the husband offered the young man, and the wife the young girl their complete wedding outfit, which had not yet been stored away, and would dress them from top to toe, inside and out. In a short time the two adventurers were not only dressed but charmingly so. They looked very handsome and were transfixed with amazement when they saw each other again; they rushed into one another's arms with passion, still half-smiling at their quaint disguise. The power of youth and the animating spirit of love completely revived them in a few moments, and only music was missing to invite them to dance.

"The sudden transition from water to firm ground, from death to life, from the circle of their families into a wilderness, from despair to delight, from indifference to passion and affection—all this at once—was almost too much for the head to grasp: it would burst or become confused. The heart had to do its best to make such a shock bearable. Since the young couple were entirely lost one in the other, some time passed before they could think of the apprehension and anxiety of those left behind. They began to feel some alarm at the thought of how they would face their families. 'Shall we run away? Shall we hide?' the young man asked. 'We shall stay together,' the girl said, clinging to him.

"The farmer, who had heard from them that their boat had gone aground, hurried to the river without asking further questions. There he saw the yacht coming downstream; with great efforts those on board had freed it and were not uncertainly sailing along, taking their chance and hoping to find their lost friends. The farmer tried to attract the attention of the people on board by shouting and signaling to them; he ran to a point where a convenient landing could be made and continued to shout and beckon until the boat headed in to shore; and what a sight it was when they landed! The parents of the two young people managed to land first; the fiancé was almost beside himself. They had hardly heard that their children were safe when the couple themselves appeared in their quaint costumes. No one recognized them until they had come quite close. 'Who is that?' the mothers exclaimed.

" 'What is that?' the fathers cried. The rescued pair knelt down before them.

" 'Your children,' they cried. 'We are engaged!' 'Forgive us!' said the young girl.

" 'Give us your blessing!' asked the young man.

" 'Give us your blessing!' both implored, while all the others stood speechless with amazement.

" 'Your blessing!' was heard for the third time, and who could have the heart to refuse it?"

Chapter Twenty-nine

The narrator paused or, rather, he had just finished his story, when he noticed that Charlotte was deeply moved. She got up and left the room with an apology. She knew the story. The incident had actually occurred between the Captain and a girl in his neighborhood, not exactly as the Englishman had told it, yet still not essentially different. Only a few details had been altered and embellished, as can happen with that sort of tale after it has passed through the mouths of many and finally through the imaginative mind of a man of intelligence and taste. The usual result is that everything and nothing is left as it was.

At the request of the two guests Ottilie followed Charlotte; and it was now Lord . . .'s turn to remark that perhaps a second blunder had been made and that his friend had recounted something well known to the family or even connected with them. "We must be careful not to make any more embarrassing mistakes," he added. "In return for all the kindness and hospitality we have enjoyed, we have, apparently, not been very fortunate in our talk. We had better try to take our leave in a tactful manner."

"I must confess that there is something special which keeps me here," his friend answered, "and for that reason I should be very sorry to leave this house without learning more about it. Yesterday, when we walked through the park with your *camera obscura*, you, sir, were much too busy looking for a place from which you could catch picturesque views to notice anything else that was going on. You turned off the main path in order to reach a less frequented spot by the lake which would offer you a charming vista. Ottilie, who accompanied us, hesitated to follow you and asked if she might go there by boat. I joined her and watched with delight the skill of my lovely captain. I assured her that never, since I had been in Switzerland, where very charming girls sometimes take the place of ferrymen, had I been rocked so agreeably on the water; but I could not resist asking her why she had refused to walk on that bypath. I thought I had noticed, in her shrinking away, a really painful uneasiness. 'If you will not laugh at me, I will give you an explanation,' she answered, without the slightest resentment. 'Although even I find the fact a little mysterious, I have never walked on that path without being overcome by a peculiar chill which I have never felt anywhere else and which I cannot explain to myself. I rather avoid, therefore, exposing myself to that sensation, especially since immediately afterward I feel a pain in the left side of my head—a pain from which I suffer at other times, too.' We went ashore; Ottilie spoke with you; and meanwhile I examined the place she had pointed out to me from a distance. I was very surprised to discover unquestionable traces of coal. I am convinced that, by digging a little more, a considerable bed of coal might be found below the surface. I am sorry, sir; I see you smile and I know very well that you listen so patiently to my enthusiastic pursuit of these things in which you have no faith at all, only because you are a wise man and my friend; but it is impossible for me to leave this place without having tried my pendulum experiment with this girl."

Every time the matter came up, Lord . . . never failed to repeat his arguments against this experiment—arguments to which his friend, in turn, always listened patiently and modestly, while persisting in his own opinion and desires. He pointed out that one should not discredit such experiments because not everyone was successful with them; on the contrary, one should test their results even more carefully and exactly; perhaps, many new relations and affinities among inorganic substances and among organic substances, as well as between organic and inorganic, might be discovered—all of them at present unknown to us.

He had already spread out his apparatus, consisting of gold rings, marcasites, and other metallic substances, which he always carried with him in a neat little box; and he now lowered pieces of metal, suspended on threads, over other pieces lying beneath them. "I do not resent the mischievous delight I can see on your face, sir, at the fact that nothing will now move for me. But this performance is really only a pretext. If the ladies should return, I want them to become curious about what we are up to."

The ladies did return. Charlotte understood what was going on at once. "I have heard a great deal about these matters," she said, "but I have never seen any results. As you have everything so nicely assembled, let me try to see if it works for me."

She held the thread in her hand: and, because she took the matter very seriously, she held it steadily and calmly; but not the slightest oscillation could be seen. Then Ottilie was asked to try. She held the pendulum even more quietly and innocently over the metals which lay beneath. But immediately the suspended piece of metal was swept away as if in a distinct swift rotation, turning first to one side and then to another with each change in the position of the tray beneath, now in circles, now in ellipses; or it swung in straight lines, as effectively as the experimenter could expect, and even beyond his expectations. Lord . . . himself was taken aback; but his friend, in his delight and eagerness, could not stop and asked Ottilie again and again to repeat and vary the experiment. The girl was obliging enough to agree, but at last she asked him to let her go, because her headache had again appeared. He was amazed as well as delighted at this and assured her enthusiastically that he could completely cure her of this trouble if she would entrust herself to his treatment. The two women hesitated for a moment, but Charlotte, who quickly grasped what sort of treatment was meant, declined his well-meant offer, for she was unwilling to permit in her domestic sphere, experiments about which she had always felt a strong apprehension.

The guests departed; and, although they have been the cause of some strange experiences, they left in the mutual hope of a meeting somewhere in the future. Charlotte now used the pleasant days to return the last of her neighbors' calls—quite a difficult task, since everyone in the surrounding country (some out of genuine interest, some only as a matter of form) had frequently called on her to inquire about her health. At home, the sight of the little boy gave her new life; and he was certainly worth her love and care. Everyone thought him an unusual child, even a prodigy. His looks, his size, his fine proportions, his strength, his health—all were delights to the eye; but the most astonishing fact was his double resemblance, which became more and more striking. In form and features the child resembled the Captain more and more; and from day to day it became more difficult to distinguish between his eyes and Ottilie's.

Because of this strange affinity, and perhaps still more because of a woman's sweet feeling of tender affection for the child of a beloved man—even though it should be the child of another woman—Ottilie was like a mother to the growing little creature or rather like a second mother. When Charlotte was absent, Ottilie stayed at home with the child and its nurse. Nanni had resentfully deserted her for some time past and had returned to her parents; she was jealous of the little boy to whom her mistress seemed to give all her affection. Ottilie continued to carry the child into the open air and gradually extended her walks with him. She always took his nursing-bottle with her in order to feed him, if necessary. But she rarely forgot to take a book along, and in this way—the child in her arm and reading as she walked—she made a very graceful *Penserosa*.

Chapter Thirty

The main objective of the campaign had been attained, and Eduard was honorably discharged with medals and other marks of honor.

He immediately returned to his small farm, where he found detailed news concerning his family waiting for him—the family which, during his absence and without their knowing it, he had kept under close observation. His quiet refuge looked very pleasant to him; many repairs and improvements had been made while he was away, according to his directions, so that the convenient arrangements in the house itself compensated for all that it lacked in size and area.

Eduard, grown accustomed to more definite decisions in a livelier sort of existence, now made up his mind to realize immediately the plans he had had sufficient time to think about. First of all he invited his old friend the Major (who had been promoted from Captain) to come and see him. Their reunion was a great joy for both. Early friendships have, like blood relationships, the distinct advantage that mistakes and misunderstandings of any kind are never fundamentally harmful to them; the old relationship is always quickly reestablished.

After a cordial welcome, Eduard inquired about the situation of his friend and hear how perfectly Fortune had favored the latter's wishes. In jesting familiarity, he asked if there was not, perhaps, some happy alliance in the offing; but his friend denied this.

"I cannot, and I must not, be secretive with you," Eduard went on. "I must tell you at once of the state of my own feelings and of my intentions. You know of my love for Ottilie; and you have known for a long time that it was this passion which drove me into the campaign. I do not deny that I wished to rid myself of a life which, without her, had no longer any meaning for me; but at the same time I must confess that I could not bring myself to feel utterly hopeless. Happiness with her seemed so beautiful, so desirable, that I found it impossible to resign my hope entirely. So many happy omens had strengthened my belief, my illusion, that Ottilie might one day be mine. A glass, engraved with our initials and flung into the air when the cornerstone was laid, did not break; someone caught it, and it is again in my possession. After I had endured so many miserable hours in this lonely place, I said to myself: I shall put myself in the place of this glass which shall be a symbol either for the possibility or the impossibility of our future union. I shall go in quest of death—not like a madman but like a man who still hopes to survive. Ottilie shall be the prize I fight for; it will be *she* whom I hope to win and conquer—in line of battle, in every entrenchment, in every besieged fortress. I shall perform miracles with the wish to be spared myself, with the thought of winning Ottilie, not of losing her. These emotions have guided me; they have helped me through all dangers; but now I feel like a man who has reached his goal, like a man who has overcome every obstacle, whose way is now plain before him. Ottilie is mine; anything that still lies between this thought and its realization I can only regard as unimportant."

"With a few strokes you eliminate everything I could and should interpose, and yet I must repeat my objections," the Major replied, "I leave it to you to recall to your memory the great value of your relationship with your wife—and you owe it to her and to yourself, not to close your eyes to it. But at the sheer thought that a son has been given to you, I must at once declare that you and Charlotte belong to one another forever; that, for the sake of this little creature, it is your duty to live united, so that, united, you can take care of his education and build a happy future for him."

"It is nothing but the conceit of parents to imagine that their presence is so necessary to their children," Eduard objected. "Anything that lives finds food and assistance; and if a son, after his father's early death, does not have such a carefree and favored youth, he may just for that reason gain a quicker training for the world, for he will early recognize that he must get on with other people, a fact which we all have to learn, sooner or later. But in our case all this is quite irrelevant; we are sufficiently well-off to provide for several children, and it is neither our duty nor to his benefit to accumulate so much property on one single individual."

When the Major began to allude to Charlotte's value as a person and to Eduard's long-standing relationship with her, the latter quickly interrupted him. "We have been very foolish, as I now see all too clearly. He who tries to realize in his middle years, the desires and hopes of his early youth always deceives himself, for each decade of a man's life has its own happiness, its own hopes and its own chances. Not with impunity does a man, driven by his circumstances or by his delusions, try to capture something that lies before or behind him! Charlotte and I have acted foolishly; should this folly last for a whole lifetime? Should we refuse to ourselves, because of some scruple, what the morals of our time do not forbid? In how many situations do not men retract their intentions and their actions, and why should it not be done in this case, where everything is at stake, not just one particular, not this or that condition of life but life's whole complexity!"

The Major did not fail to point out, with much emphasis and skill, what Eduard owed to his wife, to their families, to the world, and to his estates; but he did not succeed in making the slightest impression.

"All those considerations have passed before my mind, dear friend," Eduard said, "in the tumult of battle, when the earth shook from the continuous roar of cannonades, when the bullets whizzed and whistled, and my comrades fell to right and left, when my horse was hit and my cap riddled; these thoughts have haunted me by the still campfire, at night, under the starry vault of heaven. At such moments everyone with whom I was connected appeared before my soul; I have thought of them and deeply felt for them; I have weighed everything and drawn my conclusions; I have come to terms with myself—many many times and now for good and all.

'You, too,—why should I keep it from you—were then in my thoughts; you, too, belonged in my circle; for have we not belonged to one another for such a long time? If I have ever been in your debt, I am now in a position to pay you back with interest; if you ever owed me anything, you are now able to make a good return. I know that you love Charlotte, and she deserves this love. I know that she is not indifferent to you—and why should she not recognize your worth! Take her from my own hands! Bring Ottilie to me—and we shall be the happiest people on earth."

"Just because you wish to bribe me with such precious gifts, I must be all the more prudent and firm," the Major replied. "Your suggestion—for which in my heart I am grateful—does not make things easier but even more difficult. The question now concerns not only you, but me as well; and not only the destiny but also the good name and the honor of two men is at stake—two men of, until now, irreproachable characters, who run the risk, by such strange action—to put it mildly—of appearing in the eyes of the world in an extremely curious light."

"The fact that we have been above reproach until now, gives us a right to let ourselves be criticized for once," Eduard retorted. "A man who has proved himself honorable for a whole lifetime, makes an action honorable which would appear ambiguous in others. So far as I am concerned, I feel justified, after the trials I have taken on myself, and the difficult and dangerous actions I have performed for others, to do something for myself. We shall leave Charlotte's case and yours in the hands of the future; but neither you nor anyone else will keep me from my resolution. If any hand should be offered me, I shall be ready and willing to do what is wanted; but if I am deserted or should meet any opposition, I shall be driven to a desperate action—come what may."

The Major thought it his duty to oppose Eduard's resolution as long as possible, and he now skillfully changed his tactics by apparently yielding to his friend and by discussing only the form and the legal proceedings which would have to be undertaken in order to bring about the separation and the new unions. In this connection numerous, unpleasant, difficult, and offensive matters came up which put Eduard into the worst of tempers.

"I now see quite clearly that the fulfillment of our wishes must be taken by storm not only from our enemies but also from our friends," he cried at last. "I shall keep my eye fixed upon what I want, what is indispensable to me, and I shall seize it and certainly soon and quickly. Relationships like ours are neither dissolved nor formed without the toppling of much that once stood firm, and the giving way of much that would like to continue. Such matters do not come to a final conclusion through a process of reasoning—all rights being equal for the reasoning mind; and it is always possible to place another weight on the rising scale. Therefore, my friend, make up your mind and act; for your sake and for mine disentangle, untie and bind again these knots. Do not allow yourself to be put off by any scruples; we have already given the world reason to talk about us; people will talk once more and then forget us, as they forget anything that has ceased to be new. They will forget us and let us do what we like without being interested any longer."

The Major was at his wit's end and had no other choice but to submit to Eduard's way of treating the whole matter as being conclusively settled; while the latter gaily discussed in detail every step of their procedure, he pictured the future in the most cheerful colors and even joked about it.

Once more serious and thoughtful Eduard went on: "To give way to the hope and expectation that everything will turn out well by itself, that chance will guide and favor us, would be an unpardonable self-deception. We cannot possibly save ourselves in this manner, nor restore peace for all of us; and how should I be able to find any comfort—I, the innocent cause of all this? By my insistence I persuaded Charlotte to invite you to stay with us; and Ottilie, too, joined us in consequence of this first change. We no longer have any control of the outcome of it all; but we do have the power to counteract the harm we have done, and to direct the situation toward our happiness. Can you turn your eyes away from the beautiful and happy prospects I open up for us? Can you impose upon me, upon all of us a joyless resignation? Do you think this possible? *Is* it possible? If it is, and if we should decide to return to former conditions, would not many offensive, annoying and inconvenient things have to be suffered without any resulting good or happiness? Would the fortunate position which you hold make you happy if you were prevented from visiting me and from staying at my house? After all that has happened you must agree that this would be constantly embarrassing. With our ample fortune, Charlotte and I would only find ourselves in a melancholy situation. And if you, like other men of the world, should believe that years and separation will blunt such feelings, will erase deeply engraved impressions, those are the very years which no one wishes to spend in sorrow and resignation but rather in joy and happiness. And the final and most important argument is: even if *we*, owing to our external circumstances and our state of mind, could perhaps wait patiently—what will become of Ottilie? She would be compelled to leave our house, would be deprived of our protection, and would be harshly dealt with in a cold wicked world! Describe to me any situation in which Ottilie—without me, without us—could be happy; then you will have offered me an argument, stronger than any other, which I am willing to consider, even if I should not accept it."

This problem was not easy to solve; at least his friend could not think of a satisfactory solution. He could only impress on Eduard repeatedly how serious, how precarious, and, in many ways, how dangerous the whole undertaking was and that they should at least study with careful deliberation how to set about it. To this Eduard agreed, but on the condition that his friend should not leave him before they had arrived at an agreement about the whole matter, and not before the first steps had been taken.

Chapter Thirty-one

Complete strangers or people who are entirely indifferent to each other usually open their hearts liberally, when they are living together for some time—necessarily creating an atmosphere of intimacy. It was all the more to be expected, therefore, that our two friends, who were now living under the same roof again and saw each other daily, had no secrets left. They talked repeatedly about the earlier years of their friendship, and the Major did not conceal from Eduard the fact that Charlotte had intended Ottilie for him at the time when he had returned from his travels, and that she had hoped that Eduard would finally marry the lovely girl. Eduard was almost beside himself at this disclosure; and he now spoke without any reserve of the mutual affection between Charlotte and the Major, which, because it fitted in conveniently and favorably with his own wishes, he painted in glowing colors.

Although the Major could not totally deny this affection, he did not wish to admit it altogether. But Eduard became only the more insistent and determined. Everything was fixed in his mind, not as a possibility but as already settled. Everyone concerned had only to agree to something desired by all; a divorce could certainly be obtained; the new marriages would follow as soon as possible; and then Eduard planned to travel with Ottilie.

Among the pleasant things which imagination pictures, nothing is perhaps more charming than young lovers or young married couples who hope to enjoy their new fresh relationship in a fresh, new world, and to test and confirm the stability of their bond in many changing circumstances. The Major and Charlotte, meanwhile, would have full power to arrange and initiate any matter concerning property, money and other worldly and desirable affairs—justly and fairly and for the satisfaction of all concerned. But the point which Eduard stressed most strongly, from which he seemed to promise himself the greatest advantage, was this: that—as the child would remain with its mother, the Major would be in a position to educate the boy, to guide him according to his judgment, and to develop his abilities. Then it would not be in vain that he had been baptized by the name "Otto"—the name of both friends.

Eduard had arranged everything so perfectly in his mind that he could not wait another day to carry out all his plans. On their way to the castle they came to a small town where he owned a house and where he planned to stay and wait for the Major's return. But he could not yet bring himself to stop there immediately and accompanied his friend a little farther. Both were on horseback and rode on together, engrossed in a serious conversation. Suddenly they saw, at a distance and for the first time, the new house on the hill, its red roof-tiles shining. Eduard was all at once overcome by an irresistible longing; he wished everything to be settled this very evening; he himself would remain hidden in a neighboring village; the Major would impress Charlotte with the urgency of the matter; he would take her by surprise and, by his unexpected proposal, force her to express her feelings without reserve. Eduard had identified his desires so completely with hers that he felt certain he was meeting her determined wishes halfway, and he hoped to receive her immediate consent because he himself could not think of any other solution.

A happy outcome joyfully appeared before his eyes, and, in order that he might know the result quickly, he asked that shots be fired, or—if it had grown dark—that rockets give the signal.

The Major rode over to the castle. He did not find Charlotte there and was told that she was living at present in the new building on the hill but that today she had gone to pay a visit in the neighborhood and would probably not return until late. He walked back to the inn where he had stabled his horse.

Eduard, driven by his uncontrollable impatience, had meanwhile left his hiding place and stolen into his park along lonely paths, known only to hunters and fishermen. He arrived there toward evening in the thicket close to the lake; he saw for the first time its clear mirror spread out in its entire length.

Ottilie had gone to the lake this afternoon for a walk. She carried the child and was reading as usual while she walked. In this way she arrived at the oak trees by the jetty. The little boy had fallen asleep, and she laid him down beside her and went on reading. Her book was one of those which attract and absorb a sensitive mind. She did not think of time and hour and quite forgot that the way back to the new house was a long one by land; she sat, lost in her book and in herself—so lovely to look at that the surrounding trees should have been animated beings endowed with eyes to admire her beauty. Just at this moment slanting rays of the setting sun shone on her, tinging her cheek and shoulder with gold.

Eduard, who had, until now, managed to avoid encountering

anybody, and had found his park deserted, with no living soul in the entire surrounding countryside, ventured on and on. At last he broke through the bushes near the oaks and saw Ottilie and she saw him. He rushed to her and threw himself at her feet. After a long silence, in which they both tried to calm their emotions, he explained in a few words why and how he had come here. He told her that he had sent the Major to Charlotte and that their common destiny was perhaps being decided at this very moment; that he had never doubted her love and was sure that she had never doubted his; and that he asked her consent to their marriage. Ottilie hesitated. He implored her and was on the point of asserting his old rights and taking her in his arms, when she pointed to the child. Eduard looked at it and was startled. "Good Heavens!" he exclaimed, "if I had any reason to doubt my wife and my friend, these features would bear terrible evidence against them. Is he not the very image of the Major? I never saw such a likeness."

"Don't say that!" Ottilie replied. "Everyone says that he is like me."

"Is it possible?" Eduard said; and at this moment the child opened his eyes: two large, dark, searching eyes, deep and friendly. The little boy already looked out into the world quite intelligently, he seemed to know the two who stood before him. Eduard fell on his knees before the child and then knelt again before Ottilie. "Yes, it is you!" he cried. "The eyes are yours! Ah, but let me look only into *your* eyes. Let me throw a veil over the hour which gave this little creature his existence. Shall I shock you with the terrible thought of a husband and wife who, having become strangers, embrace each other, and by their sudden desire are capable of profaning the sacred bond! Yes! Since we have gone so far, since Charlotte and I must be separated, since you will be my wife—why should I not admit it? Why should I not speak out the cruel words: this child is the fruit of double adultery! It divides me from my wife, and my wife from me—this child that should have united us. Let it bear witness against me; let these wonderful eyes tell yours that, in the arms of another woman, I belonged to you. Feel it, feel it deeply, Ottilie, that I can atone for my fault, my crime, in your arms alone!"

"Listen!" he cried, and jumped to his feet, believing that he had heard a shot and that it was the expected signal of the Major. It was only a hunter's gun in the near-by hills. No other sound followed, and Eduard grew impatient.

Ottilie noticed only now that the sun had disappeared behind the mountains. Its last rays were reflected in the windows of the house on the hill. "Leave me, Eduard!" she said. "We have been separated for so long; we have suffered so long! Remember what we both owe to Charlotte. She is the one to decide our fate; do not let us forestall her decision. I shall be your wife if she permits it; if she does not, I must give you up. Since you believe that the decision is so near, let us wait. Go back to the village where the Major believes you to be. So much can happen that must be explained. Is it really likely that anything so rude as a gunshot will tell you the result of this talk? Perhaps he is looking for you this instant. He cannot have seen Charlotte—not that I know. He may have gone to meet her, because she left word where she was to be. There are all sorts of possibilities! Leave me! She must be at home now. She expects me and the child at the lodge."

Ottilie spoke in haste. She was trying to consider everything at once. She was happy to be with Eduard, but she felt that she must now send him away. "I beg you, I implore you, my love!" she cried, "go back and wait for the Major."

"I shall obey you," Eduard cried, with passion and desire, taking her in his arms. She held him, too, and pressed him most affectionately to her heart. Like a star falling out of the sky, hope flashed over their heads. They thought and believed that they belonged to each other. For the first time they kissed, fully aware of what they were doing; and they parted unwillingly and with aching hearts.

The sun had gone down; dusk gathered, and a damp mist was floating from the shores of the lake. Ottilie stood confused and agitated; she looked across to the house on the hill and thought she saw Charlotte's white dress on the terrace. It was a long walk around the lake; and she knew how impatiently Charlotte would be waiting for the child. She saw the plane trees just opposite; only a strip of water separated her from the path which led straight up to the lodge. Her mind, like her eyes, had already crossed to the farther shore. Her hesitation about crossing the lake with the child vanished before her urgency. She ran to the boat; she did not notice the throbbing of her heart, nor the unsteadiness of her feet, nor that her senses threatened to fail her.

She jumped into the boat, took the oar, and pushed off. She had to use all her strength and push again; the boat swayed and then began to glide out into the lake. The child was in her left arm, she held the book in her left hand, the oar in her right; suddenly she lost her balance and fell back into the boat. The oar slipped overboard and when she tried to steady herself, the child and the book slipped into the water. She caught hold of the child's clothes, but her awkward position prevented her from rising to a sitting position. She could not at first turn around and raise herself; but at last she succeeded. She pulled the child out of the water, but its eyes were closed; it had stopped breathing.

In a moment she regained her presence of mind, but her anguish was all the greater. The boat drifted almost to the middle of the lake; the oar floated far away; she could not see anyone on the shore—and what good would it have done if she had seen someone? Cut off from everything, she floated along on the treacherous water.

She tried to find help in herself. She had often heard about the resuscitation of the drowned. On the evening of her birthday she had actually seen such a thing happen. She undressed the child and dried it with her muslin dress. She hastily tore open her bodice and for the first time pressed a living being to her naked breast; but, alas! it was no longer living. The cold limbs of the poor little creature chilled her to the core of her heart. Tears streamed from her eyes; for a moment the stiffened body appeared warm and alive. She persisted in her efforts; she wrapped the child in her shawl and thought she was providing a substitute for the remedies she could not obtain, cut off as she was, as she pressed it close to her, breathed upon it, and covered it with kisses and tears.

It was all in vain. The child lay still in her arms; the boat stood still upon the water. But even in this situation her steadfast spirit did not forsake her. Sinking down on her knees in the boat, she turned to Heaven, and lifted the dead child with both arms above her breast, white as marble, and cold as marble. She turned her face to the sky, asking for help where a tender heart hopes to find it in its fullness, when there is need all about and everything else has failed.

She did not turn to the stars in vain. One by one they began to appear. A gentle breeze rose and moved the boat toward the plane trees.

Chapter Thirty-two

Ottilie ran up to the lodge; she called the physician and handed the child to him. Trained as he was for any eventuality, the doctor applied in the usual sequence one method after another to the frail body. Ottilie assisted him. She prepared and brought him the necessary items and took care of everything, although she moved as if she were in another world, for extreme unhappiness, like extreme happiness, changes everything about us. Only when the physician, after having tried every possible measure, silently shook his head and then, very gently, answered her question as to whether there was any hope, with a "No!" did Ottilie leave Charlotte's bedroom where all this had taken place; she had hardly entered the living room, when, unable to reach the sofa, she fell exhausted face downward on the carpet.

Just then Charlotte's coach drove up. The physician asked those standing about to keep back; he himself wished to meet and prepare her; but she had already entered the room. She found Ottilie lying on the floor; and a housemaid rushed in, shrieking and weeping. The physician, too, came in; and she now heard everything at once. But she could not immediately give up all hope. The physician, experienced, skillful, and always sensible, implored her not to go and see the child now; he himself left her, pretending to continue his efforts; and she sat down on the sofa. Ottilie still lay on the floor; but Charlotte raised her, lifting her to her knees, on which Ottilie's beautiful head sank down. The physician came and went several times; he seemed to be concerned with the child but actually attended the two women. It was soon midnight and the deadly silence deepened. Charlotte no longer had any illusion that her child would return to life; she asked to see it. It had been neatly wrapped in warm woolen blankets and laid in a wicker basket, which they placed at her side on the sofa. Only the little face was uncovered; it was calm and lovely.

The exciting news of the accident had soon spread to the village, and reached the inn. The Major went up to the lodge, along familiar paths. He walked around the house and eventually stopped a servant who was running to fetch something from an outbuilding. From him he heard more particulars, and asked him to call the physician outdoors. He soon came, much surprised at the sudden arrival of his former patron. He informed him of the present situation and agreed to prepare Charlotte for the Major's unexpected visit. Then he went into the house and began a conversation with Charlotte drawing her attention to other matters, leading her from one topic to another, and at last mentioning her friend, of whose deep sympathy she could be certain, since they were so close in spirit and feeling. This enabled him to speak of the Major's actual presence. She heard that her friend was at the door, and that he knew all and wished to be allowed to enter.

He came in. Charlotte greeted him with a sad smile. She lifted the coverlet of green silk which hid her dead child; and in the dim light of a candle he saw—with something of a secret shudder—the stiffened image of himself. Charlotte pointed to a chair; and so they sat opposite each other, in silence, all through the night. Ottilie still lay quietly against Charlotte's knees; she breathed gently and appeared to sleep. Dawn broke; the candle had burned down; and the two friends seemed to awaken from a heavy dream.

Charlotte looked at the Major and said, calmly: "Tell me, my friend, what strange coincidence brought you here, to take part in this tragic scene?"

"This is not the time nor the place," the Major answered in the same low voice with which Charlotte had spoken, as though afraid to waken Ottilie, "for me to be reserved, or to broach my subject gently. The circumstances in which I find you are so grave that even the important matter which brought me here loses its importance beside it."

He then told her, quite calmly and simply, the purpose of his mission, in so far as Eduard was concerned; and the purpose of his coming, in so far as his own free will and his own interests were involved. He laid both propositions very tactfully but honestly before her. Charlotte listened quietly and seemed to be neither surprised nor offended.

When the Major had finished, she answered in such a low voice that he was forced to draw his chair nearer to her. "I have never before found myself in such a situation; but in a similar crisis I have always said to myself, 'How will it be tomorrow?' I realize very clearly that now the fate of several persons is in my hands. I do not doubt what *I* must do; that can be said very quickly. I agree to a divorce. I should have made this decision earlier; by my reluctance, my resistance, I have killed my child. There are certain things on which Destiny stubbornly insists. Reason and virtue, duty and all that is sacred to us oppose them in vain. Destiny wishes something to happen which to it seems right, but does not seem right to us; and in the end Destiny will be the victor, fight against it as we may.

"But what am I saying? Destiny actually seems to take up and carry out my own wish, my own intention, against which I acted so imprudently. Did I not in the past wish to bring together Ottilie and Eduard who are so well matched? Did I not myself arrange their meeting? Have you not, dear friend, been an accomplice in this scheme? And why was I unable to distinguish between a man's stubbornness and true love? Why did I accept his hand when—as a friend—I could have made him, and another wife, happy? And now look at this unfortunate sleeping girl. I tremble for the moment when she will wake to consciousness from her deathlike sleep. How can she live, how can she comfort herself, if she cannot hope through her love to give back to Eduard what she—a tool of the strangest whim of chance—deprived him of? And she will be able to give everything back to him with her deep affection, the passion of her love. If love can suffer all, love can do still more—it can restore all. There should be no consideration of me at this moment.

"Leave me here very quietly, my dear Major. Tell Eduard that I agree to the divorce; that I leave it to him, to you, and to Mittler to start the legal proceedings; that I am not worried about my own future situation and that I have no reason to be. I am willing to sign any papers I receive; the only thing one should not demand of me is to be consulted, to think about the matter, or to give advice."

The Major rose. Charlotte gave him her hand above Ottilie's head. He pressed his lips upon this beloved hand and whispered, "And I— what may I hope for myself?"

"Forgive me if I do not give you an answer," Charlotte replied. "We have done nothing to bring about our unhappiness; but neither have we deserved to be happy together."

The Major left, feeling in his heart a great pity for Charlotte, but without really feeling pity for the poor dead child. Such a sacrifice seemed to him necessary for the happiness of them all. He pictured Ottilie with a child of her own in her arms, the most perfect compensation for the child of which she had deprived Eduard. He dreamed of having his own son on his knee, who would resemble him, and be more entitled to resemble him than the child who had died.

These hopes and fantasies passed through his mind while he went back to the inn. There he found Eduard, who had waited the whole night out of doors in vain for some signal to announce to him a successful outcome. He had already heard of the accident; but he, too, instead of feeling sorry for the poor little creature, looked at the incident, without, perhaps, quite admitting it to himself, as a providential act which had at one stroke removed all obstacles to his happiness. The Major quickly informed him of his wife's decision and could, therefore, easily persuade him to return to the village and from there to the small town where they would confer about the next steps to be taken.

After the Major had left her, Charlotte remained, deep in her own thoughts, but only for a few moments, for Ottilie suddenly lifted her head and looked at her friend with wide open eyes. She raised her head from Charlotte's lap, rose from the floor; and stood upright before her.

"For the second time," the brave girl began, with her irresistible, graceful seriousness, "for the second time this same thing has happened to me. You once told me that people often experience in their lives the same thing in the same way, and always at important moments. I see now that what you said is true; and I must make a confession to you. A short time after my mother's death, when I was a small child, I pushed my footstool close to you; you were sitting on a sofa as you are now; my head rested on your knees; I was not asleep, I was not awake. I heard everything going on around me, particularly every word which was said; but still I was unable to move, to speak, to give a sign that I was conscious—even if I had wished to. You talked with a friend about me; you felt sorry that I had been left alone in the world, an orphan; you described my dependent position and you said how uncertain the future before me was, unless an especially lucky star ruled my fate. I understood well, perhaps too well, everything you seemed to hope for me and to expect from me. I set myself rules, according to my limited insight, and kept them for a long time, and in compliance with them arranged all my actions, during the whole time you loved me, took care of me, and received me into your house; and for some time afterward as well.

"But I have strayed from my course; I have broken my vows; I have even lost my feeling for them; and now, after a terrible disaster, you have again made clear to me my present situation, which is more miserable than the first. While resting on your lap in a half-stupor, I heard your gentle voice as from another world; and I learned from you how it is with me. I shudder at myself; but again, as I did before, I have marked out for myself, in my sleep, a new course.

"I am as determined as I was before; and what I have decided you must hear at once. I shall never be Eduard's wife! In a terrible fashion God has opened my eyes to the sin into which I have fallen. I will atone for it; and no one should think of keeping me from my intention. With this in mind, my dear, my best friend, you should make your own arrangements. Call the Major back; write him that no steps should be taken. How uneasy I felt when I was neither able to move nor to give a sign when he left! I tried to rise, to cry out: 'Do not let him go with such wicked hopes!' "

Charlotte understood Ottilie's condition; she felt deeply for her; but she hoped that time and her own encouraging words would prevail upon her. But when she said a few words which indicated a better future, a relief from her suffering, and some hope, Ottilie cried, "No!" vehemently. "Do not try to persuade me or to deceive me! The instant I hear of your agreement to a divorce, I shall atone for my sin and my crime in the same lake!"

Chapter Thirty-three

Relatives, friends, and members of the same household who live happily and peacefully together usually talk more than is necessary or desirable about what they are doing and what they should do; they repeatedly inform one another of their plans, undertakings, and occupations, and, without taking one another's advice directly, discuss the whole course of their lives, as it were, in perpetual conclave. Yet, in serious predicaments (just when it would seem that people particularly need the assistance and reassurance of others) everyone withdraws into himself and acts for himself; everyone hides from others his own particular ways and means; so that it is only the outcome, the realized aims, which again become common property.

After so many strange and unfortunate incidents, a serious calm had settled on the two women, which showed itself in tender mutual consideration. The child had been very quietly laid to rest in the chapel—the first victim of an ominous fate.

Charlotte returned to her everyday life so far as she was able; and here she found that it was Ottilie who first needed her help. She occupied herself chiefly with her but in such a way that Ottilie would not notice. She knew how deeply the girl loved Eduard.

Gradually she pieced out for herself the scene preceding the accident and gathered every detail, partly from Ottilie herself, and partly from the Major's letters.

Ottilie, on her side, made life much easier for Charlotte. She was open and more inclined to talk, but she never touched on the present or on the recent past in her conversation. She had always listened attentively and observed carefully; she knew a good deal; and all this now came to the surface. She entertained and distracted Charlotte, who still hoped in her heart to see her married to Eduard, since both were so dear to her.

But Ottilie's train of thought was quite different. She had disclosed the secret of her life's course to her friend and now felt herself quite free from her former reserve and submissiveness. Her remorse and her resolution had also released her from the burden of her wrongdoing and her misfortune. She no longer needed to put any restraint on herself. Deep in her heart, she had forgiven herself, but only on the condition of a complete renunciation which would be binding forever.

In this way, some time passed, and Charlotte realized to what an extent the house, the park, the lake, and rocks and trees daily kept alive only melancholy associations for them. It was evident that a change of place was necessary; but it was not easy to decide in what manner this could be accomplished. Should the two women stay together? Eduard's previously expressed wish seemed to demand this: his declaration and his threat seemed to make it necessary; but it could not be denied that both women, with the best intention, with all their reasonableness and in spite of all their efforts, found themselves, in this life of close intimacy, in a painful situation. Their conversation tended to be evasive. There were times when one preferred not fully to understand the other; and very often a word was misinterpreted, if not by the head, at least by the heart. They were afraid of hurting each other, and this very fear was particularly painful and hurt the quickest.

If a change of place was decided upon, and, at the same time a separation (at least for a while)—the old question again arose: Where should Ottilie go? There was still that family of rank and fortune which had made unsuccessful attempts to find a congenial and stimulating companion for their only daughter. The Baroness, during her last visit at the castle and lately in her letters, had urged

Charlotte to send Ottilie there; and now Charlotte mentioned this subject once more. But Ottilie refused to go where she would meet what is commonly called 'the great world.'

"Dear aunt," she said, "let me tell you quite frankly something that it would be my duty, under other circumstances, to conceal. I do not want you to think of me as narrowminded or stubborn. A person who has had an unusual misfortune, however innocent he may have been, is marked with a terrible stigma. His presence arouses in everyone who sees him and knows about him, something like horror. Everyone imagines seeing him carry his terrible destiny like a burden; everyone is curious and at the same time terrified. It is the same with a house, or a town, where something monstrous has occurred; people are forever frightened when they enter them. There the light of day seems to shine less brightly and the stars seem to have lost their brilliance. How extreme and yet perhaps excusable is the indiscreet behavior of others toward such unfortunate beings— their familiarity and clumsy kindness! Forgive me for speaking like this, but I have suffered indescribably for that poor girl, dragged from the refuge of her room by Luciane, who tried to force her to take part in games and dancing—all with the best intentions. When the child, more and more frightened, finally escaped and fainted, and when I caught her in my arms while the guests, shocked and excited, crowded around the poor unfortunate creature with exaggerated curiosity, I did not think that the same fate would await me. But my feeling for her is still as deep and as fresh as it was then. Now I can turn this compassion toward myself,and I can be careful not to give occasion for similar scenes."

"But, my dear child, you will never be able to avoid being seen by other people," Charlotte answered. "We no longer have convents which once offered sanctuary for such feelings."

"Solitude does not constitute a sanctuary, dearest aunt," Ottilie replied. "The best sanctuary is one in which we can be active. Penances and self-denials will not save us at all from an ominous Destiny that is determined to persecute us. The world repels and frightens me only when I have nothing to do and when I am exposed to the stare of others. But when I can work with all my heart and do my duty unflaggingly, I shall be able to bear the eyes of anyone, because I need not shrink before the eye of God."

"If I am not much mistaken, you should like best to return to school," said Charlotte.

"Yes, I do not deny it," Ottilie answered. "I think it is a happy vocation to educate others in the normal, customary way, after one has, like myself, been educated in the most unusual manner. And do we not know from history that the men who withdrew into the desert because of great moral disasters were not entirely hidden and protected there, as they had hoped to be? They were called back into the world to lead the lost back to the right path. Who could have been better fitted for this task than those who were already initiated into the maze of life? They were called to give help to the unfortunate; and who could better perform this task than those who no longer had to fear any earthly harm?"

"You have chosen an unusual vocation," Charlotte said. "I shall not oppose you; you may do as you wish, although I hope it will be for a short time only."

"How grateful I am, that you will not grudge me this experiment and this experience," Ottilie said. "Unless I flatter myself too much, it should turn out well. I shall remember at the school the many tests I was put to, and how small and unimportant they were, compared to those I was put to later. I shall be so happy watching the difficulties of young growing natures; I shall smile at their childish griefs and, with a light hand, lead them out of their small errors. The fortunate person is not the right person to guide the unfortunate; it is human nature to demand always more of oneself and of others, the more one has received. Only those who are recovering from misfortune know how to foster, in themselves and in others, the feeling that even any moderate good should be enjoyed with delight."

Charlotte thought for a moment and then said, "I have only one objection to make to your plan, and it seems to me a very important one. I am thinking not of you but of another person. You know the feelings of the good and honest Tutor. On the road you have chosen, you will daily become dearer and more indispensable to him. As in his heart he already believes that he cannot live without you, he will be unable in future—after having become accustomed to your working with him—to carry on his work without your aid. You are going to give him your help in the beginning and in the end spoil everything for him."

"Fate has not treated me gently," Ottilie replied, "and whoever loves me, has probably nothing very much better to expect. Our friend is so good and sensible that I hope he will develop a feeling of friendship for me. He will see in me a dedicated person, who can perhaps atone for an enormous misfortune, to herself and to others, only by devoting herself to the Holy which is invisibly around us and is the one protection against the formidable powers which weigh upon us."

Charlotte listened to everything Ottilie said, and considered it quietly. Several times she had very tactfully sounded out Ottilie to discover if some move of hers toward Eduard might be conceivable; but the slightest mention of this, the faintest expression of hope, seemed to wound the young girl deeply; once, when she could not evade the subject, she expressed herself very clearly.

"If your resolution to renounce Eduard is so firm and unalterable," Charlotte retorted on this occasion, "you must be careful of the danger of seeing him again When we are far from the person we love, and the deeper our affection is, the more we apparently succeed in controlling ourselves, because the whole force of our passion, formerly directed outward, is now turned inward; but how soon and how quickly do we discover our self-deception when the person we thought we could renounce stands suddenly before us and seems more indispensable to us than ever. You must now do what you think is most suitable in your case. Examine your heart; you many even change your present resolution; but do it of yourself, with a free, determined heart. Do not let yourself be drawn back into the former state of things, either by chance or by surprise, because this would destroy your inner harmony and be unbearable for you. As I have said: before you take this step, before you leave me and start a new life which may lead you no one knows where, think once more—can you really give Eduard up for good and all? But, if you are determined, let us make a pact. Promise me that you will never have anything to do with him—that you will not even speak to him if he should come to see you or force himself into your presence."

Ottilie did not hesitate for a moment. She gave Charlotte her word, which she had already given herself.

But Charlotte's mind was still haunted by Eduard's threat that he would leave Ottilie alone only so long as she did not leave Charlotte. Since that time circumstances had, of course, changed so much,and so much had happened that his threat, wrung from him in momentary anguish, might be no longer considered valid, in the light of the succeeding events. Still, she did not want to risk anything or to undertake anything which, even in the remotest sense, might hurt him. She wished, therefore, that Mittler would search out Eduard's feelings and desires.

Since the death of the child, Mittler had visited Charlotte several times, although never for more than a few minutes. The accident, which, in his opinion, had made a reconciliation between her and her husband highly improbable, had made a strong impression on him; but, in his usual hopeful way, he was secretly very happy about Ottilie's resolution. He had great faith in the soothing effect of the passage of time and was still convinced that he would be able to prevent husband and wife from separating, for he took such passionate upsets merely as tests of married love and faithfulness.

Charlotte had, at the very beginning, informed the Major, by letter, of Ottilie's first declaration and had urgently asked him to persuade Eduard not to take any further steps. They should keep quiet and wait until the dear girl had recovered from her shock. She had let him know what she thought necessary about later events and decisions, but now Mittler had the difficult task of preparing Eduard for a complete change in the state of things. Mittler, however, knowing well that people will rather resign themselves to an accomplished fact than agree to something which is about to happen, persuaded Charlotte that it would be best to send Ottilie to the school at once.

Preparations for the trip, therefore, were begun as soon as he had left. Ottilie packed her things; but Charlotte noticed that she took neither the pretty dressing case nor any of its contents with her. She did not remark on this and let the silent girl do as she liked. The day of departure came; Charlotte's coach would take Ottilie, on the first day, as far as a town well known to them, where Ottilie would spend the night; the next day she would drive on to the school. Nanni would accompany her and stay with her as her maid. The temperamental little girl had found her way back to Ottilie immediately after the child's death and was now as devoted to her as before; she even seemed to wish to make good her past neglect with amusing chatter and by devoting herself exclusively to her beloved mistress. She was now quite beside herself at the prospect of traveling with her and of seeing strange places, for she had never been away from her birthplace. She kept running from the castle to the village, to her parents and relatives, to tell them about her good fortune and to take leave of everyone. Unfortunately, she happened to go into a house where a family was afflicted with measles, and at once caught the infection. The journey could not be postponed. Ottilie insisted on leaving; she had once before traveled over the same road; she knew the people at the inn, where she would stop overnight; the coachman of the castle would drive her; there was nothing to worry about.

Charlotte made no objection. She, too, hurried away, in her thoughts, from these surroundings; the one thing she wished to do before leaving was to arrange the rooms, in which Ottilie had lived in the castle, for Eduard, in just the same way that they had been arranged before the Captain's arrival. The hope of bringing back old happy times flares up constantly in us; and Charlotte had again a right, indeed a need, to hope.

Chapter Thirty-four

When Mittler arrived to talk matters over with Eduard, he found him sitting alone in his room, his head leaning on his right hand, his arm propped on the table. He seemed to be suffering extremely. "Do your headaches bother you again?" Mittler asked.

"They do," Eduard answered, "and yet I cannot hate them, because they remind me of Ottilie. I am imagining that, leaning on her left arm, she perhaps also suffers, at this same moment, and perhaps more than I do; why should I not bear it as bravely as she does? These pains are good for me; I might almost say they are a godsend, because they bring her before me more vividly and clearly—her patience, along with her other virtues. Only when we suffer do we realize fully all the great qualities that are needed in order to bear suffering."

When Mittler found his friend so resigned, he no longer concealed his mission but told the story chronologically, bit by bit, in the same way that the idea had sprung up between the two women and had matured gradually into a definite plan. Eduard scarcely made any objection. From the little he said, it seemed as though he was willing to leave everything to them to decide. His momentary pain had apparently made him indifferent to everything.

But as soon as he was alone again, he got up and began to pace up and down the room. He no longer felt his pain; his whole attention turned toward outer events. During Mittler's speech the imagination of the lover had already taken new flights. He saw Ottilie, he saw her alone, or as good as alone, traveling a road well known to him; at an inn where he was familiar with every room. He thought; he deliberated; or, rather, he did neither think nor deliberate—he only wished; he willed. He had to see her, to speak to her. Why? To what purpose? And what would come of it? These were meaningless questions to him. He did not resist; he acted.

He took his valet into his confidence, and the man actually found out the day and the hour of Ottilie's departure. The morning dawned. Eduard lost no time and rode on horseback, and unaccompanied, to the place where Ottilie would spend the night. He arrived there much too early. The landlady of the inn was surprised and delighted to see him; she owed him gratitude. He had obtained a military decoration for her son, who had distinguished himself as a soldier. Eduard, the only witness of his particular action, had brought it to the attention of the commanding general and had also defeated the opposition of some envious people. For this reason the landlady could not do enough for Eduard. As quickly as possible, she cleared the best room, which was, however, also her wardrobe and storeroom; but he told her that a young lady would arrive and take that room, and asked her to provide a small bedroom at the end of the passage for him, furnished only with the most necessary things. The landlady thought all this very mysterious; but she was only too glad to do her benefactor a favor; and Eduard showed himself very interested and helpful with all the arrangements. With what emotions he spent the long, long hours until evening! He looked around the room in which he would see Ottilie; it seemed to him a heavenly abode in spite of its strange domestic atmosphere. Many thoughts crossed his mind. Should he surprise her, or should he prepare her? At last, the latter view got the better of him; he sat down and wrote a letter which she would read as a welcome.

Eduard to Ottilie

"While you are reading this letter, my love, I am close to you. Do not be afraid; do not be shocked—you have nothing to fear from me. I shall not force myself on you. You will not see me before you give your permission.

"Think first of your situation, and of mine! I must thank you for not planning to take any decisive step; but the one you have taken is important enough. Do not take it! Here, at this crossroad, as it were, think carefully once more! Can you be mine? Will you be mine? Oh, it would be a blessing for us all, and for me an infinite joy!

"Let me see you again in happiness; let me ask you the sweet question with my own lips; and give me your answer yourself. Come to my heart, Ottilie, where you have sometimes rested and where you belong forever!"

While he was writing, he was suddenly overcome by the feeling that what he most longed for was quite close and would be here in almost no time. She will enter through this door; she will read this letter; she will actually stand before me—she, for whose appearance I have longed so many times. Will she be the same? Will there be a change in her face, in her heart? He still held the pen in his hand and was about to write down what he was thinking when the coach rolled into the yard. With flying pen, he added: "I hear you coming. For one moment only—Farewell!"

He folded the letter and addressed it; there was no time to seal it. Then he rushed into his room, from which he could later step into the passage; but the next moment he remembered that he had left his watch with his seal on the table.

She must not see these belongings first. He ran back and managed to carry them off. He already heard the voice of the landlady in the hall, coming to show the room to her new guest. He darted toward the door of his room, but it had slammed shut. The key had fallen out when he ran back for his watch and was lying inside; the lock had snapped, and he was locked out. With all his strength he pushed against the door, but it did not yield. Oh, how he wished that he could slip like a ghost through the cracks! In vain! He hid his face against the doorjamb. Ottilie came up and the landlady, seeing him, stepped back. To Ottilie he could not remain hidden for a moment. He turned round, and once more the two lovers faced each other in the strangest of circumstances. She looked at him calmly and seriously, without taking a step forward or back; but when he made a motion toward her, she withdrew a little toward the table. He, too, stepped back. "Ottilie!" he cried "let me break this awful silence! It is pure accident that you find me here now. There is a letter on the table which was written to prepare you! Read it, I implore you! Read it! And then decide what you must decide!"

She looked down at the letter and, after having thought for a second, took it up, opened it, and read it. Her face did not betray the slightest change while she read; gently she laid the letter down. Then she raised her hands, palms pressed together, and brought them back to her breast, at the same time bending forward a little and looking into Eduard's anxious eyes with a look of such pleading that he was compelled to give up all he had asked and desired.

Her gesture almost broke his heart. Her look was too much for him. He was afraid that she would fall on her knees if he insisted. In desperation, he fled from the room and sent the landlady in to her.

He paced up and down the hall. Night had fallen, and not a sound came from the room. At last the mistress of the inn came out, locked the door, and took out the key. The good woman was moved and embarrassed; she did not know what to do. Finally before turning to go, she offered the key to Eduard, who refused it. She put down the lighted candle and went away.

Eduard, completely crushed by his grief, flung himself on the threshold of Ottilie's room, weeping. Rarely have lovers spent a more miserable night so close to each other.

Dawn broke; the coachman was impatient to drive on; the landlady unlocked the door to Ottilie's room and entered. Ottilie was still asleep, fully dressed; the woman went back and gave Eduard a sign to come in, smiling sympathetically. Both stood before the sleeping girl, but Eduard could not bear this sight. The landlady did not dare to waken the sleeper and sat down opposite her. At last Ottilie opened her beautiful eyes and rose to her feet. She refused to take breakfast. Now Eduard came in again, begging her over and over to speak but one word and tell him what had decided; he swore that he would do anything she wished! But she remained silent. Once more he asked her, full of affection and passion, if she would marry him. Eyes downcast, she shook her lovely head in a gentle "No." He asked her if she still wished to go to the school. Again she shook her head, with indifference. But when he asked if she would allow him to bring her back to Charlotte, she nodded a confident "Yes." He hurried to the window to give orders to the coachman; but, with a lightning movement, she darted behind his back out of the room, ran downstairs and into the coach. The coachman drove toward the castle, and Eduard, on horseback, followed at some distance.

Chapter Thirty-five

Charlotte was completely taken aback when she saw the coach drive up with Ottilie, and Eduard following—riding at full speed into the courtyard! She hurried down and stood in the door while Ottilie stepped out of the coach and came up to her with Eduard. Ottilie took the hands of husband and wife and pressed them together; then she fled to her room. Eduard embraced Charlotte and burst into tears. He was unable to give her any explanation but asked her to have patience with him and to look after Ottilie and help her. Charlotte quickly went to Ottilie's room. She shuddered when she entered; it had been completely cleared and looked as enormous as it was depressing. Everything had been removed, with the exception of the little dressing case, which stood in the middle of the room, as no one had known what to do with it. Ottilie lay on the floor, her arm and her head resting on the case. Charlotte tried to raise her and asked what had happened; but she received no answer.

She left Ottilie with her own maid, who had come with restoratives, and hurried back to Eduard. She found him in the salon, but could get no information from him either. He threw himself at her feet; she felt his tears upon her hands; then he fled to his room. She was about to follow when she met the valet, who told her as much as he knew. She pieced the rest together herself, and at once energetically set about doing what the moment required. Ottilie's room was rearranged in no time. Eduard had found his rooms—to the last piece of paper—in exactly the same condition in which he had left them.

The three were now together again and in some sort of mutual relationship; but Ottilie continued to be silent and Eduard could do nothing but implore his wife to have the patience which he himself seemed to be lacking. Charlotte sent messages to Mittler and to the Major. The first could not be found; the latter came at once. To him Eduard poured out his heart, making a clean breast of every smallest circumstance of the events in question; and in this way Charlotte learned what had actually happened—what had so unexpectedly changed the situation, and what had caused this general excitement.

She spoke to Eduard with affectionate understanding, asking him to leave the girl alone for the present. Eduard recognized his wife's great strength of character, her love and her wisdom; but he was still dominated by his passion. Charlotte tried to cheer him and promised that she would agree to a divorce. He had no confidence; he was so disturbed that hope and faith alternately forsook him. Gripped by a kind of insane dejection, he urged Charlotte to promise him that she would marry the Major. In order to calm and sustain him, Charlotte did what he demanded. She pledged herself to marry the Major whenever Ottilie would agree to marry Eduard—under the explicit condition, however, that, for the present, the two men would go together on a journey. It was necessary that the Major go abroad for business matters, commissioned by the Court, and Eduard promised to accompany. him. Preparations were made and a temporary atmosphere of quiet settled on everyone, since something, at least, was being done.

All this time it was evident that Ottilie took hardly any food or drink and persisted in her silence. They tried to coax her, but this distressed her, and they gave it up; for are we not in general, so weak that we do not like to worry people, even if it is for their own good? Charlotte thought of all sorts of tactics, but finally she struck upon the idea of sending for the Tutor, who had great influence with Ottilie. He had written very kindly, when she had not arrived as expected; but he had not yet received a reply.

Not wishing to surprise Ottilie, they discussed this plan in her presence. Apparently she did not agree; she seemed to deliberate. At last she had apparently come to a decision. She hurried to her room and, before evening, sent the following letter to her friends.

Ottilie to her friends.

"Why should I express in so many words what you all know, my dearest friends? I have strayed from my course, and I shall not find it again. A hostile demon, who has gained power over me, seems to hinder me from without, even if I should have regained my inner peace. My intention to renounce Eduard, to leave him forever, was entirely pure. I had hoped not to meet him again. It turned out otherwise. He stood before me—even against his own will. I have perhaps taken and interpreted too literally my promise not to enter into any conversation with him. Following my conscience and my feeling at the moment, I was silent and did not speak to my friend; and now I have no words left. Quite by chance, and on a sudden impulse, I have taken upon myself a strict binding vow, which might perhaps be painful and embarrassing if taken after deliberation. Let me be faithful to it as long as my heart commands. Do not call upon anyone to mediate! Do not urge me to speak or to eat and drink more than I absolutely need! Help me through this time with your tolerance and your patience! I am young, and youth sometimes unexpectedly restores itself. Tolerate me in your presence; make me happy by your love; instruct me by your conversation, but leave my soul to me!"

The long-prepared departure of the two men was put off, since there was some delay about the Major's business abroad, and how welcome this was to Eduard! Filled with new hope by Ottilie's letter, reanimated by her comforting and promising words which justified his perseverance, he suddenly declared that he would not go at all! "How foolish it is," he cried, "to cast away rashly something indispensable which, though there may be some danger of losing it, might possibly be preserved. and what is the reason for this? Only to pretend that man is able to will and to chose. How often have I, possessed by such foolish deceit, torn myself away from my friends, hours or days earlier than necessary, because I wished under no circumstances to be forced to leave by the inevitable appointed date. But this time I shall stay! Why should I go away? Is she not already gone from me? I would not think of taking her hand or of pressing her to my heart; I cannot even think of doing this without a shudder. She has not moved *away* from me; she has raised herself *above* me."

And so he stayed on as he wished, and as he was compelled to do. But nothing could be compared to his delight in being with her. She, too, still felt the same; she, too, could not resist this blissful necessity. Now as ever they were attracted to one another by an indescribable, almost magic, power. They lived under one roof; but even when they did not so much as think of each other, when they were occupied by other things, or were with other people, they drew closer. When they found themselves in the same room, it was not long before they stood or sat side by side. Only when they were as close as possible did they find rest, and complete rest! Their being near to each other was enough; no look, no word, no gesture, no touch was necessary—just being together. Then they were not two beings; they were one person, in an unconscious and perfect happiness, at peace with themselves and with the world. Yes, if one had been detained by force at the farthest end of the house, the other would gradually have moved, nearer and nearer, instinctively and without premeditation. Life was for them a riddle whose solution they could find only together.

Ottilie was completely calm and poised and no longer gave her friends any reason for anxiety. She rarely left the others and only insisted on having her meals alone, with no one but Nanni to wait upon her.

Much that ordinarily happens to a person repeats itself more often than we think, because a person's nature is the immediate determinant of this. Character, individuality, inclination, disposition, environment and habits form together a whole, in which every human being floats, as it were, in an element, an atmosphere, in which alone he feels comfortable and at ease. It is for this reason that, to our surprise, we find human beings, about whose changeability we hear so many complaints, unchanged after many years, and unchangeable after innumerable experiences from within and without.

So in the daily life of our friends everything moved again in the old groove. Ottilie showed her obliging disposition as always in many little services, and everyone else acted in his or her way. Accordingly, the domestic circle appeared like a deceptive illustration of their former life, and it was perhaps excusable that they had the delusion that everything was as it had been.

In those autumn days, as long as the days of spring had been, they returned to the house from outdoors at about the same hour. The beauty of the fruits and flowers, peculiar to this season, made them believe that this was the autumn following that first spring; they had forgotten the intervening time. Now the flowers which had been planted in those earlier days were in bloom, and the blossoms they had seen then were now ripe fruit hanging on the trees.

The Major came and went; Mittler, too, called more often. They generally spent their evenings in the same way as before. Eduard usually read aloud; he read with more animation and more feeling; he read better, even more gaily—as one might say—than ever before. It was as though he wished to dispel Ottilie's apathy and unlock her silence through both cheerfulness and emotion. He took his seat as he used to do, so that she could look into his book; he was even restless and distracted when he was not certain that she followed his words with her eyes.

All the disagreeable and embarrassed feelings of the intervening period were blotted out. No one bore any grudges, and all bitterness had disappeared. The Major, with his violin, accompanied Charlotte, at the piano, and Eduard with his flute, again joined Ottilie's sympathetic rendering of the piano part. Slowly Eduard's birthday drew near—the birthday they had not been able to celebrate together the year before. This time it would be celebrated in their quiet friendly circle without any public festivity. They had all, half-tacitly, half-explicitly, arrived at this agreement. But the nearer this particular day approached, the more the solemn side of Ottilie's character, which until now they had rather sensed than actually noticed, increased. In the garden she often seemed to examine all the flowers; by means of gestures she pointed out to the gardener that he should spare the many varieties of summer plants and flowers; and she stood for a long while in front of the asters, which were blooming this year in great profusion.

Chapter Thirty-six

The most important thing the friends observed, however, was that Ottilie had, for the first time, unpacked the dressing case and had selected and cut out several pieces of material, enough to make a complete dress for herself. When, with Nanni's assistance, she tried to put the rest of the material back into the case, she was barely able to get in it; the space was crammed full, even after part of the material had been taken out. The younger girl could not take her eyes off all the pretty things, particularly since even the smallest accessories had not been forgotten, such as shoes, stockings, garters with embroidered devices, gloves and various other trifles. She begged Ottilie to give her one or two of these. Ottilie refused, but immediately opened a drawer of her chest and allowed the child to choose whatever she liked. Nanni hastily and clumsily grabbed something and at once ran off in raptures with her prize to show it to the others in the castle.

Ottilie succeeded at last in folding everything so carefully that it went back into the case; then she opened a secret compartment, set into the lid, where she kept little notes and letters from Eduard, together with pressed flowers, mementos of their walks together, a lock of his hair, and other keepsakes. Now she added one more—the miniature of her father—and then locked the case and hung the tiny key on a little gold chain round her neck, against her heart.

Meanwhile her friends had been stirred by hopes. Charlotte was convinced that Ottilie would begin to speak again on Eduard's birthday, because she had recently shown a secret activity, a kind of happy inner contentment; and sometimes a smile like that of a person who conceals something pleasant and enjoyable from those she loves, appeared on her face. No one knew that she spent many an hour in great exhaustion, controlling herself only by the power of her will in the moments when she was with her friends.

Mittler had been a frequent visitor of late, and had stayed for longer periods than usual. The strong-willed man knew only too well that there is but one single moment when the iron can be struck. He interpreted Ottilie's silence, as well as her refusal to break it, in his favor. Until now not one step had been taken in the matter of the divorce; he hoped to settle the future of the good dear girl somehow to her advantage; therefore he listened, he yielded, he made suggestions, and behaved as diplomatically as could be expected from him.

But he always allowed himself to get out of hand as soon as he found an opportunity to argue about subjects to which he attached great importance. He lived much in himself, and whenever he was with others, his only relation to them usually consisted in doing something for them. When he was, therefore, among friends, and his tongue loosened, as we have already often seen, his speech rolled on and on without any consideration for them—wounding or healing, useful or harmful, according to the circumstances.

On the night before Eduard's birthday, Charlotte and the Major sat together waiting for Eduard who had gone riding. Mittler was pacing up and down the room. Ottilie had stayed in her own room; she had laid out her dress and everything she was going to wear on the following day and had given her maid several directions by means of signs—directions which Nanni understood perfectly, obeying her wordless orders very skilfully.

Mittler had just come upon one of his favorite topics. He liked to maintain that—in the education of children and in the government of people as well—nothing was more stupid and barbaric than prohibitive laws and decrees. "Man is active by nature," he said, "and if you know how to give orders, he will immediately do what you tell him, and do it in the way you wish him to do it. So far as I am concerned, I should prefer to tolerate around me faults and failings, as long as I cannot impose the opposite virtues, rather than get rid of the faults without knowing anything worthwhile to put in their place. A man really likes to do the right thing for a good purpose, if only he gets a chance; he does it in order to do something, and thinks about it afterward no more than he would think about the foolish pranks he plays out of idleness and boredom.

"How often it annoys me to have to listen when the Ten Commandments are repeated over and over again in Sunday school! The Fifth is, at least, a fairly tolerable and reasonable rule: Thou shalt honor thy father and thy mother. If children take this to heart, they can practice it all day long. But look at the Sixth—what can be said for it? Thou shalt not kill. As though anyone would have the slightest desire to kill another! Men sometimes hate; they quarrel; they lose their temper, and for these and a few other reasons it may happen that one person occasionally kills another. But is it not a barbaric method to forbid children to kill or murder? If one would say: Be careful of another person's life; remove anything that could harm him; rescue him at the risk of your own life; if you hurt him, remember that you hurt yourself—these are the Commandments which should be taught in educated and rational nations; but in our Catechism they are only casually dragged in toward the end. 'What is meant by . . .'?

"But now we come to the Seventh, which is utterly disgusting! What? Should we rouse the curiosity of precocious children and induce them to pry into dangerous mysteries and excite their imagination with strange images and conceptions which tell them clearly and exactly what we wish to keep from them? It would be much better if that sort of thing were arbitrarily punished by some secret tribunal instead of being rattled off in church in front of the congregation."

At this moment Ottilie entered the room. "Thou shalt not commit adultery," Mittler went on. "How rude, how indecent! Would it not sound quite different if it read: You shall highly respect the bond of marriage; wherever you see a husband and a wife who love each other, you shall rejoice and be as glad of their happiness as you would be of a bright sunny day; if clouds should appear in their relationship, you shall try to dispel them; you shall try to calm these two, to appease them, to point out to them their good qualities, and unselfishly promote their happiness, by making them feel that any obligation, and most particularly this obligation which joins husband and wife indissolubly, is the source of the greatest happiness."

Charlotte was terribly embarrassed, particularly because she was convinced that Mittler was completely unaware of what he had said, and where he was saying it; but, before she was able to interrupt him, she saw Ottilie leave the room, with a face that had lost all its color.

"I hope you spare us the Eighth Commandment," Charlotte said with a forced smile.

"All the rest," Mittler answered, "if I can only save the one on which all the others are founded."

At this point, Nanni, with a scream of terror, rushed into the room. "She is dying! My mistress is dying! Come! Come!"

When Ottilie had reached her room with the utmost effort, the festive dress which she was to wear the next day was spread out over several chairs with all its accessories; and Nanni, who was walking up and down, passing everything admiringly in review, cried happily; "Look, dearest mistress! Look! It is a wedding gown, worthy of you!"

Ottilie, hearing these words, sank upon the sofa. Nanni saw her grow pale and faint; she ran to call Charlotte, who came at once. The doctor hurried to help; he thought it was merely exhaustion. He ordered some strong broth, but Ottilie refused it with an expression of disgust and almost went into convulsions when they raised the cup to her lips. The physician, made suddenly suspicious by the symptoms, asked what Ottilie had eaten today. The maid hesitated; he repeated his question; the girl then confessed that Ottilie had eaten nothing.

Nanni seemed to the doctor to be more nervous than was justifiable. He took her into the next room, and Charlotte followed; the girl threw herself on her knees and confessed that Ottilie had eaten almost nothing for a long time. At her urgent request Nanni herself had eaten the meals brought to her mistress and had said nothing about this, because of Ottilie's imploring, even threatening gestures; and also, she naïvely added, because everything had tasted so good.

The Major and Mittler now joined them and found Charlotte energetically helping the physician. The pale girl, beautiful as an angel, sat, apparently conscious, in one corner of the sofa. They begged her to lie down; she refused but made a sign that her dressing case should be brought to her. Then she put her feet upon it, and settled herself in a half-reclining comfortable position. She evidently wished to say good-bye; and her gestures showed her affection for the friends who surrounded her—her love, her gratitude, her apologies, and a warm farewell.

Eduard, as he dismounted, heard what had happened; he rushed into Ottilie's room threw himself down by her side, grasped her hand, and wept. Here he remained for a long time. At last he exclaimed, " Shall I never hear your voice again? Will you not return to life for me with a single word? Very well! I shall follow you, where we shall speak with other tongues!"

She pressed his hand; she gave him a long look full of life and full of love. Then, after drawing a deep breath, and moving her lovely lips soundlessly for a moment, she cried out, with a slight effort, "Promise me to live!" and then at once sank back.

"I promise!" he cried, in answer; but he only called after her; she had already passed away.

After a night of sorrow, the task of arranging the burial of the loved remains fell to Charlotte. The Major and Mittler assisted her. Eduard's condition was pitiful. When he had roused himself out of his despair and had collected his thoughts in some degree, he insisted that Ottilie should not be removed from the castle; that she should be attended, nursed and treated as though she were alive—for she was not dead, she could not be dead. They did as he wished, or, at least, they did not do what he forbade. He did not ask to see her.

Another alarm and another worry kept the friends occupied. Nanni, who had been sharply scolded by the physician, forced, by threats, to confess and then crushed with reproaches, had disappeared. After a long search she was found; she seemed to be out of her mind. Her parents took her home. The gentlest treatment did not seem to have any effect, and she had to be locked in because she threatened to run away again.

Step by step they succeeded in rescuing Eduard from complete despondency, but unfortunately for him; for now he thought clearly and saw the plain truth that he had forever lost the happiness of his life. They found the courage to suggest that Ottilie, if placed in the chapel, would still remain among the living and have a quiet and peaceful home. It was difficult to obtain his consent, and he finally gave it only under the condition that she should be carried there in an open coffin; that in the vault, she should lie under a coffin-lid of glass and a perpetually burning lamp be placed there. After all this had been arranged, he apparently resigned himself to everything.

They clothed the graceful body in the festive dress which she had made for herself; a wreath of asters was laid round her head; they shone sadly like mournful stars. For the decoration of the bier, the church, and the chapel, all the gardens were stripped of their treasures. They lay wasted, as though winter had already effaced the beauty of their flowerbeds. In the early hours of the morning Ottilie was carried out of the castle in an open coffin, and the rising sun once more flushed her lovely face. The mourners crowded around the pallbearers; no one wanted to go ahead, no one to follow; everyone wished to be close to her and enjoy her presence for the last time. Boys and men and women—not one was unmoved. The girls were disconsolate; they felt more deeply than the rest what they had lost.

Nanni was not there. They had kept her away or, rather, they had kept secret from her the day and hour of the funeral. She was closely guarded in her parents' house in a small room facing the garden. But when she heard the bells tolling she knew at once what they meant; and when the woman who was in charge of her left to see the funeral procession, Nanni escaped through the window onto the gallery, and, finding all the doors locked, climbed up into the open loft above.

Just then the procession passed through the village along the road strewn with evergreens. Nanni had a clear view of her mistress below her; she could see her more distinctly, more perfectly than those who followed the bier. Ethereal, as though carried on a cloud or a wave, she seemed to beckon to her maid, who, confused, dizzy and swaying, plunged down into the street.

With a horrified scream the crowd scattered. The crush and tumult forced the pallbearers to set the bier down. The child actually lay very close to it and seemed to have broken all her limbs. By accident or as a precaution they leaned her against the bier; with her last spark of life she seemed to be trying to reach her beloved mistress. But hardly had her limp body touched Ottilie's dress and her limp fingers. Ottilie's folded hands, when the girl jumped up, raised her arms and looked up to heaven. Then she flung herself on her knees before the coffin, looking at her mistress with rapt devotion.

Finally, she rose to her feet and cried with ecstatic joy: "Yes, she has forgiven me! What no one else could forgive me, what I could not forgive myself, God forgave though her look, her gesture, her lips. Now she again lies still and peaceful; but you all have seen how she raised herself, blessed me with her unfolded hands and looked kindly at me! You all have heard it—you are my witnesses that she said to me 'You are forgiven'! I am no longer a murderess; she has forgiven me; God has forgiven me; and no one can hold anything against me any longer."

All crowded around her; all were amazed; they listened and looked at her and at the dead girl, and no one knew what to do next. "Now carry her to her rest!" Nanni cried. "She has done and suffered her share and cannot live among us any longer." The bier was again taken up and the procession moved on, with Nanni following directly behind—and so they arrived at the church and the chapel.

There now stood Ottilie's coffin, with the child's coffin at her head, and the little dressing-case at her feet—all enclosed in a shrine of massive oak. A woman had been engaged to watch, for a time, by the body which lay so beautifully under the glass lid. But Nanni would not allow anyone to assume this office. She wished to stay without a companion and take good care of the lamp, which had been lit for the first time. She asked for this favor so eagerly and persistently that they let her have her way, in order to prevent a quite possible aggravation of her disturbed condition.

But she did not remain alone for long; for, as soon as night fell and the suspended lamp began to spread its light, the door opened, and the Architect entered the chapel, whose devoutly decorated walls seemed to him more ancient and more ominous in the subdued illumination than he would ever had believed.

Nanni was seated at one side of the coffin. She recognized him immediately; but she only pointed wordlessly to her dead mistress. And so he stood on the other side, in the strength and gracefulness of his youth, motionless, absorbed in his thoughts, his folded hands wrung in pity, his head and eyes bent toward his lifeless friend.

Once before he had stood in this way in the *tableau vivant* of "*Belisarius*." Quite involuntarily, he now assumed the same posture—how natural also on this occasion! Now as then, something of invaluable excellence had been thrown from its height; and if, in the first case, valor, wisdom, power, rank, and wealth of one man were mourned as being irrevocably lost—if qualities, indispensable to a nation and to a sovereign at decisive moments had not been valued but even rejected—in this case, many quite different hidden virtues, called forth by Nature only a short time ago from the depth of her riches, had been quickly destroyed by her indifferent hand: rare virtues with a peaceful influence which the needy world must ever welcome and mourn with profound sadness.

The young man and the girl were silent for a long time; but when she saw tears welling up in his eyes, and noticed that he seemed to be overwhelmed by his grief, she comforted him with so much sincerity, with such kindness and assurance that, amazed at the fluency of her words, he was able to control himself; in his mind's eye he saw his lovely friend living and working in another world. His tears stopped; his grief grew less sharp; he knelt down, bade Ottilie a last farewell and then left Nanni, after a warm pressure of her hand. He rode away the same night, without having seen any other person.

Unknown to Nanni, the physician had remained in the church all night; when he came to see her in the morning, he found her cheerful and perfectly calm. He had been prepared to hear wild flights of fantasy; he thought she would tell him of conversations during the night with Ottilie or of other hallucinations; but she was normal, quiet and completely in her right mind. She remembered earlier days perfectly, and everything that had happened in the smallest detail; and in nothing she said did she stray from the ordinary course of reality, except for the incident at the funeral, of which she spoke happily and repeatedly—how Ottilie had raised herself, how she had blessed her, and forgiven her, thereby giving her peace forever.

Ottilie's continuing beautiful state, which more resembled sleep than death, attracted many persons. All the people of the village and of the neighborhood wished to see her once more, and everyone enjoyed hearing the unbelievable story from Nanni's own lips—some treated it with scorn, some with doubt, but others with a strong inclination to believe her.

Any need that is not really satisfied turns man necessarily toward faith. Nanni, her limbs shattered before the eyes of the crowd, had been healed after she had touched the saintly body; why should not others as well be granted this blessing? At first, loving mothers brought their children who were afflicted with some ailment, and believed that they saw a sudden improvement. The people's confidence increased, and finally no one was too old or too weak to come to this place for comfort and relief. The crowds grew, and it became necessary to lock the chapel and—except during the hours of service—the church as well.

Eduard did not have the courage to look at his departed friend again. He lived automatically—he seemed to have no tears left and to be beyond suffering. His interest in conversation, his appetite for food and drink declined with every day's passing. His only restorative seemed to be in drinking wine from the glass, which, after all, had prophesied falsely. He still liked to look at the interlaced initials, and at these moments the serious-serene expression of his eyes seemed to indicate that even now he had not give up all hope of a reunion with Ottilie. But just as the smallest circumstance seems a good omen to the fortunate, whose happiness is increased by any chance event, the most trifling incidents frequently combine to crush and hurt the unfortunate. One day, as Eduard raised the beloved glass to his lips, he put it down, horrified; it was the same glass and yet not the same; he missed a tiny marking. He questioned his valet, who was forced to confess that the original glass had been broken not long before, and that he had substituted another from the same set, which dated back to Eduard's youth. Eduard could not be angry; his fate had been sealed by the fact; how could he be shaken by the symbol? But still he felt deeply depressed. From now on he disliked drinking anything; and he seemed purposely to abstain from food and from conversation.

But now and then he was gripped by a great restlessness. At these times he expressed a wish to eat and to drink and he began to talk again. "Alas!" he once said to the Major who seldom left him, "how unhappy I am that all my efforts are never anything more than imitations or spurious attempts! What to her has been sheer bliss becomes to me pain; and yet, for the sake of that bliss, I am compelled to accept this pain. I must follow her, follow her on this road; but my nature as well as my promise deters me. It is a terrible task to imitate the inimitable. I feel only too deeply, dear friend, that genius is required for everything, even for martyrdom."

What shall we say of the efforts of his wife, his friend, and the physician, who alternately tried to do their best in this hopeless case? At last Eduard was found dead. Mittler was the first to make this tragic discovery. He called the physician and—with his usual presence of mind—examined closely the circumstances of the death. Charlotte rushed to him; she could not repress a suspicion of suicide and accused herself and the others of inexcusable carelessness. But the physician—on natural grounds—and Mittler—on moral grounds—soon convinced her that the contrary was true. It was quite obvious that Eduard had been surprised by his end. In a quiet moment he had taken from a small box and from his wallet every memento he had of Ottilie and everything which up to now he had carefully hidden; he had spread it all out before him: a lock of her hair, flowers picked in some happy hour, all the little notes she had written him, from the very first one which his wife had handed to him accidentally and with so much intuitive instinct. All this he would not have wished to expose intentionally to a chance discovery. And now this heart, too, which only a short time before had been stirred to infinite emotions, had found the rest which can never be disturbed. And because he fell asleep while thinking of the saintly girl, one might well call him blessed. Charlotte gave him his place by

Ottilie's side and ordered that no one else should ever be buried in this vault. On this condition she made ample endowments to the church and the school—to the clergyman and the school teacher.

Thus the lovers rest side by side. Peace hovers over their burial place; gay and kindred images of angels look down on them from the vaulting; and what a happy moment it will be when, one day, they will waken together once more.

Translated by Elizabeth Mayer and Louise Bogan

ACKNOWLEDGMENTS

Every reasonable effort has been made to locate the owners of rights to previously published works and the translations printed here. We gratefully acknowledge permission to reprint the following material:

Elective Affinities translated by Elizabeth Mayer and Louise Bogan. Copyright © 1963 by Regnery Gateway, Inc., Washington, D.C. All rights reserved. Reprinted by special permission.

"Goethe's *Werther*" and "Zu Goethe's *Wahlverwandtschaften*" by Thomas Mann, from: Thomas Mann, *Gesammelte Werke in dreizehn Bänden, Reden und Aufsätze 1* © 1960, 1974 S. Fischer Verlag GmbH, Frankfurt am Main.

THE GERMAN LIBRARY
in 100 Volumes

Gottfried von Strassburg
Tristan and Isolde
Edited and Revised by Francis G. Gentry
Foreword by C. Stephen Jaeger

German Medieval Tales
Edited by Francis G. Gentry
Foreword by Thomas Berger

German Humanism and Reformation
Edited by Reinhard P. Becker
Foreword by Roland Bainton

Immanuel Kant
Philosophical Writings
Edited by Ernst Behler
Foreword by René Wellek

Friedrich Schiller
Plays: Intrigue and Love and Don Carlos
Edited by Walter Hinderer
Foreword by Gordon Craig

German Romantic Criticism
Edited by A. Leslie Willson
Foreword by Ernst Behler

Heinrich von Kleist
Plays
Edited by Walter Hinderer
Foreword by E. L. Doctorow

E. T. A. Hoffmann
Tales
Edited by Victor Lange

German Literary Fairy Tales
Edited by Frank G. Ryder and Robert M. Browning
Introduction by Gordon Birrell
Foreword by John Gardiner

Heinrich Heine
Poetry and Prose
Edited by Jost Hermand and Robert C. Holub
Foreword by Alfred Kazin

Heinrich von Kleist and Jean Paul
German Romantic Novellas
Edited by Frank G. Ryder and Robert M. Browning
Foreword by John Simon

German Poetry from 1750 to 1900
Edited by Robert M. Browning
Foreword by Michael Hamburger

Gottfried Keller
Stories
Edited by Frank G. Ryder
Foreword by Max Frisch

Wilhelm Raabe
Novels
Edited by Volkmar Sander
Foreword by Joel Agee

Theodor Fontane
Short Novels and Other Writings
Edited by Peter Demetz
Foreword by Peter Gay

Theodor Fontane
Delusions, Confusions and The Poggenpuhl Family
Edited by Peter Demetz
Foreword by J. P. Stern
Introduction by William L. Zwiebel

Gottfried Benn
Prose, Essays, Poems
Edited by Volkmar Sander
Foreword by E. B. Ashton
Introduction by Reinhard Paul Becker

German Essays on Art History
Edited by Gert Schiff

Max Frisch
Novels, Plays, Essays
Edited by Rolf Kieser
Foreword by Peter Demetz